Punjabi Centuries

Punjabi Centuries

Tracing Histories of Punjab

Edited by

Anshu Malhotra

Orient BlackSwan

PUNJABI CENTURIES: TRACING HISTORIES OF PUNJAB

ORIENT BLACKSWAN PRIVATE LIMITED

Registered Office
3-6-752 Himayatnagar, Hyderabad 500 029, Telangana, India
e-mail: centraloffice@orientblackswan.com

Other Offices
Bengaluru, Chennai, Guwahati, Hyderabad,
Kolkata, Mumbai, New Delhi, Noida, Patna

First published by Orient Blackswan Private Limited 2024
This Paperback edition published by Orient Blackswan in 2024

ISBN 978-93-5442-660-5

041931

Typeset in
Minion Pro 11/13
by Le Studio Graphique, Gurgaon 122 007

Printed in India at
Kensington Printing & Packaging, Noida 201 301

Published by
Orient Blackswan Private Limited
3-6-752 Himayatnagar, Hyderabad 500 029, Telangana, India
e-mail: info@orientblackswan.com

Contents

Abbreviations

ACK	Amar Chitra Katha
BJP	Bharatiya Janata Party
BSF	Border Security Force
CJM	Chief Judicial Magistrate
CRPF	Central Reserve Police Force
CSM	Central Sikh Museum
DAV	Dayanand Anglo-Vedic
DSGMC	Delhi Sikh Gurdwara Management Committee
FIR	First Information Report
IAS	Indian Administrative Service
ICS	Indian Civil Service
IPC	Indian Penal Code
IPS	Indian Police Service
NDA	National Democratic Alliance
PCMS	Punjab Civil Medical Services
PPA	Punjab Purity Association
RSS	Rashtriya Swayamsevak Sangh
SAD	Shiromani Akali Dal
SC	Supreme Court
SCERT	State Council of Educational Research and Training
SGPC	Shiromani Gurdwara Parbandhak Committee
TADA	Terrorist and Disruptive Activities Act
VHP	Vishwa Hindu Parishad

Images

ACKNOWLEDGEMENTS

This volume has been long in the making. It follows my journey from the History Department, Delhi University to relocation at Global Studies at the University of California Santa Barbara in the midst of a family medical crisis. While my readjustment was only beginning, the Covid 19 pandemic disrupted all normality, bringing life as we knew it to a 'virtual' standstill. Some friends who were associated with the volume were unable to participate; however, I wish to acknowledge their intellectual input that began this work, especially Samiksha Sehrawat. Other contributors kept their faith, or were arm-twisted into keeping it—I am grateful to them all.

Many old and new friendships have helped me see through this tough time of transition—my deepest appreciation for the support of Inderpal Grewal and Nicole Ranganath in California; Farina Mir and Will Glover in the US; and Yogesh Snehi in Delhi. I remember with nostalgia my last conversation over tea with the late Professor J. S. Grewal, the preeminent historian of Punjab, at his house in Chandigarh in September 2018. They don't make them like him anymore—gentle, kind, and immersed in scholarship. My gratitude also to Professor Indu Banga for her genteel concern over the years.

I will also like to thank the team at Orient BlackSwan, starting with Roopa Sharma, who plugged on with this volume despite multiple delays, and Nilanjana Majumdar, Anjali Aggarwal Gupta, and Proteeti Banerjee, who have helped bring it to completion.

I am grateful to my colleagues at Global Studies for welcoming me. I miss the banter and intellectual exchange with my friends and colleagues at Delhi University—Parul Pandya Dhar, Aparna Balachandran, Farhat Hasan, as also Razi Aquil; Upinder Singh and Seema Alavi who are now at Ashoka University; and Ratna Raman, a friend over the years in fun and sorrow.

My family has always been my pillar of strength. My interest in the history and cultures of Punjab comes from my mother Swaran, who missed her Punjab every single day while living in Delhi—her loss in 2020 amidst all the troubles was yet another blow during those dark days. The jollity, love, and caring of my sister Poonam is incomparable; and the larger *tabar* when we are together is the balm to the soul. My partner Satyajit, and my sons Mihiraan and Milind make life possible and pleasurable—you know how much you matter.

One

Punjabi Centuries

Tracing Histories of Punjab(s)

Anshu Malhotra

Everyone who lives in, thinks of, remembers and writes about Punjab imagines an entity that is particular to them. This is because the historical and territorial imaginary that is Punjab has been politically and spatially unstable and mutating, although from early times, the region's identity has remarkably been cast around its rivers and *doab*s (interfluves)[1] (Kumar 2019). Additionally, the recent history of this region has constructed different political, territorial and imagined spaces, some still referred to as Punjab and others absorbed into different spatial and emotive nomenclatures, like Haryana. What Punjab means to whom may vary: from the two Punjabs, Indian and Pakistani, post the brutal partitioning of colonial Punjab in 1947; to the state restructuring of 1966 after the demand for 'Punjabi Suba'; to the imaginings of a 'Sikh/Khalsa' homeland from the 1980s to the mid-1990s, often with support of Sikhs from the global diaspora (Singh and Shani 2022); or those for whom Partition meant the loss of a territory called homeland, such as for 'Punjabi Hindus' of Delhi or the 'Hindu Punjabis' of the British diaspora (Raj 2003). In the same vein, what one holds dear about Punjab, the sense of belonging and the embracing of a 'Punjabiness' or *Punjabiyat*, the ambiguous term imbricated in affect and charged with emotional and cultural investment, is hailed variously by people. Territory, culture, language, religion, caste or even a primordial affiliation beyond, or a hybrid of these taxonomies, may be invoked to adumbrate the term's layered complexity. Punjabiyat, lodged under the skin, seeped into the being and granularly experienced, exceeds and encompasses the myriad qualities it evokes (Malhotra and Mir 2012: xiv).

The title of this book, *Punjabi Centuries*, harks back to one such imagination; that of Prakash Tandon (b.1911), when he published *Punjabi Century* in 1963, giving an account of Punjab—his inheritance, knowledge and experience—of 1857–1947 (Tandon 2011[1988]). The specificities of his own social and cultural context shaped what he wrote, just as he fashioned his past in a particular, articulate and performative self-presentation (Malhotra and Lambert-Hurley 2015). He was a Hindu Khatri from the town of Gujrat on the banks of river Jhelum, and as a child traversed with his parents many towns and villages of the newly settled Canal Colonies. He travelled to England for higher education, coming back to work in India along with his Swedish wife. After his father retired from serving the colonial government's irrigation department, he helped to settle his parents in Lahore's Model Town, where eventually he, along with his brothers, had also hoped to retire.[2] The trauma of Partition permanently tore Lahore and Gujrat from their lives. The Punjab of Tandon's inscriptions was 'West' Punjab—a Punjab he lamented was snatched forever from him as his family moved to 'Hindustan', to Delhi and later to Bombay.[3] The enormity of Tandon's loss is best captured in his own words:

> Today we have no one left in Gujrat. All the Hindus came away at partition. It is strange to think that in all the land between Ravi and Chenab, from Chenab to Jhelum, from Jhelum to Indus, in the foothills and in the plain down to Panjnad, where the five rivers eventually merge, land which had been the homes of our biradaries since the dawn of history, *there is no one left of our kind* (Tandon 2011[1988]: 223–24; emphasis added).

Yet, Tandon's wrenching from Punjab, eloquently described in the trope of the flow and confluence of its rivers, remembered in the brotherhood of the ancestral town and bemoaned in the alienation of people of his ilk from it, was not permanent. One may say that his *Punjabiyat*, howsoever estranged, asserted itself, and he wrote two more volumes that in some ways connected him to Punjab—*Beyond Punjab* and *Return to Punjab*—assembled together in the *Punjabi Saga* (Tandon 2011[1988]).

The tale of Tandon's continuous relationship with Punjab—lived, cleaved, abandoned, reconnected—could be the story of many others, constructed from their specific and multitudinous vantage points. In this introduction I use Tandon's reminiscences, along with those of others like Lajpat Rai and Ruchi Ram Sahni, as gateways to enter the histories and cultures of Punjab. The ostensible privileging of a few voices must be seen as a conduit to lead into diverse Punjab(s); the anchoring in the memoirs is a literary and historical device that propels a conversation with the past. The memoirs are written from given caste, class and community viewpoints, and therefore have their limitations; they are also steeped in epistemologies that encouraged privileged men to narrate their (public) lives. However, for all the construction of purposive subjectivities and hegemonic ambitions, these memoirs are not devoid of interest: in what they say, are silent about, what they want us to see, what they hide. It is in the peekaboo with the past that they lead us into, obscure, or are oblivious of, and a future they hint at and look forward to that we can begin a dialogue with a lived past in its many complexities and contradictions. It is important to draw attention to the messiness of the past where diverse points of view collided, some captured in these memoirs, others not, but all worthy of attention.

This volume is not the first to adapt Tandon's title for their work; Indu Banga did it for her erudite edited volume *Five Punjabi Centuries* (Banga 1997). So, what makes Tandon's work attractive? Tandon, as noted, wrote from a specific perspective. He was a high-caste Hindu Khatri, the sort who made the best of what they saw as opportunities opened for people like them under colonialism—his use of the phrase from his history textbook '*angrezi raj ki barkaten*' (Tandon 2011[1988]: 18)—the blessings of the English rule—steeped in the logics of colonial historiography, resonated with many of his generation. Tandon's was an insider's ethnographic account of the ways of the Khatris: their towns, homes and architecture, customs and rituals, but most of all, how they took to colonial education and professions like fish to water. Such ethnographic writing mimicked British administrator–ethnographers like Horace Arthur Rose, Denzil Ibbetson or Malcolm Darling, and carried sociological and antiquarian interest. It also fulfilled for the British the need to know about, categorise and dominate the people they ruled. Like the English, Tandon too had his informers with whom he conferred, women and men who helped him to get 'tradition' right. Writing with an ethnographic bent itself was not new.

Ganesh Das Badhera's fabulous *Char Bagh-i-Panjab* (1849; see Grewal and Banga 1975) (which likely emulated the celebrated Punjabi Mughal *munshi* Chandar Bhan Brahman's erudite, eloquent and trendsetting *Chahar Chaman*; Kinra 2015) was written petitioning the British to consider the case of the Khatris as educated and proficient professionals, and can be considered ethnographic in its panoramic stance to make legible the Punjabi peoples for the British. However, its worldview was pre-modern. This can be seen in the enchantments of the holy and learned personages of different localities of Punjab that unfold in its pages; Badhera's interweaving of Punjabi romantic *qisse* within his topographical mapping of Punjab, a making of potent mytho-history; along with attention to his own genealogy. Genealogy was a salient form of knowledge, of apprehending and connecting to one's past. Badhera's was an effort to explicate a Punjabiness that he could speak of with authority, rather than as an example of antiquarian curiosity. Tandon's sociological study too was suffused with keen interest, but sparked by what came to be an aspect of modernity: the grasping, inscribing and freezing of the 'pre-modern' world before it transforms forever (Burke 2016[1978]), not to mention also the spatial sundering for him. Badhera's vernacular history, delivered in classical, cosmopolitan Persian, at a time when all languages became vernacular in relation to English, as argued by Partha Chatterjee (2008), was different from the auto/biographical vernacularity of Tandon, penned in English.

A striking reason for Tandon's success with *Punjabi Century* was the spirit of *joie de vivre* and Punjabi indomitability that pervades its pages. Punjabis, whatever the circumstances, Tandon seems to suggest, make the most of life and chances given; even after Partition, as Ravinder Kaur (2018[2007]) notes, mythologising Punjabi hardiness and success. Tandon himself had a successful career after studying accountancy at Manchester University and eventually serving as chairman of the multinational company Hindustan Lever Limited, besides being associated with the Indian Institute of Management, Ahmedabad, and the Punjab and Sind Bank. Significantly, this *esprit de corps* has come to be an aspect of Punjabiyat itself, lending its sheen to Punjabis. These include 'agricultural' Jats and Jat Sikhs: the beneficiaries of the colonial state's indulgence with regards to entitlement to land, and later in postcolonial Punjab of the Green Revolution; the soldiers in the British Indian Army; the Punjabi Muslim landlords of vast tracts in Canal Colonies; the 'non-agricultural' Hindu and Muslim urban middle classes; and the diasporic Punjabis, sometimes even Dalits, at least those who made their fortunes in leather manufacturing and trading in the early twentieth century, or through migrating abroad. Perhaps this self-aggrandising myth has helped Punjabis survive different dislocations. The longevity of this myth and its ownership by the Punjabis therefore makes it difficult to comprehend and easy to overlook the fragile and fragmented lives of many Punjabis earlier and now: for example, the pastoral and other inhabitants of Punjabi *bars* and scrubland of colonial Punjab (Bhattacharya 2018); the young Sikh men, the 'sent away boys' who migrated to escape the violence of the Indian state post operation Blue Star in 1984 (Chopra 2011; Gill 2016); the farmers committing suicide in contemporary Indian Punjab; and more recently, their fears of new farm laws and the power of corporates on their produce, their wives burdened with unpaid debts (Padhi 2012); and the Dalits fighting for dignity and recognition of their contribution to the histories of Punjab and Sikhism (Hans 2016).

Punjabi identity, then, is complex, contingent and ever reconfiguring. Some of the thematic strands mentioned earlier will be picked up by our contributors. However, since any volume can only introduce a few themes and issues, this volume confines itself to the latter half of the nineteenth century into the twentieth century, and sometimes into our present period. The chapters reflect the ongoing interests of some of the scholars of Punjab, and are not meant to suggest any comprehensive view of its past or present. Still, the chapters introduce some important issues that presently engage scholars and provide frames to understand Punjab. Let us begin with the politics of Punjabi language that rages in different, but analogous, ways wherever Punjabis reside.

Language, Reformism and Print Culture in Punjab

Many scholars have devoted time and effort to explain the complexity of the language politics of Punjab(s). This is because the language Punjabi, written in Gurmukhi and Shahmukhi scripts, and occasionally in Devanagari, had never received state patronage until the postcolonial Indian Punjab started promoting Punjabi in the Gurmukhi script. As Farina Mir's path-breaking work shows, despite Persian being the language of administration and court under the Mughals and Ranjit Singh, and the colonial state backing Urdu, Punjabi still flourished, occupying the domain of pleasure and affect (Mir 2010). It was through the vibrant print culture of Punjab, Mir argues, seen in the proliferation of *qisse* and circulating in the two scripts, that 'Punjabi literary formation' emerged, where reticulate webs were created among the writers, publishers and consumers.

The contemporary politics of Punjabi is no less fraught with complexities. With regard to the Punjabi movement in Pakistan, where Punjabi elites wield power in the state but where the nationalist credentials of the state are expressed in promoting Urdu, interest in Punjabi is seen as manifesting symbolic capital (Ayers 2012) or in demonstrating a more complicated class politics (Murphy 2018). Thus, the manner in which, in the colonial period and under reformist influence, the specific coalescing of religion, language and script took place—Muslim/Urdu/Shahmukhi; Hindu/Hindi/Devanagari; Sikh/Punjabi/Gurmukhi—has been shown to be facile and unrepresentative of the situation on the ground. Here, I revisit the link between reformism and the language/script conundrum for the reason that the conversation on the question of language has mostly bypassed the relationship of Punjabi Hindus to Punjabi. To an extent, this is a function of the Hindus in Punjab who, in the throes of the communal overtones of the Punjabi Suba movement, in the 1951 census and then again in 1961, declared Hindi to be their mother tongue. This helped to carve out a Hindi-speaking Haryana, and for the first time a Sikh-dominated Punjabi-speaking Punjab (Singh and Shani 2022: 121–23), which continues to have a substantial Hindu population of 38.5 per cent (Population Census 2011). However important this Hindu stance may have been in making political calculations, it does not exhaust the question of Hindus' relationship with the Punjabi language; and it might be worth bringing in more historical and contemporary perspectives to further complicate an already entangled question.

At a few junctures in his account of colonial Punjab, Tandon discusses the question of Punjabi language. The picture he paints is one of multilingual ease, both in written and spoken forms, but also of complex change. Speaking of Punjabi as a language without its own script, Tandon 'communalises' the question of language and script (a little differently from what we see above in the Punjabi Suba movement) by suggesting that the Sikhs invented Gurmukhi by modifying the Sanskrit alphabet in order to avoid the 'sacrilege of recording their holy book, the Granth Sahib, in Persian script, the script of the Muslims against whom they had revolted' (Tandon 2011[1988]: 65). The ease with which Tandon links Muslims and Persian is striking, given that in the same breath he also mentions all Punjabis being bilingual, 'speaking Punjabi and reading and writing Persian' (ibid.). With the introduction of Urdu by the British and Hindi being taught to women in Arya Samaj schools, Tandon goes on to speak of the troubles this caused—some couples were unable to communicate with each other in writing as men and women were proficient in different scripts, although they spoke Punjabi at home. As men learnt Urdu and English (in Tandon's words, these languages came to acquire a 'snob value'), 'Punjabi was relegated to the home, the women and the illiterates. The language consequently began to lose its purity' (Tandon 2011[1988]: 66). Tandon then goes on to characterise Punjabi as 'slow, indelicate and lusty', an unrefined language (ibid.).

Some of Tandon's observations need to be highlighted and unpacked. The linking of Persian and Muslims, on the one hand, and the assumed antipathy of Sikhs towards Persian, on the other, are of course a function of the politics of Tandon's time rather than reflecting an earlier historical situation. All elites, including the Sikh, conducted business of the court in Persian during Ranjit Singh's time, to give just one example. Anne Murphy has recently shown the complex Sikh language heritage where Sikh sacred texts produced in languages ranging from Sadhukkari, Braj and Persian—and not Punjabi—were inscribed in Gurmukhi (Murphy 2018). Yet, what Tandon wrote of was commonplace in Punjab from the last decade of the nineteenth century. Bhai Vir Singh, the Sikh polymath associated with Singh Sabha polemics, deployed the same formula in his very popular 1898 novel *Sundari*, establishing a link between Muslims and Urdu, Farsi and Arabic as languages in which they, improbably, conducted everyday conversations (Malhotra 2020). The formula linking language to community was at least partially a result of the manner in which history was taught in Punjab's schools, which divided history into distinct blocks of Hindu, Muslim and British periods (Tandon 2011[1988]: 18; see also Asif 2020). This was also part and parcel of the emerging academic, nationalist and popular history conflicts: the researching, claiming, manipulating and inventing of history for the imagined nation, which were undertaken in many parts of India from the nineteenth century. Where was history to be produced, in the cloister that was the academy or in popular fora? Were communities to be linked to their perceived places of 'origin', and their relationship to the nation judged accordingly (Chatterjee 1993: 76–115; Chakrabarty 2015; Guha 2019)?

A complex portrayal of making language choices comes from the memoirs of Lala Lajpat Rai (b.1865), the Agrawal Bania nationalist leader from Punjab, tied lifelong ideologically to the Arya Samaj, the Hindu reformist organisation that wished to recreate the achievements of a celebrated Vedic past. Rai's *Atma Katha* ('Self-Story'), published in chaste Hindi in the Devanagari script, followed the pattern delineated by Udaya Kumar for public men's autobiographies at this time: a view from an individual's perspective (an important man in public life) on what were seen to be historically significant times, with meagre discussion of private life and intimate matters (Kumar 2008). However, despite the eschewing of the private, almost unconsciously Rai adumbrates a psychological conflict with his father, Radha Krishan, a government school teacher of Farsi, who had studied in a Farsi *madrassa* established by the British. The conflict with pater unfolds on the question of language: Which language was to be adopted, owned and propagated? Rai depicts his father as attracted to Islam, deeply impressed with the Koran, who read *namaz* and kept *roza*, and though he never converted to Islam or openly become a Muslim—*khulamkhula Musalman*—it was because of the fear that his wife would leave him with their children (Rai n.d.: 20–25).

In his account of his father, it is Rai's mother who emerges as the hero. She was from a *kesdhari* (who kept unshorn hair) Sikh family with one of her brothers being a *granthi*, a ritual reader/interpreter/exegete of the sacred Granth Sahib. It is she who is shown to be patient and tolerant of her husband's Islamic bent and Muslim friends, and as responsible for maintaining staunch (*kattar*) Hindu ritualistic practice at home (Rai n.d.: 23–24). Rai entered public life in his teens around 1882 at the time of the Hindi–Urdu controversy in north India, and strongly supported Hindi and the Arya Samaj, though he, at the time, did not know the Devanagari alphabet, but indexed the language and script pairing as natural (ibid.: 37, 53, 144). The language politics of Punjab and his father's love for Farsi and Arabic feature repeatedly in the *Atma Katha*. Rai also laments his inability to learn Sanskrit, underlining it as a failing on his part. Sanskrit was embraced by the Arya Samaj as the genitor of Hindu culture and a key to unlocking the textual treasures of its past. Learning Sanskrit, and through it the ancient and glorious 'Hindu' past, or its learning along with keeping abreast of Western education became one of the issues of tussle within the Arya Samaj. Rai gives a copious account of the conflict, which often degenerated into fracas, between the 'Mahatama' wing of the Arya Samaj and its 'cultured' wing, the latter associated with the Dayanand Anglo-Vedic (DAV) educational institutions to which he belonged. However, what is also noteworthy is his lack of regret at giving up on learning Arabic, taught at the Government College, Lahore, under the aegis of G. W. Leitner, the young Hungarian Orientalist principal of the institution and promoter of Indian languages, including the classical ones. Rai presents the break with Arabic, a language his father was proficient in, as a result of a faceoff with his teacher, Mohammad Husain Azad (the literary figure famous for his commentary on and canonisation of Urdu literature, the *Ab-i-Hayat*)—another authority figure—whom he calls out for advertising his Iranian 'origins' while ironically asking Bengalis to keep off Punjab (ibid.: 90, 145).

Rai's is an emotionally enmeshed relationship with the paterfamilias and his language, where the son, his politics (the father initially disliked the Arya Samaj) and his language (Hindi) eventually triumph; the father is later shown to become a *Vedanti* (monist) and altogether more tolerant of the Samaj (Rai n.d.: 22).

It will not be an over-reading to suggest that the father–son *contretemps* here mirror the larger question of making political and linguistic choices in the shaping of the nascent nation; and the disowning of a past also meant repudiating the relationship with an 'intimate other', the Muslim, and what that figure came to represent. Interestingly, in the heroics of the mother Rai portrays, the mother tongue—*ma boli*—does not feature. Punjabi is nowhere discussed in the autobiography, though he did sponsor and help edit for a while the English-language newspaper *Panjabee* (ibid.: 174) that ostensibly invokes an encompassing identity, and though language knowledge as an attribute of a person surfaces repeatedly in the autobiography.[4] It is also noteworthy that there is no 'problematising' of the Hindus' relationship with the Sikhs, and the seamless assimilation of his Sikh mother in the Hindu household is not deemed worthy of comment. Undoubtedly, such marriages were common enough not to evoke comment, just as bringing up one son in upper-caste Hindu households as a kesdhari Sikh was an established practice (Kaur 1986; Nanda 2018).[5] The reason this stands out in Rai's writing is because the Sikh members of the Arya Samaj—Jawahir Singh, Ditt Singh and Maya Singh—left it in a huff because of prominent Aryas' attacks on Sikhism, and joined the Lahore Singh Sabha; again, an incident on which Rai is silent (Singh 1965: 58). It seems this moment was not seen as serious enough to elicit comment, but became a definitive one for the Sikh reformist movement, as noted by the Singh Sabha activist and a convert to Sikhism, Bhagat Laxman Singh, in his *Autobiography* (Singh 1965).[6] While there will be occasion to discuss the Hindu–Sikh relationship, as seen in some personal narratives later, the question of language in these high-caste narratives attests to a period when the language and religious community equation was being constructed by a few public men skilfully deploying print and publishing. However, the situation on the ground remained fluid, and despite the language polemics initiated by the end of the nineteenth century, the Punjabi people did not disown their multilingual culture.

Here, it may be useful to bring in the discussion on print culture, language and education. In Chapter 2, Purnima Dhavan takes us back to a period in Punjab when the print medium came to be established and began to shape people's mental and cultural habits, two decades after the British conquest of this region. The 1870s were surely a time of great flux in Punjab—the British had begun making definitive administrative, civil and legal changes in society, along with establishing the new revenue policies, and the effects of these changes must have seemed like enormous disruptions to life as the Punjabis knew it. There was, however, a quality of indeterminacy as to where the change would lead. The publishing industry, as Dhavan notes, was trying to gauge its market and shape it simultaneously. There was a continuity of older reading habits now beginning to be available in printed forms. The two texts that Dhavan studies—*Baran Anva* (a seventeenth-century text on religious, legal and moral issues) and *Pakki Roti* (a catechist-type text teaching the basics of Islamic religion and practice)—were experiments in understanding the needs of the Punjabi publics and in guiding them to certain kinds of texts. While the *Baran Anva*, with its prolixity and assumption of a degree of advanced knowledge on the part of the reader, did not succeed much as a publishing venture, the *Pakki Roti*, available in a chapbook format and shunning bias and polemics, was a success.

Dhavan uses the two texts also to explore the pattern of using multiple languages in Punjabi publications, indeed the comfort with multilingual texts; she uses them to introduce the conversations and debates taking place on the language of instruction and the nature of education to be imparted in Punjab. The *Baran Anva* in Shahmukhi script was in archaic Punjabi, which in printed forms in the nineteenth century was provided with glosses in Persian or Urdu.

It is in this context that we have to see the importance of Dhavan's stepping into the debate on imparting indigenous education in the languages of Punjab—classical and mundane—that was significant in the nineteenth century. Showing the ongoing polemics between those like G. W. Leitner (then the principal of Government College, Lahore, and the force behind Oriental College) and his support for indigenous forms of knowledge and its dissemination is important. He had the backing of some Punjabi elites organised in the Anjuman-i-Punjab and the governmental institutions with their schooling system, which seemed a failure in contrast to earlier forms in which education was available to the people. It was only by the late 1880s and the 1890s that the language politics and educational polemics reached an apogee—one that began to demarcate people through religion, language and script that Rai exemplified; and a politics in which the Arya Samaj and the Singh Sabha participated with gusto. And even then, the pleasures of Punjabi stayed. Most people retained the ability to be comfortable with a multiple language and script landscape of Punjab.

However, did the politics that Rai speaks of come home to roost? Did the Hindu Punjabis, a minority in colonial and postcolonial Indian Punjab (Nair 2011; Tuteja 2021), wilfully sunder their relationship with Punjabi, especially those who no longer resided in Punjab? Later in his memoir, Tandon remarks that his children, brought up in Bombay, went to local schools where they spoke English while using Hindi at home, and that 'they never learned Punjabi' (Tandon 2011[1988]: 229). The story is, once again, more complex. The Punjabis who lived in Punjab claimed to speak Punjabi at home (Paul Brass, cited in Kaur 2018[2007]: 222) till the language and state reorganisation politics of the 1950s and 1960s created divisions between Hindi and Punjabi speakers. It is then that many Hindus of Punjab made definitive claims of being Hindi speakers, as noted above. However, Kaur noticed that among those who left Punjab earlier, for instance, the Punjabi Hindu residents of Delhi, with whom she conducted her fieldwork in 2001, the older generation spoke to their age group in Punjabi but switched to Hindi or English with the younger members of their family, as the latter languages were seen to have greater purchase in India. Among the reasons Kaur discusses for this was a perceptible rise of Hindu–Sikh tension, post the demand for a Khalistani state, and the continuing Akali–Sikh and Hindu–Arya rivalry (though the Hindu right and Akalis became political partners in Punjab subsequently). On the other hand, today, when Punjabi Jat-Sikhs, who consider Punjabi an intrinsic part of their Jat identity, lose their ability to read Punjabi in Gurmukhi script—for instance, when they reside outside Punjab and learn Hindi in Devanagari script in school—see this diminishing relationship with Gurmukhi as diluting their Jat identity (Mooney 2011: 124). Of course, the more important attributes of Jat identity constitute ownership of land, their self-description being that of the Jat-zamindar (Kaur 1986: 233),[7] along with kinship networks, dominance over the postcolonial Punjabi landscape and increasing links to the global Jat diaspora.

The 'Hindu Punjabis' (rather than the Punjabi Hindus of Delhi) of the British diaspora may speak Punjabi at home but conflate it with Hindi and generally cede Punjabi as a Sikh language (Raj 2003: 70–75). They paradoxically build their identity as Punjabi (as do many Delhi Punjabis) with the memories of Partition and the loss of a homeland (ibid.). The psychological wound of Partition and of losing a place called home, and having no territory to make a claim to, is passed down to the next generation, an inheritance of trauma (Kabir 2005; Nanda 2018). Thus, caste, community and language, and their constitutive role in creating Punjabi identity, could play out in different ways in contemporary India and among the diaspora. While speaking of the 'ethnic amnesia' of the Delhi Punjabis, Kaur also comments that her respondents identified Punjabi as being a crude, vulgar and unsophisticated language, 'best put to use during quarrels' (Kaur 2018[2007]: 223). This description of Punjabi is very close to that of Tandon's almost a half-century before, who identified Punjabi as losing 'purity' as men abandoned it and it was relegated for use only in homes. Tandon then went on to describe the ritualistic 'quarrels' between women where they put to use their Punjabi in sharp vituperations; but he also spoke of Punjabi's use in love, as seen in Punjabi qisse (Tandon 2011[1988]: 67–70).

This 'low' cultural and symbolic valence attributed to Punjabi for the Punjabi Hindus—as not being men's language—or a language confined to the realm of the home, women, low-caste, abuse and desire is just another characterisation of the language, as we have seen. It enjoys high value in both Indian and Pakistani Punjab, which albeit manifests differently, not to speak of the diverse Punjabi diaspora, particularly the Sikhs amongst them, who try to hold on to their culture through becoming patrons of the language. Perhaps it is due to the ingredients of pleasure and desire that the language continues to flourish; for example, among the Punjabi Hindu migrant community in Mumbai that has played a foundational role in Hindi cinema (Daiya 2020: 21). Punjabi's deployment in 'Hindi' film songs is ubiquitous, the 'impure' and wildly popular mix of Urdu, Hindi and Punjabi lyrics, where the politically incompatible languages pleasurably intermingle, and where Punjabi still alchemically connotes desire (Malhotra and Mir 2012: 51); or the popularity of Punjabi music—lyrical and bhangra pop—that rules the charts in India and among the Punjabi diaspora (Ballantyne 2007). Bhangra, in its recursive movements between India and the diasporas, has been creolised or 'douglarised' with many inflections—Black music, Caribbean beats, Bollywood and more—making Punjabi global in myriad ways (Dudrah 2002; Kalra 2000; Roy 2013).

Chapter 3 by Nicole Ranganath discusses the diasporic context and its relationship with the Punjabi language. She leads us into the poetic and musical self-exploration of two Punjabi women in California. What makes Ranganath's essay important is her subject. Few scholars have focused on the lives of diasporic Punjabi women, their experiences or sense of displacement in distant places that were not home to begin with. How this 'world-making' occurred is what Ranganath explores: How did women adapt to new places and cultures, creating new affective associations with fictitious kin, establishing new friendships and professional associations? It is the intensity of emotion brought on by dislocation that can be discerned in the Punjabi songs these women shared with Ranganath.

A remarkable aspect of California's diasporic women's lives that Ranganath highlights is their hypermobile childhood, which finds stability and a long stay in a place only in California, where they arrive in their early youth. Harbans Panu was born in Malaysia, before moving to Punjab and then California. Mohinderjit Thiara was born in Burma, and then moved to Punjab, Iran, Punjab and California, in that order. This hypermobility is a comment on the enterprise of the intrepid Punjabi and Sikh peoples. From the late nineteenth century, they started exploring the world as colonial connections, through recruitment in the army and the police force, began to open new opportunities for themselves, and carried their language and cultural habits along. The popular Punjabi aphorism that one is likely to meet a Punjabi anywhere on earth is a recognition from within the community of their peripatetic proclivity and willingness to adapt to new circumstances.

Another aspect that Ranganath illuminates among the diasporic women is their emotional and territorial link with Punjab, despite their having spent little time in Punjab. This connectedness with Punjab, and with Punjabi language, is crucial to them. The songs the women write, to make sense of their feelings and emotions at particular times in their lives, are in Punjabi, even when the women are polyglot; each knows at least three languages. The link with Punjab/Punjabi is magnified if we examine the content and theme of the songs as also their form, which borrows heavily from women's Punjabi folksongs. Thus, the relationship with given folk genres—marriage songs, singing in the voice of Hir or emulating the love of the famous lovers Hir and Ranjha—is deepened and amplified as they are adapted to express personal emotions. The language of allusion and mimetics that they take recourse to renews a cultural relationship with an existing reservoir of connection with Punjab and Punjabi.

The politics of Punjabi language is then multifarious—marked by abandonment, renewal, passion, pleasure, desire, embarrassment, grief, love, joy—the language adapted to the needs and sentiments of the diverse Punjabi peoples in the multiple localities they reside in. What Ranganath recounts is the way in which the diasporic women of California carve their own relationship with it. The question it opens is of the making and expressing of gendered identities. Let us look at how gendered identities were constructed from the late nineteenth century onwards.

Gendered Identities and Education: Naming and Namelessness

Men

Like Tandon, many other men wrote and published their auto/biographies throughout the twentieth century, with Rai's *Atma Katha* written probably in 1915, an early example of modernist life-writing.[8] A striking feature of these personal narratives is the palpable excitement that shoots through them when discussing the prospects of new education and the opportunities it opened for men of high castes. In Rai's writing, for example, education becomes a quest—achieved despite the humble circumstances of his home, constant ill health (examinations and bouts of fever coincide) and recurring failures. Once a degree was attained and a government job secured—for that was what most aimed for—the educational qualification came to adhere to their names as suffixes, badges of honour worn for all subsequent time, modern personas proclaimed. When Rai went to Government College, Lahore, he enumerated and named the people he came to know thus: '(1) Pt. Gurudutt M.A.; (2) Lala Hansraj B.A.; (3) Rai Shivnath Sahab Engineer; (4) Diwan Narendranath Sahab M.A. (5) Prof. Ruchi Ram Sahni M.A.' (Rai n.d.: 38). This became the manner in which he introduced every male personality he came across, often also indexing the particular branch of the government bureaucracy he worked in. The colonial government in turn conferred titles on men who served it loyally, adding loftiness to their names. This is how Pran Nevile (b. 1922), another alumnus of Government College, put it in his memoirs centred around Lahore when discussing the new neighbourhoods that came up there, including Model Town: 'Here, the houses were mostly owned by retired government officials, many of whom had during their service earned titles of Rai Sahib, Khan Sahib, Sardar Sahib, Rai Bahadur, Khan Bahadur and Sardar Bahadur' (Nevile 2006[1993]: xix). Similarly, Tandon not only narrates his own sojourn to Lahore and England for acquiring education, but also of his father Ram Das who became a civil engineer after studying at the prestigious Roorkee Engineering College (Tandon 2011[1988]: 32). Even more relevant to the discussion here is the litterateur Ved Mehta's biographical sketch of his father, 'Daddyji', dedicated to the successful career-making of Amolak Ram Mehta (b.1894), who after initial education at Government College, Lahore, went on to simultaneously pursue public health at the University College, London, and tropical medicine and hygiene at the London School of Tropical Medicine (Mehta 1972: 73–84).

In most such accounts of men contriving middle-class life-worlds, some motifs recur—a journey to Lahore, sometimes to London/*vilayat*, and the important role played by the Arya Samaj in their lives. The Arya Samaj could be replaced by a Brahmo Samaj, for example, in the life of the aforementioned Ruchi Ram Sahni (b.1863), or the Singh Sabha as in the life of Bhagat Laxman Singh (b.1863); or other associations proliferating in Lahore at this time. The Arya Samaj, according to Tandon, began to fulfil the role of a caste *biradari*, the brotherhood at the intersections of caste-based conviviality and discipline, as people moved to new places in transferable jobs and left their close-knit intimacies of native towns behind, and as rules of endogamy became elastic. The Arya Samaj could be a passion, as for Rai who, after practising law first in Hisar and then in Lahore, finally dedicated his time fully to its activities. For others, like the father Harbans Lal of the incomparable Sahni brothers, the actor Balraj (b.1913) and the

Hindi litterateur Bhisham (b.1915), the Samaj was a distraction, an outlet for their public and charitable activities (Sahni 1981).

William Glover, when discussing the transmutations that occurred in Lahore as it started to grow 'modern' in the second half of the nineteenth century, has spoken of the imaginative constitution of the city as much as its material growth (Glover 2008: xv). At least part of the imaginative project that was Lahore was possible because it became a hub of education in Punjab. Although the literacy rate in Lahore was less than 5 per cent in 1901, Glover writes, 'Lahore had 5 liberal arts colleges, 3 professional colleges, 28 secondary schools, 112 primary schools, and several religious institutions offering instruction' (ibid.: xii). Government College, the premier liberal arts institution in Lahore, was a destination almost all our auto/biographers speak of and the time spent there emerges almost as a rite of passage for adult high-caste males. Alternatively, the Arya Samaj's D.A.V. school and college were also in Lahore, with which Rai was deeply involved. If Rai's struggle for education was fashioned by him as a contest to overcome bodily and familial frailties, Ruchi Ram Sahni's memoirs make his attempt to acquire education a monumental physical effort powered by sheer will—his journey from Dera Ismail Khan to first Jhang and later to Lahore was an arduous undertaking on foot, on camel, fording rivers and surviving a whirlpool in the mighty Indus (Burra 2017). Eventually, he came to study at the coveted Government College and later teach science there as well, encountering racism and prejudice from his British colleagues. In Bhisham Sahni's biography of his elder brother Balraj, the move from Rawalpindi to Government College, Lahore, becomes one of finding the right place for his restless métier while ducking their father's inappropriate choices of professions for him (Sahni 1981).

Lahore then was the exciting cosmopolitan space where people from different parts of Punjab came, for what Glover calls, 'living the Lahore life' (Glover 2008: 193). In his careful and nuanced reflections on the urban landscape of Lahore, through the material and architectural developments taking place, as much at the behest of the colonial state and British presence as of Indian and Punjabi agency and sensibility, Glover delineates the transformations taking place there. Others too have spoken about the men and women who created and consumed the spirit of being a 'Lahori' (Nevile 2006[1993]; Sidhwa 2005: xv). Educational and professional opportunities were a primary motivation to migrate to Lahore. Equally attractive was the excitement of socialising in the bazaars and cosmopolitan entertainments of the city. Pran Nevile, in his Lahore memoirs, discusses the performance of the musical genius K. L. Saigal in Lahore in 1937 as he speaks of the mellifluous talents of the women performers of Hira Mandi (Nevile 2006[1993]: 91–95; 53–60), some of whom went on to make careers in theatre, cinema, radio and recording companies (Shah 2016).

Radha Kapuria's chapter (Chapter 7) takes us to the early twentieth century in Lahore and discusses the Punjabi contribution and connection to the cultural project of classicising, modernising and nationalising music and its pedagogy, undertaken by the Maharashtrian Brahmin musician Pt Vishnu Digambar Paluskar. This was the time when indigenous musicologists were grappling with new technologies (Weidman 2006), working towards preserving or mourning the demise of the *guru–shishya* (teacher–disciple) traditions or reinventing their repertoires. Kapuria examines why Lahore and later the older and established Harballabh music festival based in Jalandhar became the arenas for Paluskar's reformist projects. Lahore, Kapuria notes, nurtured an emerging middle-class of high-caste Hindu men from varied organisations, all keen to reorganise life and manners. Theirs was the Punjabi contribution to the nationalist urgings taking root in diverse fields in India, including music. The devotionalism and sacralising of musical performances; the democratisation of the performative space and the disciplining of the auditory practices of the hearing and consuming public; and the challenge to the secretive and Muslim-dominated *gharanedar*s (musical traditions), which were central to the complex musical projects initiated by Paluskar

(Bakhle 2005), could all be experimented with in Punjab. Thus, the first Gandharva Mahavidyalaya was established in Lahore in 1901 by Paluskar. Thus too, the Harballabh festival of Jalandhar, started in 1875 within a devotional framework, could give Paluskar a ready platform to establish his musicological sensibility. However, the cleansing and nationalising projects, which meant both wresting control of musical pedagogy from women, Muslims and lower-caste musicians, on the one hand, and reimagining the context and content of public performances, on the other, had their limits, Kapuria argues. The gharanedar musicians continued to have patronage, for instance, in princely domains like Patiala. The 1924 invitation to the Harballabh festival, an archival fragment unearthed by Kapuria, is interesting in this regard. Paluskar came here regularly, sacralising Harballabh by performing gratis, in contrast to his commercialising of the performance context otherwise. The invitation shows the continuing hold of older forms of musical performances like the *Jhiron ka geet*, *Kafian* and *Shabad-Sakhi* (all forms specific to Punjab), along with traditional *Bhajan Mandli*s (troupes singing devotional songs), suggesting that musical tastes changed slowly and that older performative traditions held their own despite newer restructurings. The calibrated change discussed here endorses the notion that indigenous forms, whether in music or houses people lived in, as shown by Glover, continued to be meaningful to people.

Women

If access to education, names with honorifics, and travel to and congregation in bustling urban centres like Lahore became a part of the life trajectories of some high-caste middle-class men, what were the routes and routines that shaped the life of women? There are some life patterns for women that can be discerned from the men's life writings; women's personal narratives in Punjab began to appear a little later, though women had started to participate in public life, for instance, through the print medium, as some of the contributors here discuss.[9] In most of the accounts mentioned above, men tell us the names of the women who were important in their lives, though the narratives are so focused on men's public and professional lives that the details of homes where women resided, with a few exceptions, are relatively thin, albeit not entirely absent. Everyone, of course, had a name—whether a Punjabi one, a Sanskritised one under the influence of the Arya Samaj[10] or with the innovation of a 'Kaur', posited by the Sikh reformers, as shown by Doris Jakobsh (2003: 219–28). In memoirist literature, where men fashioned specific projections of their public selves, the naming of women would, in the minimum, accede a degree of individuality and subjectivity to them, making them co-dwellers of the modernity that they so consciously inhabited.

Tandon's writing captures a way of life, as mentioned earlier, and gives details of rituals and rites associated with birth, marriage and death, aspects of life where women were importantly present. It is therefore striking that he does not mention the name of his mother. His mother is introduced as coming from a Vinayak Khatri family from Hadiabad, Kapurthala state. Though he tells us of his father's failed experiments at 'Westernising' her with humour (there was an improbable photo of hers in English clothes) (Tandon 2011[1988]: 39) and provides some information on her characteristic habits, she remains nameless. It is as if being a wife and mother, and the perpetuator of a Khatri lineage, was the sum of her life. Another startling example comes from Ruchi Ram Sahni's memoirs. He mentions the name of his mother, Gulab Devi, and father, Lala Karm Chand Sahni, and of his three brothers; but not of his sister, who is twice referred to as their 'unmarried sister' (Burra 2017: 28, 44). The cryptic reference to her gives a clue as to how some young women were perceived by men—married or waiting to be married—cogs in the clan's demand of marriage and motherhood. It is not that women did not have personality, which may find expression after motherhood and in advanced years. Most men mention specific personality traits of irrepressible women (Rai's reference to his grandmother, who could communicate with her dead sister-in-law and in her persona answer people's queries is noteworthy; Rai n.d.: 19); it is that their clan roles, the making of connection through their own circulation, at least in the eyes of men, overrode other aspects of their lives. However, as education spread and lifestyles changed with government employment, transferable jobs and urban living, women began to be educated and named—we hear the names of all of Ruchi Ram's children: five sons and four daughters. The celebrated litterateur Amrita Pritam (b.1919), in her autobiography, *Rasidi Ticket*, even gives a story of her naming—her name was the synonym of her father's pen name Piyush (nectar)—a story that affirms her salience in his life even as she struggled to define her relationship with him (Pritam 1976: 3).

Daughters were often brought up with curbs not placed on men. From Bhisham Sahni, we hear of the carefree life of his brother Balraj; his trips from Rawalpindi to Murree or Kashmir were commonplace. His account of the constraints on the lives of their two sisters, Vedwati and Savitri, is worth quoting:

> Our two sisters studied in the girls' school run by the Arya Samaj. But strangely enough, Father discontinued their studies even before they had reached the middle standard. These two sisters were brought up under strange restrictions. We had a balcony on the first floor of our house, facing the road. Our sisters were never permitted to go to the balcony, or to peep out of the windows of the house. They were expected not to laugh loudly or sing loudly. If, by any chance, their voice became loud enough to be heard by our neighbours, Father's harsh reproof would be heard from his office below (Sahni 1981: 9).

Some education, but not too much, was the motto, even for the Arya Samajis of the time, though the Mahatama wing of the Arya Samaj had opened the Kanya Mahavidyalaya for girls' education in Jalandhar, and the Singh Sabha started the Sikh Kanya Mahavidyalaya in Ferozepur, both in the early 1890s.[11]

To begin with, the smattering of education women received was to make them eligible in a new modern marriage market, as

Rochana Majumdar notes for Bengal (Majumdar 2010). In the new colonial social formation, men's education in newly established institutions, their employment, ability to travel cities and continents gave them a subjecthood and a cultural power that placed them in a disproportionate advantage in relation to women. It was the men (and their parents) who came to command the marriage market. In my earlier work I have shown the valence placed on the renewed enunciation of the ideal of the *pativrata*, and the new and often impossible demands placed on women as daughters, wives, mothers and daughters-in-law (Malhotra 2002). The men's position as subjects who exercised choice in the modern marriage market comes through in Mehta's biography of his Daddyji. With his education in the UK and later in the US, where Dr Amolak Ram Mehta went as a Rockefeller Foundation Fellow, his high-paying job as a public health officer in Punjab, his clubbing ways and hobnobbing with the Punjabi and British elite, Amolak Ram was 'in great demand in the marriage market and there were many proposals'. Ved Mehta describes his father's expectations from the woman he sought to marry:

> My wife should be her own dowry. She should be presentable, she should be fluent in English, and she should be musical. I would like her to be able to give good parties, and sing and play the harmonium for my guests. I want her to be modern and free of superstitions. I would, of course, like her to come to my clubs with me, and be able to walk and talk with the Indian and English wives (Mehta 1972: 132–33).

When Amolak Ram married Shanti Devi—he came to know her name only at the time of marriage when he was given the choice to 'rename' her (and presumably remould her according to his needs)—he did not realise that she could neither speak English, having learnt only Hindi in the little education she received in an Arya Samaj school, nor sing, play the harmonium or be free of 'superstitions'. Shanti's parents used subterfuge to manoeuvre in an increasingly unfavourable marriage market, to offset the enormous disadvantages that emerged from being parents of a girl. Nevertheless, Mehta's parents had a successful marriage that produced six children.

Women who managed to have a good education, often with the help of the men in their lives—fathers, brothers, husbands—increasingly came to be in a position to enter public life on their own steam. An excellent example of the advancement through the backing of the father is Pandita Ramabai, and of brother and husband, Rokeya Sakhawat Hossain, women who can be defined as early Indian feminists who entered public life despite odds stacked against them (Chakravarti 1998; Sarkar 2008; Vishwanathan 2001[1998]). Three chapters in this volume showcase the growing educational achievements of women in Punjab from the late nineteenth to the twentieth and into the twenty-first centuries; and their confidence in negotiating the public world as writers, professionals and as self-conscious bearers of autonomously and discursively produced modernity.

Arti Minocha in Chapter 4 complicates our understanding of Punjabi women as they came to construct and project their subjectivities in the print public sphere in the late nineteenth and early twentieth centuries by bringing in a transnational perspective that shaped them, and not just the men, in new ways. By exploring the potential of the print medium to engage in the life of the imagination, shaping the self through writing and conjuring collectivities through invoking reading publics, the more privileged women of the middle class created their autonomous beings with more daring and intellectual labour than has hitherto been acknowledged. Their subjectivities exceeded those of reformist and nationalist imaginaries they either imbibed the lessons of domesticity and spirituality that their men gave them (Walsh 2004) to enter the public sphere (Chatterjee 1993) or rejected reformism altogether to chart distinct trajectories in the face of, and in opposition to, reformist/nationalist frames. Examples of the latter are Pandita Ramabai who converted to Christianity, set up transnational networks to raise funds and did varied work for women in Maharashtra (Kosambi 2016; Grewal

1996); or the recalcitrant Rakhmabai who refused to cohabit with a dissipated husband to whom she was married as a child (Chandra 2008[1998]) in defiance of nationalist pleas. The two women in Minocha's chapter are a novelist, Susila Tahl Ram who wrote *Cosmopolitan Hinduani*, and a journalist and travel writer, Hardevi who wrote *London Yatra* and *London Jubilee*. These women constructed themselves as 'traveling subjects' as Inderpal Grewal has discussed, their upper-class, emerging feminism forged through gendered European travel (Grewal 1996: 16).

Tahl Ram's novel teems with women from diverse backgrounds—Anglo-Indian, Hindu, Muslim—who support and give succour to each other, a putative conceiving of a cross-cultural sisterhood. The most significant character of the novel is Amar Devi, a 'Hinduani', matching some details of the life of Tahl Ram, the author, just as she mimics Tahl Ram's upbringing in England, suggesting some autobiographical inflections in the novel. The juxtaposing of 'cosmopolitan' with 'Hinduani' envisages an alternate transnational alignment. This points to global networks that were shaping the imperial world (Burton 2003; Fisher 2004) along with multiple ways in which the local and the regional impinged on imaginative frames of the time. Yet Minocha also hints at a more ambivalent incorporation of the Muslim in the novel, 'naturalising' the Hindu as the rooted inhabitant of the nation. After making the assumption of Hindu belongingness, a more encompassing cosmopolitan outlook could be fashioned. The novel is written in English, adding another dimension to its cosmopolitan engagement, though a cosmopolitan imaginary did emerge strongly in the vernacular, as Minocha's discussion of Hardevi shows.

Hardevi's two travelogues, written when she took the trip to London to attend Queen Victoria's golden jubilee celebrations, can be viewed as products of her expanding horizons, excitement about which pushed her to share her growing expansiveness with her presumably less fortunate 'sisters' back home in Punjab. As noted earlier, we have many accounts of the making of this salient and transformative journey from India to England from men—Tandon, Amolak Ram, Lajpat Rai, Ruchi Ram. This mobility that increasingly became available to upper-class/caste men opened the world of the coloniser to complex and layered understandings of the operation of power in the European context, as also that of the colony. How the experience of travel, and the encounter with the unfamiliar, created possibilities of reimagining the self for women is presented here, in tandem with scholars of global histories who have read women's lives against a background of travel and its impact on their lives (Colley 2008; Grewal 1996; Lambert-Hurley and Sharma 2010). Minocha discusses not only how Hardevi deploys local and national frames to incorporate the Queen and her domesticity to her own understanding of *pativrata dharma* or Aryan culture, but also how her subject positions vary according to circumstances and contexts. Certainly, travel for Hardevi worked for imagining a modernity that brought in fresh perspectives to the local, allowing for rethinking and refurbishing institutions, politics and power that defined what being a Punjabi woman was about.

Anne Murphy in Chapter 5 brings in an even more self-assured engagement with print and public in the writings and academic career of the celebrated litterateur Dalip Kaur Tiwana (1935–2020). Tiwana, according to Murphy, demonstrates how the Progressive Writers Movement, which took birth in the mid-1930s, was important in imagining both modern nationalist literature and its ambition; and the place of women in society and its reimagining with reformism as a motivating force. With few women actually participating in the movement, Murphy nevertheless discusses the centrality of the figure of the woman, in the literary output associated with the movement. Women, Murphy posits, were represented often as victims of society; however, through the writing of their lives, their subjectivities and desires were spoken of and shaped, making them constitutive to the construction of a nationalist imaginary. Against this background, Murphy analyses the oeuvre of Tiwana, showing both the centrality of women in her writing, embedded as her characters are in familial relationships, the significant ambit of Tiwana's writing; but also her disquiet with the feminist cause. Tiwana's multilayered women lead complicated lives woven into the fabric of society which is patriarchal, a patriarchy that women have to negotiate and compromise with to acquire power. Her women are their own persons, no doubt; however, they do not challenge patriarchal social and cultural formations. Rather, they often exult in fulfilling the roles that society assigns them. These complex gendered roles and negotiations are seen in a number of her novels and stories. A good example is her *Mata Dharati Mahatu* that conceptualises and fleshes out the lives of the mother and the three wives of Guru Gobind Singh. Here you see historically important women narratologically fulfilling the demands of hetero-patriarchally imagined heroines—beautiful and dutiful—and garnering praise for ideal behaviour. Murphy also shows how Tiwana was invested in scripting her autobiographical narratives; she analyses her *Nange Pairan da Safar*—the first part of her four-part autobiography.

In contradistinction to the men's memoirs discussed here, Murphy indexes a complex self-presentation and fashioning, as also a temporal flux in Tiwana's writing. Tiwana, in her portrayal, comments on her own being and becoming as she converses with real and spectral characters. In the various genres of Tiwana's writing, Murphy shows her to be steeped in her local environment and locates her agency as not nurtured by liberal feminism but as negotiated within her Punjabi Malwai culture and ethos. As a university professor, as a producer of highly valued literature and as an agential performer of the self, Tiwana embodies Punjabi women, complex and compelling, shaped by history and culture.

With Inderpal Grewal's Chapter 6, we enter a contemporaneous moment where she brings to us a Punjabi woman who is not only confident about her professional career, but also willing to go to lengths to defend its integrity and her name. Grewal fleshes out the growth of the security state with its extensive and systematic deployment of violence as it developed in the last two decades of the twentieth century in Punjab, the period associated with Sikh secessionism, and a demand for a separate homeland of Khalistan. She discusses in particular the 'super cop' K. P. S. Gill, the director general of police between 1988 and 1990 and again during 1991–95, who was alleged to have used unaccounted-for violence as state policy with impunity (Kaur 2019). He was alleged to not only routinely carry out extra-judicial killings of those narrativised as 'militants', 'terrorists' and 'enemies of the state', but also use his machismo to enact gender politics that in the long run undermined his public standing, otherwise burnished through receiving the Padma Shri honour. A case was brought against him by Rupan Deol Bajaj, an officer of the Indian Administrative Service (IAS), of 'sexual harassment' under Sections 354 and 509 of the Indian Penal Code. She won the case in every court it was tried in, including the Supreme Court. The case exposed the deep-seated patriarchal nature not only of postcolonial Punjab but of India in general, which constitutionally guaranteed non-discrimination on the basis of gender, among other protections. Grewal builds up her arguments of the securitisation of the state and its relentless use of violence against those deemed as threats to the sacralised nation by linking it to the colonial legacy of validating hyper-masculinity as a desirable quality, and historically the excessive deployment of violence in Punjab.

The colonial state's violent masculinity is visible not only in its recruitment of those labelled 'martial' in the Indian Army, the Jat-Sikhs idealised among them (Imy 2019; Singh 2014; Tan 2005), but also in the manner in which it consistently used excessive force to quell any movement that it viewed as a threat (Wagner 2016). The state frequently deployed violence on its north-western borders, especially in Afghanistan, and against the Punjabi populace—for example, the Kuka reformers in 1872; the Ghadar revolutionaries in 1915; in Jallianwala Bagh in 1919; or against the revolutionaries of the Hindustan Socialist Republican Association (HSRA), like the youthful and charismatic Bhagat Singh in 1931. The very moment of the birthing of the new nation of India (and

Pakistan) was mired in hideous violence in Punjab against those seen to be the 'other'. This violence showed itself in egregiously patriarchal forms as narrated by the fiction of that time, and also shown by the spate of scholarship on Partition (Butalia 1998; Manto 2008; Menon and Bhasin 1998; Roy 2018). The many gendered manifestations of this violence, for instance, when the abducted women were given no choice in the states' insistence on their return to the nations claiming them on the basis of religion, showed the deficiencies in the promise of citizenship made by the Indian state (Das 1996, 2007). Given this background, Bajaj's assertion of her right to redressal in the courts is important. It also underscores her elite status, both as an IAS officer and as belonging to the dominant landowning Jat caste (also Gill's caste) that has dominated postcolonial Indian Punjab's Akali politics. Pertinently, Grewal shows the social construction of Bajaj as an 'immodest' woman who married a Hindu man outside the Jat community. The casting of Bajaj as immodest for having flouted the rules of patriarchal endogamy shows how the gendered stakes of idealised behaviour continue to weigh heavy against women, despite the power some may wield. The very law that allows for criminalising the 'attack on a woman's modesty' expects the woman to be living within patriarchal respectability, not challenging norms through sexual autonomy and individuated agency.

The changing and uneven contours of Punjabi women's lives—from being embedded in kinship relationships that sometimes erased their names to defending the respectability of their names and selves publicly at other times—are thus captured in the chapters in this volume. In the late nineteenth and early twentieth centuries, to what extent do we find examples of politics of sharply etched Sikh, Hindu and Muslim identities, the kind that Grewal alludes to—the very basis for the demand for ethno-nationalisms like the Khalistan movement, or earlier, the Pakistan one, or indeed the way India is being imagined today in exclusivist Hindu terms? Let us explore the questions of religious and caste identities in the next section.

Religious and Caste Identities

In self-representational writing discussed in this Introduction—of men entering the public life of professions and civic reform associations, looking for employment in and patronage of the colonial state in an atmosphere of competitive politics—the overt view most accounts exude is of communal truculence, with a few exceptions like Ruchi Ram Sahni. Caste features only occasionally here as most men were high caste and, for the most part, speak with pride of their caste status, but little about the power relations that structured caste in society or its contestations. They often concerned themselves with their own ilk in their writings. For example, in Rai's writing, when he speaks of '*jati prem*' or '*jati seva*' (love for/serving the community)[12] or even '*maine Hindu qaumiyat ke saath apna naata jora*' (I aligned myself with the Hindu community/nation), he is, for the most part, referring to the high-caste educated men like himself who, at this historical moment and in their imaginations, both constructed and constituted the nation; though Rai, like some Arya Samajis, was interested in the 'low-caste question' and 'conversions' (Rai n.d.: 42). However, as a growing body of scholarship has demonstrated, this was just one view in a world of diverse praxis, whether popular saint veneration, following local charismatic and performative gurus, or what Bigelow has called 'pro-social' encounters (Bigelow 2012; Dobe 2015; Malhotra 2017; Mir 2012; Snehi 2019). What has not been commented upon is how this memoirist literature that often promotes ethno-religious identities can be mined for information that is not necessarily the worldview of the auto/biographer. Though the author projects a specific self-image, there is also the historical milieu these accounts of life experiences carry, which allow them to be read against, as much as with, the grain (Stoler 2009).

Lajpat Rai's religiously mixed heritage—Hindu, Jain (his grandfather was a Jain of the Svetambara sect, which tied a cloth over their mouths) (Rai n.d.: 18), Sikh and even Islamic (if we consider his father's inclination)—has already been noted, though he chose to fashion and project only one of these legacies, his Hindu 'Arya' self. However, an involute and complex life emerges if we were to see the larger movements that Rai came to connect himself with: intermittent association with Congress politics; his involvement with the 1907 agrarian agitations of Punjab, particularly in the Canal Colonies, and his communications at the time with Muslim and Sikh lawyers and leaders; his travels to England and the US in 1914, and meeting with leaders who had transnational links to socialism, anarchism and internationalism, including the secular Ghadarites (Oberoi 2009; Ramnath 2011). In the same vein, Bhagat Laxman Singh, who converted to Sikhism in his 30s and became a Khalsa and a life-long supporter of the Sikh reformist Singh Sabha, came to be associated with both the 'Sanatani' Baba Khem Singh Bedi (who acknowledged a relationship between Sikhism and Hinduism, and whose mansion/*haveli* had frescos depicting Hindu gods and Sikh gurus) and the more exclusivist Lahore wing referred to as 'Tat Khalsa' (Asghar 2021; Asghar et al. 2021; Oberoi 1994).[13] His mixed lineage comes through in his introductory chapter itself: he came from a Kohli Khatri family of distinguished holy men, gurus with local following. The prefix 'bhagat' (*bhakta*, devotee) in his name came from the celebrated spirituality, piety and the following of these men, among whom he names Dyal Chand, a 'Vaishnava Hindu', 'Sain Sahib', his son, who cherished Gurbani and the Granth and whose followers in turn included the Namdhari/Kuka movement initiators, Bhai Balak Singh and Baba Ram Singh. Laxman Singh himself was a great-great grandson of Dyal Chand (Singh 1965: 1–7).[14] Laxman Singh thus exemplifies the doubleness that came to define life by the late nineteenth century once competitive, post-enumerated community politics became the norm: an inheritance of plural ontological possibilities and a contemporary constitution of self-containment.

A third example of hybrid religious heritage comes from the upbringing of Ruchi Ram Sahni. Sahni presents his father as being simultaneously Hindu and Sikh. His father is shown to be fond of his daily rituals of *puja* before his idols, and when he fell ill, and since he was the fondest of Ruchi Ram, he made him bathe the idols and change their clothes. Sahni also speaks of how his father made him read a chapter of the Bhagwad Gita every afternoon and to start over when all the 18 chapters were done. His father is presented as a pious Hindu who, at one juncture, is unable to tolerate the beating of a cow. Sahni, at the same time, presents him as coming from a Sikh family: 'Although my father was an extremely orthodox man and did his *puja* to the idols scrupulously every morning, he had great faith in the Sikh Gurus and, indeed my whole family was known to be a Sikh family.' He speaks of the *dharamshala* at Bhera, their native town, and its Bhais of Kariala, descended from Matidas, the eighteenth-century Sikh martyr: 'When I was about nine years of age, I was myself initiated into the Sikh faith as a *Sahjdhari* by Bhai Partap Singh of Kariala.'[15] His father daily read the *Rahora*s and the *Sukhmani* prayers while he regularly entertained Brahmans and various sadhus in Sahni's recollections (Burra 2017: 16–35).

Sahni, a secular rationalist who was a member of the Brahmo Samaj in his adult life, consciously writes about the relations between the Hindus and the Muslims in Dera Ismail Khan: 'The social relations between the Hindus and Muslims in those days were quite cordial' (Burra 2017: 24). He speaks of the seasonal trips made by the Waziris and Powindahs from further north-west to his town and his ease in conversing with them in Pushto. The keeping of pollution taboos, mentioned in almost all our accounts, is noted in Sahni's as well, but he also dwells on interaction with Muslims at various levels. Sahni notes the separate drinking water arrangements in Bannu, further west of Dera Ismail Khan, where Muslims supplied water to Hindu households, and writes of how water was poured from goat-skin bags onto pots by Muslim *mashki*s. They took the lid off with wooden sticks: 'the non-conductivity of wood so far as communal pollution was concerned', writes Sahni in sarcastic humour, as he spent his life popularising science in Punjab and combating irrational behaviour. He mentions the exchanges of gifts with Muslims on various festivals. Sahni reminisces that during the Russo-Turkish war of 1877, the agitated Muslims of the town would ask him to read the news and he read to them the *Civil and Military Gazette* daily to update them on the events (Burra 2017: 34–61).

The plural identities and the self-serving deceptions with regard to religious and caste identities that Sahni speaks of were precisely the hybridity, the muddying co-mingling, that riled the reformers, especially the Sikh ones, who felt their very existence as a people was under threat. As Tony Ballantyne has noted, these reformers adopted a double-pronged strategy to delineate Sikh identity: a recourse to an historical reconstruction of the ideal Khalsa located in the eighteenth century, on the one hand, and a sharp distinction from Hinduism whose amorphous nature, they feared, could swallow Sikh identity (Ballantyne 2007: 6–7) on the other. However, historically the Sikhs emphasised differences with the Muslims and later in the nineteenth century with the Hindus, but the anti-Muslim angst continued to prevail in myriad ways.

In Chapter 9, Kanika Singh explores the changing portrayals of Sikh sovereignty from the nineteenth century to the present through the changing representation of an event that took place in the eighteenth century—Baghel Singh of the cis-Satluj Karorsinghia *misl*'s scrimmage in Delhi in 1783. This underscores the Sikhs as not only always separately defined, but also as sovereign. Taking as her starting point the celebration in 2014 of Fateh Diwas (victory day), the power of its performative representation of an apparent Sikh victory of Baghel Singh over the Mughals, and the flying of the *Nishan Sahib* (Khalsa flag) on the ramparts of Red Fort, Singh shows its imbrication in present-day politics.[16] The claims to Sikh/Khalsa sovereignty became insistent from the 1970s and particularly during the Khalistan movement for a separate Sikh homeland. Singh also discusses the paintings available in the Bhai Mati Das museum within the sacred precincts of the Sis Ganj Gurdwara. These too focus on depictions of Sikh sovereignty, Mughal pusillanimity and, interestingly, the mediation of Begum

Samru, the ruler of the territory of Sardhana, here depicted with the (othering) symbology of a Muslim woman in a *burqa*, between the two sides. Significantly Samru, in paintings commissioned by her that underscored her power, is shown as an androgynous and commanding figure, occupying public space with authority, far from the stereotyped figure presented by Sikh painters (Rajagopalan 2018). The performative portrayals in the *jarnaili* march and the *Raj Karega Khalsa* ('The Khalsa Will Rule') play in 2014, on the one hand, and the paintings, on the other, both borrow and differ from the nineteenth-century account of Ratan Singh Bhangu in his *Sri Gur Panth Prakash* (1841). Bhangu is also keen to demonstrate the hegemonic position of the Sikhs in Delhi, not displayed through occupying the Red Fort but by negotiating for the construction of gurdwaras in Delhi. The dialogic relationship with history is an aspect of the contemporaneous identity politics of the Sikhs, as Singh shows, and in this instance, it saliently converges with the desire of the Hindu right to show the Mughals as alien conquerors.

And what do we know of the relationship between religion and the pious practices of women? Women's religiosity was particularly eclectic, as our sources in the colonial period demonstrate. I have written elsewhere of women's faith in the local and regional *pir*s of Punjab, the Sufis and Muslim holy men and their hospices, whom women visited especially for the boon of children, desire for a male child or to remove the curse of barrenness. The story of Dani Jatti and her faith in Sakhi Sarvar, and her visit to his tomb in Nigaha to save her son, exemplifies such piety (Malhotra 2002: 170–79). Hindu women, steeped in the practice of idol worship, had no qualms about expanding their pantheon of deities. The famous novelist Mulk Raj Anand, in his autobiography, made fun of precisely such eclecticism, which seemed to him ridiculous, brought up as he was in reformist times. Reformers had sought to define religion as a universal category, with each religion having specific features, and so they endeavoured to separate out different religions, attacking practices that confounded the reformers' understanding of religious exclusivism. Women, less likely to participate in public meetings of varied reformers where debates on acceptable meanings of religion and community upliftment took place, were often left to their own devices (or received new information second-hand):

> I remember how when I was a child my mother would place little brass idols of the gods and the goddesses of the Hindu pantheon side by side with a crucifix she had picked up somewhere, a picture of the Aga Khan, and of Guru Nanak.... That always seemed to me to be incongruous... (Anand 1975[1946]: 29).

However, Anand's mother's mode of worship was the norm rather than the exception, women being more recalcitrant than pliant to new moves. Here is a similar description from Reena Nanda, a biographer of her mother, referring to her grandmother:

> Maanji's devotion to the Guru Granth Sahib did not prevent her from reading the Gita or from observing Sanatani rituals like the aarti. The large lithograph of Guru Nanak on the wall had a small shelf below with her icons of Sri Ram, Sri Krishna, and Durga Mata. For her, these deities and her *Vahe* Guru existed in a shared world of religious piety (Nanda 2018: 38).

How relevant is this manner of religiosity—hybrid, fluid, porous, incorporating, appropriating, syncretic—concepts through which we may make sense of it in our times? In today's differentiated frames, has it become a relic of the past or does it continue to flourish amidst us? In Chapter 8, Yogesh Snehi brings into focus a persistent, stubborn aspect of popular religiosities of Punjab, one that does not draw much scholarly attention. Mesmerised by the dominant idiom of religious identity that aligns with statist sanction, the Indian Punjab today is seen as a land of the Sikhs, especially post the state's reconstruction in 1966. Sikhs, who are 58 per cent of the state's population (Population Census 2011), are in turn seen to be defined in their religious practice by the Granth, the gurdwara and the line of ten gurus. At a cursory glance, the casual observer will see just this religious idiom in the Indian Punjab, particularly as it seems to uphold the power of the dominant Jat Sikhs as of the party politics of the Akalis. However, the plurality of identity and the multiple ways of seeking spiritual solace—the simultaneous adhering to the dominant ethos and participating in local traditions—is an aspect of the Punjabis' cultural practice that deserves study. In recent years, the multitudinous *dera*s of Punjab—particularly with Dalit following, including the Ravidasi Sachkhand Ballan—have received attention (Ram 2009). It is important to acknowledge that 32 per cent of Indian Punjab's population is Dalit, against 21 per cent of Jat Sikh; the focus on Dalits is thus a sound corrective (Population Census 2011).

Turning his attention to three popular shrines with mixed caste following—Gurdwara Samadhan Baba Jalan Das at Naushera Dhala; Bhairon Nath shrine in the Durgiana complex near the Golden Temple in Amritsar; and the shrine Ghuram Sharif dedicated to Pir Bhikam Shah of the Chishti-Sabri order and Gurdwara Milapsar in Patiala—Snehi shows how these connote the tenacious hold of popular religiosities on Punjabi peoples. However, Snehi also points out the varied ways in which the Sikh dominant idiom and the nation-state formation, what he denotes as the 'territorialising' power of the state and cultural formations that work with it, impinge on the histories and spaces of these alternative religiosities. Baba Jalan's dera, for instance, once in the very heart of the Majha region of Punjab, now finds itself in a contentious border region that impacts the way its devotees and its managers deal with it. The Durgiana complex has increasingly come under the power of the right conglomerate through the management of the Vishwa Hindu Parishad (VHP), marginalising some specific shrines like the Bhairon Nath which do not fit into the overall scheme of a sanitised and 'one size fits all' Hinduism. Or, even the Ghuram Sharif establishment that now contends with a virtually totally non-Muslim following and what that means to the semiotics through which it engages devotees.

Contention with authorities itself is not new as the history of these shrines shows so eloquently; for instance, the clash of Jalan Das with Shahjahan, the Mughal emperor. What is also not new is the manner in which dominant religious mythologies have impacted these sites and religious personas; for example, we see both the Ramayana story and Nanak's early life story contouring the imagining of the life of Baba Jalan Das; or the manner in which Pir Bhikam Shah's life is meant to have entwined with that of the tenth Guru Gobind from the time of the latter's birth in Patna. This recourse to 'allegory and allusion' has been vital to the pre-modern imaginations, what A. K. Ramanujan formulated as the non-pressure for originality that modernity obsesses over (Malhotra 2017; Ramanujan 2013). Thus, contention and reconciliation continue to be part of what Snehi describes as the 'archive of everyday' religiosity. Snehi tracks these contemporaneous alternate imaginations, and this is important in challenging the homogenising of pluralistic traditions that began in earnest in the late nineteenth century.

An aspect of the contemporaneous religious landscape of Punjab is the visual manifestations of an increasingly assertive Dalit presence—Ravidasis (formerly Chamar), Balmikis, Mazhabi (formerly Chuhra) and Christian (Misra 2021)—as seen in their religious spaces and deras. The question of the erstwhile 'low castes' and 'untouchables' had taken salience in the late nineteenth-century politics centred around enhancing community numbers, with the Arya Samaj initiating the 'shuddhi' or purification ceremonies in order to incorporate them into Hinduism. This occurred in an environment of competitive politics for their attention, to offset the Hindus' minority status in colonial Punjab; though the sincerity and long-term commitment of these inclusive agendas displayed ambivalence at best (Adcock 2012; Malhotra 2006). The low-caste communities, however, began to assert their identity, some in the second half of the nineteenth century by converting to different Christian denominations via the multiple missions that were operating in Punjab (Harding 2008), and by the first quarter of the twentieth century, for example, through movements like the Ad-Dharm that represented Dalit aspirations. Its leader Mangoo Ram had emigrated to the US, been involved in Ghadar politics and then returned to start the movement, though the changes were already being experienced in sub-regions like the Doaba in Punjab. His transnational mobility and experience were important in his political development, as was the intermittent and contested support of the Arya Samaj (Juergensmeyer 2013).

The significance of Dalit assertions and challenging of caste-based power dynamics today can be underscored when we see the egregious treatment that was meted out to them at the hands of the upper Brahmanical castes in colonial Punjab. Reconstructing a scene around her grandmother, Nanda describes this ordeal of the daily humiliations that was their lot:

> For Maanji maintaining purity from polluting elements was as vital as her Darbar Sahib. The *chudas*, *achhoot* (untouchable), the carriers of human excreta, were a necessity, but they had to be controlled by her to minimize their polluting presence. Every day when the *chudi* (the sweeper woman) arrived to empty the toilets, it was as if a tornado had struck the house. She had to cross the courtyard—Maanji's sacred space—to reach the mezzanine toilets, and Maanji became hysterical, scuttering around removing every object in sight: clothes, shoes, stools—anything that lay in the *chudi*'s path.... Woe betide the hapless woman if she ever accidentally touched anything (Nanda 2018: 39).

A similar scene is recounted by Ved Mehta about his great-grandmother when he narrates his father and younger brother's short trek to the school:

> The brothers would take care that they did not accidentally come in contact with sweepers, tanners or any other untouchables along the way, for Manji had given them strict instructions to throw away the food if they should be so defiled.... As an added precaution, Manji kept a vessel of Ganga water to purify them (Mehta 1972: 25).

While these accounts tell us of the world of colonial Punjab and its upper castes' prejudices against 'untouchables', the more contemporary caste conflicts in Punjab have been between the dominant Jats and those challenging this dominance and asserting their distinct identity, particularly the Ravidasis. In this context, it must be borne in mind that the colonial state, by constructing a fundamental social and economic division between the 'agricultural' and 'non-agricultural' castes through statutory laws like the Land Alienation Act (1901), made land ownership by castes like the Jats a basis for their dominance in Punjab (Barrier 1966; Bhattacharya 2018; Hans 2016). The 'non-agriculturists' included the upper castes of Punjab like the Khatris, Aroras and Baniyas, whose relationship with trading, shopkeeping and the professions became cemented (Jones 1989), excluding investment in land on their part, on the one hand, and the low castes and Dalits who provided various services to the higher castes through the *jajmani/sepidari* system or worked on land, often denigrated as '*kamins*' by the landowners, on the other. The colonial period, then, deepened a relationship of agriculture-practising castes like the Jats with land to an unprecedented degree, and had a deleterious effect on those who may labour in the fields but not own one.

The colonial print publics, as they developed, allowed for horizontal caste linkages to be forged, which began to change the way caste came to play a role in political and social life. In postcolonial India, Nicola Mooney's anthropological study of the urban Jat Sikhs of Ganganagar in Rajasthan, near Punjab, shows the significance of their real, imagined and desired circuits of connection across rural Punjab on the one hand, and on the other, diasporic and transnational Jat communities, what she calls the Jats' 'rural nostalgias and transnational dreams' (Mooney 2011). The aggravating social, cultural, ecological and economic crises of Punjab in recent years have only further grown the desire of the youth to migrate out of Punjab (Gill 2016); and the 'West' has come to encompass aspirations of modernity, progress and freedom from the oppressive gender and caste norms that are perceived to dictate life in Punjab (Mitra 2021).

Dalits also began to participate in cross-region caste associations from the colonial period. The Ravidasi networks in Punjab, India, and the diaspora are a case in point, developing their identity as a separate religious one (Jodhka 2016). In Punjab and the diaspora today, Dalit identity is often seen in the Ravidasia gurdwaras and their liturgical and ritual practices, which, while in many ways framed within the dominant Sikh idiom (setting up a gurdwara, a holy book in the form of the *bani* of Bhagat Ravidas), asserts their difference. These competitive politics of representation have sometimes led to conflict between the Jats and the Ravidasis, as happened in Vienna in 2009 when two leaders of Dera Sach Khand, including its head Sant Niranjan Dass, were shot dead by a few young men. Earlier in 2007, the Dera Sacha Sauda leader's imitation of the tenth Guru's dress and demeanour had also led to violence in the streets of Punjab (Baixas 2007). More recently, these caste contestations manifest themselves in the popular Punjabi music industry where the lyrics of songs, the accompanying visuals or the tweeted responses to them on social media exacerbate conflicts (Judge 2015).

While contemporary Indian politics is not explicable without some understanding of caste solidarities, caste has stayed relevant in other social and cultural ways too. Bringing the historical and the contemporary together in Chapter 10, Gurpreet Bal discusses the role played by the Khatri community of Amritsar in the early settling of the city, and links it to their presence in the city today. Giving us a glimpse of the manner in which the Sikh gurus, themselves all Khatris from the time the fourth Guru Ram Das first settled Amritsar, then called Ramdaspur, Bal takes us through the gurus' later relationship with the city. She notes the important changes of the eighteenth century, the time of the misls, and the significant moments of desacralisation of the holy Harimandir, but also the manner in which the markets, the *katra*s, and the business community of the Khatris bounced back each time. As a city associated with manufacture and trade, enhanced by its location on caravan routes, it flourished in the relatively calmer period under Maharaja Ranjit Singh, both as a holy city and as a business hub. Bal also takes us through the more recent sufferings of the city during Partition, but demonstrates its resilience through demographic changes and business disruptions. Similarly, she underlines the plasticity of the Khatri community in adjusting to the changing politics of governments, the difficult period of militancy, as also the evolving business environments.

Bal builds her arguments about the Khatri community and its continuous reinvention as a business and trading people through a study of their social capital: their historic social and caste organisation (the *dhai*, *char*, *barah*, *bawanjah*, the endogamy-based categories), marriage and kinship networks, risk-taking and deliberate dispersing of interests and kin, and business sense honed and developed over generations and built on systems of credit and trust. Her chapter is an interesting parallel to the way in which some of our Bania and Khatri auto/biographers—Rai, Tandon, Mehta, Singh, Nanda, Ruchi Ram Sahni, Bhisham Sahni—describe both the historical endogamous organisation of the Khatris and their adaptation to the new professions as they developed in India. Ruchi Ram's memoirs are particularly interesting from the perspective of an antiquarian interest in Khatri upbringing as he recounts his childhood: learning multiplication tables (*pahara*), complex mathematical formulae passed down from father to son, the *landé* writing characters specific to merchant *mahajan*s, apprenticing with big shopkeepers from a young age, using *hundi* credit currency and his paternally inherited cloth shop growing into a big general store. His later journey to English education and professorship at the Government College, Lahore, has already been referenced (Burra 2017). It is important to underscore the ductility of caste as a social, cultural and political unit that seems to forever mutate and reinvent.

* * *

This Introduction has taken a brief look at a few of the plentiful issues that help us delve into the meanings of Punjab and Punjabiyat for the people for whom this affiliation remains evocative, howsoever they may associate with it. Just as Punjabis domicile in multiple locations and nations, practice different religions or none at all, adhere to varied caste groupings or discredit caste, speak Punjabi or not, write it in different scripts or are illiterate, understand and interpret history in myriad ways, this introduction has sought to highlight multivalent standpoints from which we can approach what it means to be a Punjabi. The path to underscore this diversity of world-making for different Punjabis has been trodden through the voices of some who were vocal and voluble; but these have been used as entry-points to suggest that there are other voices and ways of thinking and being. The chapters this volume brings together are also introductions to questions that are complex, and moreover bring up just a few of the many problematics that engage scholars of Punjab. A historiography of Punjab, the heuristics of Punjabi pasts, the privileging of academia and popular understandings of the past—all impinge on how we understand Punjab and Punjabiyat, the object of our research, and sometimes identity as well. This is a contribution towards that ongoing project.

Notes

1. The region was referred to as Pentapotamia in Greek sources and Pancanada in epic and Pauranic ones, before the Persian term Punjab emerged. The autochthonous regional development is now being traced to the *gana-sangha* period (Kumar 2019).

2. On the making of Model Town and the ideas of town planning that went into it, see Glover (2008: 99–158).

3. The Punjabi local use of 'Hindustan' as the area of the Gangetic plains in north India beyond Punjab is different from the manner in which the term has recently been evoked by Manan Ahmed Asif (2020: 2–6) when commenting on the pre-colonial imagination, or even the

manner in which the term was evoked by Iqbal in 1904 or Bhagat Singh in 1928.

4. Rai, for example, introduces one of the leaders of the 1907 agitations in Punjab, Ajit Singh, as someone who earned a living teaching Urdu, Farsi and Hindi to the English. Ajit Singh was the uncle of popular Indian revolutionary Bhagat Singh. Similar is his description of Pandit Lekhram, whom he calls the first *shahid* (martyr) of Arya Samaj, as someone who knew Arabic, Farsi and Urdu well (Rai n.d.: 208, 132).

5. Reena Nanda comments on this: 'In Lalaji's era, the two faiths were not considered separate or exclusive. In fact, several Punjabi Hindu families had a tradition that the first son should be brought up as a Sikh' (Nanda 2018: 27).

6. Bhagat Laxman Singh comments on it in his autobiography. Ditt Singh wrote a searing critique of Arya Samaj's founder Swami Dayanand in his *Swami Dayanand Naal Mera Sambaad* (Malhotra 2017: 211).

7. Kaur noted that Jats in Punjab were so secure in their Sikh identity that many did not wear the 5Ks, did not keep unshorn hair, trimmed their beard and were not punctilious in visiting gurdwaras. Kaur's fieldwork in the Piplanwala village in Doaba region was in 1981–82, at the beginning of the Sikh militancy in Punjab. She commented that other Sikh castes like Khatris and Ramgariyas were more careful about maintaining Sikh symbols. This has been commented on by McLeod too (Kaur 1986; McLeod 1976).

8. Rai's book does not carry the date of publishing, but there are enough internal clues that allow for the date of its writing to be discerned.

9. I have written on the autobiographical narrative of the nineteenth-century woman Piro (Malhotra 2017); however, her composition was pre-modern. Amrita Pritam's autobiographical sketch *Rasidi Ticket* was written in 1976.

10. Bhisham Sahni narrates the hilarious story of how he was first named Yudhishther, but their aunt could not pronounce it and confused it with 'register', so a less tongue-twisting name was found for him. For their sister Veeranwali, the opposite happened. Her Punjabi name was replaced by an appropriately Sanskritised one, Vedwati (Sahni 1981).

11. Balraj Sahni was sent by his father to a 'gurukul' type of school, advocated by the Mahatama wing of the Arya Samaj, though his father belonged to the college/D.A.V. faction of the Samaj, so he could learn proper Hindi and Sanskrit. He later rebelled against this style of

education and went on to study in a D.A.V. school in Rawalpindi (Sahni 1981: 10–12).

12. The word *jati*—species—connotes community here.

13. Baba Khem Singh Bedi's *haveli* had frescos that depicted Hindu gods along with Sikh gurus (Asghar 2021; Asghar et al. 2021).

14. Such diversity was significant among Sikhs not only in the nineteenth century (Oberoi 1994) but also today, including in the diaspora (Takhar 2014).

15. *Sahajdhari* is derived from the word *sahaj* (spiritual bliss). Under the influence of Sikh reformers who encouraged everyone to adopt the Khalsa model, sahajdhari came to mean someone who did not keep *kes*, or unshorn hair, that is, a *mona*, and also a 'slow adopter' of the Khalsa way.

16. This mythic moment came to be re-enacted on 26 January 2021 by a breakaway group during the farmers' agitation in Delhi (Malhotra 2021).

References

Adcock, C. S. 2012. 'Brave Converts in the Arya Samaj: The Case of Dharam Pal'. In *Punjab Reconsidered: History, Culture and Practice*, eds Anshu Malhotra and Farina Mir, 261–86. New Delhi: Oxford University Press.

Anand, Mulk Raj. 1975[1946]. *Apology for Heroism: A Brief Autobiography of Ideas*. Delhi: Arnold Hienemann.

Asghar, Muhammad. 2021. 'Cultural Syncretism: An Investigative Study of Nineteenth Century Sikh Fresco Paintings in Baba Sir Khem Singh Bedi's Haveli in Punjab/Pakistan'. *Early Popular Visual Culture* 19 (1): 21–37.

Asghar, Muhammad, Muhammad Arshad Rehmani and Qurrat-ul-ain Sikandar Ali. 2021. 'Haveli Paintings: Further Explorations of Baba Sir Khem Singh Bedi's Haveli in Punjab/Pakistan'. *South Asian History and Culture* 12 (1): 75–92.

Asif, Manan Ahmed. 2020. *The Loss of Hindustan: The Invention of India*. Cambridge: Harvard University Press.

Ayers, Alyssa. 2012. 'Language, the Nation and Symbolic Capital: The Case of Punjab'. In *Punjab Reconsidered: History, Culture and Practice*, eds Anshu Malhotra and Farina Mir, 35–61. New Delhi: Oxford University Press.

Baixas, Lionel. 2007. 'The Dera Sacha Sauda Controversy and Beyond'. *Economic & Political Weekly* 42 (40): 4059–74.

Bakhle, Janaki. 2005. *Two Men and Music: Nationalism in the Making of an Indian Classical Tradition*. New York: Oxford University Press.

Ballantyne, Tony. 2007. *Between Colonialism and Diaspora: Sikh Cultural Formations in an Imperial World*. New Delhi: Permanent Black.

Banga, Indu. 1997. *Five Punjabi Centuries: Polity, Economy, Society and Culture*. New Delhi: Manohar.

Barrier, N. G. 1966. 'The Punjab Alienation of Land Bill of 1900'. Monograph and Occasional Paper Series, No. 2, Duke University.

Bhattacharya, Neeladri 2018. *The Great Agrarian Conquest: The Colonial Reshaping of a Rural World*. Ranikhet: Permanent Black.

Bigelow, Anna. 2012. 'Post-Partition Pluralism: Placing Islam in Indian Punjab'. In *Punjab Reconsidered: History, Culture and Practice*, eds Anshu Malhotra and Farina Mir, 409–34. New Delhi: Oxford University Press.

Burke, Peter. 2016[1978]. *Popular Culture in Early Modern Europe*. New York: Routledge.

Burra, Neera. 2017. *A Memoir of Pre-Partition Punjab: Ruchi Ram Sahni, 1863–1948*. New Delhi: Oxford University Press.

Burton, Antoinette. 2003. 'House, Daughter, Nation: Interiority, Architecture, and Historical Imagination in Janaki Majumdar's "Family History"'. In her *Dwelling in the Archive: Women Writing House, Home and History in Late Colonial India*, 31–64. New York: Oxford University Press.

Butalia, Urvashi. 1998. *The Other Side of Silence: Voices from the Partition of India*. New Delhi: Penguin Books.

Chakrabarty, Dipesh. 2015. *The Calling of History: Sir Jadunath Sarkar and His Empire of Truth*. Ranikhet: Permanent Black.

Chakravarti, Uma. 1998. *Rewriting History: The Life and Times of Pandita Ramabai*. New Delhi: Zubaan.

Chandra, Sudhir. 2008[1998]. *Enslaved Daughters: Colonialism, Law and Women's Rights*. New Delhi: Oxford University Press.

Chatterjee, Partha. 1993. *The Nation and its Fragments: Colonial and Postcolonial Histories*. Princeton: Princeton University Press.

_____. 2008. 'Introduction: History in the Vernacular'. In *History in the Vernacular*, eds Raziuddin Aquil and Partha Chatterjee, 1–24. Ranikhet: Permanent Black.

Chopra, Radhika. 2011. *Militant and Migrant: The Politics and Social History of Punjab*. London: Routledge.

Colley, Linda. 2008. *The Ordeal of Elizabeth Marsh: A Woman in World History*. New York: Anchor Books.

Daiya, Kavita. 2020. *Graphic Migrations: Precarity and Gender in India and the Diaspora*. Philadelphia: Temple University Press.

Das, Veena. 1996. 'National Honour and Practical Kinship: Of Unwanted Women and Children'. In her *Critical Events: An Anthropological Perspective on Contemporary India*, 55–83. New Delhi: Oxford University Press.

———. 2007. *Life and Words: Violence and the Descent into the Ordinary*. New Delhi: Oxford University Press.

Dobe, Timothy S. 2015. *Hindu Christian Faqir: Modern Monks, Global Christianity and Indian Sainthood*. Oxford: Oxford University Press.

Dudrah, Rajinder K. 2002. 'Drum 'n' Dhol 1: British Bhangra Music and Diasporic South Asian Identity Formation'. *European Journal of Cultural Studies* 5 (3): 363–83.

Fisher, Michael H. 2004. 'Becoming and Making "Family" in Hindustan'. In *Unfamiliar Relations: Family and History in South Asia*, ed. Indrani Chatterjee, 95–121. Ranikhet: Permanent Black.

Gill, Harjant. 2016. *Sent Away Boys*. New Delhi: Public Service Broadcasting Trust and Tilotama Productions.

Glover, William. 2008. *Making Lahore Modern: Constructing and Imagining a Colonial City*. Minneapolis: University of Minnesota Press.

Grewal, Inderpal. 1996. *Home and Harem: Nation, Gender, Empire, and the Cultures of Travel*. Durham: Duke University Press.

Grewal, J. S., and Indu Banga (translated and edited). 1975. *Early Nineteenth Century Panjab: From Ganesh Das's Char Bagh-i-Panjab*. Amritsar: Guru Nanak Dev University.

Guha, Sumit. 2019. *History and Collective Memory in South Asia, 1200–2000*. Seattle: University of Washington Press.

Hans, Rajkumar. 2016. 'Making Sense of Dalit Sikh History'. In *Dalit Studies*, eds Ramnarayan S. Rawat and K. Satyanarayana, 131–51. Durham: Duke University Press.

Harding, Christopher. 2008. *Religious Transformation in South Asia: The Meanings of Conversion in Colonial Punjab*. Oxford: Oxford University Press.

Imy, Kate. 2019. *Faithful Fighters: Identity and Power in the British Indian Army*. Stanford: Stanford University Press.

Jakobsh, Doris. 2003. *Relocating Gender in Sikh History*. New Delhi: Oxford University Press.

Jodhka, Surinder S. 2016. 'From Zaat to Qaum: Fluid Contours of Ravi Dasi Identity in Punjab'. In *Dalit Studies*, eds Ramnarayan S. Rawat and K. Satyanarayana, 248–69. Durham: Duke University Press.

Jones, Kenneth W. 1989. *Arya Dharm: Hindu Consciousness in 19th-Century Punjab*. Delhi: Manohar.

Judge, Paramjit S. 2015. 'Dalit Culture and Identity: Valorisation and Reconstruction of Tradition among the Chamars in Punjab'. *Economic & Political Weekly* 1 (34): 53–60.

Juergensmeyer, Mark. 2013. 'Ad Dharm'. In *Brill's Encyclopedia of Hinduism*, Vol. 5, ed. Knut A. Jacobsen, 359–65. Leiden: Brill.

Kabir, Ananya Jahanara. 2005. 'Gender, Memory, Trauma: Women's Novels on the Partition of India'. *Comparative Studies of South Asia, Africa and the Middle East* 25 (1): 177–90.

Kalra, Virinder S. 2000. 'Vilayeti Rhythms: Beyond Bhangra's Emblematic Status to a Translation of Lyrical Texts'. *Theory, Culture & Society* 17 (3): 80–102.

Kaur, Mallika. 2019. *Faith, Gender and Activism in the Punjab Conflict: The Wheat Fields Still Whisper*. San Mateo: Palgrave Macmillan.

Kaur, Ravinder. 1986. 'Jat Sikhs: A Question of Identity'. *Contributions to Indian Sociology* (n.s.) 20 (2): 221–39.

Kaur, Ravinder. 2018[2007]. *Since 1947: Partition Narratives among Punjabi Migrants of Delhi*. New Delhi: Oxford University Press.

Kinra, Rajeev. 2015. *Writing Self, Writing Empire: Chandar Bhan Brahman and the Cultural World of the Indo-Persian State Secretary*. Oakland: University of California Press.

Kosambi, Meera. 2016. *Pandita Ramabai: Life and Landmark Writings*. New York: Routledge.

Kumar, Ashish. 2019. 'Early Panjab: From a Gateway to a Metaphor—A Historiography'. *Research Journal, Social Sciences* 27 (1&2): 1–28.

Kumar, Udaya. 2008. 'Autobiography as a Way of Writing History: Personal Narratives from Kerala and the Inhabitation of Modernity'. In *History in the Vernacular*, eds Raziuddin Aquil and Partha Chatterjee, 418–48. Ranikhet: Permanent Black.

Lambert-Hurley, Siobhan, and Sunil Sharma. 2010. *Atiya's Journeys: A Muslim Woman from Colonial Bombay to Edwardian Britain*. New Delhi: Oxford University Press.

Majumdar, Rochana. 2010. *Marriage and Modernity: Family Values in Colonial Bengal*. Durham: Duke University Press.

Malhotra, Anshu. 2002. *Gender, Caste and Religious Identities: Restructuring Class in Colonial Punjab*. New Delhi: Oxford University Press.

———. 2006. 'The Body as a Metaphor for the Nation: Caste, Masculinity, and Femininity in the Satyarth Prakash of Swami Dayanand Sarasvati'. In *Rhetoric and Reality: Gender and the Colonial Experience in South Asia*, eds Avril Powell and Siobhan Lambert-Hurley, 121–53. New Delhi: Oxford University Press.

———. 2017. *Piro and the Gulabdasis: Gender, Sect and Society in Punjab*. New Delhi: Oxford University Press.

———. 2020. 'Bitter Sweet Imaginings: Form, Gender and Religion in Bhai Vir Singh's Sundari'. *Sikh Formations* 16 (1&2): 41–65.

———. 2021. 'Kisan Morcha: History, Identity, Politics—Sikh Identity in the Indian Farm Protests'. *Berkley Forum*, 1 March. Available at https://berkleycenter.georgetown.edu/responses/kisan-morcha-history-identity-politics (accessed on 8 August 2023).

Malhotra, Anshu, and Farina Mir (eds). 2012. *Punjab Reconsidered: History, Culture and Practice*. New Delhi: Oxford University Press.

Malhotra, Anshu, and Siobhan Lambert-Hurley 2015. *Speaking of the Self: Gender, Performance and Autobiography in South Asia*. Durham: Duke University Press.

Manto, Saadat Hasan. 2008. *Bitter Fruit: The Very Best of Saadat Hasan Manto* (edited and translated by Khalid Hasan). New Delhi: Penguin Books.

McLeod, W. H. 1976. *The Evolution of Sikh Community*. Oxford: Clarendon Press.

Mehta, Ved. 1972. *Daddyji*. New Delhi: Penguin Books.

Menon, Ritu, and Kamla Bhasin. 1998. *Borders and Boundaries: Women in India's Partition*. New Delhi: Kali for Women.

Mir, Farina. 2010. *The Social Space of Language: Vernacular Culture in British Colonial Punjab*. Ranikhet: Permanent Black.

———. 2012. 'Genre and Devotion in Punjabi Popular Narratives: Rethinking Cultural and Religious Syncretism'. In *Punjab Reconsidered:*

History, Culture and Practice, eds Anshu Malhotra and Farina Mir, 221–60. New Delhi: Oxford University Press.

Misra, Shubhangi. 2021. 'How Christianity is Growing among Mazhabi Sikhs and Valmiki Hindus in Punjab's Villages'. *The Print*, 2 December. Available at https://theprint.in/india/how-christianity-is-growing-among-mazhabi-sikhs-valmiki-hindus-in-punjabs-villages/775047/ (accessed on 3 April 2022).

Mitra, Diditi. 2021. 'The Business of Postcolonial Immigration: Marketing of Immigration Services in Punjab, India'. *Visual Studies* 37 (4): 363–77.

Mooney, Nicola. 2011. *Rural Nostalgias, Transnational Dreams: Identity and Modernity among Jat Sikhs*. Toronto: Toronto University Press.

Murphy, Anne. 2018. 'Writing Punjabi Across Borders'. *South Asian History and Culture* 9 (1): 68–91.

Nair, Neeti. 2011. *Changing Homelands: Hindu Politics and the Partition of India*. Cambridge: Harvard University Press.

Nanda, Reena. 2018. *From Quetta to Delhi: A Partition Story*. New Delhi: Bloomsbury India.

Nevile, Pran. 2006[1993]. *Lahore: A Sentimental Journey*. New Delhi: Penguin Books.

Oberoi, Harjot. 1994. *The Construction of Religious Boundaries: Culture, Identity and Diversity in the Sikh Tradition*. New Delhi: Oxford University Press.

_____. 2009. 'Ghadar Movement and its Anarchist Genealogy'. *Economic & Political Weekly* 44 (50): 40–46.

Padhi, Ranjana. 2012. *Those Who Did Not Die: Impact of the Agrarian Crisis on Women in Punjab*. New Delhi: Sage Publications.

Population Census. 2011. Available at census2011.co.in (accessed on 20 August 2020).

Pritam, Amrita. 1976. *Rasidi Ticket*. New Delhi: Nagamani Prakashan.

Rai, Lajpat. n.d. *Atma Katha*. Lahore: Rajpal and Sons.

Raj, Dhooleka S. 2003. *Where Are You From? Middle-Class Migrants in the Modern World*. Berkeley: University of California Press.

Rajagopalan, Mrinalini. 2018. 'Cosmopolitan Crossings: The Architecture of Begum Samru'. *Journal of the Society of Architectural Historians* 77 (2): 168–85.

Ram, Ronki. 2009. 'Ravidass, Dera Sachkhand Ballan and the Question of Dalit Identity in Punjab'. *Journal of Punjab Studies* 16 (1): 1–34.

Ramanujan, A. K. 2013. *The Collected Essays of A. K. Ramanujan*, ed. Vinay Dharwadker. New Delhi: Oxford University Press.

Ramnath. Maia. 2011. *Haj to Utopia: How the Ghadar Movement Chartered Global Radicalism and Attempted to Overthrow the British Empire*. Berkeley: University of California Press.

Roy, Anjali Gera. 2013. 'Black Beats with a Punjabi Twist'. *Popular Music* 32 (2): 241–57.

Roy, Haimanti. 2018. *The Partition of India: Oxford India Short Introductions*. New Delhi: Oxford University Press.

Sahni, Bhisham. 1981. *Balraj: My Brother*. New Delhi: National Book Trust.

Sarkar, Mahua. 2008. *Visible Histories, Disappearing Women: Producing Muslim Womanhood in Late Colonial Bengal*. New Delhi: Zubaan.

Shah, Vidya. 2016. *Jalsa: Indian Women and Their Journeys from the Salon to the Studio*. New Delhi: Tulika Books.

Sidhwa, Bapsi (ed.). 2005. *City of Sin and Splendour: Writings on Lahore*. New Delhi: Penguin Books.

Singh, Bhagat Laxman. 1965. *Autobiography* (edited and annotated by Ganda Singh). Calcutta: The Sikh Cultural Centre.

Singh, Gajendra. 2014. *The Testimonies of Indian Soldiers and the Two World Wars: Between Self and Sepoy*. London: Bloomsbury Academic.

Singh, Gurharpal, and Giorgio Shani. 2022. *Sikh Nationalism: From a Dominant Minority to an Ethno-Religious Diaspora*. Cambridge: Cambridge University Press.

Snehi, Yogesh. 2019. *Spatializing Popular Sufi Shrines in Punjab: Dreams, Memories, Territoriality*. London: Routledge.

Stoler, Ann Laura. 2009. *Along the Archival Grain: Epistemic Anxieties and Colonial Common Sense*. Princeton: Princeton University Press.

Takhar, Opinderjit K. 2014. 'Sikh Sects'. In *The Oxford Handbook of Sikh Studies*, eds Pashaura Singh and Louis E. Fenech, 350–59. Oxford: Oxford University Press.

Tan, Tai Yong. 2005. *The Garrison State: The Military, Government and Society in Colonial Punjab, 1849–1947*. New Delhi: Sage Publications.

Tandon, Prakash. 1963. *Punjabi Century: 1857–1947*. London: Chatto and Windus.

———. 2011[1988]. *Punjabi Saga 1857–2000: The Monumental Story of Five Generations of a Remarkable Punjabi Family*. New Delhi: Rupa & Co.

Tuteja, K. L. 2021. *Religion, Community and Nation: Hindu Consciousness and Nationalism in Colonial Punjab*. New Delhi: Indian Institute of Advanced Study and Primus Books.

Vishwanathan, Gauri. 2001[1998]. *Outside the Fold: Conversion, Modernity and Belief*. New Delhi: Oxford University Press.

Wagner, Kim A. 2016. 'Calculated to Strike Terror: The Amritsar Massacre and the Spectacle of Colonial Violence'. *Past and Present* 233 (1): 185–225.

Walsh, Judith E. 2004. *Domesticity in Colonial India: What Women Learned When Men Gave Them Advice*. New Delhi: Oxford University Press.

Weidman, Amanda. 2006. 'Guru and Gramophone: Fantasies of Fidelity and Modern Technologies of the Real'. In *Cultural History of Modern India*, ed. Dilip Menon, 154–75. New Delhi: Social Science Press.

Two

A Feast for the Heart and Mind

Print Culture, Polemics and Religious Debate in Punjab in the 1870s

Purnima Dhavan

Recent studies of colonial Punjab argue against a simplistic understanding of the impacts of colonial education systems and colonial language policies on the emerging print culture and religious nationalisms of the nineteenth century. For example, Farina Mir's important study of early Punjabi print culture in colonial Punjab has successfully demonstrated the significant degree to which print culture in colonial Punjab grew independently of state support; here, unlike in other provinces, state funds were directed at publications in Urdu, the language of both state-funded education and government, rather than Punjabi (Mir 2010: 67–71). Indeed, these studies offer an important corrective to an earlier view of colonial Punjab as a hotbed of polemical contestations, with pamphlets and tracts being used to draw sharp boundaries between the multiple faith communities in Punjab, and in which communal mobilisation was propelled by the emerging print culture, particularly in the decade of the 1880s and 1890s (Jones 1976).

Although early print culture in Punjab certainly had important connections with religious identity and education, even the publication of expressly religious pedagogical texts did not necessarily reflect a deeper connection to modern reform movements or a deepening of sectarian identity, as this chapter will demonstrate. Early print culture was influenced by continuities with manuscript traditions, established audiences for certain genres and by the preferences of local markets long before religious reform groups became active in the 1870s (Mir 2010; Stark 2007). Although there were growing polemics around these issues, the connection between language, script and religious identity would harden after the 1870s (Malhotra and Mir 2012: xxx). While Punjabis did express preferences for particular scripts or languages during campaigns directed at changing colonial policies on education and personal law, the bulk of Punjabis consumed print culture in multiple scripts and languages. This chapter examines two well-known vernacular books on Islamic religious practice and law in order to examine the disparate trends and debates about education, law and morality with which these works engaged, and the ways in which these did not always align neatly with the themes broached in the polemical literature of this period.

In the earliest decades of printing in Punjab, there is considerable evidence that popular demand shaped what publishers chose to produce. Entertainment and education, however, were not the only motivators for authors and publishers to select what to write or print. A closer look at the critical decade of the 1870s, when print culture first began to expand, but which also saw the rise of early reform groups such as the Arya Samaj, demonstrates the complex ways in which authors and publishers sought to produce marketable books, mould public opinion and engage with colonial polices that were already having a significant impact on communities in Punjab. Beyond the educated groups in urban settings, there was also an emerging market in affordable books in smaller towns and rural areas where smaller schools and religious shrines were well-established. Such works often focused on religious themes, but in eclectic ways (Malhotra 2017: 210–21). For example, vernacular print material related to *sharia* law could offer readers advice about normative rituals, but often also offered pragmatic perspectives on legal matters related to marriage, inheritance and taxation. While reformers, publishers or educators may have wished readers to use such information in specific ways, as recent works on legal disputes in colonial Punjab demonstrate, Punjabis used such knowledge in creative ways for divergent purposes (Ivermee 2014; Nelson 2011). Not all print ventures were successful; some enjoyed long print runs and others sold only a few hundred copies. A renewed focus on the successes and failures of these early attempts to produce marketable books helps us to better understand the complicated processes that shaped Punjabi print culture and in turn the degree to which it may have influenced the religious self-fashioning of readers, state institutions and colonial policies in later decades.

To do so, I will focus on texts that have conventionally been understood as the earliest forms of instructional material used to teach Punjabi Muslims elementary aspects of their faith. Early seventeenth-century materials such as Maulavi Abdullah's *Baran Anva* ('Twelve Treatises') were re-circulated during the 1870s in both print and manuscript form.[1] Shorter works authored in the nineteenth century, such as *Pand Namah*, *Pakki Roti* and *Mithi Roti* were also widely available in print (Rahman 2001). The profusion of these Punjabi texts and their popular identification as basic instructional materials for vernacular religious education for Muslims appears to have been cemented by the end of the 1870s. Memorials submitted to the Hunter Commission of 1882 explicitly identified *Baran Anva* and *Pakki Roti* as Punjabi texts written in Shahmukhi, used to educate 'lower classes and women' (Jalal 2000: 120). This characterisation, however, distorts the complex and often divergent motivations of diverse agents in publishing and purchasing such texts. It also misrepresents the dissimilarities of these texts in terms of their pedagogical goals, likely readers and content. Focusing particularly on *Baran Anva* and *Pakki Roti* is useful in illuminating the ways Punjabi readers and publishers sought to engage colonial policies, particularly in terms of their impact on religious education and legal codes. Publishers sought to create a market for religious texts, even as these groups were constricted by colonial policies, but were also alert to new trends. To do this, I will begin by comparing the very different content and production of these two texts, and the ideal imagined reader sought by early publishers. Second, I will turn to the wider debate in colonial Punjab about the merits of secular religion and growing demands by Punjabis for access to religious education. Since publishers of these texts were aware of these issues and also of the growing interest in topics of religious reform, inheritance and personal law, this likely shaped their selections of texts to publish. I will end by revisiting how the mischaracterisation of these two texts in both the Hunter Commission of 1882 and in later literature distorts the complex ways in which Punjabis read, consumed and transmitted these texts by the late nineteenth century.

OLD TEXTS IN NEW FORMS

The author Maulavi Abdullah Abdi's *Baran Anva* was a collection of treatises originally authored in the Mughal period during the reigns of Jahangir (r. 1605–27) and Shah Jahan (r. 1628–58). The author was born in the village of Malka Hans in Multan but spent his adult life in Lahore. Several manuscript copies of his work exist, dating from the seventeenth to the nineteenth century (Shackle 1977: 39–43). While *Baran Anva* may broadly be described as a didactic text for Muslims, the 12 essays within it actually covered several different genres and themes, including a description of Islamic legal rules (*fiqh*), prayers, instructions on how to perform ablutions, rituals and a wide variety of topics covering the organisation of civil life and ethical behaviour (*akhlaq*). Abdi's work had earned enough status as a learned text in pre-colonial Punjab; in fact, when Ranjha poses as an accomplished scholar in Varis Shah's famous *qissa*, *Hir*, this is one of the texts he claims to have mastered (Rahman 2001: 35). The text itself was written in verse and its colloquial Punjabi is inflected with what Christopher Shackle (1977) has described as 'Multani forms'.

For nineteenth-century Punjabi readers, this archaic Punjabi was difficult to read; therefore, all of the published versions of this text included Urdu or Persian glosses in the margins of the work (Abdi 1855, 1879). This fact alone should make one pause and reconsider the alleged simplicity of this vernacular text, which is taken as a given by the few scholars who have discussed it, as well as its utility as an educational text for those with little formal learning in Punjabi in the nineteenth century. Certainly, further thought must be given to the conditions that created a brief period of renewed popularity for this text in the print culture of 1870s' Punjab.

While the presence of a multilingual work was not unusual in the print culture of 1870s' Punjab, certain features of the printed *Baran Anva* invite a closer look to understand who the target audience of this text may have been in the 1870s. Although written in Punjabi, this text was neither easy to read for colonial readers nor was it intended as an introductory text on Islamic practice for a mass audience. Indeed, *Baran Anva* was part of a more complicated linguistic heritage. Here it is helpful to take seriously Anne Murphy's cautionary argument that Punjabi, like other early South Asian languages, should not be subsumed within the often teleological accounts of the development of modern languages. Similar to other pre-modern literary formations, Punjabi developed alongside literary and oral forms of Sadhukari, Braj and Rekhtah, incorporating features that can be found in latter-day versions of all of these (Murphy 2018: 69). These forms could range from popular oral genres to elite literary textual forms. Indeed, early Punjabi print texts in the Shahmukhi script inhabit a wide variety of genres and registers, particularly the poetic. These could include poetic forms such as *masnavi* or *ghazal*s, with vocabulary derived from Persian, Arabic and Rekhtah/Urdu, as well as genres like *barah masa* and *dohra* and vocabulary also found in Braj, in addition to Punjabi poetic genres like *vars* and *kafi*. Indeed, the incorporation of these forms, present in the works of pre-modern Punjabi poets, continued in early Punjabi print culture, both in reprints of earlier works and new compositions. Some of these features would have been very familiar to Punjabi speakers of the nineteenth century as these also circulated in oral performance and literature. But the archaic and regional features of Abdi's language, as well as the formal Arabic phrases from the Quran found throughout the work, may have posed some barriers for nineteenth-century Punjabi readers, requiring some form of translation or explanation to accompany the text for modern readers of Punjabi. The earliest edition printed in Delhi in 1855 came with a Persian gloss. Before the twentieth century, the only other editions of this work were printed in Lahore in 1874 and 1879 with marginal translations as well. It would seem the twentieth-century editions of this text are reprints of the 1879 edition. Within these editions, marginal notes in Urdu catered to an audience that had been formally educated in Urdu but was familiar with spoken Punjabi, as were many educated Punjabis at this time. Sheikh Ilahi Baksh and Muhammad Jalaluddin, the previous publishers for one edition of this work in Lahore, likely the 1879 version, appear to have assumed that for their audience, neither the archaic dialect of the work nor the classical Arabic vocabulary would be easily accessible; therefore, explanatory notes in Urdu were provided as a helpful aid to readers. A later, twentieth-century reprint of this version of the *Baran Anva* described the *Baran Anva* as the '*yadgar*' or memento of Sheikh Ilahi Baksh, explaining that this was the first attempt to create an Urdu translation from the previously printed Persian gloss (Abdi 1930: 2). Ilahi Baksh is identified as one of the three biggest booksellers of this period in Kanhaiya Lal's nineteenth-century history of Lahore (Lal 1977: 68).

In the decades following annexation, few schools in Punjab taught Punjabi in Shahmukhi script formally, with Urdu being the formal medium of education in state-supported schools. In contrast to the Punjabi verses of *Baran Anva*, the Urdu gloss in the marginal sections of the printed versions is in simple prose, often summarising rather than translating the text. The conventions within book production in colonial India as well as in Quranic hermeneutics appear to have influenced this bilingual annotation. Both translation (*tarjumma*) and commentary *(tafsir)* were well-established in scholarship related to the study of the Quran (Zadeh 2012: 14). Many practices found in hand-written manuscripts were continued in the lithographed texts, with both interlinear translations of scripture and prose commentary on margins in print copies of the Quran, sometimes with both techniques found in the same text (ibid.: Figure 2). In the case of Abdi's print versions of *Baran Anva*, modern European conventions of translation are not present. Rather, prose summaries in Urdu as well as brief commentaries on key themes in the margins of the text (*sharh*) were offered to aid the bilingual literate reader, who was assumed to be educated in Urdu but unfamiliar with the archaic Punjabi of the main text. Further, the printed editions also 'updated' the language of *Baran Anva*, using more standardised forms of spelling and orthography closest to the spoken language of Lahore to aid readers. In the endpiece of the printed text of one such edition, advertisements for commentaries on well-known works of *hadith* and fiqh further suggest that the printed versions of this text were never intended for a semi-literate or beginning learner of Punjabi, but rather for those well-versed in reading complex prose words and seeking to enhance their knowledge of Islamic studies in the diverse genres of fiqh and hadith by accessing works written in Punjabi and Urdu. One advertisement, for example, offers another book, *Riyaz al-Faiz*, by the same publisher, authored by the Arabic professor at Oriental College, Lahore, Faiz ul Hassan, promising a commentary of important Islamic materials in Persian, Arabic and Urdu ('Abdī 1930: 407).

It is also illuminating to compare the print versions of *Baran Anva* with the other print works with which it is often compared, namely far shorter texts such as *Pakki Roti*. While the print editions of *Baran Anva* often cover between 330 and 400 printed pages, those of *Pakki Roti* are often only about 16 pages. Some editions frequently combine this text with works of other Punjabi authors such as Ghulam Rasul and Muhammad Din, which frequently created a longer and more lucrative text for booksellers. These were distinguished in title as *Pakki Roti Khurd*, meaning the smaller version, versus *Pakki Roti Kalan* indicating the longer version of this text (Blumhardt 1902: 31–33). While the authorship of this text is not secure, there is little evidence within the text that would point to an earlier origin than the nineteenth century, despite claims to the contrary (Shahbaz 1973: 23). In contrast to *Baran Anva*, not a single version of this shorter Punjabi text was printed with marginal commentaries; although many had complete diacritics throughout the Shahmukhi script Punjabi text to guide new learners in sounding out the words, it was assumed they understood the content (Anonymous 1868–69: 2).[2] The text of *Pakki Roti* is also structured quite differently, containing not verse but prose questions posed by the author about the elementary aspects of Islamic faith and ritual, with written responses. For example, the shorter version of the text begins: '*Je ko puchhe, bismillah ki mani kihri hain? Tun akh, ji ye shuru karnan men is kitab nun nal nam khuda tala di jehra rozi denda hain, har jin nun*' ('If someone asks, what is the meaning of bismillah? You should answer, it begins this book with the name of God, the exalted, who provides each being with their daily need')[3] (ibid.: 2). This may be why many catalogues describe it as a Muslim catechism. This difference in length also translated to the considerable difference in price, indicated in the flyleaf of each book, with *Pakki Roti* often priced at Rs 2 or less while *Baran Anva* cost considerably more, one marked at Rs 12 (Abdi 1879, 1930; Anonymous 1868–69).

These facts suggest that both the target audience and the marketing of these two texts by their earliest publishers were quite different. *Pakki Roti* was produced as an affordable chapbook for elementary religious instruction in Punjabi, in different versions by different presses, but *Baran Anva* was printed for more advanced scholars and readers, particularly those who could afford the higher price. *Baran Anva* also had fewer editions due to a smaller audience, and its audience was assumed to be comfortable with the scholastic Urdu used in its marginal commentaries, which was also taught in state-funded schools. These important differences in content, target audience and pricing for the two books are helpful in understanding how these texts may have fit into the pedagogical and scholarly debates in colonial Punjab during the crucial decades of the 1870s. More importantly, as Punjabi texts which explicitly engaged with religious instruction for Muslims, these were not used by the government schools in the province. Therefore, the likely purchasers of both texts could only have been students, their families and teachers who wished to explore such material in Punjabi outside of the state schooling system, but with very different levels of educational ability. To get a finer sense of how these printed texts engaged with debates about education in colonial Punjab, let us first get a sense of how dramatically educational institutions and the core curricula transformed during the early decades of colonial rule.

Educational Debates in Colonial Punjab and the Market for Print

In the decades after the annexation of Ranjit Singh's kingdom, colonial officials attempting to set up an educational system in Punjab found steady competition from the established local institutions which predated colonial rule. This singular fact is perhaps hard to grasp when reviewing colonial records as these records were quick to bemoan the lack of enthusiasm Punjabis displayed for state-supported schools and the low levels of literacy in the province, giving the impression of educational vacuum in the province. Even though officials offered different explanations for low enrolment in government-funded schools, most faulted the haphazard way in which the colonial educational system was initially set up. By the early 1880s, even the colonial government's own records illustrated a falling literacy rate for males at 4.73 per cent when in the 1850s, at the time of annexation, it had been recorded at 6 per cent (Allender 2006: 285). Although the original plan set up by the colonial department of education was to introduce village-level schools through a 1 per cent agricultural tax, by the 1860s, most schools were in fact operating in district towns and cities, and catered to upwardly mobile urban populations. Even if rural children could have accessed these schools, instruction within government-run schools remained erratic in its pedagogical intent, shaped more through the budgetary and political priorities of the colonial state rather than the instructional needs of the students it was meant to serve. After 1857, the under-resourced and poorly supervised *halkabandi* scheme for village schools dissolved (ibid.: 44–46).

Colonial officers were aware of the vast urban tilt in school enrolment subsidised by rural taxes, and also the uncomfortable fact that Muslims, a sizeable group in colonial Punjab, were significantly under-enrolled. Many officers from the Viceroy Lord Mayo to provincial ones attributed this to the absence of 'moral' education in government schools, which remained resolutely secular in orientation (Ivermee 2015: 47). Critics of the system believed that both the linguistic focus and secular nature of colonial schooling made it offensive to Muslim parents, who preferred to enrol their children in schools where they could learn Arabic, or a familiar vernacular, and learn to read the Quran, while imbibing the moral and social values prized by their own families. Officials alarmed about this trend encouraged the government to offer support to schools where Arabic, Persian or Urdu was taught, but this posed other challenges to established policies of the state. While the colonial government continued to provide 'grant in aid' to schools which taught in Indian languages, in Punjab, these were usually missionary schools, and schools receiving those grants were explicitly prohibited from teaching religious subjects (ibid.: 90).

The entry of Gottlieb Leitner and his Indian allies in the Anjuman-i Punjab was to prove a turning point in these debates and eventually lead to lasting changes in the educational landscape of Punjab. Leitner took up his position as principal of Government College, Lahore, in 1864, when he was not quite 25, having received a Ph.D. from a German university a few years earlier (Diamond 2011: 27–29). As a trained linguist, he had formerly studied Arabic in Ottoman Turkey and was considered a Hafiz (one who has memorised the Quran) (Leitner 2002a: 11–12). Unlike other colonial officials, Leitner was quick to seek the support of Punjab's elite landowners, scholars and religious hierarchy. The support and resources these individuals provided, either in person or through the Anjuman, were critical to the critiques of the colonial education system Leitner unleashed in multiple letters, memoranda and reports. These were first articulated publicly in print in Leitner's 1870 essay *Theory and Practice of Education, with Special Reference to Education in India*, and later detailed in his *History of Indigenous Education in the Punjab*, published in 1882 (Leitner 2002b). What began as Leitner's critique of English as a medium of education in the lower grades quickly turned into fervour for what Leitner and his Anjuman allies described as 'vernacular education'. In *Theory and Practice*, Leitner expressed doubts whether all of the school children the state wished to educate in English, a language viewed as a path to employment, would ever find gainful employment in the limited jobs open to them (1870: 9–10).

Leitner also offered a sweeping critique of the memory-based curriculum in government schools that did not prioritise learning but memorisation. Assessment was done only through examinations, which at that time were the sole means of attaining a degree (Leitner 1870: 9, 19). Leitner also saw proof of the failures of the colonial educational system in the fact that the elite of Punjab, and not just Muslims, stayed away from government-run schools. Thus, the current system failed at every level—in its goal of educating the masses, its hopes for reconciling the elite to colonial rule or offering Indians pathways to career advancement. By contrast, Leitner presented his own successful work, and that of his Anjuman colleagues, in trying to transform Punjab's first college into Punjab University. Leitner claimed that the broad support it received from all classes of Punjabis was largely due to the fact that the new university demonstrated respect for Punjab's languages and literatures (2002b: 23–24).

Leitner's embrace of these local elites was critical for his later work. This network of professional contacts within the Anjuman-i Punjab, Oriental College and the Punjab University Senate also played key roles in creating, circulating and consuming print culture. While these associations and individuals did not universally share all of Leitner's passions, they were firm supporters of his attempts to create an educational system which would favour Indian languages, both classical and vernacular. Many members of these groups were also members of nascent religious reform movements (Leitner 2002b: 113–44). How much these associations transformed Leitner's own thinking can be seen in his later work, *History of Indigenous Education in the Punjab*, wherein colonial educational efforts were unfavourably compared to pre-colonial schooling in preparing diverse Punjabi groups for participation in different professions, high and low, as well as becoming informed and engaged members of their local communities.

Leitner's *History of Indigenous Education* offered a sharp and harsh critique of the failures of government educational policy and inaction in Punjab. Central to his premise was the argument that the Punjab government had misstated figures about indigenous schools and their curricula in official reports and documents. By severely undercounting, and in some cases omitting, local schools attached to mosques, temples, gurdwaras, *deras* and private homes, some 300,000 pupils who had been enrolled around the time of annexation and the roughly 120,000 pupils who were currently enrolled were not included in government figures. In sheer numbers, the indigenous school system vastly outperformed the government-run schools in terms of enrolment (Leitner 2002b: 16). Further, Leitner attributed revocation by the colonial government of hundreds of religious and private endowments as the primary cause of declining literacy. These had been made by Punjabis of diverse backgrounds to support schooling and were intended to be grants in perpetuity. Using his networks to collect exhaustive information about the curricula in those schools, Leitner fiercely contested the idea that Punjabis did not value education or that the mostly religious curriculum of those schools was limited in scope. In detailed chapters, Leitner examined the Punjabi, Arabic, Persian, Hindi and Sanskrit texts used in these schools, evaluating the methods of instruction much more favourably than those created by the department of education. Leitner concluded that the continuity of indigenous education in such large numbers in Punjab 'is a living protest of the people against our educational system, as well as its strongest condemnation' (ibid.: 72).

The testimony of prominent members of Punjab's Muslim, Sikh, Hindu and Christian communities, many of whom were Anjuman members, was also a key part of the evidence presented by Leitner (2002b: 113–44); the detailed lists of scholars and professionals in Punjab were also meant to illustrate its continuing claims to living scholarly traditions (ibid.: Part V, 1–32). While Leitner was undoubtedly skilled at self-promotion, and his deployment of connections with Punjab's landed families and respected indigenous scholars was used to build his own career, far too many scholars have narrowly focused on Leitner's engagement with colonial institutions and print culture without detailing why the elite and scholarly families of Punjab would readily ally themselves with Leitner. It is important to note that many of the testimonies used by Leitner in his *History of Indigenous Education* were extracted from formal testimonies given to the education commission, and thus while some of the witnesses were formally allied with Leitner, such as Maulavi Faizul Hassan, the instructor of Arabic at Oriental College (ibid.: 115; Part II: 114), and also editor of many early print works in Lahore, others were unaffiliated with him. One such organisation was the new nationalist organisation, the Lahore Indian Association, formed after the visit of Surendra Nath Bannerjee to Punjab in 1877 (Mittal 1986: 80). Their views on education, however, publicly aligned with those of Leitner and his other Punjabi allies. The Lahore Indian Association noted in its testimony: 'The Government might keep some control over these schools so subsidized by extending the supervision of its controlling agency over them; but it should not force its own scheme of instruction nor insist upon particular books being taught' (Leitner 2002a: 130). Leitner even included the testimony of Christian missionaries, a group he frequently mocked, who advocated that the government support indigenous schools but leave them under local indigenous leadership, and make optional the study of religions in their plurality (ibid.: 142–43). The message from these disparate groups of witnesses was clear. Educators, parents and every religious community in Punjab wanted the government to financially support schooling, but not interfere in the day-to-day running of schools or influence curricular choices. Without these conditions being met, many Punjabis would continue to educate their children privately, and not in government-run schools and colleges. Further, these testimonials and Leitner's own notes suggested that the thriving print market in Punjab was already producing a great deal of instructional material for these schools in accessible formats for Punjabi students. Affordable chapbooks such as *Pakki Roti* and similar books intended for religious instructions in faith-based schools for Hindus and Sikhs likely were part of this market. There were even options for parents and teachers who wished to provide a broad ethical education with no overt affiliation to any single religious community, such as the Akhlaq text written by Kanhaiya Lal in Persian (Lal 1977: 15).

The lobbying efforts of groups like the Anjuman-i Punjab, and branches of the Arya Samaj, Brahmo Samaj, the Indian Association, prominent chiefs, educators and bureaucrats dovetailed with Leitner's own agendas regarding educational reform and greater local indigenous control over education. They offered full-throated support for education in Indian classical languages and vernaculars—although they often disagreed on which language was the best medium of instruction—and were invested in creating more curricular materials in those languages.

While some members of these groups may have engaged in polemics on different religious or political matters, they were united in their criticism of colonial educational policy. This is likely why, using their support, Leitner opted for advocating a plurality of languages for instruction. This differed greatly from the government's own investment in developing curricular materials in Urdu and English alone. Leitner's push to have his college transformed into Punjab University and made a centre for legal training in vernaculars, in particular, found sympathetic support not only in these groups but also with Viceroy Lord Lytton during their 1877 correspondence. As Tim Allender has noted, there was a great surge of litigation in Punjab all through the 1860s and 1870s as laws about property, revenue assessments and civil matters changed rapidly, intensifying the need of the colonial state for 'trained intermediaries' (Allender 2006: 168–74). Although it is true that Leitner did not actually follow through on many of the promises made to create new Urdu curricula, his ability to swiftly raise money to support Punjab University, and particularly the Oriental College, from Indian donors, and his efforts to demonstrate local demand for the courses offered by Punjab University in religious law were successful and created new opportunities for Indians. When officials in the colonial hierarchy expressed doubts about the quality of instruction in the vernacular or their utility in offering usable professional credentials through degrees, Leitner and his Punjab University College colleagues were quick to point out the 106 degrees their institution had granted in law, 9 in engineering and 22 in medicine versus none at Calcutta University (Government of India 1960: 261).

The failure of the colonial educational policy in Punjab to create a system of education now appears clear. Scholars of colonial schooling in Punjab, such as Tim Allender, are right to point out the role played by the chronic under-funding, political rivalries among administrators such as William Rice Molrand Holroyd and Leitner, and the heavy investment in the use of Urdu which ignored local preferences for the medium of education (Allender 2006:

285). It is also true that the 'grants-in-aid' system and investment in secular education were neither homogenous within the colonial governmental hierarchy nor were they consistently applied after 1857. As Robert Ivermee's work demonstrates, after Lord Mayo's resolution of 1871, the 'grants-in-aid' system was conjoined with Muslim religious teaching in colonial institutions in some places (Ivermee 2015: 141). Certainly, Punjab's Oriental College was an important centre for this development. Considering these developments from the perspective of the colonial state and its objectives, however, leads to a narrow reading of this evidence. As Farina Mir's (2010) ground-breaking study of print culture in Punjab has demonstrated, there were important cultural transformations in Punjab that were directly influenced by colonial policies, but some others, such as the burgeoning print market in Punjabi, evolved from the investment and desires of Punjabis, and harnessed themselves to new institutions and technology. At the same time, Punjabi print culture maintained great cultural continuities with earlier forms of cultural expression and self-fashioning. To use Mir's words, 'when colonial language policy drew vernaculars into the state apparatus, in the early nineteenth century, Punjabi continued to function largely as it always had at the margins of state discourse' (2010: 158). The same could be said for access to schooling in vernaculars, which had intimate ties to both print culture and debates about the medium of instruction in Punjabi schools. It is useful to question if the province's vernacular schools or published curricular materials in vernaculars were actually visible to the state or included in government data. Leitner's critique of government educational statistics, testimonials by Punjabis and the government records themselves suggest that they were not.

Certainly, despite many ideological differences among these commentators, it is very clear that even the raw number of smaller rural and urban schools, particularly those attached to religious institutions or private homes, were not enumerated with any accuracy by the state. Indeed, as Leitner emphasised, the state role in the erasure of those numbers was deliberate as their pedagogical quality, instructional approach and curricular materials were all dismissed by officials as unworthy of comparison to state schools which, at least according to Leitner, had a dismal record themselves; however, as his investigations indicated, far more students were enrolled in the former than in the government schools (Leitner 2002b: 1–16). One can make a similar case for the limited utility of data about vernacular publishing during the 1870s when the capacity of the state to fully track and document materials was still limited. Major Holroyd, director of public instruction in Punjab and one of Leitner's main antagonists, admitted as such in 1879 when discussing the failure of many vernacular publishers to register their copyright: 'In the Punjab and North-Western Provinces the practice seems to prevail among publishers of vernacular books of noting on the covers of their publications the fact of their having been registered under the Legislative Act, when no step has been taken towards the accomplishment of that object. This reprehensible practice should be discouraged' (Government of India 1879: 152). Both the *Baran Anva* and *Pakki Roti* are certainly part of the distorted archival record due to such practices, with both print editions and handwritten copies circulating among readers, but these were not always officially documented and some editions had no date or details of publication. They also demonstrate the active participation of authors, publishers and readers working outside of the scrutiny of colonial systems.

The manner in which such texts were documented by colonial authorities may also distort knowledge about the readers of these texts. While religious materials associated with Punjabi Muslims are invariably linked in government discussions of education with Arabic, Persian and Urdu texts, and that of Sikhs with Punjabi, catalogues of surviving print and archival material tell a more complicated story. Punjabi Muslims were already buying and reading texts with a religious focus, but which could also be read for literary value or even entertainment. Colonial genre categories were by nature reductive. In the India Office Collection, the two surviving editions of *Baran Anva* from the 1870s (1874 and 1879) from Lahore as well as the nineteen editions of *Pakki Roti* printed during the 1870s are grouped under Punjabi books and described as printed in 'Arabic characters'. Other Shahmukhi Punjabi books are also mentioned in the same list as printed in 'Persian characters'. The commentary for *Baran Anva* is said to be in Persian, although clearly Urdu was the language for the marginal notes in these editions. More strikingly, these are listed among over 30 other Punjabi books in Shahmukhi script judged to have 'religious' content (Blumhardt 1902: 31–33). These categories of genre, as with the categories of 'Arabic' and 'Persian' script, seem arbitrary as some literary works also have religious themes and either genre could be used for pedagogical purposes. Clearly Arabic and Urdu were not the only languages through which Punjab's Muslims sought knowledge about Islamic prayers, rituals and traditions, or even literacy in their vernaculars.

CRAFTING PRINT MATERIALS FOR VERNACULAR SCHOOLING

With these larger Punjabi educational contexts in mind, it is easier to see why publishers thought *Baran Anva* and *Pakki Roti* would appeal to Punjabi educators, scholars and parents. Both texts offered instructional perspectives on Muslim religious practice in a text format familiar to Punjabis. Both the prose form of the question and response in *Pakki Roti* or the versified commentary of *Baran Anva* had precedence (Shackle 1977: 28–29). Publishers also appeared to be aware of the changing needs of their readers and adapted to the new contexts of colonial Punjab. The printed versions of both texts added frameworks which significantly added to their appeal for contemporary readers of the 1870s. Some of these features would prove to be highly successful and widen the appeal of texts; for example, *Pakki Roti* can be considered a great success as a commercial product, with both the short and long versions of this text going through multiple editions. *Baran Anva*, by contrast, demonstrates some of the miscalculations by publishers about assessing readers' interest in the themes of this text and colonial debates about religious and legal education for Punjab's Muslims. Already designed for a much narrower scholarly and elite market, as evidenced by the Urdu and Persian marginal commentaries in early print editions, some of the more inflexible and archaic themes of *Baran Anva* alienated the readers its publishers were hoping to reach, and other parts of the texts touched on matters that became highly politicised in the years following publication in 1874 and 1879. This may have reduced the appeal of this text for an educational context in later decades.

During the decades-long debate on religious education, the different publishers of *Pakki Roti* deftly avoided some of the more polemical aspects of the debates. In the short version of this text, the 46 questions and responses focused solely on topics that had wide acceptance among Muslims in Punjab—monotheism, obligatory prayers, discussions about fasts, ritual ablutions and the necessity of observing dietary rules (Shahbaz 1973: 48). It rarely ventured into areas associated with sectarian or ideological conflict at that time, and even when, for example, listing the names of the first four caliphs, it avoided language that would give offence to Shias (ibid.: 45). Further, as the title of *Pakki Roti* suggests, the content was readily digestible as 'well-cooked bread', and not the presumably half-baked ideas presented in new institutions.

The longer version of this text engaged with Punjab's broader connections with Sufi mystical literature. A common addition in the longer version of *Pakki Roti* was the versified *Si Harfi* of Ghulam Rasul, an acrostic in which each letter of the alphabet is used to introduce a verse related to a specific attribute of God mentioned in the Quran. Sometimes, verses in praise of the Qadri Sufi Abd al Qadir Gilani or Muhammad Ghaus were also included, creating connections with popular Sufi lineages in Punjab (Anonymous n.d.: 80). Thus, purchasers of *Pakki Roti* were presented with a choice: those favouring a mystical and locally revered Sufi path could use the longer text and read the core responses of *Pakki Roti* within a broader Sufi framework. This last section of the longer format included simple Urdu verses also, which would be intelligible to beginning learners of this language in the new colonial schools. Others, according to their preference, if inclined towards a less mystical path or hoping to spend less money, could select the shorter version which omitted these sections. Nor was there any formula to what could be appended to the longer version of the text, giving publishers some creative flexibility. The variation in spelling and phrasing across editions also demonstrated the locally produced and somewhat amateurish quality of this affordable chapbook.

By contrast, it was the much more polished and expansive nature of the *Baran Anva* which made it less profitable for publishers and less amenable to re-packaging. A more polished and scholarly framing did not necessarily create a more marketable product. Yet, it is also easy to see why keen observers of Lahore's print market and cultural trends may have thought this text had possibilities. Much like the period of its own creation in the seventeenth century, in the 1870s, Punjabis were also approaching a heady period of access to new forms of cultural self-fashioning, education and self-discovery. In the 20 years since annexation, the city of Lahore had grown in size. Observers and participants of this period of Lahore's history documented its explosion of schools, booksellers, civic bodies and cultural groups which were potentially the consumers of the new emerging market in Punjabi printed texts. In addition to groups like the Anjuman-i Punjab, transplants like the author Kanhaiya Lal, who originally came to Punjab as executive engineer for the province's public works department and stayed on to continue his career in Lahore, were centrally involved not only in the remaking of Lahore's built environment but also in shaping its contemporary culture through works that explored Lahore and Punjab's history, communities and literary culture. Kanhaiya Lal and his readers were deeply interested in antiquarian topics, but also in the education and curricular debates of this time. Lal authored textbooks on pragmatic modern subjects such as mathematics in Urdu, and also a treatise on moral ethics in Persian, built on the long-established practice of using fables to impart moral tales (Lal 1977: 1–18). A Hindu *kayasth*, originally educated in a madrassa and later earning a degree in Roorkee's engineering programme, Kanhaiya Lal, like many educated men in Lahore, was a voracious reader and consumer of many different texts in multiple languages (ibid.: 3–4). This was also the case with the other scholars of this time, including Kanhaiya Lal's younger colleague and fellow amateur historian, Syed Latif, whose father was a well-known publisher and newspaper editor in Lahore (Ivermee 2014: 1081). For well-informed publishers like Ilahi Baksh, one of the publishers of *Baran Anva*, these multilingual scholars with their antiquarian interests and linguistic skills, not to mention the resources to maintain large libraries and ability to fashion public tastes, were likely the ideal readers for a new edition of *Baran Anva*.

Kanhaiya Lal's recollections of this period also help to flesh out other groups that may have been potential readers of the printed *Baran Anva*. In his work, Lal mentions the ongoing struggles to re-instal *qazis* in colonial courts to help judges interpret matters of Islamic law. One prominent family of hereditary qazis in Lahore was particularly active in mobilising petitions and appeals to the government (Lal 1977: 75). The need for qazis to formalise all ritual, legal and civic matters in the Muslim community is an important theme of the work of Abdi, who saw their role as foundational to all civic order: 'Islam prevails in a city in which the ruler hears the command of the Qazi' (Abdi 1930: 38). Agitation on this issue continued all through the 1870s, yielding some success, but was short-lived. In 1883, the Punjab government's appointment of qazis was halted due to a lawsuit regarding the appointment of qazis. Two years later, the granting of degrees in Hindu law and Muslim law ceased at Punjab University as the institution switched its focus to promoting Western learning (Ivermee 2014: 1095). While the agitation for the application of Muslim personal law would continue, its brief success was in the 1870s where it cross-cut with issues of education and professional opportunity for older elite families. After this, a successful legal career for Punjabi Muslims implied the study of colonial law, not the Sharia or fiqh.

In other ways, Abdi's approach to fiqh may have been less appealing to his colonial readers. While Abdi encouraged personal discernment and self-study, there were limits to his acceptance of Muslims' questioning or reinterpreting matters he felt were sacrosanct. These included aspects of ritual or legal life which Abdi felt were not open to personal or historical interpretation. In this, Abdi's understanding was very different from the actual practices of many Punjabi Muslims at this time. One key and extremely fraught topic in colonial Punjab regarding fiqh was the laws of inheritance. Abdi, in contrast with Mughal and colonial practice, explicitly valorised the sharia over customary law and particularly on matters of female inheritance, providing particularly detailed analysis of the rights of daughters and widows to inherit, complete with diagrams (1930: 262–66). As Matthew Nelson's work in the colonial archives demonstrates, while a variety of practices had coexisted in pre-colonial Punjab in terms of land tenure and inheritance, both colonial revenue systems and strategic actions by revenue payers aligned to enforce a system of agnatic (all-male) ownership and female disinheritance (2011: 13–14, 31). Abdi, by contrast, was extremely critical of Mughal attempts to innovate taxation beyond forms of land tax permissible under Sharia, and was just as immovable on the rights of women to inherit a partial share of their parental or marital inheritance (Abdi 1930: 69–70; 262–66). This may well have appealed to some colonial religious reformers or those who wished to advocate for women's right to inherit a share of their family property, but this was a small group in colonial Punjab, to judge by the data on this issue. As Nelson notes, in colonial Punjab, ideological commitments to Sharia continued in principle although customary law prevailed in practice (2011: 12). This, of course, did not preclude knowledgeable actors, including women, to petition for rights to land and property based on Islamic legal codes (Ivermee 2014: 1079, 1088).

Rising interest in these topics may well have led the publishers of texts like *Baran Anva* to presuppose that its in-depth discussion on such topics within Abdi's text would interest readers. They may also have assumed that the emphasis within the text on forming informed opinions and challenging local customs based on their non-conformity with actual works on hadith and fiqh would appeal to the emerging reformers, but this was not to be. Likely, Abdi's own inflexible reading of fiqh and critique of customary practices limited the appeal of his work to colonial readers who may have admired the sentiments animating his works, but who would have found his blunt critique of familiar practices, both spiritual and mundane, quite uncomfortable. Other than offering his withering opinion of Sufi leaders, Abdi was highly critical of mystical poetry and music, which would remain popular in the colonial period (Abdi 1930: 47). Abdi also had little patience for new forms of dress and fashionable appearance in his own time, enjoining his readers to dress and groom themselves in the manner of the prophet, preserving their beards. Nor were his frequent references to the work of the devil in everyday life in accord with the sensibilities of the late nineteenth century (ibid.: 19). Thus, while *Pakki Roti*'s brevity may well have made it more marketable for the readers of the 1870s, Abdi's prolixity, particularly in its pungent critiques of practices well-entrenched in Punjab even two centuries after Abdi's time, narrowed the appeal of his work to those with more scholarly, antiquarian or reform interests, a very narrow group within the already narrow subsection of literate readers. Moreover, for those who truly were interested in the matters of fiqh discussed by Abdi, by the 1870s there were many more accessible works in vernaculars available in print, as evidenced by the advertisements attached to copies of the *Baran Anva*.

Conclusion

Reviewing the context of the 1870s, it is clear why Abdi's text enjoyed a brief decade of interest in the period, but was only reprinted once, in 1930, after that decade. It was never intended as an instructional text designed for mass education; as interest in the themes it covered waned, it appears to have lost its audience. By contrast, *Pakki Roti* continued to be published for a long time in a variety of formats as its place as a basic educational text for Punjabi-speaking Muslims was more secure and its contents more accessible to readers of that period. Also important to note in any contrastive analysis of these two texts is the larger engagement *Pakki Roti* had with the diverse practices of Punjabi Muslims, easily combining and sustaining not only Sufi devotional sentiments but also conforming in its shorter versions to more reform-minded ideas by focusing on the core of shared practices and beliefs and avoiding sectarian differences. By contrast, while Abdi's text had much in common with the emerging reformist and revivalist voices in that era, and could easily have been adapted to the new forms of polemic print culture beginning to emerge in Punjab during the 1870s, it is interesting that this text, in fact, did not find a larger audience; nor does it seem that the publishers associated with its early publication intended it for that use. Judging from the advertisements and other publications in the text published by Ilahi Baksh, it seems likely that this text was intended to draw its audience from among those elite, educated Punjabis interested in the larger issues of religious education, fiqh, the role of qazis in civic life and the rights of women. However, while Abdi certainly had much to say about these themes, his detailed and often outright polemical approach apparently did not resonate with the audience his publishers had hoped to reach. While the archaic language of the text may have some role to play in this, it is also important to note the methods key players in these debates used to build influence and consensus. As demonstrated in the discussion of vernacular and religious education in the 1860s and 1870s, groups like the Anjuman, religious reformers and new nationalist groups often found that they were more effective in finding consensus on a common principle. Thus, in championing teaching in vernaculars such as Punjabi, Hindi or Urdu, or advocating for religious education, rather than championing their separate causes, much like Leitner, they agreed to lend their support to this common principle advocating for education in Indian languages instead of emphasising their different approaches to it.

For such a group, which often had members with affiliations across different civic organisations and communities, a work like Abdi's had less appeal, even if some individuals in those groups may have shared some of his beliefs. This difference between individual beliefs and organisational tactics could help explain the great internal diversity that all of Punjab's religious communities continued to enjoy through the long nineteenth century. The common tactical goals shared by Punjab's educated and landed elite in later organisations with very divergent orientations, such as the landlord-dominated Unionist Party, as well as the diverse cultural groups formed later by the progressive Urdu writers from Punjab also met with success due to their collaboration on select issues. A unity enjoined by tactical goals was prioritised in these early decades over differences of ideology in order to achieve a shared goal of local control, often by educated elites, over the new civic opportunities emerging in Punjab.

Notes

1. Of the three manuscript copies of Abdi's work in the India Office collection, Mss. No. B12 was written in the nineteenth century while Mss. No. B42 contains different essays written earlier by more than one writer and later rebound in the nineteenth century. Additional fragmentary copies of Abdi's work survive, but some have been miscatalogued. For example, Mss. No. 64 in the collection of the Punjab Languages Department, Patiala, is labelled 'Dinyat Panjabi' but is actually Abdi's

work. A digital copy of this can be found at http://www.panjabdigilib.org/webuser/searches/displayPageContent.jsp?ID=3942&page=1&CategoryID=3&Searched=Deneyat (accessed 28 August 2023).

2. A digital copy of *Pakki Roti* can be found bound with several other chapbooks from the same time, A.H. 1285, 1868–69 CE. See http://www.panjabdigilib.org/webuser/searches/displayPageContent.jsp?ID=36852&page=30&CategoryID=1&Searched=Pakki+Roti (accessed 28 August 2023).

3. Author's translation.

References

Anonymous. 1285 AH/1868–69. *Pakki Roti*. Lahore: Āftāb Ālam Press.

Anonymous. n.d. *Pakki Roti Kalan*. Lahore: Samant Singh and Sons.

Abdullah 'Abdi'. 1855. *Baran Anva*. Delhi: Matba-i Qadiri.

_____. 1874. *Baran Anva*. Lahore.

_____. 1879. *Baran Anva*. Lahore: Ilahi Baksh.

_____. 1930. *Baran Anva*. Lahore: Ilahi Baksh.

Allender, Tim. 2006. *Ruling through Education: The Politics of Schooling in the Colonial Punjab*. New Delhi: New Dawn Press.

Government of India. 1879. *Selections from Records of the Government of India, Home, Revenue, and Agricultural Department. No. CLIX.* Reports on Publications Issued and Registered in the Several Provinces of British India During the Year 1878. Calcutta: Office of the Superintendent of Government Printing.

_____. 1960. *Selections from Educational Records of the Government of India*. Delhi: Published for the National Archives of India by the Manager of Publications.

Ivermee, Robert. 2014. 'Shari'at and Muslim Community in Colonial Punjab, 1865–1885'. *Modern Asian Studies* 48 (4): 1068–95.

_____. 2015. *Secularism, Islam and Education in India, 1830–1910*. London, New York: Routledge.

Blumhardt, J. F. 1902. *Catalogue of the Library of the India Office, Vol. II, Part III: Hindi, Panjabi, Pashtu, and Sindhi Books*. London: Eyre and Spottiswoode.

Diamond, Jeffrey M. 2011. 'The Orientalist–Literati Relationship in the Northwest: G. W. Leitner, Muhammad Hussain Azad and the Rhetoric of Neo-orientalism in Colonial Lahore'. *South Asia Research* 31 (1): 25–43.

Jalal, Ayesha. 2000. *Self and Sovereignty: Individual and Community in South Asian Islam since 1850.* London, New York: Routledge.

Jones, Kenneth W. 1976. *Arya Dharm: Hindu Consciousness in 19th-Century Punjab.* Berkeley: University of California Press.

Lal, Kanhaiya. 1977. *Tarikh-i Laahaur.* Lahaur: Majlis-i Taraqqi-yi Adab.

Leitner, Gottlieb William. 1870. *Theory and Practice of Education, with Special Reference to Education in India.* Lahore: Public Opinion Press.

Leitner, G. A. 2002a. *Writings of Dr. Leitner.* Lahore: Sang-e Meel Publications.

———. 2002b. *History of Indigenous Education in the Punjab.* Lahore: Sang-e Meel Publications.

Malhotra, Anshu. 2017. *Piro and the Gulabdasis: Gender, Sect, and Society in Punjab.* New Delhi: Oxford University Press.

Malhotra, Anshu, and Farina Mir. 2012. *Punjab Reconsidered: History, Culture, and Practice.* New Delhi: Oxford University Press.

Mir, Farina. 2010. *The Social Space of Language: Vernacular Culture in British Colonial Punjab.* Berkeley: University of California Press.

Mittal, Satish Chandra. 1986. *Haryana: A Historical Perspective.* New Delhi: Atlantic Publishers and Distributers.

Murphy, Anne. 2018. 'Writing Punjabi Across Borders'. *South Asian History and Culture* 9 (1): 68–91.

Nelson, M. 2011. *In the Shadow of Shari'ah: Islam, Islamic Law, and Democracy in Pakistan.* New York: Columbia University Press.

Rahman, Tariq. 2001. 'Islamic Texts in the Indigenous Languages of Pakistan'. *Islamic Studies* 40 (1): 25–48.

Shahbaz, Malik. 1973. *Pakki Roti (khvurd): Tanqid, Tabsire Te Purani Nasr Di Ṭor Samet.* Lahore: Taj Book Depot.

Shackle, Christopher. 1977. *Catalogue of the Panjabi and Sindhi Manuscripts in the India Office Library.* London: India Office Library and Records.

Stark, Ulrike. 2007. *An Empire of Books: The Naval Kishore Press and the Diffusion of the Printed Word in Colonial India.* Ranikhet: Permanent Black.

Zadeh, Travis. 2012. *The Vernacular Qur'an: Translation and the Rise of Persian Exegesis.* Oxford: Oxford University Press.

Three

Soundscapes of the Self

Music and Identity Assertion among Diasporic Punjabi Sikh Women in California, 1950s–2000s*

Nicole Ranganath

On 11 June 2005, the local Punjabi Sikh community gathered at Ullrey Memorial Chapel in Yuba City, California, to offer their respects to a prominent farmer, Harsev Singh Thiara. After the customary scriptural recitation by a Sikh priest, the unexpected happened. Mohinderjit Kaur Thiara walked up to the podium and sang a love song she wrote for him, 'Deson pardes'. Her intimate lyrics expressed her love for her departed husband and the pain of separation she felt in her *des* (homeland, that is, Punjab) before she joined him in *pardes* (foreign land, meaning California) in 1954. This is the only time in collective memory when a local Punjabi woman of her generation proclaimed her romantic love for her husband in public. To do so at a funeral remains almost unthinkable today.

*I wish to express my appreciation to my family and colleagues for their generous feedback. I am indebted to Rajinder K. Tumber whose passion for Punjabi women's history made this research possible. I am also grateful for the generous funding from the California Humanities and the UC Davis College of Letters and Science.

This chapter examines the rare autobiographical songs composed by the first generation of women from the Punjab region in north South Asia after they settled in California's Sacramento Valley at mid-century.[1] Music plays a crucial role in creating common ground that connects people in a universal language of shared feeling. Through the course of extensive oral history research among the first generation of Punjabi women who settled in Yuba City, I discovered two elderly women, Mohinderjit Kaur Thiara and Harbans Kaur Panu, who had composed beautiful songs about their lives traversing pastoral landscapes in the Indian Ocean region before arriving in California.

This is the first study exploring autobiographical songs composed by the first generation of South Asian American women. The songs offer rare insights into women's interior emotional lives—into their loneliness, sorrows, desires and aspirations. Music represents a particularly powerful vehicle for understanding the continuities and disjunctures in transnational cultural flows, which I refer to as 'soundscapes' (aural cultural flows) (Appadurai 1996).[2] The discovery of these songs is especially valuable given that women's lives remain largely neglected in South Asia diaspora studies. Equally important is the fact that women barely exist in the public record of early South Asian migration to North America. Moreover, elderly Punjabi women are generally relegated to the private sphere of the home, rarely garnering public attention within the community and in the broader American society. The fact that *bibian* (elderly women) composed poetry will come as a surprise to many in the local Punjabi community.

Music provides a window into the transformations of Punjabi women's interior emotional lives in the diasporic context. I argue that the nexus between gender, history and migration is central to gaining insights into women's assertions of identity through soundscapes. In particular, the diasporic framework is critical to understanding women's urge to compose original songs as well as the conditions that allowed them to create music. The liminal space that these women inhabited between cultures gave them an outsider's perspective and status, enabling them to give voice to emotions that remain unacceptable in everyday life in Punjabi society. In addition, the hypermobility of their lives created ruptures in emotional and geographical connectedness that prevented them from bonding with other people through music. In essence, they created songs in search of listeners.

Historical Background

The first significant number of Indians migrated to the west coast of North America in the 1890s. The majority were men from farming families who left Punjab in northern British India seeking economic opportunity. They migrated as soldiers and police officers throughout the British Empire to Asia, Africa, the Americas, Europe and the South Pacific. In western North America, Punjabi migrants built railroads and laboured in the lumber mills before settling in California's Central Valley where they farmed land reminiscent of the rich alluvial fields of Punjab (Jensen 1988; La Brack 1988; Leonard 1997; Shah 2012).

Punjabi men faced enormous challenges in establishing families in the United States. Many had already married before they left Punjab. Initially, they planned to return to their families in their ancestral villages in Punjab to purchase land with their savings. However, very few men were able to bring their wives due to the intensifying racial antipathy against Asians in the early twentieth century, which led to a wave of exclusionary legislation that barred immigration from India (and most of Asia) in 1917 and 1924. Due to the *Bhagat Singh Thind v United States* Supreme Court decision in 1923, South Asians were denied US citizenship along with other civil rights, including land ownership (Lopez 1996). The vast majority of their wives were left behind in Punjab for decades. Indian migrants had the lowest proportion of women among all Asian migrant groups in the US—there were just 100 Indian women for 1,572 men in 1930 (Leonard 1992: 23). Hundreds of men decided to return to India while others who stayed married Americans of different ethnicities, especially women from Mexico (Leonard 1997).[3]

There is little documentation of the history of Punjabi women in the United States. Rattan Kaur was the first Punjabi woman known to arrive in the United States in 1910. Her daughter, Kartar Kaur Dhillon, who was born in California in 1915, was one of the first Punjabi girls born in the US (Das 1923: 10; Dhillon 2012).[4] A handful of other Punjabi women arrived before World War II. When US citizenship was restored and immigration from India resumed on a limited basis in 1946, Punjabi men bought land and started sponsoring their sons, wives and other family members. The first significant number of Punjabi women arrived in the United States beginning in the early 1950s. Upon their arrival, Punjabi women encountered a small community of Punjabi men living as bachelors in ramshackle farm labour camps. The South Asian American community had dwindled from approximately 6,656 in 1910 to 2,405 in 1940 due to racially exclusionary US immigration policies and the passing of the early settlers (Chakravorty et al. 2017: 14; Jensen 1988).[5] The history of this first generation of Punjabi women in the Yuba City area is documented in my oral history research project (Ranganath 2020).

Historiography

This chapter builds on Anshu Malhotra and Siobhan Lambert-Hurley's pioneering work theorising the relationship between gender, history and autobiographical writings in South Asia. I define autobiographical writing broadly to include women's song-writing as another 'portrait of memory' that illuminates women's self-conceptions (Malhotra and Lambert-Hurley 2015). In this chapter, I contend that the diasporic context plays a crucial role, whether implicitly or explicitly, in understanding the poetry composed by Punjabi women.

Music is a powerful medium for sharing emotions that connect the singer/composer with a community of listeners. The purpose of Punjabi music, as with other cultural forms, changed dramatically in the modern diaspora. The ancestors of the women in this study spent their lives in small villages in Punjab. They listened to, sang and taught folk songs to younger people in their families and villages. Punjabi folk music was mainly performed by women, venting intense emotions that were collectively shared by other women that would otherwise be taboo to express in everyday life (that is, frustrations with husbands and mothers-in-law, mourning a daughter's departure after marriage, bereavement and sexual flirtation). Typically, women sang folk songs at important rites of passage (births, weddings, funerals) and at festivals. Due to the global migration of Punjabis beginning in the late nineteenth century, the continuity of these soundscapes was increasingly ruptured.

The meaning that women derived from music was also transformed, reflecting the changes in their identity and life circumstances outside of Punjab. This study suggests that women's need to create original music also came from a new assertion of the self that emerged within the diasporic context. In other words, these women's music reflects the notion of the *Punjabiyat*, a capacious idea of the Punjab region transcending narrow local and sectarian identities. The concept of Punjabiness has become increasingly globalised over the last 150 years. This attempt to understand diasporic Punjabi women's music is part of Malhotra and Mir's broader effort to historicise the shifting ways that an imagined Punjab is 'lived, experienced, and vitalized' by diverse peoples from the region (Malhotra and Mir 2012: xvi).

Methods and Ethics

In a larger project funded by the California Humanities, I interviewed over two dozen elderly Punjabi American women, especially those who formed part of the first generation to arrive in the United States from the late 1940s to 1970. In 2017, I gathered the life histories of this unique cohort of female pioneers, documenting their impressions of the South Asian American community in the decade before the 1965 Immigration Act dramatically increased South Asian migration to the US.[6] For the first time, women publicly discussed their tremendous contributions to the establishment of Punjabi peach farming as well as the growth of South Asian American religious and cultural institutions.

The process of gathering Punjabi women's history in the Yuba City area required patience and collaboration. In the fall of 2016, I formed a working group with three daughters of the first cohort of Punjabi women settlers in Yuba City. Initially, elderly women in the community were reluctant to talk about their lives for fear of what people would say in the community. It was the encouragement by the trusted daughters in the community that gave elderly women the courage to speak publicly. Our collaboration resulted in the first documentary tracing the history of California's Punjabi women, *Jutti Kasoori* (Walking into the Unknown) (Ranganath 2018). It was fortunate that we documented this generation of women's life histories in 2017. By 2020, many of these rich repositories of history and knowledge had already passed.

I did not discover the existence of women's original songs until after the larger project had finished. Only during informal conversations did two women discuss the songs they had composed. This finding would not have been possible without the longstanding deep bonds that the families of Rajinder K. Tumber and Sharon Singh had with the women who composed the poetry. Mohinderjit Kaur Thiara and Harbans Kaur Panu openly shared their personal experiences and the poetry they composed. Neither woman expressed concern about what people would say about them.

Out of respect for these women's desire to be acknowledged and heard publicly, I have included their actual birth names in this publication with their written consent. Every woman interviewed was given the right to make the final decision about whether to publicly release part, all or none of their interview as per the consent form. The interviews were conducted in Punjabi women's homes in Punjabi and English. The private setting was critical to help women feel comfortable in sharing their intimate experiences and emotions in a safe space.

Diasporic Punjabi Women's Music

'Love may indeed be a universal feeling, but culture and language play a role in defining it at every stage,' asserts Francesca Orsini in her history of love in South Asia (Orsini 2006: 1). The subcontinent offers a particularly rich field of ideas, idioms and legends about love of every kind, such as familial, romantic and spiritual. The heart of the women's songs created by Mohinderjit Kaur Thiara and Harbans Kaur Panu concerns their intense emotions of love, loss and longing within the diasporic context.

A careful analysis of their soundscapes reveals a great deal about the transformations in women's identities in the diaspora. In their musical compositions, Mohinderjit and Harbans borrowed most frequently from Punjabi women's folk songs, although they showed familiarity with other musical and poetic genres in Punjab, the Middle East and America as well. Their songs reflect the hybrid identities of these two women who were influenced by diverse cultural and musical traditions.

Harbans and Mohinderjit chose to compose their songs in the Punjabi language. This is notable because both women lived the majority of their lives, including their childhoods, in multilingual countries outside of India. Harbans learned Tamil and Punjabi as a little girl in Malaysia, and she also learned Hindi as a teenager in India and English after arriving in the US. Mohinderjit is fluent in English, Hindi and Farsi in addition to Punjabi. Yet both women clearly felt a special affinity for Punjabi, choosing to express their innermost feelings in their *māṃ bolī* (mother tongue).

Mohinderjit's and Harbans' songs also reflect their transnational experiences in the broader Indian Ocean world. Mohinderjit's songs are inflected with cultural and religious influences drawn from her youth in Iran. She intersperses concepts and devotion for the divine borrowed from Islam and the Hindu faith as often as the Sikh faith.

Both women heard and participated in diverse soundscapes in multiple countries in the Indian Ocean region before settling in the Yuba City area after World War II. They actively joined small gatherings that performed *sabad kirtan* (Sikh devotional music) (Kaur 2016). Mohinderjit's family played an important role in the development of Sikh institutions and devotional music in the community. Before the first Yuba City *gurdwara* (Sikh house of worship) opened in 1971, Munsha Thiara's home in Live Oak served as a centre of religious musical gatherings. According to Mohinderjit, hers may have been the only local family that sent their daughters to Punjab to learn devotional music in the 1960s and 1970s. In addition to Sikh devotional hymns, the women also enjoyed Hindi film music and popular American music.

This chapter draws from Raheja and Gold's approach to understanding women's expressive traditions in north India, particularly the complex relationship between women's language and dominant power relations in the family and in society more broadly. Raheja and Gold's *Listen to the Heron's Words* explores 'the words in which [women] construct and communicate alternative self-perceptions and alternative vantage points on their social world' (Raheja and Gold 1994: 2). Their focus on women's communication also highlights the complexities of understanding and rendering women's subjectivities. Indian women's voices have been largely expunged from history. In dominant discourses, 'the Indian woman has all too frequently been portrayed as a silent shadow, given in marriage by one patrilineal group to another, veiled and mute... and unquestioningly accepting... her own subordination' (ibid.: 3–4). Folk music highlights the nuanced ways in which women negotiate power hierarchies. Women actively critique and subvert gender norms, often in the same breath as they acquiesce to and maintain them.

Within north Indian women's folk music, the songs composed by Harbans Panu and Mohinderjit Thiara most closely resemble two genres, *barahmasa* (seasonal songs) and wedding songs. At the heart of the barahmasa genre is the abandoned woman who 'pines for her absent lover or husband and describes her pitiful state, month after month, against the backdrop of seasonal changes and ritual events' (Orsini 2010: 143). The voice of this genre is feminine, expressed in a folksy vernacular with stock images of nature that are metaphorical for emotional states. This chapter analyses how the barahmasa genre would appeal to diasporic women who experienced extensive separations from their husbands and who also created nostalgic songs about their youths in rural Punjab years after they had settled abroad. Both women also wrote powerful songs about their separations from their families as young brides in Punjab. Although Harbans and Mohinderjit drew heavily from north Indian women's folk music, their original songs also reflect the dramatically altered geographies of memory, affect and connectivity in the diaspora.

Harbans Kaur Panu

Harbans Kaur Panu (born in 1941) was part of the first generation of Punjabi women to settle in the Yuba City area (Image 3.1).[7] After her birth in Malaysia, she moved to a village near Amritsar, Punjab, when she was six years old. She fondly remembers her childhood, especially her parents' warmth and love. Having learned Tamil in Malaysia, she often spoke this south Indian language to her parents as a young girl. Her father was modern in his thinking and cherished his daughters as much as his son. He even distributed sweets when his daughters were born, a ritual that was only customary for the birth of sons. Her main regret was that she received only five years of education: 'I wish I had become a lawyer, a schoolteacher, a nurse or a doctor or something.'[8] But her family was more concerned with preparing her for marriage.

IMAGE 3.1: Harbans Kaur Panu, c. 1990, Yuba City, CA.
Courtesy: Harbans Kaur Panu.

When she was 20 years old, she married a peach farmer named Rashpal Panu. Soon after, she joined her husband in Yuba City in 1961. She never forgot her sadness about leaving her family as a young bride. She vividly remembered her fear as she departed for America: 'When I leave Delhi, I was so scared because I don't know English [*sic*]. I didn't know where I was going. No one was there who is gonna take care of me if my husband [was] not there.' Her four-day trip to the US was traumatic: 'I loved my dad a lot, but I had my mom's milk for five years. [*laughing*] I really missed my mom. The entire journey I spent crying. I developed a fever when I got here.'[9] Fortunately, another Punjabi woman came to the hospital to take care of her. Afterwards, she helped Harbans to do her grocery shopping and adjust to her new life.

In her early days in Yuba City, she recalls encountering a great deal of hostility from the local white community. Her friendships with other Punjabi women formed a lifeline for her. 'The amount of love I received when I got here, I don't think I received even that much love from my family.... The [ladies] were my friends, they were my parents, they were everything to me.' She remembered Harbhajan Kaur Takher with deep affection: 'She loved me like a little baby.' Slowly she started enjoying her life in California. She loved wearing American clothes and she learned English while watching soap operas. She worked for decades, helping her husband on their 15-acre peach orchard by pruning, thinning and irrigating. During her 26 years working at the Sunsweet fruit packing house, she created friendships with people of different backgrounds. 'I worked for 26 years. There were people of all races, and I loved them all.'[10] Harbans also enjoyed performing *seva* at the gurdwara and socialising with other Punjabi women.

She raised six children and has 12 grandchildren. Despite her initial struggles adjusting to her new life, she described America as heaven. She offered this advice to young people: 'Pain and happiness are a part of life.... It is your choice to spend your life crying or laughing. Always stay with love, and your life passes with happiness.'

Harbans Kaur Panu's Poetics of Loss

Harbans composed beautiful songs about her life, especially to soothe herself during emotionally difficult times. After her eldest son died in a motorcycle accident at the age of 21, Harbans believed she might succumb to her all-consuming grief. Composing her first song, 'Why didn't you remember me?', was an act of survival:[11]

> *Ik mera chan tara si*
> He was my moon and stars
> *Mainu lagda bara pyara si*
> I really loved him.
> *Par ik din uhne apni surat baddlan vich chipai si*
> But one day he hid his face in the clouds
> *Uhnu yad kion na meri ai?*
> Why didn't he remember me?
> *Chann ve, uhnu yaad kion na meri ai?*
> My moon, why didn't you remember me?

The song ends with this verse:

> *Lakhan mausam bit gae*
> Countless seasons passed
> *Lakhan mausam ae*
> Countless seasons arrived
> *Par jane vale phir lot ke murke kade na ae*
> But those who left never came back to me
> *Haye Rabba, phir murke kade na ae*
> Oh God, they never came back to me.[12]

The act of composing this lamentation helped her live past her intense grief. In a major departure from the composers of Punjabi folk music, Harbans did not compose her songs to be performed in front of audiences during rites of passage or at festivals. She composed poetry to heal herself. In addition to her deep reservoir of sorrow, she also expressed her anger at her son for abandoning her as well as her feeling of helplessness to prevent loss.

Harbans' song resembles the barahmasa folk song in many respects, including the association between seasons and emotions. The most striking similarity is the voice of the heroine who despairs at the loss of her loved one. Her lamentation for her departed son is especially poignant given the intimate relationship between mothers and sons in Punjabi culture. Harbans likens her son to the moon and stars, which is a common trope in north Indian music and poetry. She employs the motif of the passing seasons to express her profound grief for her son as well as her beloved family members whom she had lost over her lifetime. The use of 'countless seasons' is an evocative way of expressing her experiential sense of loss across a temporal plane that feels both infinite yet also agonisingly slow as measured by the passing of each season. Every season brings a recurring sense of dread and disappointment when loved ones fail to return. Harbans' profound loss is only tempered by her belief in the partial re-incorporation of the lost son inside her body:

> *Par uh mere dil vich rahinde a*
> He lives in my heart
> *Par uh muhon kujh nahin kahinde a*
> But he doesn't speak.

The identity that Harbans asserts in her poetry reflects her diasporic life experience. First, she lived the majority of her life far from her family due to her move to California while her extended family lived in India, England and other distant countries. Second, there is a conspicuous absence of any references to places in her poetry that is likely due to the many dislocations she experienced in life. She sought comfort in a sense of belonging with nature and the cosmos rather than with a sense of rootedness in any geographical place. Her poetry is evidence of a sense of self that is removed, even disembodied, from a specific place. Third, she may have felt the need to create her own songs, her own lullabies to comfort herself, due to the absence of her mother and other female kin.

'Daughters are always someone else's' is Harbans' poignant song about her departure as a young bride from her family home in a Punjabi village at the age of 20.

> *Babul, terian akhkhan kion bhar aian?*
> Beloved father, why did your eyes well up in tears?
> *Babul, dhian te hundian paraian*
> Beloved father, daughters are always someone else's

Chad jana babul da khera
I am going to leave my father's village
Chad jana amra da vehara
I am going to leave my mother's home
Jithe nal sahelian main khedian si lukan michian
Where I used to play hide and seek with my friends
Babul, dhian te humdian paraian
Beloved father, daughters are always someone else's.

Then the final two verses:

Tun kion hoia udas ve vira?
Why have you become sad, brother?
Tun te amri de dil da hira
You are the diamond of our mother's heart
Vekhi kidhre bhul na jai apni ma dian jaian
Don't forget your mother's daughters
Babul, dhian te humdian paraian
Beloved father, daughters are always someone else's
Babul, terian akhkhan kion bhar aian?
Beloved father, why do your eyes well up with tears?

Ih bani rit purani
This is an old custom
Peke chad ke sahure jana
Leaving the parents' home for the in-laws' house
Tera babul dosh na koi
You are not to blame, beloved father
Turdian lekh likhaian
Traditions are simply continuing
Babul, dhian te humdian paraian
Beloved father, daughters are always someone else's
Babul, terian akhkhan kion bhar aian?
Beloved father, why do your eyes well up with tears?
Babul, dhian te humdian paraian
Beloved father, daughters are always someone else's.

Harbans' song resembles a sub-genre of Punjabi folk wedding songs known as *lambe git* (long songs) in which the bride's family mourns their daughter's departure from home after marriage. What is unusual is that Harbans composed a song about her own departure as a young woman after marriage rather than expressing her emotions through the hundreds of folk songs dedicated to this theme. Harbans' poetry also reveals the process by which people remember the loss of loved ones, and how every new loss taps into a well-spring of sorrow. She wrote this song in response to her daughter's wedding, which then tapped into her reservoir of unresolved grief about her separation from her family decades earlier. The only occasion where Harbans performed one of her songs in public was at her retirement from the Sunsweet fruit packing house in the 1990s. Her feeling of sadness at leaving her friends at work brought this sad song to her heart.

What is striking about Harbans' song is her generosity of spirit. A key aspect of her reconciling with her past is her act of forgiveness. She exonerates her father for giving her away to her in-laws by accepting that her loss is part of the flowing stream of continuity of patrilocal family traditions.

Harbans' third sad song, 'Why did my memory not come to you?' expresses her grief after her husband's death:

Mahi ve, mahi ve
My darling, my darling
Tun tur gion pardes
You left for abroad

And then these two verses:

Das chithian kidhdhar nun pavan?
Where should I address my letters?
Koi de ke na gia sirnavan ve
You didn't give me your full name.

Once again, she experienced the loss of a loved one as a departure abroad without any way to find that person (no location, no address). She exclaims: '*Mere dil vichon nikalan hava ve*/Air is coming out of my heart.' The image of air/wind coming out of Harbans' heart is another metaphor for her imagined communion with the cosmos and her departed loved ones.

Harbans' only joyful song describes her feelings during her second son's wedding, she told me. However, the lyrics of her song refer to her brother's wedding. Again, the emotions she feels in the present in the United States were refracted through the memory of her joyful feeling at her brother's wedding in her youth in Punjab. The song is a celebration of an extended family at her brother's wedding. In contrast to the mixed feelings at a daughter's wedding in which a family member is lost or given to another family, a male family member's wedding is cause for great celebration. This song is filled with vibrant details in which her large extended family enjoys the wedding. The song closes with Harbans' intense feeling of joy:

> *Iho jihian khushian Rabba sabh te dikhave*
> God should bring such a joyful day to everyone
> *Iho hi a meri e dua*
> This is my prayer
> *Ni ajj asin nachna a*
> We're going to dance today
> *Nach-nach khushian de nal te dharti nun putna hai*
> I'm going to dig up the earth dancing.

Mohinderjit Kaur Thiara

Mohinderjit Kaur Thiara (born in 1937) has lived a remarkable life (Image 3.2).[13] After her birth in Burma, she grew up in Iran before marrying Harsev Singh Thiara in Punjab in 1951. A few years later, she joined her husband and his family on their peach farm north of Yuba City, making her one of the first Punjabi women to settle in the area after World War II. Outspoken, unconventional and fearless, Mohinderjit is also unusual in that she composed over 50 songs and even produced a CD.

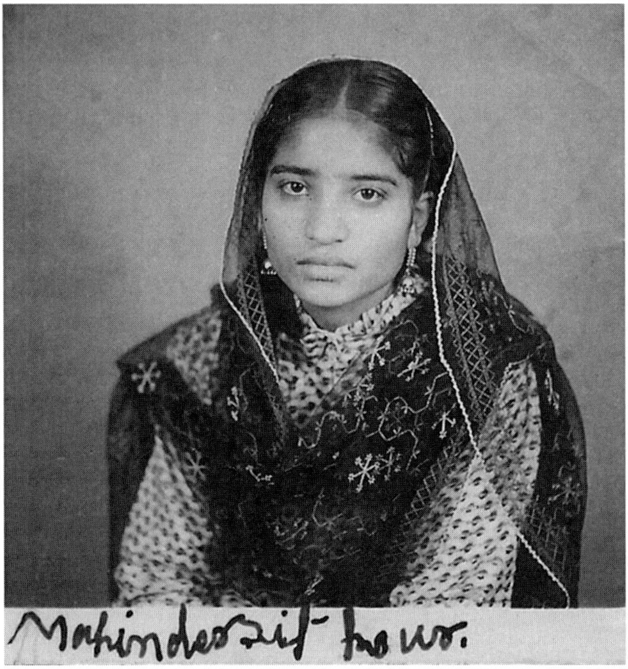

Image 3.2: Mohinderjit Kaur Thiara, India, 1954.
Courtesy: Mohinderjit Kaur Thiara.

Her father, Udham Pal Singh, loved adventure. During World War I, he served as a railway station master in Iraq. In the 1930s, he moved his family to Burma to work as a lineman for the Burmah Oil Company. During World War II, Udham spent one month walking from Burma to Punjab. Shortly after, he secured a contract as a foreman for the British-owned Anglo-Iranian Oil Company in Abadan, Iran. He and his family lived there for nine years until the nationalisation of Iran's oil industry forced them to leave the country. Afterwards, he and his wife remained in his ancestral village in Punjab.

Kartar Kaur Thanderi, Mohinderjit's mother, was the dominant force in the family. According to Kartar's son, 'Whatever we are is due to my mother. She had that much influence.'[14] She was highly intelligent and ambitious to advance her family. Her tall, elegant frame was often draped in a sari or a fashionable Punjabi suit. A shrewd businesswoman, she made the decisions in selecting sites for land acquisitions for the family. She also made sure that the family's two-storey home was visibly taller than the neighbouring homes. Unusual for a woman of her time, she treated her daughters and sons equally. She insisted that all of her children should receive an education and that they also learn to play the harmonium to perform Sikh devotional music.

Mohinderjit's mother also played a public role as a village leader. She was a vocal advocate for women's education and an opponent of the dowry system. She formed a women's committee to address local issues of concern to women (such as social problems related to men's alcohol consumption) and to improve and modernise the village. She also helped raise funds for the local gurdwara. No one dared make noise as they passed by their home out of respect for the matriarch.

Mohinderjit inherited many of her mother's personality traits. She is a natural leader who speaks her mind and makes financial decisions in her family. She also sponsored many of her relatives to join her in the United States.

Mohinderjit spent her childhood and adolescence in four countries—Burma, Iran, India and the United States. She completed a fifth grade education and learned multiple languages—Farsi, Punjabi, Hindi and English, and a little Burmese. In 1951, she returned to Punjab to marry Harsev Singh Thiara, and joined his family a few years later north of Yuba City in 1954. Mohinderjit exclaimed, 'Everyone in my family says that I'm the lucky one. Wherever I went, I brought money to the family!'[15] She enjoyed an exceptionally privileged lifestyle. In the 1950s and early 1960s, the majority of Punjabi women in Yuba City lived in dilapidated buildings on farms where Indian men had lived as bachelors for years. It took most families at least a decade to accrue the capital to buy their first family homes. Women and their children had to work long hours on the peach farms alongside the men in the early years. By contrast, Mohinderjit's husband's family owned a successful peach farming business. She moved into a large home on a sprawling property with hundreds of acres of fertile land. The family even hired a maid to perform the household chores.

The family's prosperity was due to the longstanding labour and sacrifices of her husband's uncle, Munsha Singh Thiara, who was one of the first Punjabi settlers in the area. Arriving in the US in 1907, Munsha had lived a lean, frugal existence as an itinerant farm worker in the early years but eventually built a successful farming business (Miller 1950).

Mohinderjit was an important member of the local Punjabi community. She also learned English quickly and made it a point to befriend people from diverse religious and ethnic backgrounds. With her family's love of music, her home was a gathering place for Sikh devotional music and prayers before the local gurdwaras were opened.

She has seven children and 10 grandchildren.

Mohinderjit Kaur Thiara's Poetics of Longing

Mohinderjit's songs provide a rich window into her interior emotional life. The poetry, combined with in-depth oral history, offers a complex portrait of a bright, unconventional woman with an extraordinary life history. The central impulse for her creative expression was desire: yearning for romance, adventure and freedom from the constraints of societal expectations of a woman of her background. When she was a little girl, Mohinderjit dreamed of becoming a Bollywood film star. This was a highly unconventional aspiration for a Sikh girl from a respectable family growing up in the 1940s.

It is difficult to determine the precise dates of her compositions or her initial motivation to compose poetry. However, most of her songs were composed in California and most focus on her youth in Punjab. Why was Mohinderjit one of the only Punjabi American women of her generation who composed songs in Gurmukhi (one of three scripts for the Punjabi language) and English, and even produced a CD? In the local Punjabi community, Mohinderjit is known for her non-conventional behaviour and attitudes. She is fearless in speaking her mind and getting in anyone's face to voice her opinions. Mohinderjit also had the financial means and time to write. More important, she had the time and space to reflect on her life. Isolation triggered nostalgia and the desire to express her own feelings about her life. There is a deep desire to connect with people through music; however, in her new home, she was mainly able to connect by performing at family gatherings. Her mother's influence was also powerful—she was raised in a family in which she was socialised to express herself and to value music and education. As a member of a well-respected, affluent family, she also felt secure enough to boldly express emotions that remain taboo for women in the community.

Mohinderjit's peripatetic early life is evident in the plurality of linguistic, cultural and religious influences in her poetry. Roughly a quarter of her songs reflect the Sufi tradition of *ishq* (love) in which the poet expresses a longing to be united with the divine or a lover. In describing the divine, she borrows heavily from the Islamic faith, using the terms Allah and Rabba. She also seems equally comfortable imagining devotional worship in *mandir*s (Hindu temples) as in the Darbar Sahib.

The four main preoccupations in Mohinderjit's songs concern (i) her imagined youth in Punjab, even though she largely grew up in Burma and Iran; (ii) romantic love, especially the pain of separation from her husband; (iii) excitement about moving to America; and (iv) the loneliness of her later life in the United States.

The first predominant theme in Mohinderjit's songs is an imagined nostalgia for a childhood in Punjab that she never experienced, shuttling from Burma to Punjab to Iran to Punjab to the US. Her songs about Punjab contain many of the stock tropes from the barahmasa folk song, including the stereotypical images associated with nature (for example, the arrival of the black rain clouds). 'The Cold, Cold Wind Blows' is an evocative song about a *theeyan* (women's festival), a favourite subject of Punjabi women's folk songs. The theeyan festivals occur during the arrival of the rainy season in Punjab; it is a time when women return to their home village where they traditionally gathered together to sing and dance. In this setting, it is socially acceptable for women to voice their complaints about topics that would otherwise be taboo, such as vexing mothers-in-law, sorrows and hardships in their lives, and difficulties with husbands.

> *Ṭhandi thandi vagdi hava vich bulle vagde*
> The cold, cold wind blows, filled with fierce winds
>
> *Saun da mahina ghatan charh aian*
> The rainy season has arrived and dark rain clouds have gathered…
>
> *Arsha ton aian parian, rang-birange gihne pa ke,*
> *nange pairi, pairi jhanjaran*
> Angels came from the sky wearing colourful necklaces and anklets on their bare feet
>
> *Nach-nach pavan dhamalan dharti te*
> They forcefully dance on the earth…
>
> *Chal sajna mele chalie, mele aian theeyan da*
> My friend, let's go to the fair. The women's festival has come.

This song closely resembles a traditional Punjabi women's folk song. There is an emphasis on natural elements that represent metaphors for intense feelings of foreboding and excitement. The language is informal, in the style of an ordinary village girl caught up in the anticipation of joining the fair. The imagery conveys women embracing their power, in the forcefulness of their joy in dancing, taking charge of the bullock carts, and the fierce winds signalling the arrival of their special festival.

The second dominant theme in Mohinderjit's poetry is her longing for her lover, which presumably was her husband living abroad in the United States. However, her lover's identity is ambiguous in the song. Her love poems invoke the concept of ishq, or an intense longing for a lover or God, which is borrowed in Punjabi music from the Perso-Arabic cultural influence in South Asia. It appears that her songs were influenced by Bollywood films. According to Rachel Dwyer, Hindi film music is one of the most popular forms of poetry in India with 'a rich idiom of love' that 'draws on a whole range of Indian lyric traditions, including the folksong and the Hindu devotional lyric, but is most closely connected with the Urdu lyric'. For Mohinderjit, 'songs allow things to be said which cannot be said elsewhere, often to admit love to the beloved, to reveal inner feelings, and to make the hero/heroine realise that he/she is in love' (Dwyer 2006: 292).

Mohinderjit's love songs fashion herself and her lover in the immensely popular ballads of the doomed Punjabi lovers, Hir and Ranjha (Deol 2002; Malhotra 2017; Mir 2006, 2010; Singh 2016). This narrative tells the story of the tragic love between an intelligent, beautiful woman named Hir, who defies her powerful family who oppose her relationship with her lover, Ranjha. Many of the popular songs about Hir and Ranjha concern their painful separation after the heroine is forcibly married to another man. This legend often ends with both lovers taking their lives by consuming poison rather than living apart. Mohinderjit makes her identification with Hir explicit by asserting in her songs: 'Hir should exist with the name, Mohinderjit Kaur.'

The two songs that Mohinderjit spontaneously sang for me expressed her longing for her husband during the difficult years of separation after marriage (Image 3.3). Again, Mohinderjit casts herself and her husband as the most popular romantic figures in Punjab, Hir and Ranjha. In the song 'Hir cries out', she describes the distress she felt after the train took her Rānjha away to a foreign land. She is left behind crying at the *charkha* (spinning wheel), making clothes in Punjab. She pleads with the Ranjhas (the husbands) not to forget their wives back home '[as] our blossoming youth fades'.

IMAGE 3.3: Harsev Singh and Mohinderjit Kaur Thiara as newlyweds, Punjab, India, 1951.

Courtesy: Mohinderjit Kaur Thiara

Mohinderjit sang the second song, 'Deson pardes', at her husband's funeral. She negotiated this final loss of her husband through her memory of her earlier painful separation after marriage when he left for California and she remained in Punjab. The song is a dialogue between herself and her husband, imagined as the tragic romantic legends, Hir and Ranjha.

Deson pardes ae te, main tur chalia
[Ranjha] I'm going far away, leaving home for a foreign land
Dikhin kite bhul na javin mere pichle piar
[Hir] Don't forget your first love
Hir merie ni bhul javin mere pahile vale piar
[Ranjha] My Hīr, forget your first love

Jan valia das ja apna than te tikana
[Hir] Tell me the address where you're going
Jithe likh likh rudna dian chithian main tainun pavan
[Hir] Where can I send my love letters to you?
Sajna, main tainun pavan
[Hir] Darling, [tell me your address] so I can send them to you.
Na mera than te na hi mera tikana
[Ranjha] I don't know where I'm going. I have no address or place
Ni dil apna main tere dil vich rakh jana e Hire merie
[Ranjha] I'll keep my heart in yours, my Hīr
Ni dil apna main tere dil vich rakh jana
[Ranjha] I'm going to keep my heart in yours
Jane valia, ajj teri Hir kukan mardi
[Hir] Departing lover, your Hīr calls out to you.
Chadd ke na javin Ranjha rondi apni Hir nun
[Hir] Don't leave me crying, Ranjha, your Hir is crying
Hir kukan mardi
[Hir] Your Hir calls out to you.
Chadd ke na javin Ranjha rondi apni Hir nun
[Hir] Don't leave me crying, Ranjha, your Hir is crying.

Mohinderjit's song is a powerful testament to the collective experience of the thousands of wives who were left behind in Punjab after their husbands migrated all over the world beginning in the late nineteenth century. This source material is valuable given the paucity of research on the transformations in women's lives in Punjab as British colonialism took hold of the region in the late 1800s and their husbands dispersed throughout the world.

In her third theme, Mohinderjit describes her mixed emotions about leaving Punjab for America. In her song, 'Let's go, friend, to America' she proclaims, 'There, one is equal to forty.' The song reflects her sense of her own ambition to act in the world, saying, 'My earth is like gold.' The poem continues stating that the seeds she plants yield large harvests and bring abundance and wealth to her family. Mohinderjit conveys a powerful sense of her female agency and optimism in these songs. In contrast to her sad songs about leaving home after marriage, her songs about leaving for America are bittersweet:

> *Ajj tor de sajna nun*
> Today, darling departs
> *Sagnan de nal ni, asin dur-durade jana*
> With blessings, we're going far away
> *Asam mur ke ni auna*
> We're not going to return

Despite her sadness at leaving her loved ones in Punjab, she took comfort in joining her beloved.

A fascinating aspect about Mohinderjit's preoccupation with her idyllic childhood in a Punjabi village is that she grew up primarily in Burma and Iran. Therefore, the large number of songs about her youth in Punjabi represents fantasies of a life that differed significantly from the one she lived in multiple countries. Yet they express the enduring deep cultural connection of Punjabi women who settled abroad with their familial villages in Punjab. Of the dozens of songs Mohinderjit wrote, nearly all concern her actual or imagined life in Punjab as a young woman. Mohinderjit's poetry is a rich historical source for understanding the complex ways that 'the idea of Punjab, or Punjabiness might live in the imagination' (Malhotra and Mir 2012: xvii).

The fourth theme in Mohinderjit's compositions concerns her loneliness of her later years in America. Of the dozens of songs she wrote in America, very few describe her life in her adopted country. Most of her songs about her new life reflect feelings of isolation, loneliness and alienation from society. One song exclaims, 'No one recognises my sorrows.' She adds, 'Everyone says, "God, God"/I haven't seen God ever.' It appears that she became more isolated after her husband's passing, 'People taunt in my world/No one recognises my hidden pain.' Her songs about her later years are filled with her feelings of emptiness, loneliness and despair after her husband's departure, 'I didn't receive any love.'

CONCLUSION

This chapter asserts that the diasporic context is essential for understanding the motivations of two women who wrote their own songs, as well as the conditions that enabled them to create musical poetry. Their songs represent the intense feelings of loneliness felt by the first generation of Punjabi women who lived on isolated farms in the Yuba City area while their husbands worked long hours in the orchards. Their songs also reflect diasporic Punjabi women's early life experiences in Punjab, especially the trauma of leaving their family home after marriage.

However, the life histories of Mohinderjit and Harbans also differed from other Punjabi women who settled in the Yuba City area in the 1950s and 1960s. Both women lived in multiple countries in the Indian Ocean world before settling in California, whereas most women of their generation migrated directly from their in-laws' villages in Punjab. Perhaps the hypermobility of their youth created a desire to immerse themselves in an imagined youth in a Punjabi village. Mohinderjit and Harbans shared the urge to express their unique emotions as individuals within the emergent space of the diaspora. Their female ancestors would generally have participated in the venting of the collective emotions of sadness, grief and joy in traditional folk songs. Some elderly Punjabi women found their voices to articulate profound emotions in California. Harbhajan Kaur Takher, one of the pillars of Yuba City's Punjabi American community and Harbans Kaur Panu's dear friend, remarked, 'In India, we didn't really talk. *I started talking when I got here*.'[16]

Their new lives of relative affluence in rural America also provided the time as well as the physical and emotional space for women to pursue writing. For instance, Mohinderjit married into a wealthy, well-established farming family where she was one of the few Punjabi women of her generation who enjoyed the luxury of domestic help that gave her the time to pursue music. Solitude can spur retrospection and creativity.

The same emotional and physical isolation these two women experienced in Yuba City that motivated them to express themselves creatively through music also disrupted the social bonds in which folk music was shared and enjoyed with family and friends, and then passed down across generations in Punjabi villages. By contrast, there were few occasions in which Harbans and Mohinderjit performed their songs for audiences. Harbans composed music for herself. Despite her desire to become famous, Mohinderjit rarely enjoyed the opportunity to perform her songs, and mainly did so at family functions. In short, the diasporic context both created the intense desire for social connection through music while simultaneously rupturing the social fabric in which music could be intimately shared and enjoyed within communities. Punjabi women did gather in rural California to enjoy Punjabi folk songs and dances at weddings, and more recently at the tremendously popular theeyan festivals. However, a few women felt the need to innovate by expressing their unique emotions privately rather than continuing the performance of traditional Punjabi musical forms—Punjabi folk songs and/or sabad kirtan devotional music—in California. These women sang for themselves to heal and honour emotional losses or relive joyful moments from their youth. As they sang their poignant songs about their unusual lives in private, they no longer formed a part of the circles of connectedness in Punjabi village soundscapes in which their mothers' and grandmothers' voices were once heard.

NOTES

1. When discussing people who migrated from the Punjab region to the United States, I use the term Indian when referring to migrants who left before India's independence in 1947. I employ the more inclusive term of South Asians to describe the peoples of Punjabi heritage who came from both India and Pakistan after Partition in 1947.

2. The term 'soundscape' is based on Arjun Appadurai's influential concept of 'scapes' (cultural flows) in modern diasporas (Appadurai 1996).

3. Karen Leonard (1992) documents 378 marriages between Indian male migrants and women of different racial and ethnic backgrounds, primarily from Mexico, between 1913 and 1949 in the western United States.

4. The Dhillon family's arrival in the United States is well-documented. A 1923 study notes the arrival of Bakshish Singh Dhillon as the first Indian known to enter the US in 1899: 'He has been back and forth several times and finally returned to this country in 1910 with his family' (Das 1923: 10). See also Kartar Kaur Dhillon's autobiographical account of her family, 'The Parrot's Beak' (Dhillon 2012).

5. According to official records, 6,656 Indians arrived in the United States between 1899 and 1913. See also Jensen (1988). The size of the Indian American community in 1940 is derived from the US census (Chakravorty et al. 2017: 14).

6. Elderly Punjabi American women, first group interview by Nicole Ranganath and Davinder Deol, 17 December 2017, Yuba City, CA; Elderly Punjabi American women, second group interview by Nicole Ranganath and Davinder Deol, 17 December 2017, Yuba City, CA.

7. Biographical information about and photograph of Harbans Kaur Panu were sourced from Harbans Kaur Panu interviews by Nicole Ranganath, 18 December 2017, 22 January 2019 (with Rajinder K. Tumber) and 8 August 2019 (with Rajinder K. Tumber), Yuba City, CA.

8. Harbans Kaur Panu, interview by Nicole Ranganath, 18 December 2017, Yuba City, CA.

9. Ibid.

10. Ibid.

11. The four songs composed by Harbans Kaur Panu were recorded by Nicole Ranganath, 8 August 2019, Yuba City, CA.

12. I am grateful to Dr Kuldeep Singh, Punjabi Language and Culture Lecturer, University of California, Davis, for his invaluable collaboration in translating the songs from the Punjabi language.

13. Biographical information about and photograph of Mohinderjit Kaur Thiara were sourced from Mohinderjit Kaur Thiara interviews by Nicole Ranganath and Rajinder K. Tumber, 15 February 2019 and 12 August 2019, Live Oak, CA.

14. Mohinder Singh Ghag, interview by Nicole Ranganath, 23 February 2020, Yuba City, CA.

15. Mohinderjit Kaur Thiara, interview by Nicole Ranganath and Rajinder K. Tumber, 12 August 2019, Live Oak, CA.

16. Harbhajan Takher, interview by Nicole Ranganath and Davinder Deol, 16 December 2017, Yuba City, CA.

References

Appadurai, Arjun. 1996. *Modernity at Large: Cultural Dimensions of Globalization*. Minneapolis: University of Minnesota Press.

Chakravorty, Sanjoy, Devesh Kapur and Nirvikar Singh. 2017. *The Other One Percent: Indians in America*. Oxford: Oxford University Press.

Das, Rajani Kanta. 1923. *Hindustani Workers on the Pacific Coast*. Berlin: Walter de Gruyter & Co.

Deol, Jeevan. 2002. 'Sex, Social Critique and the Female Figure in Premodern Punjabi Poetry: Varish Shah's "Hir"'. *Modern Asian Studies* 36 (1): 141–71.

Dhillon, Kartar. 2012. 'The Parrot's Beak'. 4 October, South Asian American Digital Archive. Available at https://www.saada.org/tides/article/the-parrots-beak (accessed on 24 August 2023).

Dwyer, Rachel. 2006. 'Kiss or Tell? Declaring Love in Hindi Films'. In *Love in South Asia: A Cultural History*, ed. Francesca Orsini, 289–302. Cambridge: Cambridge University Press.

Jensen, Joan. 1988. *Passage from India: Asian Indian Immigrants in North America*. New Haven: Yale University Press.

Kaur, Inderjit N. 2016. 'Multiple Authenticities in Motion: Styles and Stances in Sikh Sabad Kirtan'. *Yearbook for Traditional Music* 48: 71–93.

La Brack, Bruce. 1988. *The Sikhs of Northern California, 1904–1975*. New York: AMS Press.

Leonard, Karen. 1992. *Making Ethnic Choices: California's Punjabi-Mexican Americans*. Philadelphia: Temple University Press.

Leonard, Karen Isaken. 1997. *The South Asian Americans*. Westport: Greenwood Press.

Lopez, Ian Henry. 1996. *White by Law: The Legal Construction of Race.* New York: New York University Press.

Malhotra, Anshu. 2017. *Piro and the Gulabdasis: Gender, Sect, and Society in Punjab.* Oxford: Oxford University Press.

Malhotra, Anshu, and Farina Mir, eds. 2012. *Punjab Reconsidered: History, Culture, and Practice.* Oxford: Oxford University Press.

Malhotra, Anshu, and Siobhan Lambert-Hurley, eds. 2015. *Speaking of the Self: Gender, Performance and Autobiography in South Asia.* Durham: Duke University Press.

Miller, Allan P. 1950. 'An Ethnographic Report on the Sikh (East) Indians of the Sacramento Valley'. MA thesis, University of California, Berkeley.

Mir, Farina. 2006. 'Genre and Devotion in Punjabi Popular Narratives: Rethinking Cultural and Religious Syncretism'. *Comparative Study of Society and History* 48 (3): 727–58.

———. 2010. *The Social Space of Language: Vernacular Culture in British Colonial Punjab.* Berkeley: University of California Press.

Orsini, Francesca. 2006. *Love in South Asia: A Cultural History.* Cambridge: Cambridge University Press.

———. 2010. 'Barahmasas in Hindi and Urdu'. In *Before the Divide: Hindi and Urdu Literary Culture*, ed. Francesca Orsini, 142–77. New Delhi: Orient BlackSwan.

Raheja, Gloria Goodwin, and Ann Grodzins Gold. 1994. *Listen to the Heron's Words: Reimagining Gender and Kinship in North India.* Berkeley: University of California Press.

Ranganath, Nicole, director. 2018. *Jutti Kasoori* ('Walking into the Unknown'). Sikhlens.

Ranganath, Nicole. 2020. 'Double Passage: Marriage and Migration in Punjabi American Women's Narratives'. *Journal of Sikh and Punjab Studies* 27 (1): 65–94.

Shah, Nayan. 2012. *Stranger Intimacy: Race, Sexuality, and the Law in the North American West.* Berkeley: University of California Press.

Singh, Surjeet. 2016. *Oral Traditions and Cultural Heritage of Punjab.* Patiala: Punjabi University.

Four

Women and Print Cultures in Colonial Punjab*

Arti Minocha

Introduction

This chapter studies the formation of colonial print publics in Punjab, the gendered subjectivities that could be constituted on grounds of print, and middle-class women's deployment of print to articulate the self. The formation of public and print cultures that Bhabha terms as 'one of the most artful technologies of colonial power' (1985: 148) has largely been aligned with the emergence of communal and national identities, especially in print historiographies of colonial Punjab. Print histories also generally adopt a closed spatial framework, most often that of a province or nation, and consequently produce discrete and isolated historical accounts, thus missing the history of vibrant cross-cultural exchange and influence. Recent studies have questioned the assumption of a unidirectional flow of print technology, especially

*Parts of this chapter have been previously published as 'Writing England through Indian Eyes: The Mode of Travel Writing', *Journal of the School of Language, Literature and Culture Studies* 20 (Spring/Autumn): 52–65, 2016, and 'Alternative Literary Modernities: A Voice from Colonial Punjab', *The Zeitschrift für Anglistik und Amerikanistik* [A Quarterly of Language, Literature and Culture] 66 (1): 35–48, 2018.

in the context of nineteenth-century imperialism, and argued for the study of print cultures as sites for connections and mutual influences across the territorial confines of province and nation.[1]

The newly emergent print spheres incubated new discursive possibilities for women to inhabit public spaces, participate in public discourse, mobilise their political agency, and establish associational and print networks. Literary tastes and genres such as travel writing, novels, pamphlets and periodicals evolved at the intersection of local genres, oral and performative practices, and transnational connections. It is these connections between transnational exchanges of ideas, print networks, gendered identity formation and literary writing that this chapter explores. Transnational perspectives on print also allow us to examine the evolution of genres in response to multiple inflections, beyond the binaries of 'tradition' and 'influence'.

The research-intent in this chapter is two-fold: first, to probe, through archival research, the absence of women as agents in literary and print historiographies of colonial Punjab; second, if they were an inevitable part of the 'print publics', then to examine their presence in 'print publics' through possibly new, transnational grids of relationships and social imaginaries beyond the local, provincial and national boundaries that usually frame the study of print cultures. This will be done through two narratives by Punjabi women that imagine and explore the possibilities of establishing gendered solidarities across provincial, national and communitarian borders.

The first is Susila Tahl Ram's English novel titled *Cosmopolitan Hinduani*, which was published in Lahore in 1902. I will examine the narrator's notion of a gendered 'cosmopolitanism' and her attempt to go beyond the fault lines of religion to articulate a liberal and modern political subject, while reworking the cosmopolitan/local binary. I will also analyse the literary and linguistic practices through which the narrator enunciates a self-fashioning that she calls 'cosmopolitan'. If Susila Tahl Ram, in her novel, records a woman's fictional aspirations to mobility and her desire to visualise a transnational sisterhood, Hardevi in her travel writings fictionalises her embodied and corporeal travel experiences to London. Her travel writings in Hindi, titled *London Yatra* (1888a) and *London Jubilee* (1888b), were written for her 'sisters' in Punjab and sent from London to Lahore for women readers. The chapter will examine the implications of writing back to an imagined readership in the language chosen and the reconfiguration of the self and the nation in relationship to the imperial centre that she visits. These narratives give us a rich account of the first stirrings of the political and literary subjectivity of women in the 'modern' print cultures of colonial Punjab.

The Idea of 'Print Cultures'

The term 'print cultures' is used here to refer to the representational space that opened up, especially in nineteenth-century India when the medium of print came into the hands of private individuals rather than being monopolised by the colonial state. This space afforded the generation of public opinion on issues that were perceived as 'common good' through debates and discussions in newspapers, periodicals, books and pamphlets. Though ideally accessible to all, the print space consisted of groups and communities with different interests, powers of negotiation and accessibility to the print medium, and therefore the use of the plural 'print cultures' to suggest that there were various competing and contending groups claiming to represent public interest. In nineteenth-century Punjab, most of these efforts at public good or public spirit were centred around community identity, access to press, books, education and the printed word, and access to these was important in the constitution of middle-class masculine identities.

The understanding of print cultures as terrains of power allows us to think of print not as a given medium of knowledge-creation but as a space where historical subjects acted and operated. If colonial forms of knowledge and taxonomy were imposed and language hierarchies created by education systems in colonial societies, the subjects themselves exercised resilience through generic innovations, linguistic choices and well-entrenched traditions of oral and scribal cultures. Print was thus a locus of their agency.

Women in Print Cultures of Punjab

Although few studies have brought women into the ambit of this investigation, women inhabited, constituted and left their mark on print cultures in colonial Punjab in various ways. They modulated oral and written cultures into new genres of expression, negotiated modes of subjectivity with the reform discourse, contested the reform idealisation of women, and imaginatively delineated affective communities of belief, gendered kinship, transnational solidarities, and literary and linguistic sensibilities. Despite very few sources being available to document women's participation in the material processes of print, they are visible as editors of periodicals, writers and consumers of print material and, in a few cases, as owners of presses. Late nineteenth-century jail reports for Punjab, especially the Lahore female jail, indicate women's labour as an important part of the jail press.

Middle-class women in Punjab gained material access to publishing and print largely through educational institutions and presses set up by reform organisations in the second half of the nineteenth century. Inhabiting print cultures offered new sites to women to imagine and address new publics and develop 'public opinion'. It helped shape and circulate ideas about new social imaginaries and forms of collectivity, such as the ones that Hardevi, Susila Tahl Ram and the anonymous women in the periodicals wrote about. According to Warner, publics do not imply conversation and deliberation amongst already existing actors, but a 'poesis' (2002: 82). Thus, he emphasises the role of the literary and the imaginative in the creation of publics. Imagining gendered solidarities can also be seen as a precursor to the evolution of formal women's organisations and networks later in the twentieth century.

However, women's narratives cannot simply be idealised as alternative counter-discourses since they were subject to material, political and commercial contingencies of publication, control, censorship and access to the press. In the context of colonial Punjab, women's entry into the spheres of print and writing as agential could only follow from a material access to the reform presses and therefore sharing 'in the material and moral privileges of the emergent social elite' (Devika 2007: 16). My attempt has, therefore, been not to valorise the idea of women's agency or to claim 'authenticity' of their voices or even to enumerate women's writing as an adjunct to the established canon, but to examine the various modes of subjectivity available to them at a specific historical time.

One of the modes of subjectivity that became possible on grounds of print was a claim to professional authorship and the 'intellectual' work that it involved. For middle-class educated women, inclusion into this sphere of writing also meant cultural power and self-affirmation. In the narratives of Susila Tahl Ram and Hardevi, discussed later, their desire to write partly comes from the authority and credibility that they would gain from authorship. This desire of women to enter the domain of creativity and authorship and chart their own 'modern' literary evolution is also seen in literary writing in women's periodicals of the time. In *Bharat Bhagini*, the periodical edited by Hardevi, for example, an entire series was devoted to learning the craft of writing, including the technical aspects of metre, rhyme and genre. For women like Hardevi, Kamala Satthianadhan and Sarala Devi Chaudhurani,[2] print activism became allied with their social activism and attempts to create early social networks and women's movement in Punjab. For the anonymous women who contributed letters, essays and poetic works, the periodicals became a medium to share pain, anger, aspirations, discontent, embodied experiences and affective desires. It is these writings and anonymous letters from women sharing a collective language of everyday dilemmas, domesticity, aspirations and rights, written from as far as Burma, Canada,

America and Penang, that give us the first evidence of imagined collectivities in print.

Transnational Print Networks

Even though the writing that emerged at this time in Punjab can be largely located in the politics of language and religion, it must not be viewed exclusively through the frames of communal, provincial and nationalist identity formation because these borders had been rendered porous by the movement of people and the enormous traffic of publications between India and the world. Oral and written accounts of travellers from Punjab to the West, sometimes published in England, records of Indian publications and publications about India sold in England, booklists of foreign publishers such as Macmillan with India-specific titles, autobiographical records and communications of foreign publishers with authors in India, records of social and print networks in locations in India and outside, missionary records and records of 'inflammatory' material sent by international post intercepted and proscribed by the Punjab government provide a huge array of archival materials that show this traffic of publications between India and the world.

The publishing houses of Longman, Macmillan, Allen and Unwin, Trubner, and Thacker and Spink had flourishing trade links with India by the second half of the nineteenth century, selling textbooks for schools and books for English readership.[3] Catalogues in *Trubner's American, European and Oriental Literary Record* (1882), published in London, record the huge sale of language-teaching primers in many Indian languages and dialects such as Persian, Hindi, Sanskrit, Bengali and Kaithi published in Roman script for Europeans as well as Indian students. In fact, Hardevi's *London Yatra* finds a place in *Trubner's Record* of 1889 (p. 135) among important books published in India.

The British press of the time, especially women's periodical press, evinced a great interest in the culture and society of India, as did organisations such as the Victoria League in London that helped women students from India in London and the National Indian Association (set up by Mary Carpenter in Bristol in 1870) that worked to support Indian students in England and women's education in India. The *Journal of the National Indian Association* (published during 1871–1933 in London and titled *The Indian Magazine* from 1886) reported Hardevi's travel writings and treatise on the kindergarten system that were published in India (*The Indian Magazine*, No. 220, April 1889). This description of Hardevi's work in a publication in London perhaps merits a rethink on the audiences that her books would have found, though they were addressed to 'Punjabi sisters' back home, and invites us to think about the transregional and transnational publishing networks as an important part of identity formation, especially for women's groups in India and England.

Cosmopolitan Hinduani

Published in 1902, in the context of bitter print wars between Hindus, Sikhs and Muslims, the novel *Cosmopolitan Hinduani: Depicting Muhammadan and Hindu Life and Thought in Story Form* by Susila Tahl Ram was probably the first attempt at a novel written in the language by a 'Hindu lady' (*Reports on Publications Issued and Registered in the Several Provinces of British India* 1902) from Punjab. The title indicates the author's intent to rise above the communal anxieties and identity politics of much of the vernacular literature of the time by claiming a cosmopolitan outlook. While she claims a cosmopolitan identity, the word 'Hinduani' in the title attaches this identity to gender and religion as well, which were important markers of identity in early twentieth-century Punjab. The expansiveness inherent in the idea of the cosmopolitan seems to be antithetical to the local embeddedness indicated in the use of the word 'Hinduani'. It is therefore interesting to see how the articulation of cosmopolitan womanhood and transnational solidarities connects with the local realities of education, home and marriage for women.

The idea of cosmopolitanism has generated immense theoretical, political and literary analysis. Largely grounded in European political theory and having a genealogy from the Stoics to Immanuel Kant, it has been variously defined as 'outlooks, processes and ethico-political practices' for 'recognizing multiple identities' and 'building transnational institutions' and networks beyond the nation-state on the basis of universal human values (Rovisco and Nowicka 2011: 1). It is also assumed that the idea of the cosmopolitan, like other flows of ideas and political thought in the history of the empire, could have been only from the metropole to the colonies. A shift in the analysis of cosmopolitanism to an empirically grounded category rather than a theoretical concern located in European thought by Pollock et al. (2000) and their call for archival sources to document lived practices of cosmopolitanism was an important turn in this enquiry because it drew attention to the plurality and modes of practices from non-Eurocentric locations. This shift opens ways to examine issues of agency, subjectivity and power relations in cosmopolitan identities in the non-Western and colonial contexts. That the local and cultural rootedness of the novel can coexist with the transnational proves that narratives of cosmopolitanism can have different historicities and trajectories; they are products of specific colonial encounters and are specific articulations of a desire for a political subjectivity.

The novel was written in a context where models (mostly male) of cosmopolitan and 'progressive' networks were available in the literary and political domains. A. O. Hume, Dadabhai Naoroji, Josephine Butler, Annie Besant, and Margaret and James Cousins were examples of people who were establishing cosmopolitan networks. Narratives of cosmopolitanism articulated from the non-West, a possibility that Bhabha terms 'vernacular cosmopolitanism' (Bhabha 1996: 191–207), can offer interesting counter-narratives to the ideas of European cosmopolitanism.

The author of the novel, Susila Tahl Ram, has since remained only as a trace in the files of the colonial government and not much is known about her life, other than that she wrote and translated school textbooks through the Arya Samaj reform press. Amar Singh, a Rajput nobleman and officer in the Indian army, writes in his diary that Susila Tahl Ram was brought up in England and married Tahl Ram, an Arya Samaj follower who was a 'rascal' (Rudolph et al. 2002: 382). She did not want to breach Hindu laws; otherwise, she would have divorced him and gone to England to learn creative writing. Amar Singh further informs that she did not want to take up employment as a governess in any royal family in India because the status of an independent writer would have been far more respectable than that of a governess (Rudolph et al. 2002). Thus, carefully charting her way through an upper-class marriage and respectability, Susila Tahl Ram worked her way to press and authorship. She resurfaces in print again in a few articles in *The Indian Ladies Magazine*,[4] including a memoir, 'First Impressions of Zenana Life' (1902c), and reports written in Hindi for a Jullundar girls' orphanage.

The Plot

The novel is set in a fictional town called Zinatabad in late nineteenth-century Punjab, which forms the context for political intrigues, love relationships, and association between the British and the Indians. The five subsections narrate stories of different families and characters, but these are linked through the central figure of Amar Devi whom the novel terms 'the New Woman of the Nineteenth Century' (Tahl Ram 1902a: 172). Consciously employing the tropes of the European realist novel—the omniscient narrator and realist narrative—it begins as a love story of an Anglo-Indian woman, Rose Green (daughter of Major Green, an English officer serving in India, and Golab, the Persian beauty whom he marries) and Dilawar Jung, her cousin whom she has grown up with. Rose has been brought up by her widowed aunt, Gulzar. The trope of the love story was quite central to the Western novel, and here it is simultaneously placed within the popular historical and literary traditions of the *Bagh-O-Bahar* (tales by Amir Khusro, translated as 'Garden and Spring' by Duncan Forbes in 1857) and the *qissa* (oral story-telling tradition), Dilawar being referred to as 'the Majnun of the nineteenth century' (ibid.: 130).

Through the intermeshing of sub-plots, Rose is deceived into marrying Yusuf, a cunning upstart who has access to the local princely household as well as the Residency. At the Residency, Rose is introduced to Amar Devi, daughter of Rai Gyan Chand, a London barrister, who has been given an appointment at Zinatabad and has set up house there with his daughter. Amar Devi has been brought up in England and Ireland and given a liberal education by her father, who was at St John's, Cambridge, and kept his terms at the Inner Temple. Their house at Zinatabad becomes a focal point for discussions on reform, women's uplift, child marriages and widow re-marriage. Amar Devi is shown to be an educated, confident and articulate woman who has firm and progressive views on caste and gender reforms. She is eager to forge friendships across communities and aims to bring together 'the English, the Hindu and the Mohammedan' (ibid.: 58). It is through her that the novel raises many important questions of the time—women's education and marriage, their location within religious communities and the nation, and the idea of women's collectives that can conceptualise their 'liberation' from their own point of view. It is also through Amar Devi's ability to engage in public reasoning to argue out these ideas that the novel makes a claim over print space as a dialogic space.

The novel then turns the focus on the personal and public lives of the characters who inhabit the court, the Residency and the middle-class drawing rooms of the Zinatabad society. The plot weaves itself through Rose's torturous marriage and the nascent love relationship between Amar Devi and Ugarsen Sarma, whose new, tender masculinity makes him acceptable to her and their marriage is imminent at the end of the novel. His brief presence in the novel shows him as a soft, caring and tender person who is prevented from being overly chivalrous by Amar Devi. It is perhaps this non-assertive masculinity redefined with interest in books and music that endears him to Amar Devi.

The paradigms of progress and liberation within which both the colonial administration and the reform movements situated their efforts at women's reform are critiqued in the novel. The narrative indicts the reformers in Punjab for having failed to touch the lives of women. A trenchant critique of the hypocrisy of the men involved in the reform movements comes through the character of Nand Kumar, a pleader, 'whose voice ominously rolled from the Bar to the platform of the Congress' (Tahl Ram 1902a: 191), but he is silent when his father compares young girls to dangerous 'bundles of snakes' who 'must necessarily be united in wedlock before attaining the remarkable age of twelve' (ibid.: 192). This complicit silence continues through his child-wife Hira's torture at the hands of his mother and Hira's motherhood at the age of 15 years.

Equally unacceptable is the response of Mr Egerton, a colonial British patriarch and Rose's benefactor, when he gets to know that she is unhappy in her marriage. His offer to rescue her, a typical attitude of an Englishman to rescue an Indian woman from a Muslim husband, is undercut by Rose's rebuke, 'And you are gracious enough to hold out the hand of salvation' (ibid.: 111). The narrator thus stakes her claims to make visible these lived and affective women's histories that neither British saviours like Mr Egerton nor the high-minded Indian reformers can ever fathom or have the legitimacy to represent, their pretensions on women's reform notwithstanding. The novel seeks to intervene into the 'women's question' at two levels—questions of representation of women in colonial and reform narratives, and the everyday material experiences of women.

Networks and Communities of Affect

The narrator holds the plot together by connecting stories of various middle-class women who play out their social roles as wives, lovers, friends, mothers and daughters, but have personal desires and longings. The print affords the narrativisation of collective spaces and nurturing relationships between women, which were otherwise looked upon with suspicion by reform patriarchies. The life stories of various women characters criss-cross each other when they live together at Amar Devi's house to help Rose recover from a deceitful marriage and a corrupt husband. The Anglo-Indian Rose, her British friend Mrs Jenkins, her Muslim aunt Gulzar Begum and the Hindu Amar Devi come together to provide to Rose 'sunshine and the geniality of her deserted friends' (Tahl Ram 1902a: 153) and nurture her physically and emotionally. These sub-plots foreground the emotional, material and psychological support that middle-class women provide to each other. Thus, an inclusive collectivity of women that transcends religious, caste and race barriers is envisaged as a liberal and promising future for women at the end of the novel.

This imagination of an idealised community or sisterhood, however, can only provide a brief alternative in a society marked by anxieties on account of class, caste and religion. Hindu women's cultural practices, prescribed as appropriate to modernity, encode and structure class, caste and gender relations in the frame of the novel. Lower-class women and servants visiting the *pir*s (saints) 'to see the tamasha' (popular performances) (ibid.: 104) are thus looked at with suspicion. Having claimed a legitimacy to tell women's stories authentically, the narrator is, however, conscious of a disconnect between educated middle-class women and women from other class and caste locations. These fractures were symptomatic of the complications in feminist positions that evolved in the early twentieth century through organisations such as the All India Women's Conference (1926), Women's India Association (1917), National Council for Women in India and

Bharat Stree Mahamandal (1910, Lahore). The cosmopolitan modernity scripted by such early twentieth-century organisations often used the language of liberalism to demand women's rights, but was nevertheless shot through with questions of class and caste. In this respect, the novel foreshadows the fraught responses and interventions of these institutions and organisations to the 'women's question'. Questions about the representativeness of certain women's organisations and groups continued to be raised as women's participation was invited to discuss the issue of franchise at the round table conferences held in London between 1931 and 1933.

Fractures are evident again as the narrator casts a detached, almost colonial gaze at Muslim women inside the *zenana*s. Amar Devi observes that within the Muslim palace, slave girls are instructed in singing and serving spicy food that marks 'Mohammedan cookery' (Tahl Ram 1902a: 90). The Begum is quite hidebound due to her incarceration within the palace and is curious about the modern garments worn by Amar Devi. Although the zenana is seen as an important contact zone to visualise friendships that need to be forged despite cultural differences, the narrator's description suggests an estrangement that borders on detachment. When a doctor visits the zenana, for example, the zenana is covered by dark sheets in which a round hole is cut. As the doctor's arrival is announced, the veils are drawn deeper. Hafiza Begum[5] shows her throat to the doctor through the hole with her tongue protruding through it. Amar Devi remarks, 'It is, indeed, fortunate that Lady Dufferin has taken so deep an interest to have medical women prepared for the Zenana' (ibid.: 89). In view of the violent contestations between the Sikh and Hindu identities at the turn of the century and the assertion of a separate Sikh identity, it is noteworthy that the novel completely erases the presence of a distinct Sikh community. Perhaps the naturalisation of Hinduism as a normative reflects such attempts in the public sphere of nineteenth-century Punjab.

The desire to establish transnational connections is also reflected in the narrator's description of her Munich visit where she finds that Munich University has still not opened its doors to women, and that therefore there may be some commonality in women's agenda in different nations of the world.

The story offers a contrast between two 'New Women of the Nineteenth Century' (Tahl Ram 1902a: 172), Amar Devi and Kusum. While Kusum, a graduate, is full of disdain for her 'unenlightened sisters', Amar Devi is shown to be more inclusive:

> Though nurtured and educated in a different atmosphere to her narrow-minded sisters, nevertheless, Amar Devi invariably found something in common to evoke sympathy. Besides being a Cosmopolitan and catholic in her views she moved freely among them, and instead of ferreting and unpleasantly harping on their fossilised prejudices, that would have severed them as far as the Poles, her warm, genial nature tended to draw them closely together. Indeed, it was remarkable that at times, the stringent caste-rules relaxed most radically, and toning the differences, blended the divergencies into a pleasant bond of friendship (ibid.: 182).

The trope of friendship, however troubled, is extended from drawing rooms and Residency gatherings to the zenana, a powerful place of cross-cultural interaction and point of contact for British women as well. Solidarities thus envisaged as a desired future are created through the frame of social experiences of women, and the friendship and empathy between them, and this constitutes an emphatic imaginative and political act in the novel.

Association and Friendships with British Women

The cosmopolitan desire of the novel also leads to its interpellation into the field of circulation of ideas between colonies and the metropolitan centre, which was made possible by the increasing book trade and print transactions at the end of the nineteenth century and the possibilities of exchange between British women and their colonial counterparts. The second half of the nineteenth century saw the employment of more British women as educators and doctors in an attempt to humanise the face of the empire. Increased cultural and social exchanges between British and native women became possible at different sites and 'contact zones' (Pratt 1992), thus forming mutually constitutive relationships between women. These also began to be articulated in newer vocabularies of the social and medical welfare of Indian women. It is in this context of the changing languages of relationships that the narrator in the novel examines the terms on which links between native and British women could be established. The cosmopolitan imaginary of the novel involves associations and friendships between the British women at the Residency at Zinatabad and the native women, which are nevertheless undergirded by race and class differences, making them only tenuous.

The narrator debunks the idea of the innate superiority of the stature and practices of British women in Victorian society. The location of the British women in India within colonial patriarchies often led them to internalise and replicate the discriminatory moralities in which they were embedded. The British women in the novel are shown to have 'deviated' from the moral qualities of sympathy and compassion which would have resulted in healthier relationships with Indian women. Their relationships with native women are also seen as occasionally impelled by the desire to seek the exotic in the zenanas.

A desire for modernity, then, cannot simply be a desire for normative referents from the West. The novel offers a sharp satire on the ideas of hygiene and pollution of the British 'ladies' and their attempt to codify and demarcate identities through bodily practices: describing a Residency event where Rose feels weak and faint and so she sinks into a chair, the narrator comments:

> Mortified and faintness seizing her, she sinks into a chair, when the ladies fearing contagion from one who seems to be plague-stricken, gingerly draw away their disinfected skirts;

> while those nearest her dreading the foul breath turn away their heads in loathing (Tahl Ram 1902a: 123).

The cosmopolitan desire to reach out, then, cannot be idealised after all as it is riddled with conflicts. The desire for women's collectives that the novel visualises is based on affective communities through empathy between women and connections through quotidian experience. However, historical contradictions, even in this fictional conceptualisation of sisterhood, are very evident.

The New Woman

Amar Devi's cosmopolitanism is set within two seemingly contradictory paradigms—an individualist will for self-cultivation and betterment (which comes from travelling and exposure to the West), along with a desire to define collective politics for women, even outside of the nation. The 'New Woman' is envisaged as a socially and politically conscious subject, claiming an agency in defining her own ethics, needs and desires, and not simply as replicating Western ideals. The template on which the New Woman is predicated is clearly the liberal citizenship model which allows her to claim an entry into the field of power and to be a part of the nascent public sphere in India, and not merely imitate an imperial Western project.

The novel's claim of a cosmopolitan subjectivity for women is also a claim to unhindered mobility without any patriarchal protectionism and offers a challenge to spatial restrictions that were a part of the morality defined for women. Travel and the cultural experiences that come with it become a metonymic claim over public space. The novel is spatially and temporally organised around the movement of women such as Amar Devi—between Zinatabad, London, Munich, zenanas, the Residency, gardens, roads and various locations in India—and this distance is traversed alone by women. The print space made it possible for this mobility to be performed in the act of writing itself, to reach out to a national and transnational readership.

The choices for marital alliance and the idea of 'home' for the 'New Woman' also need to be renegotiated as they become part of the cosmopolitan imaginary of the novel. The domestic and the intimate are not simply played out in the interiors of homes, but now need to be discussed in drawing rooms, Residency and clubs in a mixed gathering of men and women. The novel brings about a structural shift in the spaces inhabited by women, from the interiors and women's quarters to drawing rooms and public locations outside the home, and a simultaneous shift to a psychological interiority and intellectual spaces now claimed by women.

Reformers argued that the 'power' and social significance of women lay in their roles as mothers, homemakers and keepers of morality. The novel shifts this premise of empowerment to the idea of individual self-fulfilment of women. While Amar Devi ends up subscribing to the view that a woman is responsible for keeping her house in order, functionally and morally,[6] and that her education must also cater to this requirement, Kusum resents this functionalist idea of women's education and the new morality that ultimately tethers her to domestic duties.

Most reformers of the Singh Sabha and the Arya Samaj, including Lala Lajpat Rai, who supported women's primary education that reinforced domestic duties and motherhood were, however, very sceptical of higher education that would 'unsex them' (Jones 1989[1976]: 106). Kusum critiques reform ideas of women's education and deportment as means to regulate and structure the lives of women in newer ways. Although overshadowed by the more non-confrontationist approach of Amar Devi, the discursive possibilities of Kusum's ideas cannot be fully contained by the plot of the novel and form an important counter to the debates about women's education at the beginning of the twentieth century: 'She desires us to know enough chemistry to keep the pots boiling, and geography enough to know the different rooms in the house. Yes, to be sure, no better than accomplished cooks and play-things of men,' says Kusum (Tahl Ram 1902a: 183). The juxtaposition of the characters of Kusum and Amar Devi as two 'New Women of the Nineteenth Century', therefore, confounds any attempts at homogeneity within the reform concepts of women's education and shows an understanding of how women were implicated in the new hierarchies and power structures of liberal reform.

Apart from women's journals in the vernacular and English languages, books in circulation in Punjab on the 'management' of the new household provided conceptual resources from the West. Some of these books that were available in translations as well were Isabella Beeton's *Mrs Beeton's Book of Household Management* (1861), Catherine Beecher's *American Manuals* (1841–69), and Flora Annie Steel and Grace Gardiner's *The Complete Indian Housekeeper and Cook* (1888) (mentioned in *Thacker's Indian Directory* 1895). Thus, the print space was a new frontier where meanings of domesticity, marriage and home were being negotiated.

Location in Hinduism

In a context where religious formations and reform organisations attempted to preserve tradition and 'vernacularity' on the backs of women (Pollock 2002: 53), appropriating practices of cosmopolitanism can be seen as an attempt to rewrite modernity from women's point of view. Yet this cosmopolitan modernity of Amar Devi simultaneously needs to hold on to a local, Hindu affiliation to mark identity and cultural difference from the West. At the end of the nineteenth century, social reform legislations initiated by the colonial state (for example, the Age of Consent Act, 1891, and the Rakhmabai case, 1884[7]) had aroused widespread agitations from revivalists on the grounds that these amounted to interference with Hindu customs and were meant to anglicise women. These fears were concretised by Pandita Ramabai Saraswati's conversion to Christianity in 1833 and her stringent critique of brahmanical patriarchy in her book, *The High Caste Hindu Woman* (1887). In these circumstances, the location of the protagonist within Hinduism is perhaps an act of self-preservation and would have given her cosmopolitan desires greater acceptability.

The danger of being ostracised as a deracinated cosmopolitan in a society that was increasingly anxious about defining a 'Hindu' identity[8] would have presented itself as a very real possibility to the author. The simultaneity of a cosmopolitan consciousness with its location within the Hindu religion becomes clear towards the end of the novel when another sub-plot involving low-caste characters is resolved by their inclusion within the fold of a liberal Hinduism. As Ram Saran, a low-caste character who has returned after being educated in London, is taken back into the Hindu fold, it is clear that the ideas about unhindered social mobility 'imbibed from a free country' (Tahl Ram 1902a: 259), that is, England, sit ill with the reality of caste dissensions in India:

> Ram Saran being warmly welcomed by his relations and kinsmen, his spirits overflowed with delight and genial fancies. In hilarity as humbly bowing, with folded hands to the elders, he beamed all round, with much questioning and many drawing him out in all directions, he felt that he was in the London drawing room among independent people. The higher rose his spirits, the more breezy became his speech, savouring of heresy, and with the time-honoured, intricate customs of the East being graciously pronounced as 'fudge'. As he unreservedly uttered the radical views imbibed from a free country, a cold shudder ran down the orthodox backs... (ibid.).

A liberal and cosmopolitan politics then necessitates a more liberal Hinduism that can rise above 'unscientific ideas' of pollution and embrace all castes within its fold: '"Do foul germs emanate from the lowly alone and not from the Twice-born?" questioned the Cosmopolitan Hinduani' (Tahl Ram 1902a: 256). A liberal history of Hinduism is invoked to make it more consonant with a cosmopolitan outlook and to suggest that the ideas of equality idealised in Hinduism need to be brought back. At the end of the narrative, Hinduism thus becomes a benevolent, expansive universalism with a cosmopolitan past rather than a narrowly defined identity and a definite set of practices. In fact, the 'Hinduani' appears to be more a turn towards civic subjecthood than a revivalist claim of authentic religious identity.

The Arya Samaj (1875) sought to promote a reformed Hinduism through emphasis on modern education and Hindu religious beliefs removed from superstition and caste prejudice. Though Dayanand Saraswati, the founder of the Arya Samaj, in his book *Satyarth Prakash* (1908[1875]), advocated *shuddhi* (purification to allow untouchables and non-Hindus into the Hindu fold) for the outcastes as part of reform and a more 'liberal' Hinduism, its relationship with the lower castes was quite uncertain at the end of the nineteenth century. Political interest in bringing more people into the Hindu fold, on the one hand, and the power of the upper-caste communities, on the other hand, made this attempt at caste elimination quite difficult, at least at the end of the nineteenth century. The novel can thus be seen as engaging with ideas of a reformed Hinduism that were current in the nineteenth century.

Cosmopolitan Language and Aesthetics

The linguistic and aesthetic practices in the novel are crucial to the narrator's insertion of herself as a gendered subject in the cosmopolitan imaginary, especially when language was entangled with issues of modernity and religious identities in colonial Punjab. Official reports on the books published in Punjab indicate that the preferred languages of expressing the literary were the competing vernaculars, while English was the language of power and scientific knowledge that came from the West. These reports also reveal interesting language transactions between English and the vernaculars and translation activity in the scientific domain to render scientific knowledge into the vernacular, especially books on women's health (*Reports on Publications* 1867–1921). Is this choice of English language for the novel, then, a matter of 'vernacular anxiety'[9] or does it imply a conscious choice of audience that is instrumental to the conception of the 'cosmopolitan' outlined in the novel?

The novel evidently seeks to address audiences outside the province and the nation through language. Local terms are translated into English and explained to readers who may not be familiar with local practices. For example, 'Aftab Jan arrived accompanied by two men, one of whom she addresses as Qazi—a priest who ratifies marriages among Muhammadans' (Tahl Ram 1902a: 35). In another instance, Dilawar says to Rose, 'This image, thy photo shall ever encircle my breast as a *tawiz*—amulet' (ibid.: 15). The novel makes an attempt to imagine such a 'socio-textual community' (Pollock 2003: 27) and reach out to transnational audiences through the choice of language. It is consciously interpellated into a field where networks of print, the social reach of language, community formation and cultural power coalesce.

The strategic deployment of the genre of the social realist novel can be seen as crucial to the framing of the 'New Woman'. The new genre of the realist novel in eighteenth-century England marked the need for a new form to inscribe stories of 'real' individuals in a changing world. Realism as a narrative mode was suited to 'subjective individualism' (Mukherjee 1984: 76) and was thus a reflection of an ideological shift in the way that an individual was conceptualised. The tensions between individual desires and social obligations, which were a crucial element of middle-class self-fashioning in colonial India, could be effectively framed through conventions of 'rational causation' (Aquil and Chatterjee 2008: 9–10) in the novel. By the end of the nineteenth century in Punjab, the novel had been fully appropriated by the reform machinery to project idealised and gendered affiliations to religious communities.[10]

The novel *Cosmopolitan Hinduani* is then an attempt to enter and counter a space that was already mediated and encoded for women and to negotiate a new matrix of power relations in print space. The cosmopolitanism envisaged in the novel is a desire to script a new modernity for Punjabi women of the late nineteenth–early twentieth centuries through education, cultural experience of the West, mobility, renegotiated domesticity and marriage, literary space and a transnational sisterhood.

LONDON YATRA AND LONDON JUBILEE

Hardevi's travel writings are instances of how print was not only appropriated by women writers to consolidate local identities, but also used to project newer ones outside national boundaries. Hardevi was a resident of Lahore and travelled to London to witness the 1887 golden jubilee celebrations of the accession of Queen Victoria to the throne. The rarity of such a venture for women and the urgency to communicate her experiences to her 'sisters in Punjab' are visible in the two accounts of her travel, *London Yatra* and *London Jubilee*. In these books addressed specifically to Punjabi women, Hardevi maps her travel to the city of London that promised a new mobility and modernity, especially to women. She wrote the account of her journey on the ship and a visual description of the Jubilee celebrations as a citizen-subject of the empire, as a social commentator and, above all, as a woman morally and ethically committed to her community of women back home.

This community is envisaged by the author as a gendered solidarity of 'Punjabi sisters' ('*Punjab deshiya bhagini samaj*'; Hardevi 1888a: i) that would overcome the caste, class and communal divide that troubled Punjabi society of the time. Thus, the travel narrative, in imagining and addressing a specific gendered community, also attempts to create one back home. The author asks the women of Punjab to read her books for their satisfaction and development and also read them out to other 'sisters' who were illiterate. Reading a book thus becomes a material marker of modernity and an activity that would shape a new literary sphere for women. Hardevi asks her sisters to conceive of a 'modern' self through the trajectories of education, mobility, redefined domesticity and family.

A significant part of Hardevi's second book, *London Jubilee*, is a biographical reconstruction of the interiority of the Queen's marital home and her conjugal life, which is seamlessly accommodated within the constructions of a modern, educated, *pativrata* (loyal and dutiful to the husband) woman. In doing so, not only does she assimilate the new world of England into her own cultural vocabulary, but she also draws British and Indian women into a sympathetic continuum. Writing travel thus becomes a means to claim and dramatise both physical mobility and a conceptual space of possibilities for a modern, gendered self, a space where new iconographies could be appropriated and created.

In the first part of this analysis, I attempt to glean details about Hardevi's life and writing from archival sources and place the story of her travels in the larger frame of the culture of travel and travel writing in the colonial context. This is to see how the representation of the empire and the self was mediated through travel experience, race, class and gender in the narratives of several other travellers that were published at this time. These narratives also help us understand how travellers inhabited multiple subject positions, ranging from the assimilative to the critical and combative towards the empire, depending on contextual needs. In the light of these shifts in subject positions, I argue that this cross-cultural encounter cannot be reduced to simplistic analytical categories of dominance and resistance or mimicry and rebellion.

I also analyse Hardevi's *London Yatra* and *London Jubilee* to examine how her travel mediates the 'reconstitution of a female politics of the local'[11] and modes of apprehending the self and the community of women in Punjab. I will examine her deployment of a specific mode of subjectivity whereby she could be a willing participant in creating the spectacle of a liberal empire and simultaneously negotiate with this idea of liberalism to demand more for women in Punjab.

Hardevi's Life and Writings

The sources that allow us to piece together Hardevi's biography and affiliations include the quarterly lists of books published in Punjab, mention of her activities in the *Journal of the National Indian Association* (begun by Mary Carpenter in 1871 and published in London) and the editorials in *Bharat Bhagini*, a Hindi monthly for women started in 1889 in Lahore and edited by Hardevi (the periodical ceased to exist in July 1911). The editorial details in *Bharat Bhagini* mention the editor as Srimati Hardevi, daughter of late Rai Bahadur Kanhya Lal, executive engineer, Lahore, and wife of Roshan Lal, barrister-at-law. The periodical had 500 listed subscribers within and outside Lahore, and anonymous letters to the editor would come from as far as Malaya, Penang and Burma. Catalogues of publications reveal another book on women's reform titled *Striyon pe Samajik Anyay* ('Social Injustice on Women') (1892) written by her.

Hardevi's access to press would have been made possible through Hindu reform groups and, therefore, ostensibly aligned with their identity politics. Thus, the use of Hindi language and the constructions of the modern 'Arya' woman in the periodical *Bharat Bhagini* and the two travel narratives are quite in consonance with the politics of the Arya Samaj and the Nagari Pracharini Sabha at the end of the nineteenth century, which came to be centred around a Hindu identity promoted through the Hindi language. Through her travel writing and editorials, she also attempts to divest the Hindi language of 'impurities', create appropriate literary tastes for the modern woman and therefore create a community in language.

As the editor of *Bharat Bhagini*, she reiterates the claim of Hindi to represent Arya women, but at the same time she moves between languages in her own writings and writes in Urdu as well. Soon after her travel to England, where she had occasion to observe the Montessori system of schooling, she wrote a book in Urdu, *Talim-i-Tiflan Yani Zakhira-i-Talim* ('Children's Education, that is, the Treasure-house of Knowledge'), 'depicting the defects in the system of training and indigenous education of children, and the brutal conduct of the generality of teachers who resort to corporal punishment. The book contains also an account of the modes of training children pursued in England' (*Reports on Publications* 1888). Her affiliation with the reformist press notwithstanding, she frequently critiques Hindu reformers for failing women's cause through her ironic and bitter editorials in the *Bharat Bhagini*.

Two observations emerge from the above. First, despite the 'one language, one community' formula being fervently espoused by reformist organisations to create linguistically bound communities, this was defied by the expediency of using multiple languages to address different audiences, even by Hindu women, for whom Hindi had been prescribed by the Arya Samaj. Second, women from within the reform presses used the very mode of argument and rationality frequently deployed by reformist organisations to critique patriarchal reformist positions on women's reform. These movements across languages (competing 'vernaculars' and English) to address intended audiences and shifts in subject positions deployed by women indicate the dynamism of the multilingual and multidimensional cultural formations in colonial Punjab.

Travel to the West and Travel Writing

Indian travellers and writers who had been published in England in the latter part of the nineteenth century, such as Toru Dutt, Manmohan Ghose, B. M. Malabari, T. B. Pandian, W. C. Bonnerjee, Dadabhai Naoroji and Sarojini Naidu, influenced British literary and print culture through their fiction, poetry and travel writing. Travel accounts from Punjab that allow us to glimpse the West through Indian eyes include the writings of Olive Christian Malvery (an Anglo-Indian woman from Lahore) (Lahiri 2010), Raja Jagatjit Singh (1895), the Maharani of Kapurthala (Brinda 1953) and Jhinda Ram (1893), and oral testimonies of Dharam Vira and Prakash Tandon. The later part of the nineteenth century saw increased opportunities of travel from India to the Western world for education, work, apprenticeships, celebrations of jubilees, exhibitions and the Indian Civil Services (ICS) exams conducted in London. Apart from the presence of the Indian royalty, students and the middle classes, it was also the 'ayahs, lascars' and peddlers (Visram 1986) that caught the attention of the print media in England. Print became a regular space for the writing of travel experience by this middle class, literate community and provides accounts of a complex relationship with the West, of both fascination and critique.

Travel for women was quite rare till the latter part of the nineteenth century, when they usually accompanied male members of their family; for example, Aru and Toru Dutt's travel with their father in 1869. Very few women travelled for education; for example, Kadambini Ganguly in 1893 (doctor from Edinburgh), Jamini Sen for medical education in 1897, and Anandibai Joshi, who went to the US in 1883 for a medical degree. However, Inderpal Grewal has shown that women formed part of the invisible migrant labour to various parts of the world (Grewal 1996: 161). She argues that although the culture of travel was a very male construct, it was interrupted by women who used it in different ways.

The various works on transcultural mobilities by many scholars such as Peter Fryer (1984), Rosina Visram (1986), Antoinette Burton (2003, 2012), Michael Fisher (2004), Shompa Lahiri (2010), Simonti Sen (2005), Satadru Sen (2004), Ruvani Ranasinha (Ranasinha et al. 2012) and Sushiela Nasta (2002) have shown that the experiences and responses of South Asians who travelled to England were undergirded by race, class, gender and location. For our purposes, two important points emerge from this body of work. First, travel opened up new ways of performing identities for colonial subjects and rather than being regarded as passive, the agency and activism of even the invisible travellers needs to be emphasised. It is this idea of a self-conscious enactment of identities that I wish to use as a frame to discuss Hardevi's works.

Second, scholarly works have shown the deployment of a whole range of shifting subject positions adopted in travel writing that were undergirded by class positions and the reception that the visitors received in England, and their own aspirations. Sometimes, the travellers adopted the seemingly contradictory positions of both a 'seeing subject', critiquing and inverting the power hierarchies they experienced, and that of a 'mobile exhibit', participating in the liberal self-representation of the empire, and used the 'creative tension between objectification and subject formation' (Lahiri 2010: 83–84). If royalty such as Raja Jagatjit Singh and the Maharani of Kapurthala were at one end of the spectrum of the visual grandeur of the jubilees in 1887 and 1897, the mere shadowy presence of the lascars and ayahs was enough to undercut that very grandeur (Visram 1986).

Hardevi's Travels: *London Yatra*

Hardevi commenced her travel to London on 9 February 1886 from Lahore with a group of people who were going to witness the Queen's Jubilee. She points to the rarity and adventurism of two women travelling in this group and the disapproval of other women in the family and community that she had to face. In a preface addressed specifically to women, she tells them of the respect and benefits that accrue from foreign exposure. As a woman, she is aware of the cultural capital that came with education and being in the print circuit and that endowed her with a symbolic power among her peers. The dissemination of books and periodicals through community reading shows the liminal space they occupied between orality and print as well as the growth of 'reading publics' despite low literacy levels in Punjab.

In *London Yatra*, Hardevi regrets that women in Punjab do not get to travel abroad; even if they travel for pilgrimages, they are in purdah and cannot associate with each other. She rues the lack of organisations and societies where women can meet, so she dedicates her book to all women who are restricted in their narrow and oppressive domestic spaces and hopes that they derive a joy that comes from listening to other women. Many women who come to meet her before departure are very apprehensive about her free movement but she explains that purdah, which was a legacy of contact with Muslims, should not be used to imprison women. Thus, Muslim women are 'othered' even while the narrator wishes to create and consolidate a community of women. As she travels from Lahore to Bombay through the Rajputana, the diverse landscapes and histories of these lands are aggregated and tied together as a nation through the eyes and sympathies of the narrator.

After meeting with Dadabhai Naoroji and watching Parsi women freely access the thoroughfares of Bombay, she contemplates on their history and social practices (Hardevi 1888a: 11). The aggregating, sympathetic eye of the narrator again traces connections and similarity of social customs between the Parsis and the Aryas, thus assimilating them within the expansive notion of the Arya culture. Thus, mobility and travel outside home look to cosmopolitan experiences, on the one hand, but sharpen the sense of home and community, on the other.

While this awe of the modernity of Europe prevails in Hardevi's writings, the focus of her description turns to her social life on the ship, and later to the Queen's household, unlike another Punjab traveller, Jhinda Ram, a pleader at the chief court of the Punjab, who marvels at the technology of the ship and the Suez Canal as a 'triumph of the art of engineering' (Ram 1893: 3). Jhinda Ram, an educated, privileged, middle-class traveller, undertook a trip to Europe for pleasure and published his travel writing in the form of a book in English, *My Trip to Europe*. He places European technology and experience of freedom and democracy at the centre of European modernity, rather than casting an eye within home and family.

It is Hardevi's close contact with British women on the ship that first impinges on the questions of identity and difference and makes her experience power in a closed space which, Burton (2003) suggests, is a crucial interpretive category to study colonial power relations. The cruelty and discrimination of an English memsahib is apparent when she wants lower berths for herself and raises a hue and cry when it is given to an Indian child. The close contact in the ship becomes a space for the narrator to protest and ritually mark out identity through social practices of eating, social habits and dress. A similar contrast between the powerlessness of colonial subjecthood felt in India and the experience of freedom in England is made by Jhinda Ram. He marvels at the treatment he receives in London as compared with the Anglo-Indians back in India, 'Oh! What a contrast between the treatment we receive in England and the treatment we receive in India from the hands of Anglo-Indians!' (Ram 1893: 11). 'We all know, that Anglo-Indians, in India, are haughty and overbearing…Anglo-Indians in England are foremost in paying attention to Indians' (ibid.: 79). As the distance from the machinery of the colonial state increased with the shift on location, expectations from a 'liberal' British state could be negotiated more easily. Narratives such as these questioned the triumphalist self-representation of Britain as a tolerant, cosmopolitan nation (Boehmer and Nasta 2012: xix).

The journey becomes a rite of passage for Hardevi whereby social bonds with people other than the family are cultivated and evaluated and physical vulnerabilities are overcome. The self is challenged through difficulties and contingencies such as the arduousness of the journey, sea-sickness, difficulty in communication and the fear of being ridiculed. Emerging from these difficulties, she must produce a stable, confident self to explain her experiences to women back home. The narrator does that by claiming equal access to space on the ship and also commanding control over 'strange' landscapes by framing them within familiar sights in Punjab. For example, the agricultural mode of life in Egypt is compared to life in India and travel through Egypt seems to her to be a travel from Lahore to Ghaziabad (Hardevi 1888a: 52).

Savouring the cultural possibilities of travel and traversing across other cultures becomes a mode of reconfiguring the nation and its women in the narrative. Her passage through Italy and

Egypt is a story of how a woman can overcome her fears and language problems. She observes that Switzerland is a democratic country where women are free; in comparison, she is reminded of the state of Indian women, and is sad and ashamed (ibid.: 116). These comparatives thus provide a framework and justification for a gendered national identity formation.

A description of cultures, social practices and position of women in Aden, Egypt, Italy and France stretches her readers' imagination to cultures outside India and yet paradoxically reinforces their Indianness simultaneously through identity and difference. Significantly, the presence of women as conscious civic subjects is envisaged as an important part of the nation, giving to women a role in history and in the formation of the nation. The creation of a sanitised civic space for women, at one level, seems to be in consonance with the patriarchal reformist marginalisation of popular spaces for women. Yet, at another level, it is expressed in the language of the 'rights' of women to access public space and education. It is this claim to civic subjecthood as a subject in the Queen's empire that is reiterated in *London Jubilee* through participating in the grandeur of the Jubilee celebrations.

London Jubilee

London Jubilee, written shortly after *London Yatra*, is a visual description of the pomp and ceremony that accompanied the commemoration of 50 years of Queen Victoria's rule. While she describes in detail the presence of Indian royalty and their being accorded an important position in the celebrations, her focus turns to the position of Indian women as subjects of the Queen's empire and to the Queen's family life. Harking on the promise of the liberal empire to women and hailing the Queen's rule as a moment of justice and progress for women, she hopes that this liberalism will not be a mere token and will deliver substantial freedom to women in India. The stance adopted is not antagonistic to imperial authority and, in fact, the desire to assimilate into the celebratory crowd is very visible. While the close contact on the ship had resulted in a critique of the power and arrogance of colonial rule in *London Yatra*, the desire in this book is to carve out a language of rationality and cooperation to draw attention to the position of Indian women.

The narratorial voice calls for a change within the system by showing loyalty to the 'Kaiser-i-Hind', the Queen Mother, rather than use a language of resistance within the book. Yet, later in a piece in the periodical *Bharat Bhagini* on Queen Victoria's death, in a sharply worded irony directed against the British government, she comments on how poor India will be made to show 'rajbhakti' by being made to cough up Rs 50 lakh for a memorial, while the rich West will contribute Rs 25 lakh.[12] Similarly, Sunity Devee, Maharani of Cooch Behar, is awestruck when she first meets the Queen on her Jubilee in 1887:

> To us Indians she was more or less a legendary figure, endowed with wonderful attributes, an ideal ruler and an ideal woman, linked to our hearts across 'the black water' by silken chains of love and loyalty.... I was delighted to find that I had not been disappointed in my ideal, and felt eager to go back to India that I might tell my country-women about our wonderful empress (1929: 108).

Yet this is complicated by her ambiguous position on the injustice of being the Queen's subject. In many other such travelogues, we find that colonial subjecthood was constantly improvised and repositioned depending on the context and could not have been a stable entity. As Codell (2003) notes, 'Intersections of economic, political, social and gendered values and forces were uneven and groups aligned differently depending on circumstances.' Therefore, attention needs to be paid to a whole range of self-positionings and 'subjectivities between Anglicized hegemony and indigenous subalternity' (ibid.: 189).

In an important act of cultural translation, Hardevi reclaims the Queen into the making of a modern '*sugrahini*' (good householder). She projects modern conjugality onto the married life of

Queen Victoria and Prince Albert, highlighting his love for her and their partnership in bringing up children. The tender moments of the Prince taking care of his wife and her public duties after child-birth are held out as examples of ideal conjugal love. The Queen is rendered into an image of the 'Arya' woman who is highly educated, is devoted to her husband and children, and follows '*pativrata dharma*' (duties of a wife) even after the death of her husband by living a simple and frugal life. The reform movements of the time were instrumental in formulating the notion of an ideal woman and her '*stridharma*' (moral duties of a woman) within an egalitarian Hinduism and Hardevi's appropriation of the Queen into this is almost an 'insurgent act of cultural translation' (Bhabha 1994: 7). The narrator exhorts Indian women to claim their fair share of education and modernity under their benevolent ruler, who was a woman herself and was a powerful symbol of women's achievement, both in her private and public life.

While she invokes the benevolence of the Queen to negotiate reforms for Indian women, ruptures between liberal expectations and colonial subjecthood do show up. When the Queen declares that she will give all the gifts that she has received on the occasion of her Jubilee to charity, the narrator praises her but advises at the same time that the Queen should spend the money received in gifts on the colonies where the gifts have come from. One finds that strategising with the British government and seeking reform through the government were modalities that Indian women frequently adopted.[13]

Hardevi's writing of her travel experiences in print can be interpreted as a political act of constituting a self-identity as well as the identity of the 'Arya' woman, an urgent question of the time. It is an 'epistemological strategy'[14] as well because it enacts the construction of a conceptual space to articulate identity formation. In that sense, the traveller not only gains physical mobility but discursive and conceptual possibilities also open up for identity formation through travel. Hardevi's narrative creates a space for the Hindu woman to demand and negotiate rights as a civic subject rather than an object of missionary and colonial benevolence. At the same time, Hardevi's work draws our attention to the need to understand Indian as well as Western modernity as being shaped through cross-cultural encounters and cultural translations rather than through the exclusivity of national boundaries.

The literary works discussed here are perhaps tentative first attempts in late nineteenth–early twentieth century Punjab to influence the formation of not only gendered 'vernacular publics' but also transnational ones that would be useful to the project of establishing women's solidarities. At a time when ethics and moral conduct in private and public spheres were being constantly redefined for women by the reform presses and the state, they were able to imagine languages of self-articulation, participation, intervention and resistance, as in the two examples discussed above. Especially when public discourse of the time is understood as largely communal, it is important to take into account ways in which certain groups constituted 'alternative publics'. The strategies of both resistance and compliance and the history of fractures within these publics need to be recorded.

NOTES

1. Such studies include Baron et al. (2007); Eisenstein (1979); Johns (1998); and McElligott and Patten (2014).

2. Sarala Devi (1872–1945) was the daughter of Swarnakumari Debi (Rabindranath Tagore's sister) and editor of *Bharati*, a monthly journal, from 1895. She was 'one of the architects of a militant mother-centered nationalism which was to take to revolutionary terrorism in the twentieth century' (Kumar 1993: 38–39). In 1905, she married Ram Bhuj Dutt Chaudhari, an Arya Samaji Congress member, and moved to Lahore. Sarala Devi Chaudhurani is listed as keeper of Hindustan Printing Press, Lahore, where *Hindustan* (1907), an Urdu weekly and paper of 'seditious tendencies' ('Statement of Newspapers and Periodicals published in the Punjab during the year 1911', Home Political (B), no. 2–3, October 1912), was published (with a circulation of 14,484), and Dipak Rajput Printing

works, from where *Dipak*, 'a social and political journal', was published ('Statement of Newspapers and Periodicals published in the Punjab during the year 1914', Home Political Deposit, March 1916, no. 51).

Kamala Satthianadhan was a writer and editor of *The Indian Ladies Magazine*, published in Madras during 1901–18 under her editorship, and later from 1927–38. The periodical published articles on women's education, social reform and political activism, and was influential in constructing a gendered middle-class identity by negotiating conservative and progressive opinions. It was also a conscious attempt to build transregional print networks among women. However, the exclusivity and elitism of such print networks is evident in Satthianadhan's comment on her intended audience:

> a considerable number of daughters of India are taking advantage of the opportunities afforded them of a liberal English education, some of them even succeeding in winning University honours. The future of the women of India rests largely with this educated class; and more especially with those belonging to it, who, without losing what is distinctly Indian, have come under the best influences of the West (Editorial, *The Indian Ladies Magazine*, Vol. 1, July 1901–June 1902).

3. For further reference, see Priya Joshi (2002: 94) and Rimi Chatterjee (2001).

4. For example, a creative piece by Susila Tahl Ram titled 'Spring at the Kutub' (1902b).

5. Hafiza Begum is one of the begums in the *zenana* at the palace of the local Muslim raja at Zinatabad.

6. Himani Bannerji similarly points out the new moral imperatives that the 'home' is shot through in nineteenth- and twentieth-century women's magazines in Bengal. See Bannerji (2001: 147–48).

7. The Rakhmabai case was central to the debates around age of consent and restitution of conjugal rights in nineteenth-century India. Dadaji Bhikaji filed a petition for restitution of conjugal rights against his wife Rakhmabai since she refused to live with him on grounds that she was married at the age of 11 years and did not know better and that she had subsequently never lived with him. The case ended in the dissolution of her marriage after intervention by Queen Victoria.

8. Radha Kumar outlines the concerns with Westernisation and the 'Hindu' identity that split the Arya Samaj in the 1890s and the increasing identification of the 'Aryan' with Hindu (Kumar 1993: 29–30).

9. Pollock (2011: 28) uses the phrase in the context of the Sanskrit scholar Kavindracharya Sarasvati, who considered the use of vernacular a matter of shame.

10. Examples are Bhai Vir Singh's *Sundari* (1983[1898]), *Bijai Singh* (1983[1899]) and *Satwant Kaur* (1983[1900]), and Shraddha Ram Phillouri's *Bhagyavati* (1887).

11. Clark (1999: 3), who sums up Caren Kaplan's argument in Kaplan (1996).

12. *Bharat Bhagini*, 14 (1), January 1902.

13. For example, a letter by 'a Hindu lady' published in 1885 in the *Journal of the National Indian Association*. See 'Child Marriage in India', *Journal of the National Indian Association*, 7 (1885): 420.

14. Term used by Derek Gregory (1994: 33), cited by Majeed (2007: 19).

REFERENCES

Aquil, Raziuddin, and Partha Chatterjee, eds. 2008. *History in the Vernacular*. Ranikhet: Permanent Black.

Bannerji, Himani. 2001. *Inventing Subjects: Studies in Hegemony, Patriarchy and Colonialism*. London: Anthem Press.

Baron, Sabrina Alcorn, Eric N. Lindquist and Eleanor F. Shevlin, eds. 2007. *Agents of Change: Print Culture Studies after Elizabeth L. Eisenstein*. Massachusetts: University of Massachusetts Press.

Bhabha, Homi K. 1985. 'Signs Taken for Wonders: Questions of Ambivalence and Authority Under a Tree Outside Delhi, May 1817'. *Critical Enquiry* 12 (1): 144–65.

_____. 1994. *The Location of Culture*. London: Routledge.

_____. 1996. 'Unsatisfied: Notes on Vernacular Cosmopolitanism'. In *Text and Nation*, eds L. Garcia-Morena and P. C. Pfeifer, 191–207. London: Camden House.

Bharat Bhagini (Hindi periodical), ed. Hardevi. 1902–05. Lahore.

Boehmer, Elleke, and Sushila Nasta. 2012. 'Preface'. In *South Asians and the Shaping of Britain, 1870–1950: A Sourcebook*, eds Ruvani Ranasinha, Rehana Ahmed, Sumita Mukherjee and Florian Stadtler, 1–15. Manchester: Manchester University Press.

Brinda, Maharani of Kapurthala. 1953. *Maharani: The Story of an Indian Princess*. New York: Henry Holt.

Burton, Antoinette. 2003. *Dwelling in the Archive: Women Writing House, Home, and History in Late Colonial India*. New York: Oxford University Press.

———. 2012. 'Epilogue: Salaam, Great Britain: Thinking Through Resistance in an Age of Global Empire'. In *South Asian Resistances in Britain, 1858–1947*, eds Rehana Ahmed and Sumita Mukherjee, 161–65. London: Continuum.

Chatterjee, Rimi. 2001. 'Macmillan in India'. In *Macmillan: A Publishing Tradition*, ed. Elizabeth James, 153–70. Houndmills: Palgrave.

Clark, Steve, ed. 1999. *Travel Writing and Empire: Postcolonial Theory in Transit*. London and New York: Zed Books.

Codell, Julie F., ed. 2003. *Imperial Co-Histories: National Identities and the British and Colonial Press*. London: Associated University Press.

Devee, Sunity. 1929. *Autobiography of an Indian Princess*. London: John Murray.

Devika, J. 2007. *En-gendering Individuals: The Language of Re-forming in Early Twentieth Century Keralam*. New Delhi: Orient BlackSwan.

Dharam Vira. Tape Transcript, Mss. Eur. T66, British Library.

Eisenstein, Elizabeth. 1979. *The Printing Press as an Agent of Change: Communications and Cultural Transformations in Early-Modern Europe*, 2 vols. Cambridge: Cambridge University Press.

Fisher, Michael. 2004. *Counterflows to Colonialism: Indian Travellers and Settlers in Britain, 1600–1857*. New Delhi: Permanent Black.

Forbes, Duncan, tr. 1857. *The Bagh-O-Bahar* [Garden and Spring]. London: W.H. Allen.

Fryer, Peter. 1984. *Staying Power: The History of Black People in Britain*. London: Pluto.

Gregory, Derek. 1994. *Geographical Imaginations*. Cambridge and Oxford: Blackwell.

Grewal, Inderpal. 1996. *Home and Harem: Nation, Gender, Empire and Cultures of Travel*. London: Duke University Press.

Hardevi. 1888a. *London Yatra*. Lahore: Oriental Press.

———. 1888b. *London Jubilee*. Lahore: New Imperial Press.

———. 1892. *Striyon pe Samajik Anyay* [Social Injustice towards Women]. Allahabad: Con Press.

Johns, Adrian. 1998. *The Nature of the Book: Print and Knowledge in the Making*. Chicago: University of Chicago Press.

Jones, Kenneth. 1989[1976]. *Arya Dharma: Hindu Consciousness in 19th-Century Punjab*. New Delhi: Manohar.

Joshi, Priya. 2002. *In Another Country: Colonialism, Culture and the English Novel in India*. New York: Columbia University Press.

Kaplan, Caren. 1996. *Questions of Travel: Postmodern Discourses of Displacement*. Durham: Duke University Press.

Kumar, Radha. 1993. *The History of Doing: An Illustrated Account of Movements for Women's Rights and Feminism in India, 1800–1990*. New Delhi: Zubaan.

Lahiri, Shompa. 2010. *Indian Mobilities in the West, 1900–1947: Gender, Performance, Embodiment*. Basingstoke, Hampshire: Palgrave Macmillan.

Majeed, Javed. 2007. *Autobiography, Travel and Postnational Identity: Gandhi, Nehru and Iqbal*. Basingstoke, Hampshire: Palgrave Macmillan.

McElligott, Jason, and Eve Patten, eds. 2014. *The Perils of Print Culture: Book, Print and Publishing History in Theory*. Basingstoke, Hampshire: Palgrave Macmillan.

Mukherjee, Meenakshi. 1984. 'Reality and Realism: Indian Women as Protagonists in Four Nineteenth Century Novels'. *Economic & Political Weekly* 19 (2): 76–85.

Nasta, Sushiela. 2002. *Home Truths: Fictions of the South Asian Diaspora in Britain*. Basingstoke, Hampshire: Palgrave Macmillan.

Phillouri, Shraddha Ram. 1887. *Bhagyavati: Strishiksha ki Apoorv Pustak*. Harigyan Mandir: Phillour.

Pollock, Sheldon. 2002. 'Cosmopolitan and Vernacular in History'. In *Cosmopolitanism*, ed. Carol Breckenridge, Dipesh Chakraborty, Sheldon Pollock and Homi Bhabha, 15–53. Durham: Duke University Press.

———. 2011. *Forms of Knowledge in Early Modern Asia: Explorations in the Intellectual History of India and Tibet, 1500–1800*. Durham: Duke University Press.

———, ed. 2003. *Literary Cultures in History: Reconstructions from South Asia*. New Delhi: Oxford University Press.

Pollock, Sheldon, H. K. Bhabha, C. A. Breckenridge and D. Chakrabarty. 2000. 'Cosmopolitanisms'. *Public Culture* 12 (3): 577–89.

Pratt, Mary Louise. 1992. *Imperial Eyes: Travel Writing and Transculturation*. London: Routledge.

Raja Jagatjit Singh of Kapurthala. 1895. *My Travels in Europe and America 1893*. London: Routledge.

Ram, Jhinda. 1893. *My Trip to Europe*. Lahore: Mufid-I-Am Press.

Ranasinha, Ruvani, Rehana Ahmed, Sumita Mukherjee and Florian Stadtler, eds. 2012. *South Asians and the Shaping of Britain, 1870–1950: A Sourcebook*. Manchester: Manchester University Press.

Reports on Publications Issued and Registered in the Several Provinces of British India. Calcutta: Office of the Superintendent of Government Printing, 1867–1921, IOR/V/25/960, The British Library.

Rovisco, Maria, and Magdelena Nowicka, eds. 2011. *The Ashgate Research Companion to Cosmopolitanism*. Surrey: Ashgate.

Rudolph, Susan Hoeber, Lloyd I. Rudolph and Mohan Singh Kanota, eds. 2002. *Reversing the Gaze: Amar Singh's Diary: A Colonial Subject's Narrative of Imperial India*. Boulder: Westview Press.

Saraswati, Dayanand. 1908[1875]. *Satyarth Prakash*, tr. Durga Prasad. Lahore: Virjanand Press.

Saraswati, Pandita Ramabai. 1887. *The High Caste Hindu Woman*. Philadelphia: The Jas B. Rodger's Printing Company.

Sen, Satadru. 2004. *Migrant Races: Empire, Identity and K. S. Ranjitsinhji*. Manchester: Manchester United Press.

Sen, Simonti. 2005. *Travels to Europe: Self and Other in Bengali Travel Narratives, 1870–1910*. New Delhi: Orient Longman.

Singh, Bhai Vir. 1983[1899]. *Bijai Singh*. Delhi: Bhai Vir Singh Sadan.

____. 1983[1900]. *Satwant Kaur*. Delhi: Bhai Vir Singh Sadan.

____. 1983[1898]. *Sundari*. Delhi: Bhai Vir Singh Sadan.

Tahl Ram, Susila. 1902a. *Cosmopolitan Hinduani: Depicting Muhammadan and Hindu Life and Thought in Story Form*. Lahore: The Civil and Military Gazette Press.

____. 1902b. 'Spring at the Kutub'. *The Indian Ladies Magazine* 1 (8): 355–58.

____. 1902c. 'First Impressions of Zenana Life'. *The Indian Ladies Magazine* 1 (12): 355–58.

Tandon, Prakash. Tape Transcript, Mss Eur. T127, British Library.

Thacker's Indian Directory. 1895. Calcutta: Thacker, Spink & Company.

Trubner's American, European and Oriental Literary Record. 1882. Vol. 2, January to December. London: Trubner and Company.

Trubner's Record. 1889. Third Series, 1 (4), September.

Visram, Rosina. 1986. *Ayahs, Lascars and Princes: Indians in Britain 1700–1947*. London: Pluto.

Warner, Michael. 2002. 'Publics and Counterpublics'. *Public Culture* 14 (1): 49–90.

Five

Progressive Politics, Gender and the Punjabi Literary through the Work of Dalip Kaur Tiwana*

Anne Murphy

Since the early decades of the twentieth century, modern Punjabi literature has represented a domain for the articulation and exploration of a set of new political imaginaries—a testing ground, in some senses, for political ideas and affiliations that have not always found their footing on the ground of lived political practice (Murphy 2018, 2019). Modern Punjabi literary works thus express a generally progressive (*pragatīvādī* or *taraqī pasand*) set of political commitments (Singh 1987). This is in keeping

*A very early version of this chapter was discussed at the workshop 'Gender In and Out of Punjab: Regional Heterogeneity and Specificity in Transnational Asian Studies', Yale University, 29–30 March 2019; a more developed version was presented at L'École Hautes Études en Sciences Sociales [The School for Advanced Studies in the Social Sciences], Paris, in the seminar for *Projet DELI (Dictionnaire Encyclopédique des littératures de l'Inde)* [Encyclopaedic Dictionary of Indian Literature]. My sincere thanks to workshop organisers and participants in both venues, and particularly to Anne Castaing (CEIAS, Le Centre d'Études de l'Inde et de l'Asie du Sud [Centre for Indian and South Asian Studies], EHESS & CNRS, Le Centre National de la Recherche Scientifique [The National Centre of Scientific Research]), for these opportunities and feedback.

with broader trends: the history of modern vernacular literary production in South Asia is deeply tied to a broader history of leftist politics; as Priyamvada Gopal has described, 'the historical conjuncture from the early 1930s to the years immediately after independence made possible a range of historical tasks or, at the very least, a *perception* that it would be possible—and necessary—to undertake certain kinds of radical endeavors' (2005: 22). The Progressive Writers Association emerged in 1936 with this commitment to critical engagement with and reconstruction of the past and present, towards the production of a new future that would exceed the constraints of the present. Progressive interests did not, and still do not, characterise modern writing as a whole; by the early 1940s the increasingly narrow ideological commitments of some progressive writers alienated those who did not adhere to its defined programme (ibid.: 17–18; Murphy 2018). We shall see some distance from, as well as embrace of, that position in the work examined here. Still, as we will also see here, the progressive ethos marked the production of modern literature even among those who challenged an ideological status quo, as the literary engaged in the imagination and re-imagination of the nation and the world in the context of decolonisation and beyond. A critical purchase on gender inequality, it will be shown, was central to this project of re-imagination.

I explore this dynamic in this chapter through an examination of the work of one prominent Indian Punjabi woman writer, Dalip Kaur Tiwana (1935–2020), who emerged as an author in the early decades of the post-Partition period and continued writing until her death. She is, of course, not the only female writer in the first generation of modern Punjabi writers: Ajeet Cour was another senior female writer active from the 1940s to the present, and Amrita Pritam is another well-known female figure who wrote both in Hindi and in Punjabi; she is relatively better known than these other two. All three of these writers produced significant and critically acclaimed work within a field of cultural production otherwise overwhelmingly dominated by men. In turning to Tiwana, this chapter seeks to bring greater critical scrutiny to the body of work produced by a central figure in the early decades of the development of modern Punjabi literature in the Indian Punjab, as a part of a larger project that considers Punjabi's modern literary life on both sides of the India/Pakistan Punjabi border. After first exploring the central role that gender has played in the modern Punjabi literary imagination, both in the hands of male writers and those of women, I consider here the narratological modes and inhabitations of 'agency'—that problematic term—in writing by Tiwana, as she sought to inhabit the position of woman as author rather than simply as (but often alongside) woman as the site (most often for men) of progressive intervention. Indeed, as will be discussed, Tiwana's self-positioning bears an ambivalent relationship to the progressive. Foregrounding women's experiences and articulating complex understandings of resistance and empowerment, all three of the senior women mentioned sought to formulate a women's authorial voice in diverse terms. Tiwana, the focus here, did so in sometimes remarkably diverse ways, over the course of an equally striking and long career. In this way, representations of 'agency' remained a site for creative negotiation in the exploration of the intersectional forces that constituted women's subjectivity in a society marked by caste and class, as well as gendered hierarchies, and moulded within a colonial and then postcolonial frame.

Modern Punjabi literature remains a male-dominated field and the figure of the woman as the site of progressive intervention remains a construction largely managed by men. It also remains dominated by middle- and upper-class and dominant-caste actors. At the same time, we can see that Tiwana and other women writers (who cannot be addressed within the space of this chapter) worked effectively to articulate women's experiences within patriarchy in ways that exceed the formulations of gender in early reformist and progressive senses. Tiwana's location in Punjab, in particular, invites consideration of what is at stake in writing Punjabi at the state/provincial level, rather than New Delhi (where Pritam and

Cour were located after Partition). This reveals the particular vantage point of the cultural politics of representation in the vernacular in the vernacular language state, not the national centre where Punjabi is ever-present but never central.

The Punjabi Literary and the Figure of the Woman

After the Conference of Indian Progressives in Lucknow in 1935, Punjabi novelist and short-story writer Kartar Singh Duggal tells us that 'the old concept of art for art's sake was formally abandoned… [marking] a conscious shift in new writing in Punjabi from the portrayal of the privileged to that of the under-privileged' (Sekhon and Duggal 1992: 117). This was accompanied by new interests in dialect and new literary forms, including narrative fiction. The modern form of the novel emerged by 1898, with Bhai Vir Singh's well-known work, *Suṅdarī* (2003[1898]), originally serialised, like so many other early vernacular novels. The novel is set in the eighteenth century and tells the story of a young woman, who gives the novel its name, who is abducted by a Mughal official at the time of her *muklāvā*, the ceremony that marks the moment when she leaves home to commence married life. She is saved by her Sikh brother, and then decides to dedicate her life to the Sikh way. Her life and its trials—and her dedication to the Sikh path—constitute the central thematic of the novel (Murphy 2012: Chapter 4). Duggal calls Bhai Vir Singh the 'grand old man of our time' who 'upheld the torch of modernism in Punjabi literature' (Sekhon and Duggal 1992: 109); this relationship with modernism is, however, largely a feature of his poetry, while his narrative fiction maintained closer ties to the expression of Sikh reformist concerns and interests in the representation of the Sikh past (Murphy 2012: Chapter 4; 2023a). It is from his landmark text *Suṅdarī* that Punjabi modern literature is usually understood to have proceeded.

It is significant that this early work of narrative fiction in the novel form in Punjabi is centred on a woman. Bhai Vir Singh's novel, which held up its main character *Suṅdarī* as a model of chaste Sikh female fortitude, was in keeping with a far wider use of the female figure in late nineteenth/early twentieth-century fictional work to define and defend the boundaries of community and nation. As Anshu Malhotra (2002: Chapter 4) and Charu Gupta (2001) have each vividly shown, the tract literature of the period in both Punjabi and Hindi was highly regulatory in its approach to women, setting up almost impossible ideals and then chastising women for not fulfilling them; as Elleke Boehmer has argued, in such formulations 'women are more often than not cast as symbols or totems, as the bearers of tradition' (2005: 22). Gender constituted a central concern of reformist literature overall and was also tied centrally to the nationalist project, as Partha Chatterjee's (1993) foundational work on nationalist formations argued. As Anita Anantharam has noted, 'women's chastity, femininity, and productive and reproductive labor became inseparable from nationalist thought' (2012: 8), and as Antoinette Burton has described, 'the imperial public sphere was saturated with the "woman question" in [the] heady and tumultuous decades' of the early twentieth century (Burton 2003: 9). It is now widely recognised that, as Boehmer notes, 'gender forms *the* formative dimension for the construction of nationhood' (2005: 22; emphasis in original), such that, for example, as Sangeeta Ray has shown, 'the figure of the "native woman" as upper-class Hindu woman becomes the crucial site through which Indian nationalism consolidates its identification with Hinduism', linking religious, cultural and nationalist discourses through the figure of the woman (2000: 7).

The figure of the woman was central to the emergence of the novel in British India in particular, where social reformist novels by men attempted to 'reconcile indigenous literary forms and notions of the function of literature with British ideas of the same, while simultaneously making them vehicles for social reform' (Shandilya 2017: 12). In these complex literary contexts, we see the emergence of the figure of the woman in multiple terms: as the object of reform through the domestic reform novel, where male writers sought, in the words of Krupa Shandilya (2017: 4), to 'articulate a coherent vision of the reformed Indian woman'; as hero and nationalist ideal, as what Ray (2000: 13) describes as a 'site for the expression of the political and social ambitions of the upper caste and middle class as they sought to imagine a culturally powerful Indian nation grounded in a common tradition'; and as the site of activist, progressive intervention, among late colonial 'progressive' writers (Anantharam 2012: 17).

This preoccupation with the portrayal of women's lives in fiction provides a powerful continuity among otherwise quite radically diverse writers, and over time. There are important differences, therefore, between the narrative historical fiction work of figures like Bhai Vir Singh (and other early writers in both a reformist and modernist vein in Gurmukhi Punjabi) and a more radical (in terms of both politics and literary form) author such as Gurbakhsh[1] Singh *Prīt Laṛī*, who engaged in wide-ranging experiments with modern forms, from the novel to the essay (Murphy 2023b). Yet, despite the formal and political differences between such authors, there was a common concern for the status of women and their plight in a patriarchal society, as Parvinder Dhariwal (2013) has shown. Such concerns should not be taken in isolation; they were indicative of a broader interest among Gurmukhi Punjabi creative writers in portraying and critiquing hierarchical social relations: the first novel by master storyteller Gurdial Singh (1933–2016), *Maṛhī dā Dīvā* ('The Memorial Lamp', 2000[1964]), which was later made into a film released in 1989, explored feudal relationships and the impact of monetisation and agricultural development on long-standing relationships. Accomplished novelist and master of the short story form, Kartar Singh Duggal (1917–2012), equally portrayed social relations realistically, with an unflinching eye. The figure of the woman also appears in Shahmukhi[2] Punjabi, although modern narrative fiction in Shahmukhi Punjabi did not draw as many practitioners of the craft as did Gurmukhi Punjabi; in narrative fiction, Urdu was preferred over Shahmukhi Punjabi by many authors. But this was not universally true. The Christian author Joshua Fazl-ud-Din, for example, was active in publishing in Shahmukhi Punjabi in the decade prior to Partition with the journal *Punjabi Darbar* from 1928 to 1935, and he wrote novels, stories, plays, and political commentary in English, Punjabi and Urdu (Columeau 2019: 46).

The figure of the woman and concern for patriarchy were not unique to Punjabi literary domains. As Gopal has argued, the early concern for women's lives by modern literary authors followed from reformist concerns, but quickly developed in diverse ways in relation to individual authors' 'complex subjectivities as writers, political thinkers, and social beings' (2005: 3). From this, she has argued, 'emerged a body of fiction where gender came to have *constitutive* rather than merely thematic importance… [and] themes with a more familiar connection to the "woman question"—education, domesticity, and familial politics—came to intersect with questions of citizenship, political responsibility, labour, sexuality, class, caste, religion and ethics' (ibid.). Progressive literary production therefore engaged centrally with the question of gender, which intersected with a range of other interests. Yet, at the same time, as Gopal notes, 'women writers and intellectuals have no presences in these documents [associated with the Progressive Writers Movement], a fact that is all the more remarkable given their relatively high profile in Progressive literature and the salience of gender as a thematic in this body of work' (ibid.: 28). Still, she argues, we should not dismiss the PWA as inattentive to gender (ibid.: 31). Indeed, as Shandilya well notes, it is wrong to assume that the treatment of women as sites of reform was not in some way providing a kind of agential capacity for the women so imagined: 'because these women occupy center stage in social reform novels, they are also narratively produced as subjects with interiority and desires' and made visible through their inhabitation of patriarchal norms (Shandilya 2017: 15). There is a need, therefore, to understand male constructions of ideal women and women's oppression, as Shandilya notes well, 'in order to grapple with questions of social reform as they were debated in the late nineteenth century' (ibid.: 10). It is also the case that space was claimed by female writers (although not in large numbers): women writers of literary prose in the founding years of the Progressive Writers Association include Ismat Chughtai, Rashid Jahan and Qurattulain Haider, for example.

Nationalising discourses homogenise women's experiences; as Anantharam notes, 'the multiplicity of women's voices is glossed over in an attempt to construct archetypal images of the feminine; thus, an ideal womanhood comes to define national purity and legislative legitimacy' (2012: 8). The print space, as Arti Minocha has rightly noted, has thus generally 'been understood as a disciplining space' (2018: 36). But women's voices do not disappear, and it is crucial that we remain attentive to the points of their emergence, as both Anantharam (2012) and Minocha (2018) show. The emergence of women creative authors allows for possibly different relationships with the concern for reform that characterised much of tract and explicitly nationalist literature, and the preoccupation with woman-as-victim that came to be a staple of progressive literature. There is also, at the same time, a complex relationship between male constructions of women's lives and women's own articulation of women's lives. As Gopal (2005) suggests, if we seek to understand the emergence of women's voices as authors, we must understand them within the larger trajectory within which they emerge. I resort here to woman's authorship, therefore, not to claim it as an unmediated expression of women's experience or agency, nor to distinguish it in absolute terms from perspectives and positions found within men's writing. But if woman as the site of literary intervention is important, as men writing in Punjabi and other modern vernaculars clearly agreed, writing *by women* does offer an important site for the articulation of and grappling with the question of women's position in society. As I will show here, Dalip Kaur Tiwana's work expresses a complex portrait of women's power within patriarchal power structures, one which bears a sometimes ambivalent relation to both progressive interests and the broader literary field.

Woman as Author

Dalip Kaur Tiwana was born in 1935 in a village in Ludhiana district (in what became the Indian Punjab; she was therefore not forced to migrate at Partition, as was Ajeet Cour, for example) (Kaur and Bhangu 2011).[3] Kartar Singh Duggal called her, in 1992, 'the counterpart of the poetess Amrita Pritam in Punjabi letters. What Amrita Pritam says in verse, Dr. Tiwana depicts eminently in fiction' (Sekhon and Duggal 1992: 269). She has been one of the most prominent of Punjabi language prose female authors in India, rivalled only by Ajeet Cour and Amrita Pritam (who also wrote in Hindi), as has been mentioned. Tiwana's Ph.D. dissertation focused on the Punjabi short story, and she served long as a university professor, as well as chairperson of the School of Punjabi Studies, Punjabi University, Patiala; she remained based at the university after retirement. Her first novel, *Agnī Prīkhiā* ('The Fire Test'), was published in 1967 (Tiwana 2001[1967]) and her second novel, *Ehu Hamārā Jīvaṇā* ('This is Our Life'; 2013[1968]) was awarded the Sahitya Akademi award. *Ehu Hamārā Jīvaṇā*, that early award-winning book, is striking for its effort to portray the oppression of women, how women bear the burden of *izzat* or honour, how women's bodies are traded and used, how women are forced to accept what is put upon them. Tiwana attempts to understand a woman's psyche in such a context.

Tiwana's productivity is striking. In 1995, she published *Merī Pratīnidh Rachnā* ('My Representative Work'), which provides an overview of her work to date as well as representative works (Tiwana 1995). That book includes six short stories, a 'novelette' as she calls it, two novels (including *Ehu Hamārā Jīvaṇā* and one other work, described at length below), selections from her autobiographical works (mainly from *Naṅge Pairāṅ dā Safar* ['Journey on Bare Feet'], her early autobiographical work, published in 1980) and exemplary literary criticism (ibid.). The list of her representative works in that volume includes 19 novels, at that point. In the 25 years after that publication, before her death in 2020, she wrote numerous additional works including, among others, the 584-page *Kathā Kaho Urvashī* ('Tell the Tale, Urvashi') in 1999 and *Mātā Dharati Mahatu* ('The Greatness of the Mother Earth') in 2014 (both discussed below) (Tiwana 2011[1999], 2014). While it is impossible to address such a volume of work in a short chapter, I bring together here discussion of a number of exemplary works to give a sense of the breadth and tenor of her *oeuvre*. I utilise both works available only in Punjabi and those also available in English translation: in so doing, I hope to encourage readers of English to explore her work in translation.[4]

N. S. Tasneem has noted that Tiwana has a way of 'describing familiar things or introducing known individuals in an unfamiliar manner. She makes strange what is commonly perceived' (2002: 76). It is this fine attention to detail, and the rendering of psychological as well as social complexity, that marks her work; she maintained a focus on the Malwa section of Punjab, with some of its distinctive dialectical features, typical of an *aṅcalak* or regional author. Several critics have noted that her novels function, at times, as 'long short stories', to quote Kartar Singh Duggal, with their concise plots and controlled narrative development (Sekhon and Duggal 1992: 270). They have also been characterised as featuring a 'conversational' style and a 'severe economy of expression' (ibid.: 324). Her award-winning *Ehu Hamārā Jīvaṇā* reads—in terms of texture and speech—almost like a play. The same is true of her autobiography from the same period, *Naṅge Pairāṅ dā Safar*—for example, its fourth chapter transpires almost completely in direct speech, and at times descriptions seem like stage directions, with characters moving in space and time in front of the mind of the reader, as if on a stage. This reveals a complex narrative interface between narrative fiction and theatre, perhaps reflecting a strong synergy between them in the 1960s and 1970s, an awareness of performance that perhaps now has been internalised and made into prose fiction. (One can see these elements in Bhai Vir Singh's *Sundarī* as well, so there is a longer genealogy to this intersection of theatre and fictional narrative that speaks to the oral life of narrative story-telling [Murphy 2012: Chapter 4].) It also shows the close connection in narratological terms between her fiction and her autobiographical work. It would be a mistake, however, to assert too strong a relationship between any one genre and Tiwana's wide-ranging set of works. Observers have commented, for instance, on her turn away from an explicit focus on gender towards a more introspective, philosophical approach (Kaur and Bhangu 2011). Her *Kathā Kaho Urvashī*, Tasneem argues, works at a grand scale, in keeping with the grand mythological allusions of its title: Urvashi is renowned as the most beautiful of the *apsaras* or nymphs. In the Mahabharata, Urvashi desires Arjuna, and tells him of this; he rejects her, seeing her as an elder, and she curses him. Tasneem sees Tiwana's approach in this work as distinct from the local and fine grain attention of earlier works (2002: 101–02). While the breadth of the work across characters and generations is striking, it is still grounded, as is her work overall, in the articulation of the complexity of relationships, in the conversations that comprise these relationships, and an exploration of individual subjectivity within relational formations. She, therefore, demonstrated considerable range that will be discussed below, even as human relationships and gender are maintained as a focus.

Self-Narration and the Fictional

One mode of writing for Tiwana revolved around self-narration. A novelist and short-story writer, Tiwana published numerous autobiographical works as well, and many that merge with this form yet retain a fictional core. If women were a topical focus of modern vernacular fiction, it is perhaps not surprising that autobiography might emerge as an important genre among women writers. We can, therefore, see in the moments of emergence of modern narrative fiction across languages some recourse to the autobiographical among women, both in terms of that specific genre of writing and within the autobiographical haunting of the fictional narrative realm. This spectral role seems enabled by the thematic concern for the figure of the woman in progressive literary circles, enabling the claim of ownership of a female narrative voice. Gopal (2005) sees this emerge in Ismat Chughtai's semi-autobiographical work, for example. Yet, it would be a mistake to characterise women's writing in general as operating in an autobiographical mode; it is important to see the role of self-fashioning and the choices that comprise it, such that, as Anshu Malhotra and Siobhan Lambert-Hurley describe it, autobiographical practice functions as a 'self in performance' (2015: 1). Malhotra and Lambert-Hurley's explication of the long history of self-narration in South Asia, and the importance of seeing it as autobiographical, is valuable in correcting Eurocentric approaches to the genre and opens up a broader view of what constitutes the form or approach (ibid.: 7). This is particularly valuable in this case, since Tiwana's avowedly autobiographical/factual works are marked by elements of the remarkable or unreal, for example, that undermine straightforward descriptive narrative. The play of time in her novel *Kathā Kaho Urvashī* is consistent with this feature, opening with the visit of the spirit of a deceased man to his daughter and then moving back in time to the story of her life and other members of the family (Tasneem 2002: 102; Tiwana 2011[1999]). Temporal flux and the presence of spectral figures are thus both features of her fictional and her autobiographical works. Tiwana wrote a multi-part autobiography, the first volume of which was *Naṅge Pairāṅ dā Safar*. But even less explicitly fictional works are configured around self-narration. Her *Zammīṅ Puchhe Asmān*, which portrays the conflicting political loyalties and tensions of the 1980s and early 1990s in the Indian Punjab, for instance, features herself as a character—as a University Professor (Sekhon and Duggal 1992: 271).

We thus start here with her *Naṅge Pairāṅ dā Safar* (Tiwana 1980). The story begins with a woman: '*je pichhāṅh muṛ ke dekhāṅ tāṅ…sabh toṅ pahilāṅ uh amīr ghar yād āuṅdai jitthe ik garībaṇī jihī aurat rahiṅdī sī, jis nūṅ maiṅ māṅ ākhdī sī. te uh bāpū jī dī vī māṅ sī*' ('If I look back, the first thing that I remember is a wealthy house and the poor-seeming woman who lived there, whom I called "mother" and who was also the mother of my father') (ibid.: 7). This provides the frame for the work as it proceeds forward: the experience of a young woman growing up in the shadow of the lives of other women, under the control of men. She continues at the end of the first chapter, after the intrusion of her authorial voice into the narration of her childhood: '*ih shāid us amīr ghar vich rahiṇ vālī garīb aurat dā mere sir riṇ hai us ghar dī dhī hoṇ karke, jihṛa maiṅ chukā rahī hāṅ. te mainūṅ lagdā hai us amīr ghar de har baṅde ne us garīb aurat dā kujh nā kujh deṇā hai...*' ('And maybe because of my being a daughter of that house that I owe this debt to that poor woman living in a rich house, and it seems to me that every person in that house owed something to that poor woman') (ibid.: 9).

The story of her life that Tiwana tells is that of the daughter of a wealthy family, but one in which her father's alcoholism threatens ruin. She was the eldest of five daughters, before a son was born much later, and this too functions in the narrative as a weight that is borne by all. The child narrator is taken from the village by her father's childless sister to live in Patiala, a nearby city, where she at first refuses to go to school. Later, she relents, and comes to excel. The tensions in the family persist, heightened by the death of the narrator's grandfather and the worsening alcoholism of her father. Drama also surrounds the question of the girl's marriage—and the narrative technique engaged is dominated by direct speech and stage direction-like scene descriptions. The marriage occurs, but married life does not commence, and the girl returns to her family and to school. Slowly, the story of her life as a writer takes shape: she begins to write stories, she is successful, she is encouraged, she continues in school. She moves on to college. She observes injustices as they pass through her life; she comments on them, and they pass by her as if on a stage. The story of her life proceeds, with her commitment to Punjabi language and literature taking shape in some cases because of, and in some cases despite, the advice and guidance she receives. She meets the 'great writers' of her time in the home of Principal Teja Singh: Gurbakhsh Singh, Devinder Satyarthi, Balwant Gargi. She is, at the time, disappointed that they are not special: '*ih tāṅ ām jihe hī lok ne*' ('These are just normal people') (Tiwana 1980: 110). She describes her travels through her education: her completion of her Master's degree and taking up of college teaching, her emergence as a short-story writer and her achievement of the Ph.D., against considerable opposition.

The Punjabi version of Tiwana's autobiography opens with an epigraph that is not attributed to another, and so represents a statement by the author to the reader:

> *itihās itihās de saphiā ute likhe jāṇ toṅ bahut chir pahilāṅ, kujh lokāṅ de piṅḍiāṅ uppar likhiā jāṅdā hai. ih sva-jīwanī samarpit hai, unhāṅ lokāṅ nūṅ, jihaṛe itihās nūṅ āpṇe piṅḍiāṅ uppar likhiā jāṇā jarde ne.*
>
> (Much before history is written on the pages of history, it is written on the bodies of some people. This autobiography is dedicated to those who have had to endure the writing of history on their bodies.)[5]

This is representative of her authorial style: her tendency to insert direct speech—her own experience, in the first person, in some cases, and in others a third-person general commentary—within a narrative. It is meant to intrude. We see this above, in how she declares her current debt to the 'poor woman' of the rich house in which she grew up. This in some ways gives these statements their power: the violence of their temporal and logical intrusion into and upon the story. We see this, for example, at the end of the first short chapter of the work, where the author subverts chronological development in her exploration of her childhood to comment upon what she is narrating, through her own eyes in the writing present: '*Naṅge pairīṅ phirnā, mainūṅ behadd pasaṅd hai. juttī nūṅ ṭuṭṭaṇ toṅ bacāīṅ rakkhṇā bhāveṅ, is dā kāran nahīṅ*' ('Wandering in bare feet is endlessly delightful to me, even though this is not to save my shoes from being worn out') (Tiwana 1980: 9).[6]

Naṅge Pairāṅ dā Safar is thus throughout marked by a sense of temporal flux, where the intervening voice of the author sets aside chronological development to comment and characterise. As she notes at the end of *Naṅge Pairāṅ dā Safar*, '*asal vich mainūṅ āpṇī svai-jīvaṇī ithoṅ shurū karnī chāhīdī sī, kiuṅki huṇ hī maiṅ maiṅ sāṅ*' ('In truth, I should have started my autobiography here because it was only at this point that I became me') (ibid.: 150). Comments throughout the work complicate the relationship of present to past, impinging upon the past in a present voice, constituting the present self out of the past. This temporal shifting frames narration in time that moves and is fluid, yet is marked by the strong chronological development that it violates: the narrative proceeds through direct speech and minimal description, which enhances its 'nowness' and makes interventions of the present more jarring. This temporal complexity is central to her self-understanding: '*siraf ihī, ki maiṅ rabbo vālīāṅ dī dhī de nāl nāl, harkur dī dohatī vī hāṅ*' ('I am the daughter of the Rabbo clan and also the granddaughter of Har Kaur') (ibid.: 29). Here, present is imbedded in the past, and her present being bears the weight of the past and her relationships within it, with primacy to female affiliation (within the overall patriarchal order).

The play of ghosts or spectral figures in her autobiography defies conventional notions of factual prose, and it is the haunting of the imagination that runs through the work. We first hear of such spectral figures in the fifth chapter, when Tiwana again enters authorial time (that is, the time of the present, of writing) to describe herself in relation to her past. When answering—to those who might ask—the question of why she went on pilgrimage to Hardwar, she notes: '*par inhāṅ nūṅ koī kiveṅ samajhave, ki ajihīāṅ thāvāṅ ute jā ke, kade kade tuhāṅūṅ āpṇā guāchiā āpā vī nazarīṅ pai jāṅdā hai*' ('But how can someone explain to them that going to such places, one can catch sight of one's lost self') (Tiwana 1980: 29). She goes on to describe a further haunting: '*jadoṅ hazur sāhib nūṅ jāṅdiāṅ, gaḍḍī sāṅ sāṅ kardī rāt de hanere vichoṅ laṅghī jā rahī sī, tāṅ mere zihan vich, hanere vich, ikallā thakkiā, udās gurū gobiṅd siṅgh turiā jā rihā sī, te us de ghoṛe dīāṅ ṭāpāṅ mainūṅ suṇ rahīāṅ san*' ('When I was going to Hazur Sahib and the car was coming through the darkness of the night, in my mind I could see the worn out and exhausted Guru Gobind Singh walking, and I could hear the sound of the hooves of his horse') (Tiwana 1980: 29). So, we see the haunting of the author's past life in the present, the visage of the Guru, and also of course the haunting of the 'poor woman' of that 'rich house'.

The haunting returns, after chapters of nearly exclusive dialogue and the straightforward theatrical mode that characterises the work overall. We get a sense of the connection between such hauntings and the literary/imaginative through the childhood eyes of the author when she begins to read fiction:

> *kitābāṅ de pātar kitābāṅ choṅ tur ke, mere man vich aa pahuṅche, te ik āpṇā hī saṅsār siraj liā. phasalrūp ziṅdagī vich, asalī pātarāṅ dī asalīat beyakīnī bhāsī, te kālpanik pātarāṅ dī hoṅd sacch baṇ gaī. pichhoṅ is gall ne, kaī vārī, mainūṅ chhaliā hai. shāid ise kāran, dādī māṅ ākhdī huṅdī sī, ih tāṅ dhī merī, bahut bholī ai, es nūṅ nī koī val chhal āuṅdā* (Tiwana 1980: 56).
>
> (The characters came out from the books and entered my mind and created their own world. In this contrived world, the truth of actual people seemed false and the imaginary world became true. This fooled me quite a few times. Maybe this is why my grandmother always used to say that my daughter is very naïve and that she has no guile.)

This imaginary life continues to provide a kind of truth for her, when truth itself is absent:

> *āpṇe āp toṅ pār laṅgh ke, jīūṇ dā is vele mainūṅ bas iko tarīkā patā sī. uh sī kitāb paṛhiāṅ, kitāb de pātarāṅ 'ch gumm ho jāṇā. āpṇā āp bhull ke, kise pātar dī ziṅdagī jīūṇ lagg jāṇā. te haulī haulī maiṅ āpṇe āp toṅ, pār khaṛoke, āpṇe āp nūṅ turī phir rahī vī dekh sakdī sī.*
> *inhāṅ dināṅ vich, yathārth te kalpanā vichlī lakīr, bahut dhuṅdhlī ho gaī sī* (ibid.: 104).

(I only knew one way of living at this time, having moved beyond myself: to lose myself in the characters of the books I was reading. I would forget myself, and live the lives of the characters I was reading. And then, slowly, I would stand up away from myself, and could see myself from a distance.
In those days, the line between truth and the imagination became very unclear.)

Spectral figures seem to return at the end, but in a dramatically different mode, grounded in the real. She describes colleagues and students in Mohindra College in Patiala as *bhūt*, or phantoms; in this case, however, she is describing a group of people who were known by this term, and a place that was known as *bhūtwāṛā*, the place where the phantoms gathered. This was an artistic collective where writers gathered to share ideas, work, and live in common (Rode and Cheema 2021). She describes a story she wrote about them visiting her to drink tea and discuss literature:

ih sāre bhūtwāṛe de maiṁber han.
har koī bhūtwāṛe dā maiṁbar nahīṅ ho sakdā bhāveṅ maiṁbar hoṇ dā chaṅdā koī nahīṅ.
bhūtwāṛā kise saṁsthā, kise vād jāṅ kise thāṅ dā nāṅ nahīṅ ih taṅ ik ṭabbardārī hai. is ṭabbar de sāre jīāṅ nūṁ bhūt ākhiā jāṅdā hai (Tiwana 1980: 137–38).

(All of these were members of the Phantomland.
Not everyone is a member of Phantomland but there is no fee to become one.
Phantomland is not an organisation or a place or an ideology. It is a kind of family. All the people in this family are called Phantoms.)

They are found all over: '*ajj kallh, bhūtwāṛe de maiṁbar tuhānūṅ chaṅdīgaṛh, aṁbālā, pharīdkoṭ, dillī, baṭhiṇḍā, gaṛhadīvāl, kaineḍā, iṅglaiṅḍ, te amrīkā vich vī mil jāṇge, par pakkā aḍḍā ihnāṅ dā paṭiāly hī hai*' ('These days you will find members of the Phantomland in Chandigarh, Ambala, Faridkot, Delhi, Bathinda, Gardhiwal, Canada, England and the USA, but their centre is at Patiala')

(Tiwana 1980: 138). She describes their mode of living, giving a sense that their commitments are perhaps superficial and facile:

> *khulhā jihā koī ghar ih bhūt kirāe ute lai laiṅde han bhāveṅ uh ghar ik kamre dā hī hove. jihaṛā bhūt kise kamm ute hai, kirāiā us bhūt ne deṇā huṅdā hai. je kirāiā kujh chir nā ditā jā sake taṅ baṛī khushī nāl kirāe vich sārā sāmān de ke kise hor ghar vich ā jāṅde han. uṅj vī jāṇ pahichāṇ vāliāṅ nāl sāre rishte nāte toṛ ke thoṛhe hī jāīdā e. hisāb kitāb chaldā hī rahiṇā chahīdā hai.*
> *phir unhāṅ dināṅ vich samājvād nūṅ baṛī tībartā nāl uḍīkiā jāṅdā hai* (ibid.: 147).
>
> (These phantoms take an open house on rent, even if it is only one room. When some phantom has work, the phantom has to give rent. If rent can't be given for some time, then he happily brings all his things to a new house. In this way he doesn't break off with his relations. Some give and take remains with them.
> And in these days, they waited attentively for the coming of socialism.)

The novel then ends with further anecdotes about the author's life as a professor in Patiala. In this way she transitions back to the concrete and the real. We see thus the combination of the real and fantasy, woven intimately together, a sense both of a community of writers and a sense of alienation from them. We see here also a certain distancing of the author from the interests of the Left, which animated the work of so many other Punjabi-language authors of the time.

NOVELS, SHORT STORIES, NOVELLAS

But while self-narration is an important feature of Tiwana's oeuvre, both in her numerous explicitly autobiographical writings and those that are not centrally autobiographical but are marked by its features, this mode cannot be said to characterise her work overall. Neither can it be said that there is one particular approach, one perspective that she wrote from. She wrote short stories and novellas; she composed novels, short and long. She explored the inner thoughts of contemporary women; she wrote historical novels. She described women in positions of power and those who are structurally marginalised.

One of the works included in Tiwana's representative collection of her works up to 1995 is *Laṅgha Gae Dariā* ('Gone are the Rivers'), first published in Punjabi in 1990 and published in English translation in 1998 (Singh and Narula 1998; Tiwana 1990 and 1995: 151–248). This work is driven by a distinct historical focus: it portrays the state of Patiala—a 'princely state' within the British system—and the family of the wazir of Patiala state, Sardar Bakhshish Singh. The story portrays their lives at the height of their power, and the decline in their power and prestige as the world changed around them with the end of the princely state, Partition and adjustment to an independent India. The main characters of the novella are the Sardar himself, and the elder and younger *sardārnīs*, his wives: he remarries when his first wife does not produce a child. She is called the *vaḍḍī* or great sardārnī and she remains the main figure, however, and as it is stated by the second wife (and mother of the Sardar's three children, two girls and a boy) at the end of the story: 'I've only given birth to them—in fact, they belong to the elder Sardarni...' (Singh and Narula 1998: 81; Tiwana 1995: 231). One girl is engaged to a prince from Chittor, a princely state in Rajasthan; a conflict between the two states results in his abandonment of the marriage, and she spends the rest of her life in waiting. The older daughter, named Harpreet, is married into a Punjabi aristocratic family, whose son has sought his fortune in the United States; there, they divorce, and she struggles on her own. The son leads a decadent lifestyle: at the beginning of the novel, he is described as such: 'He does no work. It's difficult to say whether he is unfit for any work or whether no work is good enough for him' (Singh and Narula 1998: 1; Tiwana 1995: 151). He loses his wife as she abandons him to his drinking, and his daughter seeks to rebel. The novel ends with the return of the elder daughter, Harpreet, after the death of her father and the *vaḍḍī sardārnī*, in time to be present for her brother's death. The novel ends with his daughter's desperate plea to live with her aunt.

The novel portrays both female oppression and power. The *vaḍḍī sardārnī* lives a life constrained by patriarchy. Her value is lessened by her inability to produce children for her husband; his second wife does this. She remains powerful, however. She accepts the arrival of the second wife, and ferociously protects the interests and standards of the family; she thus remains the confidante and ally of her husband, the Sardar, and he relies on her in all things. For example, when the time comes to consider the marriages of his children (the children of the *chhoṭī sardārnī*, or younger Sardarni), he takes the elder Sardarni into confidence. When she suggests that he ask the opinion of the younger Sardarni because '*asal 'ch dhīāṅ tāṅ usdīāṅī ne*' ('after all they're her daughters'), he refuses, saying, 'On the contrary, they're your children—one doesn't win a claim to children simply by giving birth to them' (Singh and Narula 1998: 43; Tiwana 1995: 191). For another example, with the visit of the Sardar's sister, 'the hierarchy of the house became quite clear to the younger Sardarni' (Singh and Narula 1998: 13; Tiwana 1995: 163). The Sardar's sister carefully favoured the elder Sardarni, for the sake of keeping the peace and preventing her from doing harm: 'For her brother's good, it was right for her to support the elder Sardarni. If this dethroned and dejected woman ever turned desperate, she could prove dangerous. It was best to keep her under the illusion that she was still number one in the house' (Singh and Narula 1998: 14; Tiwana 1995: 163).

Tiwana here portrays the complexity of women's machinations within the working of patriarchal power in an elite household: the elder Sardarni articulates her own power within that structure and is provided with the benefits accorded to those who support it. Her investment in that structure is without fail. Indeed, the household is the locus of the entire novel: the immediate environment of the elite, Patiala household and the people within it. Those who leave disappear from the story. The character of Harpreet, the daughter of the Sardar who has gone to the United States and has therefore exited the household, returns to the narrative only when she comes back to it. She, too, does not question the underpinnings and forms of power within the household.

How do we characterise such work? The work is feminist in its focus on female characters, its sensitivity to issues of power and the family, its portrayal of the ways in which women's lives unfold in relationships and within patriarchy, and its attention to intersections of caste, class and social status with gender (although its focus is on elites). Women have agency: the elder Sardarni has the ability to act, and she does—in her own self-interest, and in the interests of the Sardar (which is clearly, to her, also in her self-interest). Her agency is directed in these two ways. The men portrayed in the novel do possess agency denied to women: the Sardar can choose his way of living and with whom he lives; his son has freedoms his daughters do not have. Women in the family who seek to pursue their own choices must leave the household, as Dolly (the granddaughter of the Sardar) seeks at the end of the novel, and as her mother achieved when she left her alcoholic husband, the son of the Sardar. That release, however, requires absolute loss, the cost of inclusion in the household. Within the household, women must behave.

We see in Tiwana's works overall radically different portrayals of women and the working of power, and perhaps a distancing from a sense of what women's empowerment means, or a questioning of its terms. For example, her short story '*Terā kamrā merā kamrā*' ('Your room, my room'), in *Merī Pratīnidh Rachnā*, represents the experience of a woman working in an office, and her thoughts about the man in the office next to hers (Tiwana 1995: 3–6). Through this, Tiwana explores a woman's inner thoughts, her desires, her sense of herself in relation to another. Tiwana expanded this story into a later novella that has been translated into English, *Twilight*, which explores the inner thoughts of a woman, Harjit, who becomes infatuated with her co-worker, perhaps (Kaur and

Ratan 2009: 3–92). It is not entirely clear how much she knows him, and how much she truly cares. She is intrigued by him as an unknown figure. She becomes entranced by her own imagination, in her conceptualisation of him. She likes him, she says to herself (ibid.: 27). She writes him a letter when he is ill, her husband finds out and assumes the worst; he then wants a divorce. Harjit has neither a lover nor a husband, and leaves her marital home. This leads to the opportunity for debate, as Harjit the protagonist comes to live in a hostel with her friend Sonal, who has unconventional views about women's freedom and the nature of women's lives:

> 'This is what our Indian traditions are, that we consider our home, husband and children as our achievements. But why is it, that the woman never becomes a man's achievement?'
>
> [Harjit responds:]
>
> 'Sonal, I feel that today's woman has lost her direction, she doesn't know what to do.'
>
> 'Harjit, woman has never herself tried to find out her direction. She is not bold enough to do so. She is not intelligent enough to create this boldness in herself,' Sonal said.
>
> 'But Sonal, what you call boldness is a misleading notion. The very idea that woman should lead a life, which is free of all attachments, is the need of man not of woman. A woman, free of all bonds, does not fetter a man. This is what he wants. A woman feels that she is living on her own terms, but in reality, even this choice is not her own.'
>
> For a few moments, Sonal was taken aback at my argument and then she said, 'Life is tragedy for a woman who can think independently' (ibid.: 51).

Twilight provides Tiwana with the space to debate with herself, for her readers, regarding the nature of women's freedom and what is at stake in the possibility of women's desire. She challenges conventional formulations of the binary between freedom and unfreedom, arguing for a woman's subjectivity that is not fully expressed through a notion of agency-as-freedom.

Kathā Kaho Urvashī (2011[1999]) is similar in its exploration of human relationships with attention to women, but it also attends carefully to men; it is also an exploration of death and its meanings and forms. The work focuses on Kuldeep, the daughter of the father whose ghost haunts the opening of the book, but in terms of narrative voice and focus, the work is dominated by the stories of Devinder and his son Arvind, who becomes the sanyasi (ascetic) Ganga Puttar. The massive work is comprised of six parts and a preface. In the preface, we see the visit of Kuldeep's father, after his death, as he seeks to understand her grief. The first part of the work relates the story of that family, of Kuldeep the daughter, but primarily of Devinder, the longed-for son (ibid.: 19) who joins the army later in life. The story follows his efforts to act as male head of the family, which does not always succeed (ibid.: 46–70), and of Kuldeep's unwavering support for and deference to him (in seeking his approval for her marriage, for instance) (ibid.: 53–54). He marries a woman named Alka and becomes the father of two sons, Angad and Arvind (ibid.: 71, 83). His marriage with Alka sours, and this part of the work ends in his suicide.

In the second part of the work, we see the family struggle with Devinder's suicide. Angad leaves India to go to the United States, and Arvind disappears (ibid.: 274). In the end, waiting and in limbo, Alka's mental health deteriorates. In the third section, we hear from Devinder, after his death: his regret at having taken his life (ibid.: 345, 351), his despair over what went wrong in his life. He blames his wife for their difficulties (ibid.: 332–34) but also admits to his own alcoholism and silence (ibid.: 334, 353ff.). We hear here about how '*ih vī ho sakdai sārī hī marad jāt dā uh mere koloṅ badalā lai rahī sī*' ('Perhaps she took vengeance on all men through me') (ibid.: 335). This theme of revenge returns through the novel as an aspect of both death and life. At the same time, we hear praise of Kuldeep, for whom there was never 'me', only 'we' (ibid.: 342). In a theme that recurs, Devinder notes that he should not have demanded so much of Alka and should have had faith in God (Tiwana 2011[1999]: 370). The importance of the spiritual path is at the core of the work.

In the fourth section, Kuldeep reads Arvind's diary, so we hear then in the first person the story of the family from his perspective. He reveals that his father always preferred his brother, perhaps because he (Arvind) looked too much like his mother or was not successful enough (ibid.: 382–83, 394, 410). We learn more about the animosity between his mother and Kuldeep. He is critical of his father's suicide (ibid.: 388, 397), but ultimately blames himself (ibid.: 405, 441); in the next section, he excuses the father's alcoholism and blames the family for it (ibid.: 481). He says that '*laggdai tusīṅ koī pichle janamāṅ dā badalā lai rahe sī*' ('It seems like you were taking revenge for some prior life') (ibid.: 423; we hear again about *badalā* for a prior life or lives on page 544). In the fifth section, we learn of what happens to Arvind after he leaves home, in third-person narration. The story follows his journey to the mountains and the beginning of his discipleship to a sanyasi named Anand (ibid.: 454). We see also Alka (ibid.: 472) and learn of the life of Shalini (ibid.: 505), a young woman Arvind was fond of, but the narrative of Arvind—now Ganga Puttar—dominates the section. Here we see full articulation of the central concern of the work with the nature of life and death: Arvind's experiments with renunciation are explorations of the nature of these states, and how one can die to the world while alive, in contradistinction to the figure of the father, who is alive (and attached) to the world while dead. He asks himself, '*par maiṅ jīūṇdā hāṅ ki mar giā hāṅ*' ('But was I alive or dead?') (ibid.: 465; see also pp. 478, 485). He says of his mother: '*uh nahīṅ jāṇdī arviṅd sacchī gaṅgā vic ḍubb ke mar cukkiā hai*' ('She doesn't know that Arvind has already drowned in the Ganga and died') (ibid.: 496).

At the end of the section, he returns to Patiala to visit his mother; he also meets Shalini's son, named Arvind. His mother recognises him (ibid.: 532). He does not acknowledge that he is her son and leaves. He tells the Sanyasi Anand that he has failed the test because he felt something for his mother when she fell in agony at his departure, after recognising him. He is told that in fact this means he passed the test: '*agar teriāṅ akkhāṅ vic pāṇī nā āuṅdā tāṅ tūṅ phelh hoṇā sī. usdā matlab hoṇā sī ki tūṅ sādhū nahīṅ sagoṅ patthar ho giā haiṅ*' ('If you had not come to tears then it would have meant you failed. This means that you had not become a Sadhu, but had become a stone') (ibid.: 534). In the final section, we open with the story of the ghost of the father, and then return to the story of Kuldeep in the third person. This then joins with the story of Arvind as she goes to find him (ibid.: 547), and we read of her further interactions with him. The book ends with the promise of Ganga Puttar to return to his family, with the Guru Granth Sahib that his grandmother once kept and which Kuldeep had given him, after he believes he hears his father's voice.

With this work we see a focus on the nature of life and death, articulated through the intense family relationships that are a hallmark of Tiwana's work overall. We also see a move away from a singular attention to women, or at least to the articulation of a woman's voice or perspective—we only hear from men in the first person in *Kathā Kaho Urvashī*, and we never understand Alka's difficult position. This is reflective of a larger move, at least in this work, away from the focus on women in oppressive contexts that characterises Tiwana's earliest work. She did, however, as in *Laṅgha Gae Dariā*, continue to bring focus to women in other works. Tiwana's *Mātā Dharati Mahatu* provides an example of this focus in a new register. Its components were published individually before the complete collection of four parts was published in 2014. On the back cover of the first hardback edition of the book, Tiwana describes a meeting between a 'Punjabi female writer' and a 'Padre', whereby a discussion ensues. The Padre notes that Christ had committed a great sacrifice for the people of the world, and the Writer responds that '*saḍe paṅjāb vicc vī bahut sāre lokāṅ ne karaisṭ vāṅg kurbānīāṅ hoīāṅ ne*' ('In our Punjab, many people have sacrificed themselves like Christ'). The Padre responds, in surprise, that Punjabis will go to hell because '*Tusīṅ paṅjābīāṅ ne dunīā nūṅ dassiā hī nahīṅ ki tusīṅ kauṇ ho, kihnāṅ dī aulād ho, kihnāṅ de vāras ho, te tuhāḍīāṅ jaṛāṅ kitthe han*' ('You Punjabis have not told the world who you are, where you come from, what you have inherited, and where your roots are') (Tiwana 2014: cover). The author then ends the note with the comment that with this book she seeks to arrive at the roots of the Punjabis through a journey of the mind.

The book is structured into four sections. Each section, which does not announce itself explicitly in this way, is dedicated to one of the women closely associated with the tenth and final embodied human guru of the Sikh tradition, Guru Gobind Singh: his mother, Mata Gujari, in the first section, and his three wives, given here in the order of their sections in the book: Mata Sahib Kaur (Sahiba), Mata Jito and Mata Sundari. The narrative of the Tenth Guru is here re-centred on the women in his life. He is central, of course, as the Guru, and mention of him and of his father, Guru Tegh Bahadur, is respectful and reverent, and forms the narrative core of the work as a whole. But the Guru is at the centre of the narrative in the course of the women's lives, and we follow their upbringing and childhoods, from their perspectives. In this, it parallels the approach of *Laṅgha Gae Dariā*, where the narrative core of the story is centred on women, not the men who generally dominate such narratives, although the women portrayed are part of the narrative *because of* their relationships with a central, powerful man. Mata Gujari's story, for example, begins with her parents' decision to go and live near the Guru at Kartarpur. Here, the story invokes stereotypical tropes of Mughal injustice and cruelty, claiming that '*musalmān hākam kuṛīāṅ nūṅ zabardastī cukk de lai jāṅde san*' ('Muslim rulers forcibly took away girls') (Tiwana 2014: 14, 19, 22; 19 for quote). Otherwise, it focuses on Gujari's childhood and her merits: her beauty and her devotion (ibid.: 16); even sadhus bow down to her as a form of the goddess (ibid.: 21).

As Gujari's story progresses, a defining feature of the book emerges: the narration of stories as a legitimate and central feature of religious life and instruction. We hear this throughout the work, although particularly in the sections on Mata Gujari and

Mata Jito; the section on the latter foregrounds her relationship with a beloved aunt, and theirs is a relationship constituted by story-telling, out of which complex philosophical conversations commence. Throughout the work, the *sākhī*s or stories of the Gurus are central, but so are the stories of Haranakhsh, Dhruv and Narasimha, sections of the Mahabharata and Ramayana, and countless other mythological tales (Guru Gobind Singh's education is described vividly along such lines as well [Tiwana 2014: 53]). We can see this as the articulation of a feminist theological domain, structured through story-telling and within the conversations and reflections among women. This is a particularly striking dimension of the relationship between Jito and her aunt, Ganga Bhua (ibid.: 186 ff.). After Ganga Bhua explains why it is important to do *pāṭh*, in simple and yet powerful terms, Jito asks her, '*ih sārīāṅ gallāṅ tainūṅ kiveṅ patā ne*' ('How do you know all of these things?') (ibid.: 228; this is a question she reiterates on page 259), her aunt replies that '*mere nānā-nānī baṛe bhagat sī. unhāṅ dā asar merī māṅ vich giā hoṇai, māṅ dī gāhāṅ maiṅ dhī sī nāle baṅde dī kamāī ik janam dī nahīṅ huṅdī*' ('My maternal grandfather and grandmother were great devotees. Their legacy was passed on to my mother and I am the daughter, who is the harvest of my mother. What people earn isn't extinguished in a single lifetime') (ibid.).

At the same time, we also see conventional assertions of the girls' 'special' beauty, and the 'grooming' of young girls as brides. Sahiba, for instance, is described as a '*chaṅd dī chāṅdanī vargī dhī*' born into her house ('a daughter like a ray of moonlight') (ibid.: 82), and later as '*apsarā vargī shakal wālī, mriganaiṇī, kamal de phull vargī*' ('with the face of an Apsara, eyes like a deer, and like a lotus flower') (ibid.: 96). Jito is described as having large eyes, a straight nose, a round face and fair skin (ibid.: 184), and although there is discussion with her aunt about internal and external beauty (ibid.: 187), Sahiba is described as Jito is described (ibid.: 311). In this way, the conventional emphasis on the beauty of women within the patriarchal narratological mode is fully maintained. And they are groomed to be good, obedient and capable wives. After being described as unusually beautiful and devout, as all the women are, for instance, when Gujari is promised into the Guru's family and accepted by Guru Hargobind, she then begins to train to become a daughter-in-law: '*istoṅ magaroṅ bishandeī gujarī nūṅ vele-kuvele vaḍḍe gharāṅ vāle taur tarīke dassdī rahiṅdī ki sahure ghar jā ke sir naṅgā nahīṅ rakhnā*' ('After this, whenever she could, Bishandei would explain to Gujari how one should behave in the homes of prominent people, such as that when in the home of her in-laws, she should never leave her head uncovered' (Tiwana 2014: 34).[7] We see this pattern in the descriptions of each of the wives of the Guru as well, such as with Sahiba (ibid.: 93), Jito (ibid.: 235) and Sundari (ibid.: 329). Sundari is told, '*utthe tainūṅ vī har tarhāṅ nāl isatrī dharam, grahiṇī dharam dā pūrā khiāl rakkhṇā pavegā*' ('There, you must give with your full attention to maintaining women's duty, the duty to adjust') (ibid.: 330). When Jito is faced with the problem of not having produced an heir, she behaves as a model wife and encourages her husband to marry another woman who can bear a child for him (ibid.: 242–43); Sundari, in turn, gives her child to Jito fully, and then is ready to take on the full role of mother when Jito moves on to learning the arts of battle (ibid.: 336, 339). This is the story of women, therefore, but it is one in which these women fit into the roles defined for them within the family. One can see such depictions as typical of any idealised representation, as is expected when speaking of the family of the Guru; the ideal here requires adherence to gendered norms.

At the same time, there is careful delineation of context throughout the work, allowing the work to function effectively as a general history of the period and of the life of Guru Gobind Singh, through the narrative woven out of these women's lives. At times, there are odd and sometimes striking inaccuracies, such as the claim that the mother of a Muslim friend of Gujari's would not eat in Gujari's house (ibid.: 40, 42) when, in fact, the reality was generally the opposite: that non-Muslim, dominant-caste persons would refuse to eat in the homes of Muslims (which we also see later in the story of Sahiba [ibid.: 89]); there is an inaccurate description of the great suffering of all non-Muslims in the period of Aurangzeb, which is not supported by the historical evidence (ibid.: 47), and an inaccurate understanding of Islam as a practised faith (ibid.: 313). The historical content is therefore at times problematic. Narratologically, however, this contextual material successfully allows the work to function on these several levels: as a general, popular history of the period and of the Sikh tradition, as a women-centred narrative of the history of the Sikh tradition and as a history of the life of the tenth Guru.

The equality of women is asserted through each of the women's stories. In Mata Gujari's story, it is associated with the formation of the Khalsa: '*Gurū nānak dev jī ne istarīāṅ nūṅ jo barābarī de hakk ditte san gurū sāhibān ne uhnā nūṅ savīkār kītā te isī mārag te chale. isatrīāṅ aṁmrit chhakk sheranīāṅ baṇ gaīāṅ*' ('The rights to equality that Guru Nanak had given to women were upheld by the Gurus and they continued it. Women took initiation [literally "nectar"] and became lionesses') (Tiwana 2014: 70). The most striking articulation of this is by Mata Jito who says (as the theme is first introduced in the story of Mata Gujari): '*Gurū ghar vich tāṅ aurat-marad vich farak nahīṅ rakkhiā giā. pher maiṅ yuddh vich kiuṅ nahīṅ jā sakdī*?' ('In the house of the Guru there is no difference between man and woman, so why can't I go fight in battle?') (ibid.: 72; articulated again on page 348). We hear much more of this in the story of Mata Jito, of course, where the Guru acknowledges her spiritual advancement (ibid.: 247) and allows her to learn to fight with her sons (ibid.: 275 ff.). Jito tells the Guru, '*sāhib sacch jāṇo tuhāḍe nāl rahiṅdiāṅ mainūṅ bhull hī giā hai ki maiṅ aurat vī hāṅ*' ('Lord, know that in truth, living with you I have forgotten that I am a woman') (ibid.: 275). She learns to fight herself and encourages her sons (ibid.: 284, 289, 292). She is later killed in battle (ibid.: 296). And in the end, as is known from history, the wives of the Guru, Sundari and Sahiba, play a leadership role within the community; this is described in detail, particularly with reference to the compilation of the Dasam Granth (ibid.: 150 ff., 357 ff.). Tiwana tells us that when Sahiba accepted that all the Khalsa was indeed her child, this was the first time in history that a woman had thought so expansively (Tiwana 2014: 357). Thus, in this telling, these figures fulfil the roles conventionally assigned to women—with the exception of Jito, who comes to see herself as taking on a new kind of role, no longer as a woman—but within these roles, all assert their experience of equality and empowerment.

This work reveals in a particularly clear way one of the central tensions that is visible through Tiwana's work: her focus on women's lives in a way that foregrounds women's experience, but, within that, the articulation of and support for what can be construed as a subordinate role for women, the fulfilment of which she articulates as a triumph of female power. Mata Sundari, for one final example, is thus valorised for her patience, as a woman who asks for nothing (ibid.: 331), just as Kuldeep in *Kathā Kaho Urvashī* is valorised for rejecting 'me' in favour of 'we' (Tiwana 2011[1999]: 342). This valorises the giving, service and sacrifice of women's lives on par with the different kinds of sacrifices and self-negation of religious positions more broadly associated with men. It cannot be denied that this position also accepts female subordination and the fulfilment of the conventional roles assigned to women. This is a women-centred position within patriarchal formations, with an ambivalent position on where to move in relation to those formations and what it means to achieve a woman-centred power within them.

Conclusions

With this preliminary exploration of Tiwana's range of work, we see the ways in which she constructed her authorial voice out of her experience as a woman and out of the experiences of women in general terms.[8] She places herself within women's genealogy, and places her writing, too, within the genealogy of women's lives. This commitment reveals itself in dramatically different ways, in her diverse works. The imaginative enters her early self-narration in relation to the trials she suffers as a woman, and she portrays herself as retreating into the world of the imagination in response to the constraints placed upon her life. She positions herself as an outsider in all things: in fulfilling (and not fulfilling) the requirements of gender imposed in the home, as an author (with a sense of distance from a broader community of writers) and in the world as a professor/teacher. Writing is configured here as a form of both assertion and denial, of participation in a world that also excludes. The figure of woman here is not the ground for reform and not an object to be liberated. She struggles to find voice through a space that can only be imagined. This is achieved partially through self-narration, but the fictional undergirds even that self-narration and exceeds it into a broad range of forms.

Anantharam's analysis of the writings of four twentieth-century Urdu and Hindi poets provides a valuable analytical frame for understanding Tiwana's work: she argues that among the four writers she examines, each negotiates:

> prescriptive constructs of femininity in her own unique way, and no single, definitive 'feminist' voice emerges through the collective study of their writings. Instead, an analysis of their work reveals a number of ideological contradictions in feminist subjectivity in South Asia. Depending on their context, they emphasize different aspects of their subjective experience as a way of signifying power; sometimes they state their commitments to an international feminist movement, and at other times they deny it, choosing alternative communities of solidarity (Anantharam 2012: 10).

Tiwana too—as shown vividly in *Twilight* but also visible in other works—has a complex relationship with notions of agency and empowerment. Anthropologist Saba Mahmood called attention to the need to account for complicating the conception of agency, for understanding 'the lives of women whose desire, affect, and will have been shaped by nonliberal traditions' (2001: 203). Mahmood's exploration of women's participation in mosques in Egypt demonstrates how modes of being associated with Islamic pietistic forms of ethics and action for women—modes that seem to embrace a subordinated position for women—must be understood outside of the assumptions implicit in much feminist and liberal theory in the search for female agency. Mahmood suggested that to understand women's participation in Islamic piety movements, we must understand that

> what may appear to be a case of deplorable passivity and docility from a progressivist point of view, may actually be a form of agency—but one that can be understood only from within the discourses and structures of subordination that create the conditions of its enactment. In this sense, agentival capacity is entailed not only in those acts that resist norms but also in the multiple ways in which one *inhabits* norms (Mahmood 2005: 15).

Tiwana wrote to produce space for consideration of the ways in which women partake of power in patriarchal structural formations, both in assertion and in submission, and how they inhabit norms both by choice and by force. Agency for her thus cannot be linked solely to an idea and praxis of liberation. That is to say, Tiwana engaged with the myriad forms of agency that are articulated within the non-liberal, non-liberatory: people participate in and produce their own forms of subjugation, as well as those of others, and achieve kinds of agency in relation to others that can entail the subversion of the assertion of self. Tiwana described this in her work with an unflinching gaze. She did not romanticise or rationalise this. When asked in a 1996 interview with Iqbal Kaur about whether men enjoy more facilities than women writers, Tiwana responded directly: 'Every man, be he a writer or not, enjoys lots of freedom in every field while the life of every woman, be she a writer or not, is full of constraints. This is a stark reality' (Tiwana and Kaur 1996: 142). She did not in any way deny inequality. But her position on equality is complex. In the same 1996 interview, she defined a liberated woman as 'The one who has her rights, the one who understands her responsibilities,' noting with reference to a question about feminism that 'So far as the equality of women is concerned, the feminist movement is O.K. but things go wrong when the difference between equal and same is lost sight.' As she noted in an interview with the author of this chapter in 2014: 'women have got some misconceptions about freedom. They think: we are equal, but they forget they are not the same, here comes confusion. They are equal, they should be equal, but not the same. So, when nature has made them different, they should accept difference' (Tiwana and Murphy 2014). Tiwana expressed, therefore, deep ambivalence about the alternatives to a patriarchal order, and what 'equality' might mean within it. 'Revolution,' she noted in the 2014 interview, 'is when you discard the old and adopt the new, and better one—but this is deviation, when you discard the old and you don't know where to go' (ibid.). Again, however, this critique is not staged in simplistic terms. When asked in the 1996 interview, 'How far are women themselves responsible for their oppression and exploitation?' Tiwana responded, 'Quite a bit! If exploitation is wrong, allowing yourself to be exploited is equally wrong. But the thoughts and the personality of a woman is determined by the society and culture whose product she is. Very few women understand the meaning of revolt and can pay the price of revolt' (Tiwana and Kaur 1996: 143). She argued that in portraying 'traditional' women and favouring married women in her portrayals, she portrays the 'evolution' and not the 'revolution' of women (ibid.: 144).

In this interview, then, as in her fiction, Dalip Kaur Tiwana neither rejected the need for liberation nor did she see it in binary terms. Women will 'not hesitate humiliating, even smashing another woman', she said, to get their sense of worth from a man (ibid.: 144). She saw this, and sought to portray it in her novels, stories and novellas: the working of power that women are both subject to and fully participate in, within a patriarchal frame. This frame of patriarchal power does not allow us to know exactly what freedom in fact is, for those within it: a lack of attachments to family and children cannot be defined as a form of liberation for many women, Tiwana suggests in *Twilight*. It is, in fact, a patriarchal order that speaks on behalf of such detachment as 'freedom'. That this frame speaks through women, Tiwana argues in *Twilight*, should not distract us, since a woman's voice is as much formed within patriarchal society as is a man's. Tiwana's position is ultimately framed in universalist humanist terms, as she argued in 2014: 'I think before anything else, in our society, maybe in other societies also, people categorise women according to relationship, she is wife, she is sister, she is mother; first of all she should be treated as human being' (Tiwana and Murphy 2014).

Tiwana's complex perspective—her clear articulation of the inequality between men and women in Punjabi society, and her doubt about what 'freedom' means in the context of that patriarchal society—may reflect the particularities of her positioning, situated in the Indian state of Punjab, in a small city, at a university founded to champion the Punjabi language. She operated far from the national centre in Delhi, and even the celebrated cosmopolitan centre of the nearby city of Chandigarh. It may be that Tiwana—and her particular view on gender—represents an example of the 'critical regionalism' suggested by Butler and Spivak (2007): here, not out of self-conscious rejection of the national, but as a located regionalism that offers a grounded perspective on women's liberation within that context (see also Anantharam 2012: 8), imbedded within a patriarchal order and challenging it from within. Location in a secondary urban centre in Punjab distinguishes Tiwana from both Cour and Pritam, who lived in Delhi after Partition, where perhaps other imagined communities and subjectivities were possible. The place of Punjab offers a particular vantage point, embedded within the patriarchal figurations of the Indian Punjab, and the forms of liberation and change that can be imagined and lived within it.

NOTES

1. Often spelled in English as 'Gurbux'. His epithet *Prīt Laṛī*, 'Chain of Love', refers to the name of the journal he founded in 1933.

2. 'Shahmukhi' refers to a Punjabi-language form of Urdu-modified/ Perso-Arabic script that has been used to write Punjabi for centuries, and is currently prominent in Pakistan.

3. See Tiwana and Murphy (2014) for Dr Tiwana's self-narration of her life story, in a video-taped interview.

4. I have not referred here to the English translation of *Kathā Kaho Urvashī*, which was unavailable to me at the time of writing: Tiwana (2017).

5. All translations are by the author, unless otherwise mentioned.

6. See also, for example, Tiwana (1980), pages 74–75, when a long description is interrupted by a paragraph of commentary on the past, or pages 82–83, when later experiences as an author intervene, without clear connection to the chronological narrative.

7. Gujari is described thus by her friend Sara: 'must have been a queen in a former life' because she is so beautiful (Tiwana 2014: 36).

8. Malhotra and Lambert-Hurley (2015: 7–9) discuss the way autobiography can 'speak for' and 'to' a larger social world.

REFERENCES

Anantharam, Anita. 2012. *Bodies That Remember: Women's Indigenous Knowledge and Cosmopolitanism in South Asian Poetry*. Syracuse, NY: Syracuse University Press.

Boehmer, Elleke. 2005. *Stories of Women: Gender and Narrative in the Postcolonial Nation*. Manchester, UK: Manchester University Press.

Burton, Antoinette. 2003. *Dwelling in the Archive: Women Writing House, Home, and History in Late Colonial India*. New York: Oxford University Press.

Butler, Judith, and Gayatri Chakravorty Spivak. 2007. *Who Sings the Nation-state? Language, Politics, Belonging*. London, New York: Seagull Books.

Chatterjee, Partha. 1993. *The Nation and Its Fragments: Colonial and Postcolonial Histories*. Princeton, NJ: Princeton University Press.

Columeau, Julian. 2019. 'Les mouvements pour le panjabi à Lahore entre 1947 et 1960' [The Movements for Punjabi in Lahore from 1947 to 1960]. Thèse pour obtenir le grade de Docteur de l' École des Hautes Études en Sciences Sociales, Histoire et civilisations [Thesis completed to obtain the degree of doctorate in the School for Advanced Studies in the Social Sciences, History, and Civilizations].

Dhariwal, Parvinder. 2013. 'The Heroine in Modern Punjabi Literature and the Politics of Desire'. Unpublished M.A. thesis, University of British Columbia.

Gopal, Priyamvada. 2005. *Literary Radicalism in India: Gender, Nation, and the Transition to Independence*. London: Routledge.

Gupta, Charu. 2001. *Sexuality, Obscenity, Community: Women, Muslims, and the Hindu Public in Colonial India*. New Delhi: Permanent Black.

Kaur, Birinder, and JapPreet Bhangu. 2011. 'Dalip Kaur Tiwana's *And Such is Her Fate*'. *Muse India* 36 (March–April). Available at https://museindia.com/Home/ViewContentData?arttype=feature&issid=36&menuid=2531 (accessed on 5 September 2023).

Kaur, Narinderjit, and Jai Ratan, tr. 2009. *Twilight; Mark of the Nose-Ring*, by Dalip Kaur Tiwana. New Delhi: National Book Trust.

Mahmood, Saba. 2001. 'Feminist Theory, Embodiment, and the Docile Agent: Some Reflections on the Egyptian Islamic Revival'. *Cultural Anthropology* 16 (2): 202–36.

———. 2005. *Politics of Piety: The Islamic Revival and the Feminist Subject*. E-book. Princeton, NJ: Princeton University Press. Available at https://hdl-handle-net.ezproxy.library.ubc.ca/2027/heb.04721 (accessed 29 April 2020).

Malhotra, Anshu. 2002. *Gender, Caste, and Religious Identities: Restructuring Class in Colonial Punjab*. New Delhi: Oxford University Press.

Malhotra, Anshu, and Siobhan Lambert-Hurley. 2015. 'Introduction'. In *Speaking of the Self: Gender, Performance, and Autobiography in South Asia*, eds Anshu Malhotra and Siobhan Lambert-Hurley, 1–30. Durham, NC: Duke University Press.

Minocha, Arti. 2018. 'Alternative Literary Modernities: A Voice from Colonial Punjab'. *Zeitschrift für Anglistik und Amerikanistik* [Journal of English and American Studies] 66 (1): 35–48.

Murphy, Anne. 2012. *The Materiality of the Past: History and Representation in Sikh Tradition*. New York: Oxford University Press.

_____. 2018. 'Writing Punjabi Across Borders'. *South Asian History and Culture* 9 (1): 68–91.

_____. 2019. 'Punjabi Literature and the Possibility of the Secular in India and Pakistan'. Paper presented at the *Centre de l'études de l'Inde et de l'Asie du Sud* [Centre for Indian and South Asian Studies], 11 June.

_____. 2023a. 'Beyond the Past: Poetry as a Notation of the Present'. In *Bhai Vir Singh (1872–1957): Religious and Literary Modernities in Colonial and Postcolonial Indian Punjab* (Critical Sikh Studies Series), eds Anshu Malhotra and Anne Murphy, 119–34. New York: Routledge.

_____. 2023b. 'The Possibility of the Secular: Sikh Engagements with Modern Punjabi Literature'. In *The Sikh World*, eds Pashaura Singh Arvind-Pal Singh Mandair, 287–99. New York: Routledge

Ray, Sangeeta. 2000. *En-gendering India: Woman and Nation in Colonial and Postcolonial Narratives*. Durham, NC: Duke University Press.

Rode, Ajmer, and Gurleen Cheema. 2021. Interview for the 'Punjabi in BC' Oral History Project. Available online at https://blogs.ubc.ca/annemurphy/research/punjabi-in-bc/writers-journalists/ajmer-rode/ (accessed on 15 October 2023).

Sekhon, Sant Singh, and Kartar Singh Duggal. 1992. *A History of Punjabi Literature*. New Delhi: Sahitya Akademi.

Shandilya, Krupa. 2017. *Intimate Relations: Social Reform and the Late Nineteenth-century South Asian Novel*. Evanston, IL: Northwestern University Press.

Singh, Bhai Vir. 2003[1898]. *Sundarī*. New Delhi: Bhai Vir Singh Sahit Sadan.

Singh, Bhupinder, and S. C. Narula, tr. 1998. *Gone Are the Rivers: Lang Gaye Dariya*, by Dalip Kaur Tiwana. Chennai: Macmillan India Limited.

Singh, Gurdial. 2000[1964]. *Maṛhī dā Dīvā* [The Memorial Lamp]. Ludhiana: Chetna Parkashan.

Singh, K. 1987. *Pragatīvādī Vicāradhārā te Pañjābī Kavitā* [Punjabi Progressive Thought and Punjabi Poetry]. Chandigarh: Aki Prakashan.

Singh, Surinder, director. 1989. *Maṛhī dā Dīvā* [The Memorial Lamp], Film, 115 minutes.

Tasneem, N. S. 2002. *Narrative Modes in Punjabi Novel*. Shimla: Indian Institute of Advanced Study.

Tiwana, Dalip Kaur. 1980. *Naṅge Pairāṅ dā Safar* [Journey on Bare Feet]. Delhi: Nagmani Prakashan.

———. 1990. *Laṅgha Gae Dariā* [Gone are the Rivers]. New Delhi: Navayug Publishers.

———. 1995. *Merī Pratīnidh Rachnā* [My Representative Work]. Patiala: Publications Bureau, Punjabi University Press.

———. 2001[1967]. *Agnī Prīkhiā* [The Fire Test]. New Delhi: Arsi Publications.

———. 2011[1999]. *Kathā Kaho Urvashī* [Tell the Tale, Urvashi]. Samana: Sangam Publishers.

———. 2013[1968]. *Ehu Hamārā Jīvaṇā* [This is Our Life]. Chandigarh: Lokgeet Parkashan.

———. 2014. *Mātā Dharati Mahatu* [The Greatness of the Mother Earth]. Chandigarh: Lokgeet Parkashan.

———. 2017. *Tell the Tale, Urvashi*, tr. Bhupinder Singh. Hyderabad: Orient BlackSwan.

Tiwana, Dalip Kaur, and Anne Murphy. 2014. Interview. Available at http://blogs.ubc.ca/annemurphy/research/modlit/indian-punjab/ and http://hdl.handle.net/2429/71964 (accessed 3 January 2024).

Tiwana, Dalip Kaur, and Iqbal Kaur. 1996. 'Of Women and Tradition: Dalip Kaur Tiwana in Conversation with Iqbal Kaur'. *Indian Literature* 39 (5) (175): 142–44.

Six

THE CIVIL SERVANT AND SUPER COP

MODESTY, SECURITY AND THE STATE IN PUNJAB*

INDERPAL GREWAL

In a postcolonial state such as India, the making of the nation-state has been an unstable project almost from its inauguration, requiring the repression of uprisings and insurgencies both at the borders and in the interior with the use of colonial-era military and police (Singh 2000). The Indian nation-state has long seen security as a key project for nation-building. How to secure the border from within as well as from outside has been a continual

*My most grateful thanks to Mrs Bajaj for sharing her memories and her documents with me. I had a wonderful research assistant, Kirin Jessel, who took notes and transcribed interviews. I could not have done this without her help. Thanks also to Kamaldeep Gill, who was kind enough to share her deep knowledge of Chandigarh and the Indian Administrative Service (IAS) bureaucracy, and her husband Sukhjit. My thanks also to Maninder and Minty Grewal for allowing me to talk about this case endlessly; to Justice Kuldip Singh for answering my questions, and Gurminder Kaur, his partner, for her insights. I also have to thank all those in Chandigarh and Punjab who were so forthcoming and open to my questions. Many thanks also to librarians at the Centre for Women's Development Studies (CWDS), Deepa Singhal, Vijay Kumar, Madhushree, Anju Vyas, and to CWDS for being so helpful and enabling my research.

project since Independence (Bhan 2013; Telford 2001). Direct and proxy wars with Pakistan and China, and insurgencies in Kashmir, Punjab, Mizoram, Assam, Ladakh and Bengal (to name just a few) have all led to a continued concern with borders, security and territoriality, as the nation-state's boundary-making is always in process. Inaugurated by communal and sexual violence during Partition, this process of security and nation-building has been a gendered and sexualised project, with numerous allegations of sexual assault by military and police, and protection of women seen as property of one patriarchy or another. As the Centre continues to enable and use violence (gendered and sexualised) for counter-insurgency, feminist engagement and activism against such state security projects and the question of the relation between feminism and the state remain important. The focus on the state and legal activism means that the use of laws that give impunity to military and security forces in counter-insurgency operations has been a focus of feminist protest (Bora 2010; Duschinski et al. 2018; Human Rights Watch 2009), even as feminist scholars and activists debate whether legal remedies are enough to address endemic forms of violence and subordination based on gender and sexuality.

In order to examine the interconnections of feminist activism, gender, security and the continued politics of territoriality, I focus on the crisis of the Indian state in the 1980s through the period of the Sikh-Khalistan movements and the Indian counter-insurgency against that movement in the state of Punjab. Most accounts suggest that Indira Gandhi's use of religious division was responsible for beginning a new phase of communalism in the service of electoral politics, especially after she declared the Emergency in 1975 and suspended all elections and civil liberties (Noorani 1990; Prakash 2019; Puri 1985). By the 1970s and 1980s, her discourse of one minority community, the Sikhs, as intrinsically violent, or as 'terrorists', became widespread in the dominant media in both vernacular and English-language press, responding also to the emerging movement for a separate Sikh nation, and after the assassination of Indira Gandhi by her Sikh bodyguard, leading to a pogrom against Sikhs in Delhi and several other Indian cities (Van Dyke 1996). In such representations, Sikh males were presented and recuperated as hypermasculine and therefore a violent threat to the nation; a long history of war, religion and military service in the pre-colonial period and during British rule over-determined a warrior masculinity within this group, enabling this representation to become weaponised by the Indian state (Chowdhry 2013b; Sinha 1995; Streets 2004). In the postcolonial state, however, the use of this masculinity for counter-insurgency by the state, deployed on both sides of the struggle, made it much more suspect, leaving openings to challenge both the state and this masculinity, even as the security state's power remained overwhelming (Axel 2001; Singh and Purewal 2013).

The particular challenge to the security state in Punjab that emerged within the Indian state's counter-insurgency operations came in the form of an incident of sexual harassment (as it was called) and its court cases, which I examine in this chapter. This is the case of Rupan Deol Bajaj v. K. P. S. Gill, often referred to in India as the 'butt-slapping case' (Admin Lawnn 2015) which, seemingly about sexual harassment, and sometimes seen as trivial, opened up questions about what militarised security meant, who it protected and what it looked like on the ground for women in the state. It is a case that the Supreme Court directed as concerning Section 354 and Section 509 of the Indian Penal Code (IPC) (though Bajaj invoked other IPC sections that the SC decided were not relevant). These statutes, though distinct from those concerning rape, are linked to them by the focus on violence against women; as feminist scholars have pointed out, they rely on notions of female respectability rather than sexual rights or sexual autonomy for women. Section 354 of the IPC concerns the 'assault of criminal force to woman with intent to outrage her modesty':

> Whoever assaults or uses criminal force to any woman, intending to outrage or knowing it to be likely that he will thereby outrage her modesty, shall be punished with

> imprisonment of either description for a term which may extend to two years, or with fine, or with both (The Indian Penal Code 1860a).

Section 509 states:

> Whoever, intending to insult the modesty of any woman, utters any word, makes any sound or gesture, or exhibits any object, intending that such word or sound shall be heard, or that such gesture or object shall be seen, by such woman, or intrudes upon the privacy of such woman, shall be punished with simple imprisonment for a term which may extend to one year, or with fine, or with both (The Indian Penal Code 1860b).

Both sections recuperate problematic notions regarding women, given that the laws came from a colonial era that reflected a Victorian view of women, and the Supreme Court came to define modesty in ways that enshrined patriarchal ideas of women's behaviour.[1] While the Supreme Court ruling of 1996 found that Mrs Bajaj was justified in drawing on these statutes to claim she had been a victim of a crime, Justice Mukherjee's ruling cited a previous case, *Punjab v. Singh*, which he said established that 'a woman's modesty is her sex and from her very birth she possesses the modesty which is the attribute of her sex' (Bajaj v. Gill 1996).[2] The enduring problem with these statutes is that, as with trials concerning rape, they have long kept women from reporting assaults because then it was their modesty that is being adjudicated in the courts. However, this eventuality did not happen in the case of *Rupan Deol Bajaj v. K.P.S. Gill* since Mrs Bajaj was open about what had transpired with her, pursued the case vigorously despite great opposition by the government anxious to protect the perpetrator, and saw herself as a role model for women to speak out. The Bajaj v. Gill case continued for about 10 years, going through the Punjab and Haryana High Court and the Supreme Court, which gave its final judgement in 2005 upholding the conviction by the High Court, and handing down to Gill a sentence of probation for three months and a small fine of Rs 200,000 (Admin Lawnn 2015).

Most analyses of the case suggest its inadequacy in helping all groups of women in the struggle against sexual harassment. Martha Nussbaum writes that the case 'divides women by caste, class, occupation, and marital status, ultimately strengthening norms of proper female conduct that are subversive of women's equality' (2003: 635). Writing about the broader question of legal feminism, Ratna Kapur (2001) has argued that much of the sexual harassment law in India has enshrined conservative sexual morality and disregarded their sexual autonomy. While there is no doubt that the statutes and the judgment are both problematic with regard to constraining women's sexuality and behaviour, a closer examination of questions of historical and social context might suggest why the case became notorious and noteworthy. I show in this chapter that the word 'modesty' came to mean much more than the lack of sexual autonomy that it is often taken to imply, and that the politics of respectability could be a broader question about power and position for women within a state continually struggling to control its borders and populations. The context of a patriarchal security state, with the collaboration of male power across state and community, requires us to engage with a more contextual understanding of modesty vis-à-vis the state, and to see how women, even those elite and powerful, struggle against forms of subordination and humiliation that emerge from gendered institutions, for which they come to blame the security state that takes away their rights. Elite women are thus torn between a feminism that allows them the claim to be models for women and the state that gives them the power to become role models by subjecting them to a state patriarchy as well as by acknowledging the gendered injustice done to them. While there is little doubt that elite class and caste status gives them access to the state, their interventions against the postcolonial security state can impact not only the politics of gender and sexuality, but also that of security and militarism.

This broader understanding would explain why the case resonated so much in the region, and why it was covered so extensively in the news. The plaintiff, Mrs Bajaj, as well as many women in the region saw the case as a victory for women against sexual harassment; Chandigarh-based newspaper *The Tribune* noted, 'Women, particularly college lecturers and human rights activists, were in an upbeat mood' after the final verdict, and politician Simranjit Mann said that the punishment 'could have given solace to other women who had suffered at the hands of Mr. K.P.S. Gill' (*The Tribune* 1996c). Though the judgement resonated more so in Punjab in the context of the violence of counter-insurgency, it continues to be mentioned as an important case, despite its limited impact on sexual harassment law.[3] The case thus requires us to think about gender in a more intersectional and contextual way, which would then address why it did not have a large impact on sexual harassment law, and would reveal how gender exists in relation to other institutionalised identities and what modesty meant to the woman at the centre of the scandal. Thus, it is necessary to turn to understanding history and culture in addition to legal judgments and case law, and to broaden the framework of feminist engagement with the state to address the violence of securitisation and militarised repression. One might even call Mrs Bajaj a 'citizen-litigant' as 'political actor', as Rohit De (2018a) terms the many marginalised persons who filed writs in the courts, though she was a much more powerful elite than the litigants that De tracks.

I suggest that despite its limited remit regarding women and sexual harassment, *Rupan Deol Bajaj v. K.P.S. Gill*, in its itinerary through different courts, did have a role in challenging the security state in Punjab on the grounds that the security of even elite women became visible as being distinct from the question of state security. The context of the period of counter-insurgency and militancy and the question of the protection of women by the security state make this case noteworthy and historically important. That the courts ruled for Mrs Bajaj and against Mr Gill said a great deal about the ability and determination of both Mrs Bajaj and the courts in challenging the security state, which had initially tried (through the Governor and the police chief Julio Ribeiro) to dismiss and bury the charges.[4] The case created headlines and speculation, grabbing the front pages of newspapers in both Punjab and nationally, revealing that police power was unchecked and problematic and that it would affect not only rural Punjab but also urban elites. Yet, it was remarkable that a woman, though an elite bureaucrat, would ruffle the waters of the security state by accusing the chief police officer of harassment, and that the courts would repeatedly rule in her favour, even if the penalties to the harasser were less than severe and admittedly nominal. Gill was not just the second-in-command to police chief Julio Ribeiro at the time, but would also later rise to replace Ribeiro. He also belonged to the Jat caste, the dominant caste in the state, as did Deol; both were Sikhs, though Bajaj had married a Hindu, a fellow Indian Administrative Service (IAS) officer, so that she was always seen as someone who had broken religious norms (though not class norms) and for whom respectability was always a concern. She came from a military family, well-known in the region for having started a school for those hoping to enter the Indian army. She was herself deeply attached to the military, as was often the case for her caste and community.

The case is thus noteworthy because of its principals, two powerful people, both government officers with a lively sense of their power and position. It continued a tradition of civil service litigation, a frequent use of court cases filed by civil servants who have had success in the courts.[5] As Upendra Baxi pointed out, the contradiction in such cases is that those who deprive others of their rights as civil servants are very careful and litigious about their own as rights-bearing citizens; Baxi also suggested, and as Rohit De points out, that such jurisprudence provided openings for others to pursue such rights claims (Baxi 2007; De 2018b). Therefore, it is not surprising that we see a civil servant filing a case against another civil servant. The case is also important because it did challenge the security state, though on the basis of two problematic assumptions: one about women's essential character of 'modesty' and the other of the Sikh male, of the Jat caste, as threatening and uncontrolled. In Punjab, it opened up questions about the ways that civil governance had been replaced by a police state since people saw Gill, a police officer, openly enacting his power over the civil administration and bureaucracy, showing that he believed that Bajaj, a civil servant, would have to submit to him. It also opened up issues of caste as two Sikhs from the Jat caste clashed in the courts, revealing that it was not just Jat culture that was patriarchal but also the police state. Moreover, it threw the heterogeneity of the state and conflicts within it into relief.[6]

THE SOCIAL AND HISTORICAL CONTEXT

During the insurgency in Punjab, the Indian state enacted a set of laws giving large-scale power to the security state. The National Security Act, enacted in 1980 to address the 'anti-social and anti-national elements', was amended in 1984 (the year of Indira Gandhi's assassination and the subsequent killings of Sikhs in New Delhi) with reference to the 'extremist' and 'terrorist elements' in the state. The terms 'terrorist' and 'extremist' were used widely in newspapers and by the state, along with terms such as 'militant', thus yoking together the representation of the insurgency as the work of religious 'extremists'.[7] In 1985, the government passed the Terrorist and Disruptive Activities Act (TADA) with a time limit of two years, but this was extended in 1987, and then in 1989, 1991 and 1993. Within this Act, terms such as 'terrorist', 'abetment of terrorist act', and 'disruptive activity' were defined broadly to enable police and security forces the maximum latitude to use violence with impunity. Under this Act, trials could occur wherever the state wanted and without the presence of the accused or his/her lawyer, with secret witnesses and in camera; bail could be denied and the arrested person could be detained without bail for one year. Finally, no government officer could be taken to any court for any actions which they had done in what was called 'good faith' in pursuant of the Act.[8] Though some of these laws have been ended, similar ones continue in Kashmir, and cases of sexual assault by the military in that region have also become famous (Human Rights Watch and Physicians for Human Rights 1993).

As a result of acts such as TADA, which was upheld by the Supreme Court, police violations, extrajudicial killings and disappearances became widespread. The Supreme Court, in its judgment upholding the constitutionality of the Act, argued that national security trumped the abuses of power, that is, people could be killed but that was allowed (*Kartar Singh v. State of Punjab* 1994). According to the National Human Rights Commission, the Punjab Police registered 17,529 cases under the Act between 1985 and 1994, when the Act expired (Human Rights Watch 2007). Former Home Minister Rajesh Pilot revealed that over 60,000 people had been detained since TADA came into force (Kumar et al. 2003) and the TADA review committee found an incorrect use of the law in thousands of cases.[9] There is little doubt that these abuses occurred because police in Punjab increased its numbers and capabilities for surveillance and gathering information, and collaborated with the Border Security Force (BSF) and the Central Reserve Police Force (CRPF) to increase counter-insurgency practices against what came to be called 'terrorism' (Lobo 1992).

The chief of police credited with ending the insurgency was K. P. S. Gill, a Jat Sikh who became notorious for his ruthlessness and his policies of rewarding policemen for killing the so-called terrorists. Gill had earlier served as director general of the CRPF and had been inspector general of the BSF in Jammu; he had also been posted in Assam where he had become notorious for his violent policing tactics (Karmakar 2017). Because of his experience with the border and with several police forces, the Central government brought him to his home state and allowed him to use similar tactics against his own Sikh and Punjabi communities. His policies included creating secret bands of policemen to carry out counter-strikes against so-called terrorists and their families as well as against anyone protesting his practices; new forms of surveillance and mapping of 'hot spots' came into use, alongside an increase in numbers of police personnel. In fact, Gill used the historical and colonial brutality of the police force (Verma 2008) and their caste and class positions within rural and urban Punjab by allowing them to use violence, including against those with whom individual policemen had personal vendettas. Policemen were rewarded on the basis of how many alleged 'terrorists' they killed in what were euphemistically called 'encounters' (Human Rights Watch/Asia and Physicians for Human Rights 1994; *The Economic Times* 2017).

Gill himself was open about his uncompromising views on security. In his account of the counter-insurgency in Punjab, as well as in later writings about security, which for him was about fighting 'terrorism', Gill advocated the 'use of coercive force…(as) a fundamental obligation and duty of constitutional government', seeing any negotiations with 'terrorists' as 'appeasement' (Gill n.d. a). As a 'security' expert and in his 'Opinion' pieces in journals such as *South Asia Intelligence Review*, *Seminar* and *The Pioneer*, and newspapers such as *The Hindustan Times*, he continued to advocate maximum force against any who he deemed 'terrorists', disdaining any political solutions, and stating that his principle was that 'there can be no compromise with terrorists; all such compromises reward terrorism' (Gill n.d. b). There is little reflection in his writings concerning the political use of terming a group as 'terrorist', and in his book on the Khalistan movement, *Punjab, the Knights of Falsehood*, he sees the movement as a political struggle by the Akali party that misused religion to advocate for a separate state and that was put down with the help of right-thinking Sikhs such as himself (Gill 1997a). Such a narrative leaves out the complex economic, political and social issues that animated the conflict, including the political relations between the then Prime Minister Indira Gandhi and the politicians in Punjab. In his words, actions and policies, Gill seemed to embody a warrior masculinity and patriarchy, one that ultimately opened him up to charges of the use of excessive force and human rights violations.

Like so many in Punjab, however, it was the Partition and its violence that forged his masculinity. His nephew, Hartosh Bal, begins his (sort of) obituary and defence of Gill's record with an incident that he tells us Gill liked to narrate (Bal 2017). According to Bal's account of Gill, when in Lahore during Partition, Gill's mother handed him a sword and asked him to kill his sister (Bal's mother) if she was in danger (of sexual assaults by Muslim men—a point not made but understood by Bal's readers). This narrative reveals how the postcolonial state is forged through patriarchy, as feminist scholars have pointed out, and it seems to be one that Gill remembered as formative (according to Bal). It is also an often repeated narrative of those who lived through the period, as it worked to enforce the idea that women were to be protected and their men were protectors, and that a woman who was raped was better off dead; it enabled male power over women and the right of men to kill their womenfolk in the name of protection (Das 2008; Jayawardena and Zakaria 2016; Kandiyoti 1991; Menon and Bhasin 1998; Mookherjee 2008; Sinha and Walkowitz 2006). Such a patriarchal notion no doubt contributed to Gill's self-perception of one who protects the nation and its border, but for whom women are subordinate—a patriarchal ideology that was shared by many in the region as well as by the state. Interestingly, though the obituary is meant to defend Gill by arguing that he reduced violence during his tenure as police chief (a case made by using information from Gill's writings and the Institute of Conflict Management), it ignores the sexual harassment case.

Gill's patriarchal masculinity, though constructed in the violence of the Partition, was also augmented by his policing work. He had gained a reputation for brutal tactics during his time in Assam, and he continued to rely on them, but also showed himself as a leader using a warrior masculinity. He asserted his power as the head of police, often going with other policemen on night-time raids against militants, with the goal of displaying a control of territory by the police and the security state. But in Punjab, he also used his religious identity, displaying his adherence to the Sikh religion and showing that he was a true Sikh, unlike the militants. He created a commando force from within the police, who were almost exclusively Sikh, and urged them to wear turbans and keep beards to display their Sikh identity; he picked those with tall physiques, dressed them in black uniforms and gave them more advanced weapons than the rest of the force. He was extremely proud of the force, referring to them as his 'boys' (Chima 2014). Joyce Pettigrew has argued that the Khalistan insurgent movement was defeated 'not by the massive array of state force' but by 'the features of traditional rural society such as family feuds and vendettas and allegiances based on friendship or on shared hatreds' (1995: 174). Though it is clear that family feuds and vendettas played a role, these features were neither wholly 'traditional' nor the sole reason for the failure of the movement. The use of counter-insurgency policing was a colonial and postcolonial feature of law and order, one that relied on local knowledge and Sikh male identity produced around the notion of the 'martial race' to claim that the counter-insurgency and the state were true Sikhs. By using his Sikh identity to show that the militants were false Sikhs—'knights of falsehood', as he would term them in a later book (Gill 1997a)—Gill's goal was to turn the population against the movement.

It is not simply the British military that determined the warrior masculinity that Gill displayed, since it came also from a longer history of struggle and military prowess (Dhavan 2014). Caste identity was also key since Gill and Deol both belonged to the Jat caste that controlled a majority of agricultural land and was also politically and religiously dominant in Punjab. In this domination, the Indian state has been complicit since it enabled the patriarchy by ensuring male inheritance over agricultural land, a law that did not change even when women's equal rights in inheritance were ensured in law through changes in 2005. Patriarchal power was such that women often gave up their rights to land in favour of brothers and husbands, as anthropologist Srimati Basu (2001) argues. Historian Prem Chowdhry (2013a) relates that after a change in inheritance laws in 1956 that threatened male inheritance (though it left out agricultural property), the courts were full of men with women in tow who were giving up their rights to land. Punjabi masculinity was not, however, wholly in service to the colonial and postcolonial state since Sikh men were active in the anti-colonial struggle; this masculinity was also revolutionary, as evidenced by Bhagat Singh and those in the anti-colonial Ghadar Party. This revolutionary history, allied to a history of religious reform, also emerged in the Bhindranwale movement in the 1980s.

Gill's cultivation of his religiosity was part of the image he created to gain support from the Sikh community, despite his use of violence against young men in rural Punjab. The government, both at the Centre and in Punjab, allowed Gill full control over the counter-insurgency operations (Chima 2014), since he was adamant that any political interference would lead to failure to suppress the insurgency. Because Punjab was a border state, the Central government enabled multiple police and military to be deployed because the insurgency was understood to be a geopolitical rather than an internal matter, as the insurgents were believed to be in collaboration with Pakistan (Claiborne 1984).

Hailed as 'supercop' and awarded a high civilian honour in India, the Padma Shri, K. P. S. Gill came to be regarded as an expert in 'security' matters, founding the Institute for Conflict Management, and until his death in 2017 he wrote a regular column on terror and policing, turning his attention especially to Kashmir and Pakistan. After the 2002 pogrom of Muslims in Gujarat, he was appointed security advisor for a brief period by Gujarat Chief Minister Narendra Modi. However, his work on behalf of the state did not lead to a high position and he ended up as the president of the Indian Hockey Federation (a position that is both valued in the nationalist context and yet irrelevant to many in the new economy), a thankless job from which he was fired after dismal results by the Indian team (Vinayak 1996). It was also an insulting appointment, given that Gill saw himself as a security expert, and it deployed a stereotype of Sikhs as athletes—bodies and not brains. But it was also the sexual harassment case against him that led to his downfall, especially when he was denied appointment as security advisor in Assam. He became an embarrassment, not just accused of enabling human rights violations[10] but also mired in a case of sexual harassment and convicted of having violated Section 354 of the IPC by 'violating the modesty of a woman' and Section 509, using 'word, gesture intruding on the privacy of a woman'.

THE CASE: *RUPAN DEOL BAJAJ V. K.P.S. GILL*

From newspaper reports, interviews with informants, court rulings and from Mrs Bajaj, whom I met in 2006, I gleaned the following story: In 1988, in the period in Punjab when the insurgency movement against the government was in full force, Mr Gill was at a party hosted by the principal secretary, the highest ranked IAS officer of Punjab state based in Chandigarh.

During the party, Mr Gill got drunk and 'molested' (her term) Mrs Rupan Deol Bajaj by beckoning her to come with him and then slapping her behind. According to Mrs Bajaj, she complained to the host and Mr Gill was sent home. Mrs Bajaj also found out later, as she related to me, that he had behaved inappropriately with a young woman at the same party, and this young woman and her parents left hurriedly without making any complaints, though others knew what had happened. She also discovered that Gill had the reputation of misbehaving and had been instructed, when appointed to his position in Punjab, not to go out in the evenings. The next day, Mrs Bajaj complained to her boss, the chief secretary (also a fellow IAS officer), at his home as well as to Mr Ribeiro, who was Mr Gill's boss as the director general of police. As Mrs Bajaj narrated to me, Mr Ribeiro wrote down the complaint but refused to do anything with it. She went to the Governor, Mr S. S. Ray, who told her that the police force 'would be demoralised' if the incident were to be made public since Gill was a leader for the police, upon which she responded that she too was a role model for women. He also offered her any job posting that she or her husband wished to have, and to end another legal case in which they were entangled.

The first information report (FIR) was accepted but later quashed on the ground that it was a trivial matter (*The Tribune* 1989), and the judicial magistrate accepted the Chandigarh Police's account that the case was 'untraceable'. Mrs Bajaj then complained to the Governor of Punjab, Mr S. S. Ray, who had been appointed as governor during this period of President's rule, and to the IAS Association and IAS Women Officers Association. She told me that Mr Ray's response was that he 'has decided to forgive Mr. KPS Gill in the interest of the nation'. She was summoned to meet Mr Ribeiro, the police chief under whom Gill worked, who put her complaint in an envelope, sealed it and told her she would have to file a writ of mandamus to have it opened. She responded by sending a copy to the press and making the complaint public. The chief secretary, her boss, told her not to make a mountain out of a molehill and that she should be afraid in the current circumstances: 'You are very lucky that nothing more happened to you.'

According to Mrs Bajaj, while she was struggling to petition the courts to lodge her case, Mr Gill filed a separate petition in the court seeking to dismiss Mrs Bajaj's case on the grounds that she was, as she recalled to me, a 'terrorist or acting at the behest of forces out to weaken Government's resolve to fight with terrorism'. The cases continued, with the Supreme Court instructing the chief judicial magistrate (CJM) to take up the case under Sections 354 and 509 (*Bajaj v. Gill*, A. I. R. 1996 S.C. at 313). It is important also to find the patriarchal logic even in the argument of the defence, as I later discovered while reading news reports, when in the hearing before the CJM, Mr Gill's lawyer, Mr Faqir Chand Aggarwal, argued that the incident could not have happened because Mrs Bajaj had not immediately sought out her husband instead of complaining to the host. As Aggarwal stated, 'Every Indian woman's husband tried to save the honour of his wife till the last drop of his blood' (*The Tribune* 1996a). Aggarwal's argument was two-fold: Bajaj was not respectable because she complained to her boss, and she was a liar because any modest woman would have complained first to her husband and then kept quiet. Thus, according to the defence, the case about modesty could not be upheld because by going to the courts and to her boss, she was, *ipso facto*, not modest.

Despite this argument, Mr Gill lost his case. Gill was fined Rs 500 and given three months' rigorous imprisonment (*The Tribune* 1996b). Though Mrs Bajaj was not present, Mr Bajaj was there and stated that the verdict 'was an indictment of the Punjab government as also the Home Ministry', naming former Punjab Governor S. S. Ray and Chief Secretary Ojha who, Mr Bajaj said, had tried to 'save' Mr Gill (ibid.). Gill appealed again but the sessions judge upheld the conviction with a fine of Rs 200,000, with another Rs 50,000 to reimburse Mrs Bajaj for expenses for the litigation, though he reduced the prison sentence to three years' probation.[11] Gill appealed once again but the Punjab and Haryana High Court upheld the verdict, though it reduced the probation period to one year (Negi 2005). Mrs Bajaj told me that she had heard that these judges who ruled in her favour were afraid for their lives because of the power of Gill and the police at the time; the CJM had to leave his house and sleep in other houses to be safe. The appeal continued up to the Supreme Court. In 1989, the Government of India awarded Gill a Padma Shri, an award given to recognise distinguished achievement in arts and public service. Ninety-five IAS and Indian Police Service (IPS) officers wrote to the prime minister, protesting the award.[12] The court cases continued until 2005 when, in a final judgment, the Supreme Court ruled in Bajaj's favour, upholding the judgements of the lower courts, awarding her Rs 200,000 as compensation which she donated to women's groups (*The Times of India* 2005).

Following the verdict, *Hindustan Times*' (2005) editorial proclaimed the judgement was 'Too modest, too late', that the verdict 'disappoints' because 'the punishment meted out has been reduced to nothing more than the equivalent of a traffic challan (violation)'. It wrote: 'This, after all, is the man who rid Punjab of terrorism.... It's another matter altogether that the accused remains to this day unfazed and unashamed by his indiscretion.' The editorial reveals the mixed reactions of many people to this case: dislike of Gill but praise for ending the insurgency. However, it is also remarkable that in 2005, the editorial supported Bajaj, even though when the scandal first emerged she was vilified in most news media for disrupting the counter-insurgency efforts of the state and for making too much of a small incident.

Mrs Bajaj recounted that she was dissuaded by all, including the then Punjab Governor S. S. Ray, to file any charges against Gill: 'He (the governor) went to the extent of requesting me not to press charge against Gill for he was fighting a national battle against terrorism. I told Ray that I didn't share his perception of national interest,' she said, adding that it would have been against the national interest of women had she kept quiet. She mentioned how several government officials in the IAS—including then chief secretary R. P. Ojha—the Governor and the Governor's security advisor asked her to withdraw the complaint 'in the interest of the nation', saying that if she went public with the complaint then 'the entire police force will be demoralized'. She went on to say that she could not agree 'since…my notion of national interest differed from theirs'. It is important to note that her career did suffer as a result, and she was given jobs that were akin to demotions (Kang 1995).

When I interviewed Mrs Bajaj in 2006, she framed her recollections in terms of her resistance to 'the silence imposed on Indian women to not complain'. The silencing of women was what she spoke about at some length, and she said she was proud that she had gone public with the accusation even though it had not been easy: 'The honour lies in not letting people know what has happened,' she said.[13] She recalled that she was brought up to be equal to men; she had been ranked very high in the IAS entrance exams and had served in prestigious positions in the civil service: 'I had held diverse positions where I've had eight to ten thousand men working under me.' She remembered that the press had vilified her, and one columnist, who was also a woman, had written, 'what was a few inches of ass compared to national honour'. Since it was a time of terror, she was told that Gill would have her 'disappear' as he had so many others, that 'it was known that Gill had power of life and death over everyone...anything could have happened'. She mentioned that since a major human rights lawyer had been killed by the police during that time, she was afraid for her life but felt that if she could not protest sexual harassment, then nobody would be able to. 'I have accomplished a precedent...a shift in the mindset of people,' she said, adding that the 'consequences of not complaining are a permanent lowering of one's self estimation, and it somehow gets that hurt internalized forever'. She continued that, on the other hand, the 'consequences of complaining are also worst...it's something that the entire society almost seeks to destroy you', but she had not anticipated that 'a mountain would fall on my head'.

In my conversation with her, it seems that it was not simply a question of modesty for Mrs Bajaj, but rather a sense of humiliation before a gathering of her friends and peers, a lack of respect evidenced by Gill for her accomplishments and position in the bureaucracy and society. It was clear that Mrs Bajaj saw herself as a leader for women, both in her role as an IAS officer and as a woman leading in the struggle against sexual harassment. She saw her case as a victory for women's struggle against sexual harassment in the workplace. For instance, in an interview with *The Times of India*, she stated, 'I have alone suffered through 18 agonizing years. For me it's not relief but there's hope for millions of working women who face similar male behaviour at the work place' (Awasthi 2005). Adding that it has sent a signal that working women should not put up with these indignities, she went on to say that she saw her case as 'not just a battle against KPS Gill but against the mindset of the administration and society that condones such acts' (ibid.). She expressed a powerful discourse of female subjectivity and struggle, through which she was simultaneously part of the state in her capacity to excel and compete but not part of the state in the subordination she experienced. In addition, what she expressed to me was her lack of power even as she saw herself as part of the powerful machinery of the state, which she had utilised by getting the support of her fellow IAS officers and which had probably protected her. She emphasised that she had spent most of her life either aspiring to be in the bureaucracy or being a high-ranked official within it; she was also the wife of another high-ranking official. To many, she would have been the image of the state's power. But in this case, she expressed that she now felt powerless, abandoned by the state and society, and subjugated to them. In the interviews that she gave to the media in 2005, she blamed 'the mindset' of the people and of the 'administration' for its refusal to address her injury (see BBC News 2017).

In my conversations with a number of people in Chandigarh in 2006, soon after the final judgment from the Supreme Court, many remembered the case vividly even though it was almost two decades since the incident had occurred, probably because the Supreme Court's ruling had just been in the news. In a context in Punjab where the time of terror from the1980s is not often spoken about in everyday interactions, its victims unheard by the courts and ignored in the press, the coverage was noteworthy. But my interlocutors expressed a variety of opinions about Mrs Bajaj. I heard people who appreciated her courage and her persistence in pursuing her case. There were others who said she had had a prior liaison with Gill, and since she had herself crossed caste and religious boundaries to marry outside her community, she was not 'what she seemed to be'. This comment confirmed the reason why Bajaj had continued to press the case to establish her 'modesty' in the face of such notions of respectability, as constituted simply by class and endogamy. Several informants, diverse in gender and caste, told me that although they detested Mr Gill, they doubted Mrs Bajaj's motives. They said that since she and her husband had been mired in other litigation around charges of corruption prior to this event, perhaps she was using this incident to get out of that problem. There were others who believed her because they were suspicious of the police and its power over the population. Here, one could note the suspicions of ordinary people vis-à-vis the elite bureaucracy, who are often seen as corrupt and too powerful (Gould 2010).

Most of those I spoke with about the case condemned the violence of the state's counter-insurgency tactics that were led by Mr Gill, though some believed that this violence was necessary to put down the insurgency. The case enabled condemnation of police tactics, with one former member of the Legislative Assembly of Punjab reported as saying that the incident had 'ripped open the all-pervading disease from which the Punjab police and bureaucracy suffered' and that 'depraved and degenerate politicians had been replaced by an equally, if not more, depraved and degenerate bureaucracy and policemen' (*The Tribune* 1988a). However, there were opinions that said that the reason why no harm had come to Mrs Bajaj, as it would have for a less privileged woman, was because she was an elite bureaucrat and part of the state. People sought motives and reasons for the victories in the courts for Mrs Bajaj, and she was seen as a complex person and not universally liked for a variety of reasons: that she was an elite bureaucrat, she was also seen as corrupt, but also because she had married out of caste and religion. She was a visible manifestation of state power, but also disliked for being so. Talk about her assault was thus a way to suggest that the state was not only corrupt, but also riven with factionalism and sexual misconduct.

Yet it was also her personal history that allowed people to question her motives and the 'modesty' argument from Sections 354 and 509. The Supreme Court's construction of modesty as an essential category for women did not completely coincide with Mrs Bajaj's notion of herself as a Jat, as a member of a powerful military family and as a powerful and experienced civil servant. It did mesh with her sense of herself as a respectable woman, even if she had crossed caste and religious lines in marriage to a fellow IAS officer. Her construction of women's modesty, as I learned, was more a matter of being respected for all these aspects rather than having any essential category of modesty. By all accounts (in ways that echoed Gill's lawyer's argument), she had been quite immodest in pursuing the case and in speaking openly about the incident. Her framework was thus not wholly coincident with the legal framework that she had used and was enjoined to use by the courts.

Institutional Contexts: *The Security State v. Civil Administration*

It was evident from my interview with Mrs Bajaj that her identity as an IAS officer and as a woman bureaucrat was important to her sense of herself. She had felt powerful in her position and abilities. She mentioned that she had done extremely well in the entrance exams to the service and that she had held high positions, managed hundreds of people and done well in her profession. While she had not reached the height of the profession, as had her husband, she had reached powerful positions. Such a career trajectory is not surprising since, within the IAS itself, women have had a mixed reception and their history in the IAS has to do with class and caste as much as with gender. One study of a survey reported that most of the women bureaucrats came from upper-middle class, upper-caste, professional and urban backgrounds, and were English-educated (Sahai-Achutan 1989). Though more recently the demographic of civil servants has been changing to include more rural elites (Fernandes 2006), far fewer women than men came from rural or poor families (Benbabaali 2008). In the service, women tended to be given the 'softer' positions in health, education and social services sectors, while men typically were given the 'field' postings that sent them to rural or isolated areas (Bhatia and Chawla 2022; Rana 2020). Such postings had consequences because the 'field' postings led to greater advancement.

Despite more women entering this elite service, the issue of sexual harassment within the service has had a history of silence (Bhattacharyya 2017), although some concessions have been made by male officers acknowledging gender bias. Sanjoy Bagchi, for instance, writes in his memoirs of his years in the service that though women in the IAS have excelled in the entrance exams, there remains a 'subtle invidious discrimination' so that competent women have been 'thwarted of the opportunity of working in the range of really responsible and challenging jobs merely because of spoken or unspoken inhibitions against entrusting the job to a woman' (Bagchi 2007: 153–54). After this admission, however, he goes on to say that while sexual harassment happens, he consulted one study of the problem and found that not one male respondent thought that this was a problem. The only two cases he had heard of were about Mrs Bajaj and of an 'uncivilized Bihari' who had 'misbehaved with a woman colleague' (ibid.: 158). In another instance, he mentions a horrifying case of assault on a woman officer, who was physically assaulted by the chief minister's party men and had acid thrown on her face, disfiguring her for life, but does not see it as a gendered form of violence. Instead, he cites this instance as an example of the politicising of the job by Indira Gandhi's government rather than an example of gendered violence (Bagchi 2007). It is possible to conclude that sexual harassment, especially of single women officers, was quite frequent, but there was no way to redress the problem since there was little sympathy from male officers or seniors who thought women made too much about a small problem. Yet it is clear from the studies that many of these women officers face large and small problems, from issues such as a lack of toilets for women in government offices to the problem of moving with the job for women with families (Rana 2020).

It is not surprising then that Mrs Bajaj's identity as an IAS officer was a key aspect of the case, as was the perception of her supposed sexual availability or lack of respectability because she had married a man of her choice instead of being in an arranged marriage. Her work status was also an issue because in the context of state security, the civil administration had lost much of its power. In the pursuit of border security, the control of governance over the state was shifted to the police.

The state came under President's rule from 1987 to 1992, under the control of the Centre, and the state government was dismissed. Though President's rule meant that the Governor of the state was in control, in Punjab it meant that it was the highest level of police which came to be in control, which ended up with K. P. S. Gill in charge from 1988 to 1990 and then from 1991 to 1995. Another police officer recollected that 'the State of Punjab finally ended up, by 1994, being a Police State—of the police, by the police and for the police', so much so that there was no other government nor rights for people (Danewalia 1997: 451). The police and Gill, given a large infusion of money, arms and personnel, became so powerful that civil administrators and government officers felt subservient to Gill and complained about their loss of authority to the then Chief Minister Beant Singh (Chima 2014). Matters came to such a head that at the time of the incident with Mr Gill, his superior, police chief Julio Ribeiro, had to intervene to restore cordial relations between the magistracy and the police. A magistrate had complained to Governor Ray that, as reported in the news, 'the role of the magistracy in the maintenance of law and order had been reduced to almost zero because of the "obstinacy" of certain SSP's (senior superintendent of police)' (Khosla 1987). Apparently, the SSPs had shown, as *The Tribune* reported, 'utter disregard for the complaints against "police excesses" received by the magistracy' (ibid.).

The civil and police administrations were clearly at odds with each other, especially during the period of President's rule and the counter-insurgency, but also historically. In particular, relations between this service and the police are generally fractious because the highest-ranking policeman remains below the rank of the highest-ranking IAS officer in the government. In the British government, too, this tension between civil service and police services was evident, and it continues from the colonial to the postcolonial state. As under colonial rule, the civil service viewed with disdain the violence of the police and distanced itself from it, even while supporting it in multiple ways. The police were used to quell nationalist movements and their brutality was well-known (Danewalia 1997); the police in the postcolonial state continued to function as it had in the colonial state because politicians used the police to repress and control their opponents. A study conducted to assess the attitudes of those in the IPS towards the officers of the IAS found hostility and resentment between these two groups (Singh and Bhandarkar 1994: 24). This issue seems to have rankled amongst many in the civil services for a long time and would have played a role in the Bajaj case.

In particular, my interviewees told me that the IAS officers in Punjab were not happy at being at the mercy of Gill, the police officer in charge of security forces in Punjab. The molestation incident, as the 'Editorial' in *The Tribune* (1988b) reported, had 'opened up the IAS–IPS rivalry which lay dormant so far'. Though Mrs Bajaj denied that such a rivalry was a cause of her complaint (Prashar 1988), many believed that this was a battle between the police and the administrative services, two branches of the government that have historically been at odds in Punjab. Indeed, during the 1980s and the 1990s in Punjab, the IAS had had to retreat before the power of the police, and the IAS officers, used to having quite a bit of power, did not like being less important; Mrs Bajaj's case, my interviewee suggested, was a proxy war between two parts of the government in a time of terror. This may explain their support of Bajaj even when it would have been dangerous to do so. In a competitive entrance exam taken by hundreds of thousands of applicants, those securing the top ranks generally join the IAS while those securing slightly lower ranks usually join as IPS officers. It is a postcolonial restructuring of the British civil service and is responsible for the civil governance of the country. Mr Gill belonged to the police force, the IPS, which is generally ranked lower than the administrative service, though it was the most powerful bureaucracy in the state because of the insurgency. These discrepancies led to tensions between the services.

For Mrs Bajaj, the period from 1988 (when the incident happened) to 2005 (when the Supreme Court upheld Mr Gill's conviction) was when she felt rejected, indeed threatened, as she recalled, by the nation she had served. Yet, at the same time, her repeated assertions stating that she was afraid of being 'disappeared' suggests that she believed that during that time, even high-status government officials in the civil services were in danger from the police; however, she was outraged that that might be the case for those in the elite services. Even while she suggested that she was unlike most Indian women who are taught to keep quiet despite the violence committed on them, she relied on the state to help her, using her contacts within it and working through the judicial arm for redress. As a high-achieving state official, she saw herself as a model for resisting the ways in which the nation was being constructed by the state—as a patriarchal and security state. By separating state and nation, she was able to position herself as both within it and outside it—aligning herself with an emerging critique of sexual harassment, but claiming that her notion of security was also about security for women, rather than for just the security state.

Reviewing the subsequent developments in sexual harassment law in India, it can be said that the Bajaj case set a precedent in the use of two sections of the IPC and ushered in an era in which legislating on sexual harassment became the foremost issue for some feminist groups. The Bajaj case has now become part of the history of feminism in India, and Bajaj herself is lauded for her determination and perseverance with the case (Upadhayay 2017). Furthermore, over the decade and more during which it made its way through the courts, the case led to a discussion and furore about the relation between women and the nation. At the time of the incident, however, most of the media, in the context of the Punjab insurgency, sided with Gill and with the security state in vilifying Sikhs, seeing the insurgent movement as a threat to the nation that must be controlled. In the newspapers, especially some of the national English-language dailies, the idea that Sikhs were intrinsically violent was used widely (Mann 2016), with the allied belief that therefore it was only from within the community, by people such as Mr Gill, that the insurgency could be put down.

Distrust and stereotypes of Sikh males, especially those of the Jat caste such as Mr Gill, were widespread.

In contrast with the many cases of sexual harassment that have emerged in security forces such as the CRPF or the local police or the military in Kashmir (Kazi 2014), Bajaj was able to mobilise vastly more support and help because of her wealth and power, as well as her courage that was imbricated with that wealth and power. It is also the case that civil servants have been very active in seeking litigation for any wrongs that they experience in their jobs, that women civil servants have fought key cases regarding gender discrimination in their jobs, and that the most important case that has been the basis for sexual harassment law, *Vishakha and Others v. State of Rajasthan*, concerned a government servant—a social worker—who had been gang-raped as retribution in the course of doing her job (De 2018b; Baxi 2001). Despite these examples, it is important to state that it is not all women who stand up against their own class and caste patriarchy for a variety of reasons, economic and social.

Yet if one thinks of the period in which the case was tried, not only was Mrs Bajaj's courage remarkable but so also were the circumstances in which she was heard. In the late 1980s, the Punjab judiciary resisted being involved in TADA cases, and the Punjab and Haryana High Court initially would not even take up Mrs Bajaj's case. After the Supreme Court ruled that the case needed investigation, the High Court went on to convict Gill of 'outraging the modesty of a woman' during the same time period when it would not hear the numerous cases involving allegations of rape, murder and torture against the state (*The Economic Times* 2011). Gill continued to state that police should not be persecuted for these abuses (Gill 1997b). Even today, the government has refused to hear many such cases (Human Rights Watch/Asia and Physicians for Human Rights 1994).

What then does this case say about gender and the state, especially the security state, as heterogeneous, patriarchal and postcolonial? It is clear that ethnic identity, that of the Sikh male of the Jat caste embodying the stereotype of the 'martial race', is to be controlled and utilised in the continued project of state-making. Gill could be used for counter-insurgency and to control his own communities as well as other minorities on other borders, but could also be humiliated. Some parts of the state lauded him, others found him guilty; the courts found he had committed a crime while the political state at the Centre gave him an award but also a sports job that showed him as a failure in upholding national pride. Across the Indian public, he is still seen as one who 'ended terrorism' in Punjab but also as one whose behaviour should have been controlled because he was not respectable. It is not only women's sexuality and victimhood that the Indian state constructs, but also a threatening masculinity that can be useful for the security state if it is controlled and kept in check.

At the same time, in upholding Bajaj's claim, the Supreme Court, as Ratna Kapur (2001) points out, reified notions of the 'modesty' of the Indian woman and constrained her sexuality. It placed her firmly in the domestic space and as needing the protection of the nation-state, even when the case in question involved a powerful woman official. But perhaps we can say more about 'modesty', gender and the state if we expand the frame to consider the question of a patriarchal state whose institutions of power relied on gender as well as caste and class. The word 'modesty', in Bajaj's account and in the context of the time, was a much more complex term. The Supreme Court defined it as the 'essence of woman', making distinctions based on a politics of respectability (Pathania n.d.). But it is more than that for Bajaj, who saw 'modesty' as connected to a respectability that came from her career and her social position, rather than her sexuality. She saw her humiliation as a disregard of her career and accomplishments, but it was also a control of her sexuality because it was implicitly connected to her marriage outside of caste and community. Gill's actions probably displayed his desire to sexualise and humiliate Bajaj because she came from the same Jat caste as him and she had violated the norms of caste and religious endogamy by marrying a Hindu and a non-Jat man.

Though the Bajaj case is sobering in the way it reveals how the state in Delhi and in Punjab as well as the community constitutes the 'Indian woman' as needing the protection of the nation, it provides space for some elite women to become national role models. Yet such women do not define themselves solely through the frameworks of the IPC or the court, but also claim their rights to a job in the civil services and a career that allows them to have fewer constraints in marriage and in economic opportunities. Sexual harassment litigation, even if it was based on a politics of respectability, indexed the struggle of Indian women to free themselves of sexual control and economic control in ways that allowed them to challenge the patriarchal contract of national security and protection.

Despite the modest gains of this case, it is, once again, a case where the state is challenged for its own caste patriarchy in the context of its security project. The use of the notion of gendered modesty reveals that the security state cannot be both patriarchal and casteist and protect women's respectability—that the security of the state and the security of women are not two separate and conflicting projects. The state's duplicity is thus made visible even as the liberal state claims to protect its women. It was no small feat to take on the security establishment and to file a writ petition against the most powerful and feared police chief in the state or to continue to persevere in the case despite opposition from high-ranking bureaucrats and politicians. This is not a case of radical or subversive feminist politics. It is a modest case, about modesty, a term stretched beyond the Supreme Court's definition to encompass a broader and robust sense of self and identity constituted by social and economic contexts. Its very modesty reveals the predatory and patriarchal power that constitutes the banal politics of state security.

Notes

1. In 2013, Section 354 was changed to add other forms of sexual harassment, stalking, and voyeurism, and to prevent the dissemination and circulation of sexual images, once again, by men of adult women.

2. 1996 AIR 309, 1995 SCC (6) 194. Available at https://indiankanoon.org/doc/579822/ (accessed on 9 January 2024).

3. It is the Vishakha and Others v. State of Rajasthan judgment which has had a greater impact in cases of sexual harassment, laying down guidelines to be followed by employers. See the discussion in Menon (2004: 144), who calls it a 'landmark' case.

4. Interview with Mrs Bajaj, Chandigarh, 7 August 2006.

5. My thanks to Rohit De for pointing this out as part of legal history and for turning my attention to Upendra Baxi's (2007) writing on the topic and De's commentary (2018b).

6. One might say that it was not Bajaj but the security state which got its 'butt slapped', even as it was able to do as it wished with regard to less powerful women and men. By this, I mean that the police was humiliated by the courts and Bajaj.

7. It was not only the national dailies that used these terms, but also newspapers within Punjab. *The Tribune* was one such newspaper, with headlines such as '4 terrorists held, woman shot at' (11 June 1987), 'PM vows to stamp out terrorism' (8 June 1987), '20-point plan to combat terrorism' (22 January 1987), 'Women bodies urged to fight terrorists' (25 May 1987), 'Students speak out on terrorism' (23 June 1988) and 'Relief for terrorist victims' families' (4 July 1988).

8. The National Security (Amendment) Act, 1984. Available at https://www.mha.gov.in/sites/default/files/2022-09/NationalSecAmndmntAct1984%5B1%5D.pdf (accessed on 9 January 2024).

9. SAHRDC, Human Rights Features, 'Defending the Indefensible: India Does the POTA Act', www.hrdc.net/sa hrdc/hrfchr58/Issue3.htm (cited in Kumar et al. 2003: 100).

10. This was especially the case for the custodial death of Jaswant Singh Khalra, in which Gill was named as a key participant and conspirator. See OneIndia (2006).

11. Kanwar Pal Singh Gill v. The State (Administration, UT Punjab and Haryana High Court, August 20, 1998). Available at https://www.casemine.com/judgement/in/56e66850607dba6b53431e9b (accessed on 9 January 2024).

12. Interview with Mrs Bajaj, Chandigarh, 7 August 2006.

13. Interview with Mrs Bajaj, Chandigarh, 2006. The rest of this paragraph is based on this interview.

REFERENCES

Admin Lawnn. 2015. 'Rupan Deol Bajaj vs. K.P.S. Gill'. 1 August. Available at https://lawnn.com/rupan-deol-bajaj-vs-k-p-s-gill/ (accessed on 4 January 2024).

Awasthi, Surinder. 2005. 'Rupan Deol Bajaj'. *The Times of India*, New Delhi, 28 July, p. 7.

Axel, Brian Keith. 2001. *The Nation's Tortured Body*. Durham, NC: Duke University Press.

Bagchi, Sanjoy. 2007. *The Changing Face of Bureaucracy: Fifty Years of the IAS*. New Delhi: Rupa & Co.

Bal, Hartosh Singh. 2017. 'Lessons Not Learnt: The Left and Right Have Distorted KPS Gill's Success against Terrorism'. Scroll.in, 9 July. Available at https://scroll.in/article/842699/lessons-not-learnt-the-left-and-right-have-distorted-kps-gills-success-against-terrorism (accessed on 4 January 2024).

Basu, Srimati. 2001. *She Comes to Take Her Rights: Indian Women, Property, and Propriety*. New Delhi: Zubaan.

Baxi, Pratiksha. 2001. 'Sexual Harassment'. *Seminar* 505: 54–59.

Baxi, Upendra. 2007. 'Introduction'. In *Services under the State*, ed. M. Rama Jois, xc–cx. New Delhi: Indian Law Institute.

BBC News. 2017. 'Taking on India's "Super Cop" after He Sexually Harassed Me'. 22 January. Available at https://www.youtube.com/watch?v=WJjtov2mXKE&ab_channel=BBCNews (accessed on 20 October 2023).

Benbabaali, Dalel. 2008. 'Questioning the Role of the Indian Administrative Service in National Integration'. *South Asia Multidisciplinary Academic Journal*, 5 September. Available at https://doi.org/10.4000/samaj.633 (accessed on 20 October 2023).

Bhan, Mona. 2013. *Counterinsurgency, Democracy, and the Politics of Identity in India: From Warfare to Welfare?* First edition. Abingdon, UK and New York: Routledge.

Bhatia, Surbhi, and Akshi Chawla. 2022. 'Why There Have Been So Few Women In India's Administrative Services'. IndiaSpend. BQ Prime, 10 January. Available at https://www.bqprime.com/politics/why-there-have-been-so-few-women-in-indias-administrative-services (accessed on 20 October 2023).

Bhattacharyya, Arundhati. 2017. *Sexual Harassment in the Indian Bureaucracy: Violation of Human Rights*. Newcastle upon Tyne, UK: Cambridge Scholars Publishing.

Bora, Papori. 2010. 'Between the Human, the Citizen and the Tribal'. *International Feminist Journal of Politics* 12 (3–4): 341–60.

Chima, Jugdep S. 2014. 'The Punjab Police and Counterinsurgency against Sikh Militants in India'. In *Policing Insurgencies: Cops as Counterinsurgents*, eds C. Christine Fair and Sumit Ganguly, 258–90. New Delhi: Oxford University Press.

Chowdhry, Prem. 2013a. 'Emerging Patterns: Property Rights of Women in Colonial and Post-Colonial South-East Punjab'. *Journal of Punjab Studies* 20 (January): 111–34.

———. 2013b. 'Militarized Masculinities: Shaped and Reshaped in Colonial South-East Punjab'. *Modern Asian Studies* 47 (3): 713–50.

Claiborne, William. 1984. 'Indian Official Accuses Pakistan of Training Sikh Guerrillas'. *The Washington Post*, 14 June. Available at https://www.washingtonpost.com/archive/politics/1984/06/14/indian-official-accuses-pakistan-of-training-sikh-guerrillas/6d4fd9b3-0bc2-4476-b6a1-614f9649ceb2/ (accessed on 20 October 2023).

Danewalia, Bhagwan Singh. 1997. *Police and Politics in Twentieth Century Punjab*. New Delhi: Ajanta.

Das, Veena. 2008. 'Violence, Gender, and Subjectivity'. *Annual Review of Anthropology* 37 (1): 283–99.

De, Rohit. 2018a. *A People's Constitution: The Everyday Life of Law in the Indian Republic*. Princeton, NJ: Princeton University Press.

———. 2018b. 'A Republic of Petty Bureaucrats: Upendra Baxi and the Pathologies of Civil Service Jurisprudence'. *Jindal Global Law Review* 9 (2): 335–50.

Dhavan, Purnima. 2014. *When Sparrows Became Hawks: The Making of the Sikh Warrior Tradition, 1699–1799*. New Delhi: Oxford University Press.

Duschinski, Haley, Mona Bhan, Ather Zia and Cynthia Mahmood, eds. 2018. *Resisting Occupation in Kashmir*. Philadelphia: University of Pennsylvania Press.

Fernandes, Leela. 2006. *India's New Middle Class*. Minneapolis: University of Minnesota Press.

Gill, K. P. S. 1997a. *Punjab, the Knights of Falsehood*. New Delhi: Har-Anand Publications.

———. 1997b. 'Text of K.P.S. Gill's Letter to Prime Minister I.K. Gujral on the Death of Ajit Singh Sandhu'. South Asia Terrorism Portal, 30 May. Available at https://www.satp.org/satporgtp/kpsgill/terrorism/97pm.htm (accessed on 20 October 2023).

———. n.d. a. 'Endgame in Punjab: 1988–1993'. Available at https://www.satp.org/satporgtp/publication/faultlines/volume1/Fault1-kpstext.htm (accessed on 4 January 2024).

———. n.d. b. 'K P S Gill: Freedom from Fear—Occasional Writings on Terrorism & Governance'. Available at https://www.satp.org/satporgtp/kpsgill/index.htm (accessed on 4 January 2024).

Gould, William. 2010. *Bureaucracy, Community and Influence in India: Society and the State, 1930s–1960s*. First edition. London and New York: Routledge.

Hindustan Times. 2005. 'Too Modest, Too Late'. Editorial, 29 July.

Human Rights Watch. 2007. 'Protecting the Killers: A Policy of Impunity in Punjab, India'. 17 October. Available at https://www.hrw.org/report/2007/10/17/protecting-killers/policy-impunity-punjab-india (accessed on 4 January 2024).

———. 2009. "Broken System: Dysfunction, Abuse, and Impunity in the Indian Police'. 4 August. Available at https://www.hrw.org/report/2009/08/04/broken-system/dysfunction-abuse-and-impunity-indian-police (accessed on 4 January 2024).

Human Rights Watch and Physicians for Human Rights. 1993. 'Rape in Kashmir: A Crime of War'. Vol. 5, No. 9. New York and Boston. Available at https://www.hrw.org/sites/default/files/reports/INDIA935.PDF (accessed on 4 January 2024).

Human Rights Watch/Asia and Physicians for Human Rights, eds. 1994. *Dead Silence: The Legacy of Human Rights Abuses in Punjab*. New York: Human Rights Watch.

Jayawardena, Kumari, and Rafia Zakaria. 2016. *Feminism and Nationalism in the Third World*. Reprint. London, New York: Verso.

Kandiyoti, Deniz. 1991. *Women, Islam, and the State*. Philadelphia: Temple University Press.

Kang, Bhavdeep. 1995. 'Brought Down A Peg'. 25 October. Available at https://www.outlookindia.com/magazine/story/brought-down-a-peg/200051 (accessed on 4 January 2024).

Kapur, Ratna. 2001. 'Sexcapades and the Law'. *Seminar* 505 (September). Available at https://www.india-seminar.com/2001/505/505%20ratna%20kapur.htm (accessed on 4 January 2024).

Karmakar, Rahul. 2017. 'KPS Gill: A "Fearsome" Police Officer Even during Assam Agitation Days'. *Hindustan Times*, 27 May. Available at https://www.hindustantimes.com/india-news/kps-gill-a-fearsome-police-officer-even-during-assam-agitation-days/story-BK0fPtNzIbjvBwqygvTvyH.html (accessed on 4 January 2024).

Kartar Singh v. State of Punjab. 1994. Casemine. Supreme Court of India. Available at https://www.casemine.com/judgement/in/5767b0fee691cb22da6d0200 (accessed on 4 January 2024).

Kazi, Seema. 2014. 'Rape, Impunity and Justice in Kashmir'. *Socio-Legal Review* 10: 14–46.

Khosla, Shyam. 1987. 'Police-Bureaucracy Clash a Fib'. *The Tribune*, 30 June.

Kumar, Ram Narayan, Amrik Singh, Ashok Agrwaal and Jaskaran Kaur. 2003. *Reduced to Ashes: The Insurgency and Human Rights in Punjab*. Vol. 1. Nepal: South Asia Forum for Human Rights.

Lobo, John. 1992. *Leaves from a Policeman's Diary*. New Delhi: Allied Publishers.

Mann, Richard D. 2016. 'Media Framing and the Myth of Religious Violence: The Othering of Sikhs in The Times of India'. *Sikh Formations* 12 (2–3): 120–41.

Menon, Nivedita. 2004. *Recovering Subversion: Feminist Politics beyond the Law*. Urbana, IL: University of Illinois Press.

Menon, Ritu, and Kamla Bhasin. 1998. *Borders & Boundaries: Women in India's Partition*. New Brunswick, NJ: Rutgers University Press.

Mookherjee, Nayanika. 2008. 'Gendered Embodiments: Mapping the Body-Politic of the Raped Woman and the Nation in Bangladesh'. *Feminist Review* 88 (1): 36–53.

Negi, S. S. 2005. 'SC Holds Gill Guilty in Rupan Deol Bajaj Case'. *The Tribune*, 27 July. Available at https://www.tribuneindia.com/2005/20050728/main5.htm (accessed on 23 October 2023).

Noorani, A. G. 1990. 'Indira Gandhi and Indian Muslims'. *Economic & Political Weekly* 25 (44): 2417–20.

Nussbaum, Martha. 2003. 'The Modesty of Mrs. Bajaj: India's Problematic Route to Sexual Harassment Law'. In *Directions in Sexual Harassment Law*, eds Catherine A. MacKinnon and Reva B. Siegel, 633–54. New Haven: Yale University Press.

OneIndia. 2006. 'Plea to Probe KPS Gill Role in Khalra's "Liquidation"'. 8 September. Available at https://www.oneindia.com/2006/09/08/plea-to-probe-kps-gill-role-in-khalras-liquidation-1157731487.html (accessed on 3 October 2023).

Pathania, Shweta. n.d. 'Case Study on Outraging Modesty of Women'. Legal Service India E-Journal. Available at https://legalserviceindia.com/legal/article-6559-case-study-on-outraging-modesty-of-women.html (accessed on 20 October 2023).

Pettigrew, Joyce J. M. 1995. *The Sikhs of the Punjab: Unheard Voices of State and Guerrilla Violence*. London, Atlantic Highlands: Zed Books.

Prakash, Gyan. 2019. *Emergency Chronicles: Indira Gandhi and Democracy's Turning Point*. Princeton, NJ: Princeton University Press.

Prashar, A. S. 1988. 'It's No IAS-IPS Issue, Says Mrs. Bajaj'. *The Tribune*, 4 August.

Puri, Balraj. 1985. 'Era of Indira Gandhi'. *Economic & Political Weekly* 20 (4): 148–50.

Rana, Akanksha. 2020. 'My Struggles to Battle Gender Roles in Indian Administrative Services'. Feminism in India, 11 March. Available at https://feminisminindia.com/2020/03/12/struggles-battle-gender-roles-indian-administrative-services/ (accessed on 20 October 2023).

Sahai-Achutan, Nisha. 1989. 'Women in the IAS (1948–74): A Study of Their Socio-Economic Cum Academic Background, and Attitude to Marriage and Career'. *Journal of Social Science* 2 (4): 579–93.

Singh, Gurharpal. 2000. *Ethnic Conflict in India: A Case-Study of Punjab*. New York: Palgrave Macmillan.

Singh, Pritam, and Asha Bhandarkar. 1994. *IAS Profile: Myths and Realities*. New Delhi: Wiley Eastern Limited.

Singh, Pritam, and Navtej K. Purewal. 2013. 'The Resurgence of Bhindranwale's Image in Contemporary Punjab'. *Contemporary South Asia* 21 (2): 133–47.

Sinha, Mrinalini. 1995. *Colonial Masculinity: The 'Manly Englishman' and the 'Effeminate Bengali' in the Late Nineteenth Century*. First edition. Manchester, New York: Manchester University Press.

Sinha, Mrinalini, and Daniel J. Walkowitz. 2006. *Specters of Mother India: The Global Restructuring of an Empire*. Durham: Duke University Press.

Streets, Heather. 2004. *Martial Races: The Military, Race and Masculinity in British Imperial Cultures, 1857–1914*. Manchester, UK: Manchester University Press.

Telford, Hamish. 2001. 'View of Counter-Insurgency in India: Observations from Punjab and Kashmir'. *Journal of Conflict Studies* 21 (1): 73–100.

The Economic Times. 2011. 'SC: Can Armed Forces Enjoy Immunity for Rape, Murder?' 17 June. Available at https://economictimes.indiatimes.com/news/politics-and-nation/sc-can-armed-forces-enjoy-immunity-for-rape-murder/articleshow/8884625.cms (accessed on 20 October 2023).

———. 2017. 'KPS Gill: The Man Who Put a Full Stop to Militancy in Punjab'. 26 May. Available at https://economictimes.indiatimes.com/news/politics-and-nation/kps-gill-the-man-who-put-a-full-stop-to-militancy-in-punjab/controversys-child/slideshow/58859296.cms (accessed on 24 October 2023).

The Indian Penal Code. 1860a. Section 354. Available at https://www.indiacode.nic.in/show-data?actid=AC_CEN_5_23_00037_186045_1523266765688&orderno=354 (accessed on 21 October 2023).

———. 1860b. Section 509. Available at https://www.indiacode.nic.in/show-data?actid=AC_CEN_5_23_00037_186045_1523266765688&sectionId=46297&sectionno=509&orderno=573 (accessed on 21 October 2023).

The Tribune. 1988a. 'Punjab DGP Asked to Resign'. 1 August.

———. 1988b. 'A Needless Controversy'. 2 August.

———. 1989. 'Quashing of F.I.R. against Gill Opposed'. 19 May.

The Tribune. 1996a. 'Verdict Reserved in Gill Case'. 2 August.

______. 1996b. 'Three Months R.I for Gill'. 7 August.

______. 1996c. 'Gill's Conviction Hailed'. 8 August.

The Times of India. 2005. 'SC Upholds Conviction of Gill in Rupan Deol Case'. 27 July. Available at https://web.archive.org/web/20120922084014/http://articles.timesofindia.indiatimes.com/2005-07-27/india/27846624_1_conviction-rupan-deol-bajaj-k-p-s-gill (accessed on 23 October 2023).

Upadhayay, Shraddha. 2017. 'KPS Gill—The Sexual Harasser Remembered As A Supercop'. Feminism in India, 31 May. Available at https://feminisminindia.com/2017/05/31/kps-gill-sexual-harasser/ (accessed on 4 January 2024).

Van Dyke, Virginia. 1996. 'The Anti-Sikh Riots of 1984 in Delhi: Politicians, Criminals, and the Discourse of Communalism'. In *Riots and Pogroms*, ed. Paul R. Brass, 201–20. London: Palgrave Macmillan UK.

Verma, Arvind. 2008. 'Policing the Police'. *India Review* 7 (2): 155–59.

Vinayak, Ramesh. 1996. 'Conviction of Supercop K.P.S. Gill Turns Spotlight on Sexual-Harassment Offences'. *India Today*, 31 August. Available at https://www.indiatoday.in/magazine/crime/story/19960831-conviction-of-supercop-kanwar-pal-singh-gill-turns-spotlight-on-sexual-harassment-offences-833762-1996-08-31 (accessed on 4 January 2024).

Seven

Pt V. D. Paluskar and the Punjab

Assessing a Complex Relationship

Radha Kapuria

Introduction

This chapter assesses the place of Pt V. D. Paluskar (1872–1931) in the social history of music in colonial Punjab. A leading reformer of Hindustani classical music, Paluskar nationalised, revived and 'cleansed' it of its associations with courtesans and lower-caste performers. Though he hailed from western India, where he spent much of his early years, his first brush with success and fame as a music reformer came in the colonial Punjabi city of Lahore.

The period under focus here is the 1890s when, across India, the emergent English-educated professional middle classes were making new articulations about their identity, centred on gender and caste. This was the decade when the famous Age of Consent Bill (1891) controversy raged, reflecting the broader tendency of gender as being the primary axis around which male elites in colonial India defined their identity in relation to those ruling them (Sarkar 2000, 2003; Sinha 1995). Beginning in the 1890s, a strong wave of the socio-religious reform movement crystallised differences between the three major communities—the Sikhs, Hindus and Muslims—paving the way for a more virulent communalism that was to define the later period from the 1920s onwards. Paradoxically, Kenneth Jones has noted similarities in the strategies and discourse followed amongst the different groups leading socio-religious reform in Punjab, such as the Arya Samaj and the Ahmadiyyas, especially in the way they adopted Western organisational and institutional models from their common enemy, the Christian missionaries (Jones 1989: 121). Across north India, vernacular languages were also harnessed to the project of defining communities more rigidly along religious lines, with campaigns to identify languages and scripts exclusively with particular ethnic and religious groups. Despite such attempts, however, a multilingual vernacular culture flourished in the Punjab, represented by the *qissa* (epic-romance) tradition in Punjabi and Urdu, moored in shared practices and widely embraced by members of all religious communities, often cutting across class distinctions as well (Mir 2010). Two other predictable axes of unity between rival religious and linguistic communities revolved around gender and caste. Anshu Malhotra's work has shown how the reinforcement of caste in late nineteenth-century colonial Punjab was in accord with the disciplining of women's bodies and defining the behaviour of the ideal domesticated *pativrata* (husband-worshipping) woman. She documents the campaign of Sikh and Hindu male reformers against traditional practices of women where inter-caste interaction was the norm, as well as the resistance of many Punjabi women to this move (Malhotra 2002).

The first section of this chapter will delineate the hitherto unexamined reasons behind the location of Pt Paluskar's spectacular first successes with musical reform in colonial Punjabi cities like Lahore. Through a focus on the city's Hindu reformist elites, I investigate the ways in which late nineteenth-century colonial Punjab constituted ready ground for the dissemination of Paluskar's agenda for Indian music. In the second section, I examine Paluskar's impact on the famous Harballabh music festival (purportedly Hindustani music's oldest), dating back to 1875, held in the east Punjabi city of Jalandhar. In the final section, I demonstrate how

Paluskar radically redefined the trajectory this festival took in the future, whether in terms of festival organisation, monetising performance or shifts in the performative space. The broader shift this chapter tracks is the rise of a newer music public and forms of pedagogy, and the re-situation of music within perspectives of nationalism and socio-religious reform along the axes of caste and gender in colonial Punjab.

Paluskar's Predecessors in Late Nineteenth-Century Punjab

As in other realms of Indian social life, the 1890s were also a watershed decade in the social history of female performers. 'Anti-*nautch*' campaigns raged all across India, focusing on outlawing professional female musicians and dancers, based on their perceived 'debased' morals. However, as elsewhere (see Morcom [2013], Soneji [2012] and Walker [2014] for west India, south India and north India, respectively), there was a gradation in the hierarchies of female performing communities in the Punjab. Apart from the campaigns to abolish the nautch (the institution of dancing for an audience by female performers) elsewhere in India, it was in equal measure the prevalence of the still powerful and wealthy courtesan in Punjab which stimulated the *Opinions on the Nautch Question* pamphlet published in Lahore in 1894. The local group responsible for its publication was the curiously titled Punjab Purity Association (henceforth PPA), which was formed with the express purpose of condemning the nautch and spearheading a Punjab-wide campaign for its abolition. The PPA also had a more intimate connection with the anti-temperance movement launched by Christian missionaries in the region; indeed, some leading missionaries of Punjab were also prominent members of the Association (Webster 1976: 199). The main motivation of the PPA was towards the creation of a new kind of Punjabi womanhood where elite and upper-caste women would be trained to embody an Anglicised modernity tempered with tradition. This would be a newly reformed strand of tradition divorced from earlier associations with community practices of singing 'obscene' songs in public, in rituals like the *siyapa* (Punjabi women's mourning ritual that involves collective weeping and wailing), for example, as has been demonstrated by Anshu Malhotra (2002: 196–98).

Inspired by nationalist reformers from Bengal like Keshab Chandra Sen, who provided a vehemently anti-nautch foreword to the PPA pamphlet (mentioned earlier), the Association solicited views from elite and educated Punjabis hailing from a range and diversity of backgrounds—Muslim, Hindu and Sikh.[1] The text offers us key insights, some inadvertent, into the role music played in the elite social life of the city, especially from the perspective of the urban gentrified classes and their musical interests. Those members of the Punjabi Anglophone elite who contributed to the *Opinions on the Nautch Question* asserted that nautch girls were, in fact, 'public prostitutes', and that whatever little merit they had accrued from their 'borrowed plumes, viz., the musical art'. Music was thus viewed as a key reason for the attractiveness of the nautch girls for young men alongside their eroticism. This recognition of the unique musical powers of the nautch girls went hand-in-hand with a call for alternative 'healthy recreations', which could most gainfully be created if young women from respectable families were taught this art. In the search for a 'respectable class' of musicians to teach 'respectable' women behind closed doors, many contributors denounced the *mirasi*s (Punjab's caste of low-status hereditary musician-genealogists) as 'men of low character' and 'a nuisance' while praising the more spiritually oriented *rababi*s (hereditary musicians tracing their lineage back to Bhai Mardana, Guru Nanak's musician-accompanist, who perform Sikh liturgical music and are proficient in performing on stringed instruments like the *rabab* or rebec).

The majority of the contributors to this leaflet hailed from the English-educated middle classes across the Punjab and, somewhat unsurprisingly, exhibited a Victorian social morality. Many contributors emphasised the importance of a substitute to the institution of the nautch, thereby exhibiting an affective interest in the music, and not simply disdain towards all music and dance.[2] The majority of the contributors are, nonetheless, somewhat monotonous in their stridently anti-nautch position, given that the Association solicited suggestions for 'some good substitute (that) will obviate the difficulty and soon put an end to the evil' (Punjab Purity Association 1894: i). Reading against the grain in a document like this yields many important insights that illustrate pre-existing nautch practices across Punjab. The most common theme invoked by each contributor concerned the supposedly insalubrious moral character of the dancing girls, who were held solely responsible for turning innocent young men into 'whoremongers' and 'budmashes' (rascals).

For example, Mian Muhammad Shafi, a barrister-at-law from Lahore working at Hoshiarpur (who went on to become one of the founding members of the All India Muslim League), mentioned that this custom was abolished as early as the 1880s by his family in Baghbanpura (Punjab Purity Association 1894: 9),[3] illustrating how indigenous elites in the Punjab had begun censuring the nautch practices within the first three decades of British rule.[4] Yet the very force with which these members of the urban Indian elite attacked the institution throws into sharp relief the ubiquity of the dancing girl in *fin-de-siecle* Punjabi society. H. C. Mukherji, a Bengali pleader based in Rawalpindi, elaborated upon the sources of the dancing girl's remarkable power, which arose from the 'union of feminine blandishment with the charms of the musical art' that 'makes her doubly attractive' to youth, transforming them into 'whoremongers' (ibid.: 16–17). Mukherji suggested that the focus should be on educating women from 'respectable' homes in the art of music and encouraging the formation of public 'music clubs'. Many contributors also referred to the ways in which nautches were a waste of money, thus articulating a classic Victorian middle-class ethic of saving money and preventing wasteful expenditure. As

Moulvi Rahim Bux put it, nautch girls 'involve a great expenditure of money, which transforms the honest earnings of many into the ill-gotten gains of a few' (Punjab Purity Association 1894: 22). The *Opinions on the Nautch Question* is exemplary of the kind of document where the discussion of 'disreputable' women was central to defining the honour of the men themselves, the women being secondary to the discourse. As delineated in numerous studies such as those by Lata Mani and Mrinalini Sinha, the idea driving most of the *Opinions* was that women's bodies and their performance practices, far from being accorded a modicum of autonomy, became a site for the definition and construction of a respectable masculinity (see Mani [1998] and Sinha [1995]). Despite the overwhelming odds stacked against practitioners of the courtesanly tradition during these years, Shweta Sachdeva has argued (for the broader north Indian sphere) that this was also the period when some courtesans reinvented their singing through the employment of the gramophone and new technology (2008: 195–306). This note of resistance and reinvention was also discernable in colonial Punjab, where we find public references to powerful and wealthy courtesans during these very years (Kapuria 2023: Chapter 3).

The authors of the *Opinions* were not isolated in the stridency of their reformist tenor, however. The Arya Samaj and other Hindu reform organisations like the Sanatan Dharm Sabha were at the forefront of redefining and recreating traditional or 'obscene' Punjabi folksongs sung by women. Mai Bhagavati, a rare example of a female Arya *updeshak* or missionary in the late nineteenth century, 'expressly intended to replace the traditional women's songs used at the time of Hindu marriages' (Jones 1976: 95). Her *Abala Mati Vegarodhik Sangit* ('Music to Prevent Impetuousness in Weak-Minded Women'), published in 1892 in Lahore, is a book of songs that inverts traditional *sithniyan* (songs sung during marriages, parodying the kin of the new family), actively converting songs laden with pleasure, love, lust and the impending union of bride and groom into songs loaded with moral strictures, ideal codes of behaviour and the praise of 'Bhagwan' or God. A few years later, at the Arya Samaj's first school for girls, the Kanya Mahavidyalaya, established in 1896 in Jalandhar, Lala Devraj Sondhi was also actively writing 'new lyrics' for Punjabi women's songs in an attempt to train middle-class and upper-caste girl students in the musical arts.[5]

The establishment of V. D. Paluskar's Gandharv Mahavidyalaya in Lahore in 1901 was thus in many ways made possible by the foundation laid by the Punjab Arya Samaj and those airing their views in the *Opinions*. Pandit Vishnu Digamber Paluskar was a Marathi musician trained in the Gwalior *gharana* (specialist school of music and/or dance, with a hereditary lineage of practitioners), who made the mass dissemination and modernisation of Indian classical music his life's mission. The vital connection of musical reform with socio-religious reform is evident in the way Paluskar's most recent biographer, the historian Janaki Bakhle, describes his 'desire to found a school for music that would return music to its traditional, unsullied origins [which] endeared him to the leading lights of Hindu reform and revival organizations outside the sphere of music' (Bakhle 2005: 144). These organisations, like the Arya Samaj and the Sanatan Dharm Sabha, supported his plan to open a school of music since 'they saw in Paluskar a willing and able proponent of their cause whose aim was to commandeer music from its mainly Muslim practitioners and return it to Hindus' (Kippen 2006: 25–26).

Though the Arya Samaj and the Sanatan Dharm Sabha were rival reform organisations in matters of doctrine, they came together on a broad Hindu devotional platform, united by the wholly new and radical proposal that upper-caste Hindus, especially women, should sing and perform (albeit religious and devotional songs only) in public spaces—practices usually associated with lower-caste, often Muslim practitioners like the mirasis, or with female musicians and dancers such as *tawa'if* (female performers of music and dance, usually elite courtesans with felicity in the arts, letters and social etiquette who traditionally serviced the

Mughal and post-Mughal nobility). In the proliferation of weekly devotional musical meetings at Lahore from at least the 1920s onwards, they also spawned a new middle-class audience for publicly performed devotional music, where earlier such music was performed exclusively in the private, domestic realm or for elite and princely patrons.

The very success and strength of the Hindu reform movement in Punjab may be linked more widely to the status of Punjabi Hindus as minorities *within* the province, and as a majority in the more nationwide pan-Indian context (Nair 2011). Kenneth Jones convincingly located the widespread popularity of the Arya Samajist message (rational, scientific, yet rooted in Hindu doctrine) to the increasing threat to Punjab Hindus from rapidly increasing Christian conversions in a majority Muslim province: 'By 1891, they represented merely 40% of the province and continued to decline in the following census reports. Theirs was a community on the defensive' (1976: 2). This newly paradoxical position of Punjab's Hindus during colonialism accounts for their peculiarly eager receptivity to Hindu reformist ideas from western Indians such as the Gujarati founder of the Arya Samaj, Dayanand Saraswati, or indeed the Marathi music-reformer Pt Paluskar, whose ideas about music for the nation placed it within a distinctly Hindu-devotional mould.

As capital of the Punjab, Lahore was thus an apt choice for Paluskar, given that it was a vital cultural centre with a strong intelligentsia, a print and publishing hub, and a public reformist drive spearheaded by the main characters whose *Opinions* we have quoted above. Pt Paluskar received a glowing reception, followed by unparalleled success in Lahore. The reasons for this are manifold: the power with which the message of Hindu reform organisations from elsewhere (the Arya Samaj from Gujarat and, a little earlier than that, Brahma Samaj from Bengal) took root, and the thriving centre for printing and publishing which Lahore had become by century's end. Because of this, in the befitting words of B. R. Deodhar, 'Panditji found Lahore *congenial to his temperament* and he started his musical mission here' (1973: 43; emphasis added).

At the inauguration ceremony of the first Gandharv Mahavidyalaya on 5 May 1901, Pt Din Dayalu Sharma of the Sanatan Dharm Sabha (who apparently suggested the name for the institute) referred to the

> ...deplorable decline in the 'divine art' in this Province [Punjab], and observed how it was now *solely practiced by low caste people* to the great detriment to the cause of pure music. The Pundit... hoped that Hindu and Mussalmans would help unitedly in the work taken up by Professor Vishnu Digambar (Rosse 1995: 27; emphasis added).

It is clear that Sharma castigated 'low caste' musicians, the bulk of whom in Punjab were Muslim, while at the same time reaching out to the elite, *ashraf* (high-born Muslim nobility, claiming a lineage back to the Prophet Muhammad) Muslims. Sharma's concern that music was 'solely practiced by low caste people' and the formal holding out of the olive branch to the 'Mussalmans'[6] show how his discourse was in tune with his fellow Lahories, whose views were solicited by the PPA. It is interesting to note the rather formal and meaningless holding out of this olive branch, given that these very hereditary Muslim musicians were the first point of attack in Paluskar's agenda for music.

The relationship of Paluskar with the Hindu elites of Lahore has been well-documented by scholars like Bakhle, as also the ethnomusicologist James Kippen. Kippen, in his work on Dattatreya Vasudev Patwardhan, a disciple of Paluskar, points out how the invitation to Lahore in 1898 was extended to Paluskar by the Sanatan Dharm Sabha, an important Hindu organisation in the Punjab. Lahore was an apt choice, given that it was a vital cultural centre, with a strong intelligentsia and budding modern public sphere. In Kippen's words, 'Paluskar had a shrewd and presciently nationalist understanding of the direction music's trajectory needed to take.... Insofar as his ambition was nationalist, he had to establish his credentials, and mission, well outside the immediate province of Maharashtra... [Lahore] was the stronghold of aggressive and proselytizing Hindu revival movements' (2006: 24).

In this way, the contemporary wave of social reform represented by the success of the Arya Samaj and Sanatan Dharm Sabha in the Punjab, with its self-conscious, modernist understanding of being Hindu, as also its extensive popularisation of *bhajan* (devotional songs for the Hindu gods) and *sankirtan* (communal singing of Hindu devotional songs), prepared a ready ground for Pt Paluskar to propagate his message (Kapuria 2013: Annexure II). Thanks to the efforts of Paluskar, by the 1920s, barely two decades following the publication of *Opinions on the Nautch Question*, music clubs patronised by 'respectable' middle-class men and women had proliferated at a remarkable pace.[7] The musical education of middle-class women had especially proceeded with a great pace in the Punjab. A sterling example of the success of this project was the emergence of middle-class female musicians like Devki Sud who, by publishing *Sangit Prabha* in Hindi in 1934 in Amritsar, arguably became one of the first Punjabi women to write on music in the public sphere.[8]

PT PALUSKAR AND THE HARBALLABH MUSIC FESTIVAL

It was east of Lahore, in Jalandhar's Harballabh Raga Mela or 'Raga Fair' (now Sangīt Sammelan or 'Music Conference'), the oldest extant festival of Hindustani classical music, that Paluskar found his most abidingly loyal audience and his keenest supporters.[9] Beginning in 1875, the origins of Harballabh Mela lay in a musical-mystical gathering of mainly *dhrupad* (the oldest extant, fairly sombre genre of Hindustani music, characterised by a meditative restraint) musicians across the Punjab as an annual death anniversary celebration of the *guru* of Baba Harballabh, the festival-founder. This festival underwent significant changes from the turn of the century onwards, by which time the introduction of railways in 1870 had brought in its wake sustained contact with the outside world, especially ideas about modernity and music as they were emerging in Lahore. Most importantly, after Paluskar visited the festival in 1898/1901 (sources disagree on the date of his first visit), he became a regular visitor, establishing close ties with the festival organisers, an association which altered the festival in radical ways. First, the predominant performance genre shifted from dhrupad to *khayal* (a shorter, more 'imaginative' form characterised by fast ornamentation and greater emphasis on the words and meaning of the musical composition or *bandish*). This was in keeping with prevailing changes across India brought about by the confluence of Paluskar's new agenda of khayal-centred music pedagogy with gramophone technology, which favoured the shorter time duration of khayal over dhrupad's lengthier form.[10] Second, and equally importantly, the festival strove toward greater formalisation and institutionalisation—and a more certain alignment with nationalist discourse as well as middle-class norms and morality.

Paluskar's establishment of the Lahore Gandharv Mahavidyalaya also inspired local music teachers at Jalandhar. Bhagat Mangat Ram,[11] who, along with his many disciples, was a regular performer at many musical meetings at Jalandhar and Lahore, set up a school of music in 1904 at the Bhakt Bazaar of Jalandhar, known simply as 'Sangit Mahavidyalaya'. According to an advertising notice reproduced in his disciple Devki Sud's *Sangit Prabha* (1934), it claimed to be the only institution across the Punjab where students from humble backgrounds could learn, without charge, 'pure classical music' along with every kind of instrument. Interestingly, by actively reaching out to those with 'humble means', Mangat Ram's Sangit Mahavidyalaya could be seen as positing an alternative to the more powerful Gandharva Mahavidyalaya established only three years prior at Lahore by Paluskar. One can postulate that the 'philanthropic' character of the Jalandhar Sangit Mahavidyalaya could have something to do with the fact that it was the city of the Harballabh, which was renowned for its open accessibility to all music lovers. Mangat Ram's success lay in the fact that his school made many students autonomous and independent musicians, several finding employment with the Arya Pratinidhi Sabha and the Pradeshik Sabha of Punjab in the capacity of '*bhajnik*' (bhajan singer), thus being the media of 'musical entertainment', albeit of a pious and devotional nature, for the public. This again establishes the new professional respectability afforded to musicians, provided it was in the garb of Hindu devotional music, an outcome of the possibilities created by reform activists of the Arya Samaj combined with Paluskar's modernisation for classical music first revealed in the Punjab.

The heroism and divinity attributed to Pt Paluskar was also reflected in stories about the extreme power that he exerted as a guru over his disciples. This was a ubiquitous practice in the world of music, as Daniel Neuman has shown us (1990[1980]: 63–64; 68). Perhaps what was new was the way in which it was through the figure of Pt Paluskar that such stories took residence in the popular memory of present-day Jalandharis. In the absolute power he commanded, whether over audiences, fellow musicians or his disciples, combined with a visible obsequiousness and public displays of devotion to the shrine of the Harballabh and his modernist reform of Indian classical music, Pt Paluskar was the one most suited to take on the mantle of patron-saint for the newly rising intelligentsia backing the Harballabh.

There are many anecdotes about Paluskar's triumphs on the Harballabh stage, two of which deserve quoting as they were narrated by Jagannath Parti, founder of the *Sangit Mahasabha* in 1922, to J. S. Bawra, the biographer of the festival. The first anecdote narrates an impromptu competition in 1912/13, mediated by Pt Tolo Ram, between Paluskar and renowned vocalist Ustad Kale Khan of the Patiala gharana, a *darbar* (court) musician at the court of the ruler of Kashmir. Even though Paluskar was himself trained by a *gharanedar* (hailing from a gharana lineage) musician, Ichalkaranjikar of the Gwalior lineage, in life-stories and hagiographies, he is consistently pitched against gharanedar musicians. This was true of Paluskar's association with Punjab's oldest music festival too. The aim of this extempore competition, as it were, was to decide which musician possessed greater facility and expertise in music through an appraisal of their skills in elaborating upon different *raga*s (melodic mode of Indian classical music, containing an established number of notes), especially their prowess with rendering the *tana*s (intricate musical units sung or played towards the end of khayal compositions, in a very fast tempo):

> Once at night he sang Raga Darbari. Khan Saheb's *swara*s (notes) were echoing in every direction…. After him Pandit Vishnu Digambar came on the stage. Prior to beginning his singing Pandit ji said in praise of Kale Khan, 'The singing has already been finished by Khan Saheb now what can I sing?' But Khan Saheb could not digest his own praise and said, 'Yes! Pandit ji I challenge you to do so.' Pandit ji had a laugh and began Raga Bihaga… Mahant (priest) Tolo Ram ji also did not like the words of Khan Saheb…. Now Mahant ji, in order to break the haughtiness of Khan Saheb, said Pandit ji you please stop singing as the performance had almost reached the end with the *tana*s. He told Khan Saheb that he also should come on to the stage, and both singers sing the *tana*s of the *raga* one after the other. Then what remained ('*bas fir kya tha*')? Both began singing. The competition lasted for almost two hours. *As the time kept getting past, Pandit ji kept moving ahead and Khan Saheb kept falling behind.* Pandit ji then drew him (Khan Saheb) close and hugging him, gave him a lot of commendation (Bawra 1998: 30–33; emphasis added).

Despite the superior position of Pt Paluskar, which this anecdote is supposed to establish, given the victory of the better musician on an *apparently* level playing field, the issues it raises are deeper. The genesis of the conflict lies in a seemingly innocent compliment to Ustad Kale Khan, which the latter could not receive in all its supposed magnanimity. Had it not been for a remarkably similar tussle with an unnamed *beenkaar* (instrumentalist who plays on the *veena*, an Indian stringed instrument) from Jaipur who similarly could not accept the praise of Paluskar, we would be compelled to take the above paragraph at face value. In both anecdotes, the reason the compliment translated itself into an affront on reception had to do with the *context* in which they were made. By 1912–13, almost a decade since Pt Paluskar made his memorable debut at the Harballabh stage, his eminence had reached an apogee, given the firm establishment of his reputation as an innovator of music with his Gandharv Mahavidyalaya at Lahore (1901). The supposed defeat of other musicians stems from an intimidation they, and especially Ustad Kale Khan, had felt in the knowledge that Pt Paluskar enjoyed priority of position in the Harballabh organisers' eyes. The refusal to accept this otherwise harmless 'compliment' should be grounded in an underlying opposition to Pt Paluskar's reform agenda. To see these instances in purely musical terms glosses over the context and deeper rationale behind the resistance of other gharanedar musicians towards Paluskar's new agenda for music pedagogy. Such instances of resistance can also be seen as a note of dissent against the pro-Hindu and anti-Muslim devotionalist stance of Paluskar's reform project.

More broadly, the resistance was firmly against the direction which public culture was taking due to the reform efforts of Pt Paluskar and Pt Bhatkhande, whereby the hold of hereditary court and gharanedar musicians was increasingly being challenged, threatening the tenuous stability of court musicians. The popularity and adulation received by Pt Paluskar from the audience as well as the organisers all served to highlight the fragility of the position of these traditional-style performers. Paluskar's seemingly adulatory, though subtly mordant, 'compliment' to Ustad Kale Khan and the Jaipur beenkaar amounted to adding insult to the larger injury of being unable to match up to Paluskar's newly feted position as 'music's saviour' across north and west India.

Paluskar's valorisation at the cost of Kale Khan and other gharanedar musicians demonstrates several strands about Paluskar's self-perception and his consistent need to mark out the 'Other' in the public realm of musical performance. Importantly, given the wide recurrence of the 'Paluskar-as-hero' trope in these stories, I would argue that they do not reflect actual fact but constitute an example of his strategy of self-representation, carried forward by his followers and hagiographers. Indeed, these very musicians whom Paluskar and his supporters set out to vilify were, in fact, the ones whose pedagogical stamp survives most prominently through to the present—their musical heirs define the parameters of elite and high-status music even today. Despite Paluskar's reform project, therefore, the older pedagogical practices associated with the gharana system were not unequivocally dismantled, but rather were reconfigured and transformed into a more inclusive and democratic institution that increasingly allowed for the training of students outside the immediate family and kin of the gharanedar musician.[12] Thus, Bakhle's (2005) narrative contrasting a triumphant trajectory for Paluskar and his followers with an arc of absolute decline for gharanedar musicians is misplaced. Instead, as my analysis attests, the recurrent trope of Paluskar's heroism in the above anecdotes reveals the frail vulnerability that he felt, as a performer, in the face of performance specialists and musical stalwarts such as Ustad Kale Khan.

Paluskar's Long-term Impact

The Paradoxes of Monetising Performance

Harballabh has been feted as a place where musicians demanded only a minimal fee or none at all, given its status as a space of devotionalism where musicians performed for more mystical reasons. Elsewhere, I have shown the origins of the festival in 1875 in a tradition of cosmopolitan devotionalism (with dhrupad music as the primary genre performed), which shifted by the turn of the twentieth century to a more Hindu devotional sphere, thanks to the efforts of Pt Paluskar, who also popularised the shorter khayal genre across India, and especially at the Harballabh (Kapuria

2015). However, the turn to greater professionalisation ushered in under Ashwini Kumar, who was charged with the organisation of the festival (on whom more below), was seen as a negative development by many old Harballabh hands, like Jagannath Parti, one of the founder members of the Sangit Mahasabha in 1922. The finger of blame was unequivocally pointed in the direction of the doyen of the Patiala gharana, Ustad Bade Ghulam Ali Khan. His insistence on a fee for performance was contrasted with the more pious (and, unsurprisingly, Hindu) performers of the past, mostly students of Pt Paluskar, who himself had inaugurated the era of a nationalised, Hindu devotional *avatar* for Indian classical music, coupled with a suspicion of tawa'if (characterised as mere 'dancing girls') and Muslim performers (Kapuria 2013: 99–103).[13]

The way in which Pt Paluskar managed to mould the Harballabh festival as per his vision of an ideal Hindu religious space preserving music since ancient times is captured in the following story, quoted with great reverence by both Bawra and also in another account by Krishnanda Shastri:

> Once Pandit Vishnu Digambar ji, while travelling to the Maharaja of Kashmir, joined in this *sammelan* (conference) on his way there. While bidding him adieu, a packet of Rs. 250/- was donated to him. He took the packet in his hand, removed Rs. 5/- from his pocket and adding it to the packet placed it on the *samadhi* (tomb of a Hindu holy person) of Swami ji and said '*This is a spot for giving, not for taking*' (Bawra 1998: 30; emphasis added).

Here we find Pt Paluskar adding, of his own volition, to the purity of the space as a shrine *for* music, where he deemed it an honour to be able to perform, as opposed to performing for monetary reasons. Ironically, the monetisation of musical performance at public concerts was one of the most decisive steps that he took towards the modernisation of Indian music. The eminent ethnomusicologist of South Asia, Bonnie Wade, informs us about the singularity of this achievement, first demonstrated at the turn of the century in Gujarat:

> In Rajkot in 1897 he initiated a practice, which he continued all his life and which was most significant for Indian music. Since only a small, selected audience would be admitted to hear a concert at a royal court or in the home of a rich person, *he decided to give his musical performances in public, charging admission fees*. By this means he wished not only to make music accessible to the common man but to provide a means for musicians to earn a livelihood independently of rich patrons. Most traditional musicians (including his *guru*) opposed him, of course, saying *that the art of music would be cheapened and commercialized* (1985: 43–44; emphasis added).[14]

Thus, Paluskar embodied a business-like acumen in demanding fees for professional concerts performed before an urban intelligentsia, whilst also retaining his devotionalism. In Bakhle's words, 'he was that rare artist whose enterprising sense of business mixed well with his religious sentiments' (2005: 154). The claim of music being cheapened and commercialised surfaced amidst the organisers of the Harballabh most vociferously in the 1950s, a decade when musicians began insisting on fees even at the Harballabh, considered a 'shrine of music'. Harballabh organisers looked back to the 'glory days' of Pt Paluskar, which were seen as untainted by the mercenary insistence on fees—a feature that had paradoxically been pioneered by Paluskar himself. Thus, the Harballabh was fashioned as the one exception to Paluskar's rule of demanding fees for public performance in most of the subcontinent.

Curiously then, the affirmation of the sacrality of the spot of the Harballabh by Pt Paluskar needs to be seen in the important context of his awareness of the nobility of his mission, the completion of which cast the Harballabh as a shrine of music, almost as a natural by-product. The obsequiousness exhibited by Pt Paluskar towards the Harballabh (as opposed to similar gestures made by a lesser-known musician) makes sense only after his primacy as a reverential figure had been established in the world of the Harballabh by the Sangit Mahasabha. This element of obsequiousness is something that the Jalandhar intelligentsia was also quick to pick up, along with his recipe for the kind of music to be performed and the norms of performance he upheld. The traits of volition, and specifically the non-monetary proclivities of musicians in the early twentieth century celebrated across the many accounts of the Harballabh (and discussed in the previous section), can thus be seen to reside in the particular connotations which Pt Paluskar actively imbued the Harballabh with. Thus, while for Paluskar, the act of not accepting money and instead donating money on Baba Harballabh's *samadhi* might have genuinely been expressive of a legitimate faith, the impact of his actions for the festival itself was problematic because any musician *not* exhibiting the same devotion at the Jalandhar festival was looked at askance by the majority of people at Jalandhar, whether patrons or audience members. This, then, is yet another example of Paluskar's agenda of imbuing a more syncretic musical cultural sphere with an overt Hindu devotionalism, an aspect which was changing the larger national cultural sphere at this time.[15]

As Bakhle succinctly reminds us, 'Paluskar's devoutness is not by itself the issue any more than is the genuineness of his faith. The real issue lies in the *commingling of music and sacrality in modern India*, not as the expression of individual private faith, but *as a paradigm of public culture*' (2005: 178; emphasis added). The Harballabh is thus a foremost example of Paluskar's exclusivist effect on what were hitherto eclectic and diverse musical meetings. By the time Pt Paluskar reached the end of his life in 1931, the mystic fluidity and 'aesthetic of inclusion' of the Harballabh's origins had been transformed into the clearly Hindu devotionalism of a modernised music.

The Birth of the Sangeet Mahasabha and the Nationalist Imperative

With the shift from the nineteenth to the twentieth century and the concomitant impact of Pt Paluskar, the organisers of the Harballabh (along with other Punjabi provincial efforts at musical congregations, for example, the Durgiana Temple Raag Sabha at Amritsar) were defining their festival in the new idiom embodied by developments at Lahore, especially in light of the leading role played by the Gandharv Mahavidyalaya there.

The Harballabh was organised and run solely under the headship of the *mahant* Pt Tolo Ram of the Devi Talab until 1922, aided by the steady flow of volunteers and materials from the residents of Jalandhar. In that year, however, thanks to the urging of a young high school teacher, Jagannath Parti, and with the agreement and leadership of other local leaders of Jalandhar, the first steps towards the setting up of a modern body were taken, as elaborated by Bawra below:

> In 1922 Shri Jagannath Parti was serving at the Sain Das Anglo-Sanskrit High School in the role of an English teacher. He had a great fondness for music and every morning he would meet Mahant Tolo Ram ji. Mahant Tolo Ram ji made him also join his efforts. With inspiration from Master Parti, Mahant ji accepted the solution of making a *sabha*. This year at the residence of Lala Mushtaq Rai Sood, a meeting of different residents of the town was called, wherein this *sabha* was named 'Shree Harivallabh Sangeet Mahasabha'. Shri Rai Bahadur Pandit Devi Chand was chosen as its President. Babu Sant Ram Ahluwalia (in whose name there is the Sant Cinema) and Rai Bahadur Mushtaq Rai were chosen Vice-Presidents. Master Jagannath Parti was chosen as the Secretary. From 1922 until 1964, he continued working in the role of Secretary. Since then he was the one who used to manage the stage (1998: 26).

This account corresponds, almost word-to-word, with the account of Jagannath Parti himself in Urdu.[16] The above paragraph squarely places the impetus for the emergence of the Sangeet Mahasabha on the local literati and other powerful elite notables of Jalandhar. The larger coincidence of the setting up of the Mahasabha in the year 1922, which marked the height of nationalist mass mobilisation around the non-cooperation movement, marking a new wave of middle-class self-consciousness and the emphasis on national universities, education and culture cannot be missed.

The active link the Sangeet Mahasabha forged with the ongoing Indian national movement is evident in the fact that the practice of singing 'Bande Mataram' at the end of each session of the Harballabh was introduced here by Paluskar.[17] Pt Paluskar and disciples would be present at many Congress sessions to conclude them with soulful renditions of 'Bande Mataram'. The Harballabh too adopted this practice of finishing each year's sitting with the singing of this national song. The first reference in newspaper reportage to the singing of 'Bande Mataram' comes from the year 1937.[18] This surely cannot be the exact date, for 'Bande Mataram' was an integral part of Pt Paluskar's agenda at all political meetings held in Lahore during the days he was setting up the first Gandharv Mahavidyalaya there during the first decade of the twentieth century (Bakhle 2005: 155).

This was also the time when and context in which the festival was first defined self-consciously as a 'Raga Mela', the name first appearing in 1933. Perhaps the reason for the epithet 'Mela' (fair) being attached is the fact that by this time numbers were swelling due to the democratisation and popularisation of music, thanks to the efforts of Pt Paluskar and Pt Bhatkhande, the impact of the fledgling gramophone industry and, most importantly, the fact that it was in the 1930s that the radio established itself in a major way in India (Goswami 1996: 149). Another reason for this epithet is the fact that by this time, the festival, under the efforts of the Sangeet Mahasabha, was actively defining itself as an upholder of classical music as per Paluskar's Sanskritised version, thereby leading to the inclusion of the crucial first half in the term 'Raga Mela', that is, 'Raga'. Prior to 1933, the festival is termed in very tentative and un-pompous terms as an 'annual symposium of musicians' (1913 and 1914), 'symposium of musicians' (1921) or simply 'anniversary of the Mahasabha' (1924).

The Performative Space at the Harballabh

With the rise of new technologies such as gramophone recordings and the subsequent widening of listening publics, the new custodians of classical music in the nationalist form at the Harballabh also strove to discipline audiences in newer ways. Elsewhere, I have delineated the process by which norms of performance and socially accepted behaviour for both the artist and the audience were established by the Mahasabha during the late 1920s. This ranged from the prohibition of the consumption of cigarettes and other addictive substances to especially the strict proscription on the spontaneous bestowal of monetary rewards by elite members of the audience on a musician, mid-performance (Kapuria 2015: 81–83). Apart from 'sacralising' the performative space of the Harballabh, such a strategy aimed to groom the elite (and lay) members of the audience in newer modes of musical appreciation. This strategy also favoured the emergent middle-class (upper-caste) performers, who were averse to being treated on par with traditionally lower-caste performers of music. Hence, saying 'no' to the money offered them was an effort to establish themselves as upholders of a hallowed tradition 'of the gods', and therefore it was important to identify the Harballabh as a space where this autonomy of the artists, as performers for the Devi (goddess), was paramount. Like Pt Paluskar did for the larger sphere of Indian music, so the doyens of the newly created Sangeet Mahasabha institutionalised the Harballabh mela itself, foregrounding new norms of purity by challenging prevailing practices that moved patrons and audience members to spontaneously reward pleasure-inducing entertainment.[19] This agenda of a 'modernisation of tradition' inaugurated by Punjab elites took inspiration from Paluskar's momentous visits to the Harballabh, which served to introduce a new disciplined ethic of performance at the Harballabh, evident in the notices issued by the Sangeet Mahasabha, which itself was formed at the height of the national movement.

This shift in the space of performance was simultaneous with a parallel shift in the content of music performed here. In terms of the more sublime or avowedly 'classical' genres, dhrupad, which enjoyed a wide following throughout the Punjab with a considerable number of practitioners, was slowly being ousted by khayal, the genre foremost in Paluskar's agenda. Many varieties of music performed here such as *sufi kafiyan* (classical form of Punjabi and Sindhi poetry, composed by popular sufi poets) and the *devi ki bhentan* (songs sung for the goddess Durga, literally, the 'gifts of the goddess'[20]), along with other popular folk genres, were also slowly sidelined. This is evident in a rare primary source, a common invitation letter printed by Pt Tolo Ram in 1924 to invite eminent people to the Harballabh (see Image 7.1).

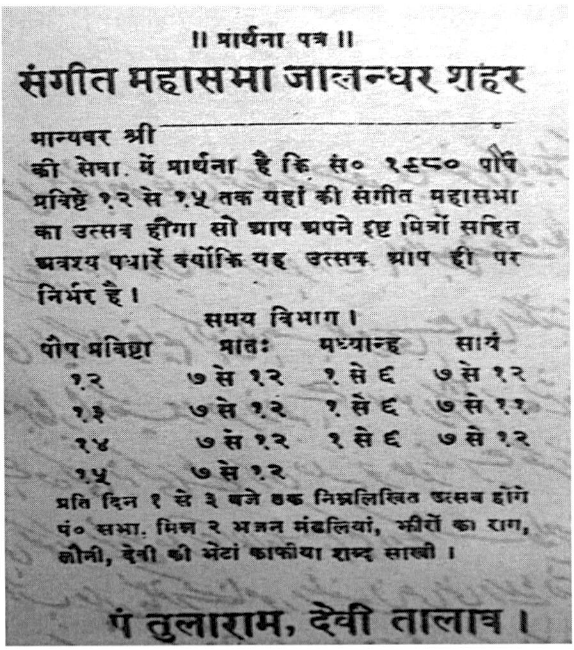

॥ प्रार्थना पत्र ॥

संगीत महासभा जालन्धर शहर

मान्यवर श्री ____

की सेवा में प्रार्थना है कि सं० १९८० पौष प्रविष्टे १२ से १५ तक यहां की संगीत महासभा का उत्सव होगा सो आप अपने इष्ट मित्रों सहित अवश्य पधारें क्योंकि यह उत्सव आप ही पर निर्भर है।

समय विभाग।

पौष प्रविष्टा	प्रातः	मध्यान्ह	सायं
१२	७ से १२	१ से ६	७ से १२
१३	७ से १२	१ से ६	७ से १२
१४	७ से १२	१ से ६	७ से १२
१५	७ से १२		

प्रति दिन १ से ३ बजे तक निम्नलिखित उत्सव होंगे पं० सभा. मित्र २ भजन मंडलियां, मीरों का राग, कौनी, देवी की भेटां काफीया शब्द साखी।

पं तुलाराम, देवी तालाब।

Image 7.1: Invitation letter-cum-advertisement printed by Pt Tula Ram in 1924 (Shastri 1997: 129).

Source: Reproduced with kind permission of the author.

As is evident, here we find an allusion that the 'devi ki bhentan' will be one of the items performed, thereby firmly establishing the range of popular pieces of music apart from the classical which were performed here right up to the 1920s. Interestingly, amongst the other kinds of musical repertoire advertised by Pt Tolo Ram are '2 *bhajan mandlis*', '*jhiron ka raga*', '*louni*', 'kafiyan' and '*shabd sakhi*'.[21] Each of these repertoires is in itself extremely interesting. The first are the '2 bhajan mandlis' referring to the wandering troupes of bhajan-singing minstrels—a practice and cultural phenomenon clearly catering to popular devotional needs—that would be performing at this Mela of classical music. '*Jhiron ka raga*' is the next item on the list, and I would propose this refers to the music performed by groups of the *jhinwar* or caste of 'water carriers', whose performances at Harballabh are also referred to by Bawra and whom colonial ethnographers recorded as playing an important ritual role in lifting the bride's palanquin at weddings in Punjab.[22] This is thus a clear reference to the presence of a variety of folk music at the Harballabh. Even more interesting is the reference to 'louni', most likely a Marathi martial song (and not a corruption of the Marathi '*lavani*').[23] Nonetheless, the fact that it was chosen as one of the musical repertoires to be printed in this notice could allude to the fact that the many Marathi musicians regularly attending the Harballabh post-Paluskar would, in fact, be exhibiting folk music from their region. This would make 'louni' an exotic attraction from a distant region that was available for consumption only at the Harballabh, hence meriting special emphasis.

After mentioning the exotic, however, Pt Tolo Ram (or Tula Ram, as his name is spelt in the notice) finds it necessary to firmly return to the familiar. The next item on the list is the much-loved sufi genre of the Punjab, the 'kafiyan' (classical form of Punjabi and Sindhi poetry, composed by popular sufi poets like Shah Hussain, Bulleh Shah and Shah Abdul Latif Bhittai), which are followed by the last item hailing from the Sikh liturgical tradition—'shabd sakhi' (sung hymnal religious stories of the Sikh gurus). The reference to the shabd sakhi also demonstrates the popularity of Sikh devotional musical traditions among the listening publics of the Harballabh.[24] The insertion of both sufi and Sikh liturgical genres of music at this festival of classical music located on a Hindu sacred site points to the older aesthetic of inclusion that marked the space of performance at the Harballabh, harking back to the more convivial origins of the festival in 1875.

Further, given that both genres are mentioned after the presumably Marathi 'louni' also enhances their status as genres *representative* of the Punjab, and hence one may surmise that many other rich genres from Punjab would have also been performed.[25] Despite the main attraction being classical and raga music, the reference is to genres that are all beyond the pale of the classical. Given the focus on raga music at this festival, the mentioning of these quintessentially non-classical items can thus be seen as a means to attract a wider audience via these more popular genres and draw them towards classical music through the backdoor, as it were. Gradually, however, such eclecticism in the performance and consumption of music created by an equally eclectic group of Punjabis began to shift towards a more rigidly fixed musical sitting focusing on the formalised classical music of a sanitised high tradition as upheld by Paluskar and his cohorts, which focused on and attracted musicians from beyond the Punjab as well.

CONCLUSION

This chapter has explored Pt V. D. Paluskar's connections to colonial Punjab through a focus on his relationship with Hindu elites in Lahore and Jalandhar—two out of three major colonial Punjabi cities (the third being Amritsar). However, Paluskar's connection to Punjab extended beyond Lahore and Jalandhar, as evidenced by his stint at centres like the city of Okara (110 km from Lahore) where he was employed by a wealthy patron, Sikh leader Baba

Khemsingh Bedi, during the months before he established the Gandharv Mahavidyalaya. Paluskar channelised the patronage offered by Bedi towards the creation of a newer, more modern and nationalist form of music. This included the devising, while he was employed by Bedi at Okara, of a new notation for Hindustani music, which he first published at Lahore in 1901 in a book titled *Sangita Balabodh* (Kippen 2006: 25). Again, Punjab's princely rulers, especially the maharajas of Kashmir and Kapurthala, also offered crucial early funding to Paluskar's music school, the official announcement for which was made in 1901 at the Lahore *haveli* (traditional home) of Raja Dhian Singh Dogra, who had been one of the Sikh Maharaja Ranjit Singh's longest-serving prime ministers in the early nineteenth century (Bakhle 2005: 148). These examples demonstrate that, to an extent, old aristocratic relationships still mattered during this period of change, even though they were increasingly directed towards a new and different goal—of freeing Indian music from its feudal patronage and the cultivation of new patrons and audiences in the form of the middle classes.

By examining the wealth of anecdotes that surround Paluskar's association with the Harballabh, this chapter has attempted to unpack the contradictions in the historical circumstances of the functioning of the festival and the officially championed discourse around it. It delineated how Pt Paluskar's visits led to a sea change in the technicalities and logistical organisation of the festival, especially in the structural ordering of its performative space. While elsewhere in India Paluskar also created new norms of more commercial performances, at Jalandhar he particularly invested performance at the Harballabh festival with a solely devotional aura and non-commercial form, one that Harballabh organisers strove to continue well after his death, right up to the 1950s. In the post-Paluskar phase, through an emphasis on practices such as the disciplining of large crowds and injunctions on audience behaviour, among others, the Sangeet Mahasabha consciously began cultivating the Harballabh festival in the mould of the modern, disciplined, urbane music concert characteristic of those held at Lahore (Kapuria 2013: 197–209). By the 1940s, then, the Harballabh had become an important and crucial centre for the nurturance, performance and consumption of classical music in a democratised public sphere of culture defined by the norms of colonial modernity. However, I also went beyond and complicated the picture with a reference to the paradoxical and exceptional position which the Harballabh occupied in the imagination of Pt Paluskar, and at the same time, the consistently celebratory, semi-hagiographic discourse circulating amongst Harballabh-*wallah*s around the figure of Paluskar. Instead of simply treating these anecdotes as stories, this chapter has attempted to detect a pattern in these tales, situating them in the wider socio-political context of early twentieth-century Punjab.

More broadly, I have argued how colonialism precipitated conditions for a new reformist agenda that was crafted for music under the leadership of the Arya Samaj in colonial Punjabi cities such as Lahore, Amritsar and Jalandhar.[26] This laid the groundwork for the subsequent success enjoyed by Paluskar's programme in redefining Indian classical music along Hindu devotional lines. Thus, the decade of the 1890s in colonial Punjabi cities prepared the foundation for the reception and propagation of Paluskar's message of a Hindu devotional music performed by domesticated, middle-class Hindu women through an attack on courtesans and mirasis, a cleansing of 'vulgar' lyrics in traditional women's songs and the conceptualisation of a new relationship between piety and pleasure in the public domain. However, the larger question, which Paluskar's engagement with music in Punjab entails for the cultural history of the region, needs to be more fully researched in a way that takes on board the many contested and controversial trajectories that music took in the aftermath of the partition of the subcontinent, and especially of Punjab, in 1947.

Notes

1. It is telling that a Bengali man's views are of central importance for this mini-reform attempt in the capital of colonial Punjab. This can be explained on account of the lead in education and other spheres that Bengali elites had over those of the Punjab, which had been colonised only relatively recently.

2. In many ways, these were later echoes in Lahore of what reformers had elsewhere already articulated two-three decades previously. Janaki Bakhle discusses the very similar views of Parsi reformer K. N. Kabraji in Bombay during the 1860s. See Bakhle (2005: 70–75).

3. Baghbanpura, located on the Grand Trunk Road, is a town near the city of Lahore in Pakistani Punjab. It is also home to the shrine of the Punjabi Sufi poet Shah Hussain.

4. The vociferous denouncements of *nautch* girls were clearly a sign of how prevalent nautches were, reflecting the centrality of the institution in Punjabi society. The very fact that caste-based 'associations' and *biradari*s (large families), such as the one in Baghbanpura, found it necessary to take collective pledges to ban them illustrates how they were a pre-eminent form of popular entertainment and crucial for the successful completion of any festivity.

5. See Sondhi (1905). For more on Sondhi, see Kishwar (1986).

6. This was a rather meaningless gesture, given that these very hereditary Muslim musicians were the first point of attack in Paluskar's agenda for music, as has been illustrated by Bakhle. See *Two Men and Music*, pp. 173–78.

7. Several voluntary music associations, such as the Lahore Sangit Sabha and Punjab Classical Music Society, were active in the period from the 1910s to the 1940s, as evident in weekly notices in newspapers like *The Tribune*, consulted by this author.

8. For a discussion of some of Sud's statements, see Kapuria (2013: Chapter 1, especially pp. 64–68).

9. A *raga* is the basic unit of Hindustani music, and refers to a melodic mode of Indian classical music, containing an established number of notes.

10. I am grateful to Bhai Baldeep Singh for this insight.

11. More famous in the oral record as also having taught *dhrupad* to a young Pt Bhimsen Joshi who visited and stayed in Jalandhar during his peregrinations across India as an adolescent.

12. Instead, the one domain in which nationalist reform succeeded indisputably was in altering the composition and expectations of the audience, the character of which shifted from an artistocratic, feudal nobility towards an emergent Anglicised middle class. The audience for such music is thus comprised mostly of the middle classes today, most of them educated in the basics of Hindustani music through the nationalist music schools of Paluskar and Bhatkhande.

13. For a more detailed account of Paluskar's reception in Punjab, see Kippen (2006: 24–26). For a more general account on Paluskar, apart from Bakhle's seminal work, see Rosse (1995).

14. This is an argument that still rages.

15. The crucial point Bakhle demonstrates is that

> we see through Paluskar's achievements...the emergence of a national cultural sphere in the early years of the twentieth century, long before the nation itself was in sight, in which Muslimness needed to be hidden from view, toned down, or reformulated. It had to *demonstrate*... its participation in Brahminic ritual, prayers, *bhajans*, *kirtans*, and *abhangs*, and attendance at temples as proof of its right to membership in the Indian nation. *This inaugurated the structural and systemic difficulty of being a musician in the public world of music without participating in Hindu forms of religiosity* (2005: 174–75; emphases added).

16. Part of a 12-page-long document in Urdu from his memoirs, reproduced in the Harballabh Sangeet Sammelan Souvenir of 1972.

17. For the Harballabh, it was the 1919 Congress that is the most memorable. In this instance, too, it was musicians from beyond the Punjab who took centre-stage, and not Punjabi ones, in what was perhaps one of the only classical music festivals that, if we were to believe Pt L. K. Pandit's testimony, Gandhi apparently attended in the Punjab. Those participating in this historic sitting included musicians such as Pandit Bhaskar Rao, Ustad Fayyaz Khan, Pyaare Imaamuddin, Master Krishna, Pandit Ram Krishna Buva, and Shri Kanhaiya Laal, among others. Noting this watershed moment, Bawra commented that: 'Prior to c. 1919 so many artistes of such high calibre had not come here together.... On the last day, amongst the listeners present were the English Commissioner of Jalandhar, the Guru(s) of Kartarpur, the Chief Minister

of Kapurthala princely state Miyan Abdul Azeez, and the ministers of Patiala and Kashmir as well' (1998: 32).

18. *The Tribune*, Friday, 31 December 1937, p. 7. Under the heading 'Jullundur Music Conference Concludes', the report in the 'Local and Provincial' column tells us, 'With the singing of the "Bande Mataram" song the conference came to a close.' References to Bande Mataram in *The Tribune* reports recur for the years 1937 and 1944. For more details, see Annexure II, 'Music and Lahore: The Constitution of the Norms of Cultural Practice', in Kapuria (2013: 197–209).

19. In the case of north India, and especially the Punjab, this is also a cultural artefact, still very prevalent at weddings and other festive occasions, when currency notes are twirled around the heads of the performers and then bestowed on them.

20. Though the literal translation is 'gifts of the goddess', given the multiple meanings the word '*bhent*' holds, '*devi ki bhentan*' could also be interpreted as 'tributes/offerings *to* the goddess', or indeed 'meetings *with* the goddess'.

21. *Jhiron ka raga* were the songs sung by the caste of 'water carriers', while *shabd sakhi* denotes the sung hymnal religious stories of the Sikh gurus.

22. The reference here is most likely to the caste of the '*Jhinwar* or water-carrier', described by colonial ethnographers as the one who

> supplies water to each house, night and morning, also in the harvest field (for which he is specially paid), and at weddings and funerals when he generally gets moderate fees in coin. He is also expected to help carry the bride's *dooly*. For ordinary work he gets grain at each harvest, calculated in various ways, and usually is supplied with daily food by the villagers turn and turnabout (*Punjab District Gazetteers* 1908: 212).

23. That this genre was popular in late nineteenth-century Punjab is corroborated in a short story by Rudyard Kipling set in Lahore. See Kipling (1899[1888]). According to Prachi Deshpande, the *louni* performed by disciples of Paluskar at the Harballabh festival of Jalandhar in the 1920s is not to be confused with the erotic Marathi genre, the *lavani* (personal communication, 29 January 2013).

24. As Niranjan Kaur Khalsa (2012) has shown, Sikh *kirtan* music was being similarly institutionalised and canonised during this period, part of the broader Singh Sabha movement for socio-religious reform across Punjab. See also Linden (2008).

25. Today, however, this broader 'aesthetic of inclusion' has almost completely disappeared and it would be unimaginable to find the organisers advertising 'shabd sakhi' or '*kafiyan*' as items of performance in the Harballabh souvenirs or invitation cards.

26. For evidence of the Amritsar literati's encouragement of Paluskar's project, see Kapuria (2023: Chapter 3).

REFERENCES

Bakhle, Janaki. 2005. *Two Men and Music*. New York: Oxford University Press.

Bawra, Joginder Singh. 1998. *Harivallabh Darshan*. Jalandhar: Sangeet Kala Manch Publications.

Bhagavati, Mai. 1892. *Abala Mati Vegarodhik Sangit*. Lahore: Anglo-Sanskrit Yantralaya. British Library shelfmark VT1589.

Deodhar, B. R. 1973. 'Pandit Vishnu Digamber in His Younger Days'. *Journal of the Indian Musicological Society* 4 (2): 21–51.

Goswami, B. N. 1996. *Broadcasting: New Patron of Hindustani Music*. New Delhi: Sharada Publishing House.

Jones, Kenneth. 1976. *Arya Dharm: Hindu Consciousness in Nineteenth Century Punjab*. Berkeley: University of California Press.

———. 1989. *Socioreligious Reform Movements in British India*. Cambridge: Cambridge University Press.

Kapuria, Radha. 2013. 'A Muse for Music: The Harballabh Musician's Fair of Punjab, 1947–2003'. MPhil. diss., Jawaharlal Nehru University.

———. 2015. 'Rethinking Musical Pasts: The Harballabh Music Festival of Punjab'. *Social Scientist* 43 (5–6): 77–91.

———. 2018. 'Music in Colonial Punjab: A Social History'. PhD diss., King's College, London.

———. 2023. *Music in Colonial Punjab: Courtesans, Bards, and Connoisseurs, 1800–1947*. New Delhi: Oxford University Press.

Khalsa, Nirinjan Kaur. 2012. '*Gurbani Kirtan* Renaissance: Reviving Musical Memory, Reforming Sikh Identity'. *Sikh Formations* 8 (2): 199–229.

Kipling, Rudyard. 1899[1888]. 'On the City Wall'. In *In Black and White*, by Rudyard Kipling, 5–52. New York: R.F. Fenno & Co.

Kippen, James. 2006. *Gurudev's Drumming Legacy*. Aldershot: Ashgate.

Kishwar, Madhu. 1986. 'Arya Samaj and Women's Education: Kanya Mahavidyalaya, Jalandhar'. *Economic & Political Weekly* 21 (17): WS 9–24.

Linden, Bob van der. 2008. 'Sikh Music and Empire: The Moral Representation of Self in Music'. *Sikh Formations* 4 (1): 1–15.

Malhotra, Anshu. 2002. *Gender, Caste and Religious Identities: Restructuring Class in Colonial Punjab*. New Delhi: Oxford University Press.

Mani, Lata. 1998. *Contentious Traditions: The Debate on Sati in Colonial India*. Berkeley: University of California Press.

Mir, Farina. 2010. *The Social Space of Language: Vernacular Culture in British Colonial Punjab*. Ranikhet: Permanent Black.

Morcom, Anna. 2013. *Illicit Worlds of Indian Dance: Cultures of Exclusion*. London: C. Hurst and Co.

Nair, Neeti. 2011. *Changing Homelands: Hindu Politics and the Partition of India*. Cambridge, MA: Harvard University Press.

Neuman, Daniel M. 1990[1980]. *The Life of Music in North India: The Organization of an Artistic Tradition*. Chicago and London: The University of Chicago Press (in arrangement with Wayne State University Press).

Punjab District Gazetteers. 1908. *Vol. XIV A, Jullundur District and Kapurthala State with Maps, 1904*. Lahore: The 'Civil and Military Gazette' Press (sole contractors for printing to the Punjab Government).

Punjab Purity Association. 1894. *Opinions on the Nautch Question*. Lahore: New Lyall Press.

Rosse, Michael David. 1995. 'The Movement for the Revitalization of "Hindu" Music in Northern India, 1860–1930: The Role of Associations and Institutions'. PhD diss., University of Pennsylvania.

Sachdeva, Shweta. 2008. 'In Search of the Tawa'if in History: Courtesans, Nautch Girls and Celebrity Entertainers in India, 1720s–1920s'. PhD diss., SOAS, University of London.

Sarkar, Tanika. 2000. 'A Prehistory of Rights: The Age of Consent Debate in Colonial Bengal'. *Feminist Studies* 26 (3): 601–22.

———. 2003. *Hindu Wife, Hindu Nation: Community, Religion and Cultural Nationalism*. Ranikhet: Permanent Black.

Shastri, Krishnananda. 1997. *Trigartapradesh Jalandhar: Aitihasik Aivam Dharmik Drishtikona*. Mai Heeran Gate, Jalandhar: Bharatiya Sanskrit Bhawan.

Sinha, Mrinalini. 1995. *Colonial Masculinity: The 'Manly Englishman' and the 'Effeminate Bengali' in the Late Nineteenth Century*. Manchester: Manchester University Press.

Sondhi, Lala Devraj. 1905. *Balodyan Sangeet, Stree Shiksha Sahitya Bhandaar Series*. Lahore: Punjab Economical Press.

Soneji, Davesh. 2012. *Unfinished Gestures: Devadasis, Memory, and Modernity in South India*. London: The University of Chicago Press Ltd.

Sud, Devki. 1934. *Sangit Prabha*. Amritsar.

Wade, Bonnie C. 1985. *Khyal: Creativity within North India's Classical Music Tradition*. Cambridge: Cambridge University Press.

Walker, Margaret. 2014. *India's Kathak Dance in Historical Perspective*. Farnham: Ashgate.

Webster, John C. B. 1976. *The Christian Community and Change in Nineteenth Century North India*. Delhi: Macmillan.

Eight

Territorialising Shrines in the Sacred Landscapes of Punjab

Yogesh Snehi

Introduction

Academic and popular debates on religion in twentieth-century Punjab have often centred on the theological and textual contours of sacred practices, and therefore peripheralised far more predominant practice-based notions of piety that revolve around sacred shrines.[1] Shrine-based faith practices were also particularly sought to be redefined and territorialised in twentieth-century Punjab. Harjot Oberoi underlines how the project of modern Sikhism entailed 'the reordering of sacred space and pilgrimage destinations, a new religious calendar (negating agrarian rhythms and their accompanying celebrations), the disciplining of the body, the cultivation of a Protestant ethic and its attendant rationality' (Oberoi 1994: 141). Colonial governmentality (see Murphy 2012: Chapter 3) as well as polemics of reformers like Giani Ditt Singh (Malhotra 2017) against the veneration of Sakhi Sarwar or Gugga Pir (Oberoi 1994: 139–203), the movement for gurdwara reform (Murphy 2012; Singh 1922; Singh 2000) or controversy over the proprietorship of Shahidganj complex (Haroon 2017) give us a window to explore the contours of these contestations. But these were not the only debates on sacred shrines, and therefore despite these reformist polemics on the historical (*itihasak*) gurdwaras, there were a plethora of popular sacred centres that continued to be important centres of faith practices later in the twentieth century—even when they struggled to cope with the impact of early twentieth-century debates, as well as the aftermath of the partition of Punjab. This chapter focuses on this *longue durée* of sacred shrines and argues that understanding them is critical to making sense of religious debates in Punjab. Territorialisation of shrines was therefore an important facet of all reformist debates in twentieth-century Punjab that sought to define religious boundaries as well as re-orient notions of sovereignty over sacred spaces.

TERRITORIALITY AND PUNJAB'S SCHOLARSHIP ON RELIGION

Territoriality has been an important marker of state discourses in colonial and pre-colonial India, articulated variedly on its landscape as Pakistan, Khalistan, Punjabi Suba, etc. The term has been employed to suggest physical borders or *sarhad* (Snehi 2020) and territory or *wilayat* (Snehi 2019: 94–125)[2] or debates around borderlands, boundaries and periphery, to designate political and spiritual domains of the state and religion. Most of these domains overlap. Therefore, the spiritual wilayat of Chishti saints, for instance, in medieval India, remained co-terminus with the expanding political frontiers of the Sultanate state (Aquil 2004: 216–20).[3] However, once these gained salience in the lived spaces, wilayat was also socially grounded and intertwined with local networks of patronage and piety.[4] The term also has implications for debates around religious identity and has been employed, though critically, by Bhakti saints in medieval India to problematise dominant identities and ritual practices.[5] Since the nineteenth century, the term has been used to situate debates on identity, religion and region, and articulate claims of hegemonic religious nationalisms. These debates employ a language of monolithic religious identity which is bereft of diversity.[6] These imagined notions of religious nationalisms, expressed as *qaum*, do not necessarily correspond to the immediate sacred landscapes of Punjab. However, aggressive religious nationalisms do pose a potent challenge to popular sacred spaces, something I will discuss in the case studies detailed in the following sections.

While arguing the contemporary construction of affective attachment to Punjab among Sikhs, Harjot Oberoi states that 'it is the intersection of history and geography, discourse and space, territoriality and metacommentary' that transformed Punjab to Khalistan (1987: 27–28). This is despite the historical instability of the region's territoriality (Malhotra and Mir 2012: xxiii). Therefore, though a pan-regional notion of a loosely held Punjabi identity may have existed, an identity-oriented Sikh, Hindu or Muslim territoriality does not seem to have consolidated before the nineteenth century. Tony Ballantyne argues that the Sikh representation of themselves in the British state involves a deliberate process of privileging a 'religious over a regional identity, thus providing little ground for inter-racial or inter-faith alliances that might have more effectively furthered Sikh political and social-economic aims' (cited in Malhotra and Mir 2012: xxiii–xxiv). Similarly, in the construction of claims on the itihasak gurdwaras of Punjab, the claims of the Shiromani Gurdwara Parbandhak Committee (SGPC) have, since the early twentieth century, been articulated through a language of territoriality and community identity which is distinct from 'Hindu' identity (Murphy 2012: 188–223). Singh Sabhaites like Giani Ditt Singh articulated this notion of territoriality in the language of a distinctive notion of piety by denouncing the 'Sikh' veneration of 'Muslim' saint mystics.[7] Scholars have also drawn our attention to the language dynamic of identity formation and argued how the growing pressures of the reform movements in the late nineteenth and early twentieth centuries tried to centre around choice of language and script to define a Hindi–Devanagri–Arya, Punjabi–Gurumukhi–Sikh and Urdu–Nastaliq–Muslim identity

(Jones 1989). These debates gave a significant thrust to the print culture (particularly tract literature) and attempted to territorialise notions of religious identity. Territoriality, therefore, has been critical in the articulation of a variety of 'modernist' aspirations that encapsulate questions of identity, language, region, religion and also sacred shrines. However, as Farina Mir argues, 'in addition to Punjabi texts' oral circulation in both rural and urban settings as aspects of social and cultural life, there was a vibrant [popular] Punjabi book trade in the late nineteenth century' (2006: 422–23).

Thus, the predominance of a narrow textual scholarship on religion in and on Punjab limits our understanding of the complex ways in which religion operates in the everyday contours of a region's sacred landscape (Snehi 2019: 1–44). This historiography has a long continuity with the colonial narratives on Punjab that gave prominence to scriptures and disciplinary texts (*rehat maryada*). Here, Oberoi's remark about the nature of the sources that historians can use to reconstruct popular religion and the ways to use them becomes relevant (Oberoi 1994: 144). Recent scholarship by Yogesh Snehi (2019), Anshu Malhotra (2017), Anne Murphy (2012), Anna Bigelow (2010) and Farina Mir (2010) adds a new dimension to sources by foregrounding aspects of shrine spaces, Bhakti, popular print culture, materiality and sacrality through significant use of fieldwork and oral history, in addition to textual sources. Snehi foregrounds the relevance of studying shrine spaces as a significant sphere of religious debates. His work focuses on Sufi shrines and takes forward Farina Mir's work that suggests that there existed in colonial Punjab a possibility of viewing practices of Sufi saint veneration as independent of formal religious affiliations. Malhotra's work explores the intersection of caste, bhakti and gendered self through the agency of Piro from the Gulabdasi sect in Punjab. Such an exploration of intersectionality is crucial to understanding the complexity of caste and gender formations. Murphy similarly adds another dimension of materiality, incorporating sacred objects, to an understanding of sacrality in Punjab, which is intertwined with ideas of textuality, though not necessarily recognised in dominant historiography. These newer readings of notions of the sacred only further the enrichment of religious debates and broaden our understanding of territoriality. This chapter proposes that sacred shrines form an almost independent domain of religious expressions and therefore constitute a significant field of research.

Sacred shrines are imbued with the charisma of the founder, and therefore embody the founding moment. Yet shrines are also informed by streams of pilgrims who visit and frequent their spaces. These pilgrims come from a diverse range of formal religious affiliations. My argument on shrines departs from the dominant discourse of the Sikh historiography in Punjab, which treats shrines as an extension of textual discourses, and therefore, in any episode of perceived deviation, requires course correction. Shrines that deviate from such disciplining are at best considered anomalies in the 'modern' religious ideals of territoriality and governmentality. There continues to be a predominance of this milieu in both theological and political manoeuvrings of the SGPC and the Vishwa Hindu Parishad (VHP).[8] The most important example of this ideal is the Gurdwara Reform Movement, which continues to manifest in everyday contours of Punjab through the authority of the SGPC (Snehi 2014). The recent controversy on the revision of the State Council of Educational Research and Training (SCERT) textbooks over the reduction of content on Sikh history (to allow students to read more of Indian and world history) similarly underlines the limits of any possibility of reimagining the textbook narrative on Punjab.[9] While this has been reported and debated as an instance of erasure and distortion of the history of Punjab, much of it has to do with the representation and dominance of Sikh history syllabus in Punjab and additionally the hold of private publishers who control the huge market for history textbooks of classes XI and XII. Both these instances highlight the power that modern and territorialised discourses on religion continue to exert on forms of text and practice. The Golden Temple is one intriguing example of this complexity of association and disciplining. Anyone who visits this shrine complex cannot miss the guards holding spears deputed along several places at the entrances, along the *sarovar* (tank), along major and minor shrines. Important symbols of the shrine's sovereignty, these guards tutor and discipline visitors on the correct code of conduct. This may range from asking women to cover their heads properly or instructing *mona* (non-turbaned) visitors/pilgrims to wear proper *patka*s. Sometimes, even a devotee may point at the formal and informal, Indian or Western caps or headgear that apparently do not align with the code of conduct inside the gurdwara premises.[10]

This constant monitoring raises some fundamental issues on debates around faith practices in South Asia that demand disciplining. Shrine visitation as a practice is also an equally complex phenomenon not necessarily guided by formal religious affiliations, as people from different faiths visit a variety of sacred spaces. Additionally, caste-based exclusions on temple or gurdwara entry are not generally practised in Punjab. Is it therefore possible to think of sacred shrines as not merely embodying and illustrative of textual norms, but as a far more complex arena of overlapping sacrality, a domain of liminality? In an attempt to seek alternatives to this historiographic dominance, my focus has been on such shrine spaces which remain fairly independent, though not necessarily untouched by dominant discourses, and try to see how these spaces struggled to find a narrative agency despite the dominant pressures of territorialisation. The following case studies foreground some of the theoretical possibilities embedded in the invocation of 'space' as an analytic in the longue durée history of Punjab. These narratives have been compiled from interviews of caretakers and devotees, popular tracts, inscriptions at sacred sites, newspaper reporting, court petitions and a sustained engagement with shrine spaces. The attempt is not to deviate from the given narrative or establish a correct narrative, but to situate this narrative in the space of its production. I have translated and paraphrased diverse narratives in my own voice, collating both oral and textual tales that had been narrativised within the premises of shrines. My attempt has been to analyse narrative strategies, their emplotment and the meaning embedded in these narratives.

While discussing 'fictional' narratives around Gulabdasi dera at Ratol, Malhotra lays emphasis on 'the moulding of the story, narrating and performing it to a culture's unique predilection' (2017: 300–01). Is it, therefore, possible to reinterpret causality by attaching meaning to memory and agency to narrative strategies? I remain wary of ascribing definitive values to popular shrines, either as abodes of peace or spectres of antagonism, discourses that are informed by identitarian politics (Snehi 2019: 52–56). Popular shrines are archives of everyday life, a mirror to understand the complex reciprocity, contestation and dissent of dominant discourses. This complexity cannot be understood by presupposing exclusivity and competition.

Gurdwara Samadhan Bhagat Jalan Das Ji at Naushera Dhala[11]

Gurdwara Baba Jalan Das has been the most recent addition in the large complex of Samadh Baba Jalan Das (d. 1664). Situated near Atari on the Indo-Pak border (Image 8.1), this sacred complex has had a continuous existence from at least the early seventeenth century. Located along an important trade link between Lahore and Amritsar, it embodies both the character of sacred spaces pre-Partition and post-Partition. In the latter half of the twentieth century, the shrine has been in the midst of Indo-Pak wars, leading to the terrible period of militancy.

Baba Jalan Das Ji, a Sandhu Jat, was born in 1586 at village Kanhaiye Ke in district Lahore and got married in village Hazrah (3 km from Naushera Dhala) before settling down with Bibi Ramki (d. 1650) at Naushera Dhala. Before Partition, Naushera Dhala was part of Lahore district. Baba Jalan was an Udasi *sant* (saint) and a contemporary of the sixth Sikh Guru Hargobind.

IMAGE 8.1: Gurdwara Bhagat Jalan Das Ji.

Source: Author.

He performed his *tap* (meditation) inside a *gufa* (cave), locally called *bhaura*. Baba Jalan is said to have met Guru Arjan Dev at Tarn Taran and Guru Hargobind at a nearby village, Bhadana, which is now in Pakistan. At a sarovar which stands along a small *linga* shrine (Image 8.2), he performed ritual bathing and finally attained *jal samadhi* (literally, union with the divine through deep meditation), never to emerge again. He composed 313 *sakhi*s (Punjabi prose) and 42 *bishnpad*s (a poetic genre associated with Mathura, and with Vaishnavas and wandering Bairagis), which were transmitted mostly orally until they were compiled in the early twentieth century. These were published for the first time in 1914 by Bawa Thakar Singh and later by Bawa Budh Singh in 1935. His compositions were also included in the *giyani* (Punjabi) coursework of Punjab University, Lahore (*Bani Bhagat Jalan Das Ji* 2013[1999]: 4). Jalan's hagiography follows repetitive motifs and templates that are borrowed from bits of stories from Nanak's early life (not paying revenue or disoriented in mundane tasks) or bits of tropes from the Ramayana (Baba Jalan, Bhai Gola and Bibi Ramki). These narratives are embedded both in the given literary motifs and embedded worldviews.

IMAGE 8.2: Shivala along the *sarovar* at Bhagat Jalan Samadhan complex.
Source: Author.

Baba Jalan's father was a lambardar (village headmen) who collected revenue from village Khairo and deposited it in the official treasury at Multan. Once, Jalan was assigned the task of depositing the revenue. He was caught in a storm and lost his way. On the way, he met a *sadh* (ascetic) who transformed his life. Overjoyed, he threw away the silver coins and immersed himself in bhakti. Angered by his failure to deposit the revenue, Shah Jahan, the Mughal Emperor of Delhi, ordered the arrest of Baba Jalan. Someone also informed the emperor that Jalan had disrespected his *tasveer* (image/painting). He sent his cavalrymen from Multan to arrest Jalan, but they turned blind. Jalan still submitted to them and got himself handcuffed, but the handcuffs were miraculously unlocked. When they reached the court of Shah Jahan, the emperor asked Jalan whether he had disrespected his image. Jalan admitted to possessing the emperor's image. He stated that when he looked at it every morning, he envisioned the Ram who made him the emperor. Jalan then performed some miracles (Image 8.3); the fodder he was carrying on his head was offered to horses but as soon as it was consumed, it was replenished again. Similarly, when Bibi Ramki offered the wood she was carrying for the emperor's

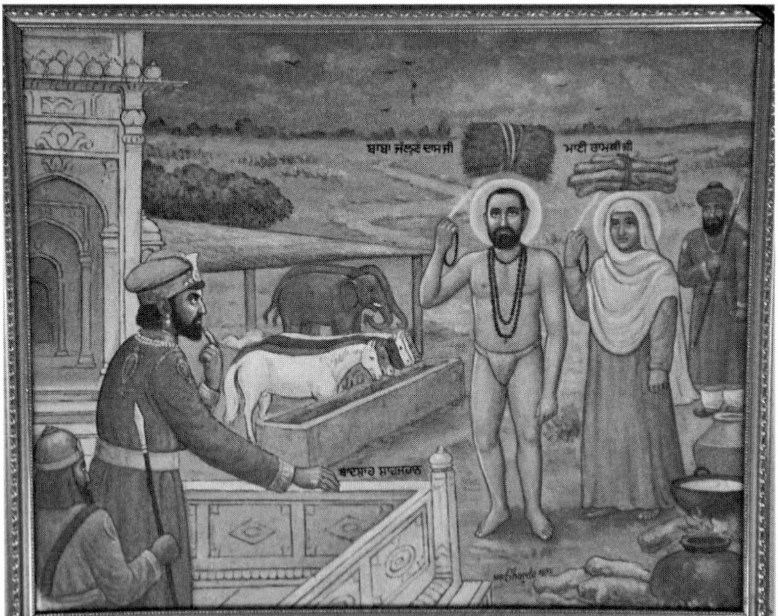

IMAGE 8.3: Baba Jalan pays a visit to Shah Jahan.

Source: Author.

kitchen, its stock would not finish. Looking at these miracles, the emperor repented his mistake. Baba Jalan was offered 2,000 *bighas* of land, which he donated to people of different castes who settled a village in his name and a *darbar* (shrine) in this village near Multan. Another village, Rampur, was settled in the Lahore district with a family of Bathan Jats from village Hadiare, Gill Jats from village Gillan, Khatris from village Naarli and Majhabis (extracted from Singh and Ghuman 2012[2005]: 7–15).

Neither of Baba Jalan's two sons, Kanshi Ram and Banshi Ram, survived. The present sacred complex at Naushera Dhala is managed by the descendants (Baba Nirmal Singh and his family)[12] of Bhai Gola, the younger brother of Baba Jalan, and his successors. The 'place of dwelling' of Baba Jalan constitutes an important centre of veneration. It was a single-storey nineteenth-century octagonal tomb structure with a large dome and small pilasters on all four sides. Bibi Ramki's tomb is adjacent to Baba Jalan's tomb. Both tombs contain their *samadhs*.[13] Baba Jalan's samadh is said to be a memorial samadh since he attained jal samadhi and disappeared inside the sacred pond (Image 8.2). These samadhs bear a peculiar similarity to the burial sites of Nath jogi ascetics, representing a linga-like tumuli. Adjacent to these samadhs, in their respective tombs, are single beds with covers. There are images and copperplate engravings of images of Baba Jalan in a loincloth (*langot*) with Bibi Ramki and Baba Gola (also in a langot). While the tomb of Bibi Ramki remains intact (Image 8.4a), Baba Jalan's tomb has recently been transformed into a three-storeyed structure with an onion-shaped dome on top, typical of late medieval structures and also of contemporary gurdwaras (Image 8.4b).[14]

Adjacent to these tombs is the grave of pir Baba Bhaur Shah, a Sufi disciple of Baba Jalan. Bhaur Shah lived in the nearby village of Bhasin (now in Pakistan) and was deeply devoted to Baba Jalan. He would reach Naushera Dhala early in the morning every day before the latter woke up. The pir assumed the name Bhaur (or nectar-seeking bumblebee) because of his deep devotion to Baba Jalan (Image 8.5a). Since Bhaur Shah was growing old, Baba Jalan

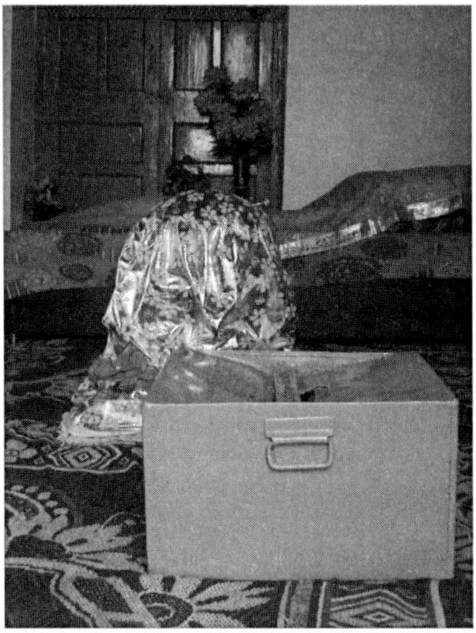

IMAGE 8.4A: Mai Ramki's tumuli.

Source: Author.

IMAGE 8.4B: Ghar Asthan Bhagat Jalan Das Ji Mai Ramki Ji.

IMAGE 8.5A: A painting depicting Bhaur Shah visiting Baba Jalan.

Source: Author.

IMAGE 8.5B: Dargah of Bhaur Shah with a *jhanda sahib*.

stopped him from coming every day, even tying him up in a cattle shed at village Bhasin. However, Baba Bhaur still managed to reach the next day and performed services for Baba Jalan. Since Bhaur did not relent, Jalan asked him to stay with him at Naushera Dhala. The pir died here and his burial place, which was inside a house earlier, has now been reclaimed and transformed into a small dargah (Image 8.5b).

In the centre of the complex is a small pond approached by steps where Baba Jalan took jal samadhi. At one corner of this pond is a small *shivala* (shrine dedicated to Shiva) where Baba Jalan performed worship (Image 8.2). Baba Nirmal Singh, the current caretaker of the *dera*, expressed his desire to appoint a priest to take care of rituals at the temple. The early nineteenth-century structure attests to the sacred complex's pre-colonial past. However, at the place where Baba Jalan performed tap (meditation) now stands a large gurdwara (Image 8.6). This gurdwara was named

IMAGE 8.6: Guru Granth installed inside Gurdwara Bhagat Jalan Das Ji. His *dhuna* (not visible in the image) is on the right.

Source: Author.

after Guru Hargobind and was established on 14 May 1999 by the earlier *prabandhak* (manager) of the shrine who got the *tapasthan* (place of meditation) demolished and apparently wanted to evict the descendant caretakers. Baba Nirmal (Image 8.7) laments the demolition of the tapasthan and opines that the gurdwara should have been constructed at some other place and not above it. After the site was restored to the family of descendants of Bhai Gola, the gurdwara was re-named after Baba Jalan. The site of the tapasthan is now marked by a concrete memorial in one corner of the two-storeyed gurdwara. Apparently, the need for a gurdwara also emerged because people from neighbouring villages who were devoted to the sacred complex are predominantly Jat-Sikh, and regularly sought the performance of *akhand path* (continuous recitation) of Guru Granth Sahib. The second storey of the gurdwara has a gallery that displays a number of paintings on the life of Baba Jalan. These paintings were commissioned by Baba Nirmal Singh, the present caretaker, in 2005.

IMAGE 8.7: Baba Nirmal Singh narrating an event from Baba Jalan's life.
Source: Author.

Baba Jalan's early disciples were Khatris of the nearby villages—Bhasin, Bhadana and Kanha. Most late medieval structures at Naushera Dhala were commissioned by these disciples. Among the newly commissioned structures is one large Diwan Hall (place of congregation) where *ragi dhadi*s, *kavishri*s and *kathavachak*s (storytellers) come and perform on festive occasions. There are two medieval wells named Ramki Khui and Chitti Khui which are no longer in use. When Baba Jalan went on 12-year-long travels, Bibi Ramki performed *seva* (service) for pilgrims at Chitti Khui. Another medieval well outside the complex is ceremoniously run on a Persian wheel during Baisakhi celebrations.[15] The sacred complex earlier contained just the samadhs, a temple, two wells and the pond. After the partition of Punjab, Naushera Dhala became a part of Amritsar district. The shrine complex is at a throwaway distance from the international border, which was fenced during 1967–68 (Image 8.8). Baba Nirmal Singh states that during the 1971 war, the Pakistan army came very close to the site, but the village was somehow saved. Guru Granth Sahib was installed in the dera in around 1973.

After the 1971 war, the Indian army wanted to construct a canal, as the first line of defence, right through the shrine complex. But due to the villagers' reservations, it later relented. During the heyday of militancy from the late 1970s to the early 1990s, the Border Security Force (BSF) did not mingle with the locals and people were not allowed to come out of their houses after evening. The BSF's camp is located right across the entrance of the shrine complex. Baba Nirmal says that things have changed for the better now. He laments two changes which were initiated in the dera's sacred complex post-militancy: the demolition of the tapasthan and the commissioning of new paintings on the life of Baba Jalan. The damage done to the cave was irreversible. There is a prevalent belief about Baba Jalan's curse—that whosoever constructs a second storey in the village does not prosper. Ironically, most new buildings in the complex are two-storey constructions and remain incomplete even after decades of construction.

IMAGE 8.8: International border fence and the boundary wall of the sacred complex of Baba Jalan.

Source: Author.

In the case of the paintings, Baba Nirmal had suggested that the Sharda painters of Amritsar make changes in the bodily representation of Baba Jalan. The new display hence altered his loincloth-clad appearance (Image 8.9a) which adorned the walls of samadh and the temple, and instead imagined a fully draped representation of Baba Jalan. These images were printed on the cover of the official life-sketch and *bani* of Baba Jalan (Image 8.9b). Baba Nirmal has tried to undo this misrepresentation by reverting to older images in the new editions of official publications.

Image 8.9a: Book cover of Baba Jalan's compositions.

Image 8.9b: Book cover of Baba Jalan's hagiography.

Source: Author.

Shree Bhairon Nath Temple and the Durgiana Tirath at Amritsar[16]

Bhairon Nath temple is one of the oldest shrines of Amritsar. It is situated close to Hathi Gate, adjacent to Durgiana temple outside the walled city. Despite the former's relative antiquity, it is the latter which has recently been given the status of *tirath* (pilgrimage centre). Durgiana temple was established in 1925, in the aftermath of the expulsion of allegedly 'Hindu' priests and Udasi ascetics ('*mahants*') from the premises of the Golden Temple in 1905.[17] Its construction coincided with the culmination of the Gurdwara Reform Movement and enactment of The Sikh Gurdwara Act, 1925. Singh Sabha reformers critiqued the practice of idol worship in the redefined precincts of the Golden Temple which was being neatly imagined as a 'Sikh' religious centre (Image 8.10). The structural similarities between the Durgiana temple and Golden Temple are truly remarkable. The former sought to compensate for 'Hindu' religious sensibilities. Gursahaimal Kapoor played a pivotal role in the establishment of this temple, which was inaugurated by Pandit Madan Mohan Malaviya. The site chosen for this temple was unusual. It was located outside the walled city and the chosen tank was actually meant to serve the ritual needs of the cremation ground. Adjacent to it were five important sites, a Parshuram temple, a Sitala Mata temple, a Hanuman temple, a Shiv Ganga temple at Dashnami Akhara and a Bhairon Nath temple. Most of these sites were in existence long before the Durgiana temple was established in 1925. The new temple mimicked the Golden Temple and was similarly located in the centre of the tank and approached through a causeway, conceived in white marble, and with a *darshani deori* (gateway) at the entrance. The stark structural resemblance between both the shrines is only a reminder of Durgiana's conceived alternative for *sanatan* (unchanged/eternal) sensibilities, which were displaced in the early twentieth century. There are smaller 'Hindu' shrines on all four sides of the tank; yet another structural resemblance with the Golden Temple plan, which also has minor 'Sikh' shrines on the periphery of the sarovar.

Image 8.10: Golden Temple and its periphery.

Source: 'An unknown bazaar print', 1860, Victoria and Albert Museum

The Golden Temple has occupied a central space in the religious practices of the Punjabi Hindu and Sikh population of

Amritsar since medieval times. Until the 1920s, there were hardly any other major centres in the city, which even closely paralleled the position of this shrine. There were several tanks in the city but the major ones were appropriated by Singh Sabhaites from the 1920s. The only major tank that was associated with 'Hindu' ritual bathing and that equalled the Golden Temple was Durgiana tank (Image 8.11). The Gazetteer of Amritsar District, 1892–93, describes the tank as:

> The Durgiana tank, which measures 541 feet by 432, lies under Fort Govindgarh, and is much resorted to by Hindus, who have surrounded it with temples and devidwaras. It has lately been put in order at a cost of Rs. 10,000 subscribed for the purpose by the Hindus of Amritsar. The principal cremation ground is close to the east corner of the tank (p. 162).

Durgiana's sacredness and antiquity depended on the transformation of this 'periphery' into a 'centre' of core *sanatani* sensibility. Appropriating the antiquity of the peripheral shrines was thus crucial for the legitimacy of Durgiana temple. Each of these has a narrative associated with it. Sitala Devi temple (as stated above) was located opposite the second entrance of Durgiana temple. The small shrine dedicated to this female deity, who is believed to cure measles, is now surrounded by an open courtyard on four sides and on one side by a large Dhanwant Kaur Dharamshala which was constructed around the first quarter of the twentieth century. Adjacent to this shrine is the Bara Hanuman temple. There is a legend associating this shrine with the story of Sita, who was exiled by Ram and stayed at Ramtirath (a large pilgrimage centre associated with Saint Valmiki) near Amritsar with her sons Luv and Kush. It is believed that when Ram was performing the Ashwamedha *yajna* (by letting a horse loose to demarcate the territory of a king), his horse was challenged by Luv and Kush at the spot where the Bara Hanuman temple is now located. When Hanuman came to confront Luv and Kush, they tied him to a banyan tree, which is believed to be the same tree located in the

1. Gobindgarh Fort
2. Bara Hanuman Temple
3. Durgiana Temple
4. Sitala Mata Temple
5. Bhairon Nath Temple
6. Shiv Ganga Temple
7. Cremation Ground
8. Parshuram Temple

IMAGE 8.11: Bird's-eye view of the Durgiana Tirath and its periphery.
Source: Google Earth image taken on 18 July 2020.

courtyard of Bara Hanuman temple. These legends have been in circulation at least since the early nineteenth century,[18] and were crucial to ascribe sacredness and antiquity to the site which can now parallel the Golden Temple's legacy. However, Bhairon Nath temple did not fit well in this sanatan scheme (Images 8.12a, 8.12b).

IMAGE 8.12A: Bhairon Nath Temple.

IMAGE 8.12B: Bhairon embossed on steel.

Source: Author.

Since the 1920s, Durgiana temple has also emerged as a source of legitimacy for contesting political ideologies. For a significant period after Partition, the management of the Durgiana Committee was with the affiliates of the Congress party. It was the Congress government which came up with a plan for the beautification of the Durgiana temple in 2005. In 2007, with the change in the mayorship of Amritsar and the hold of the BJP government, and the corresponding control of the VHP over the managing committee of Durgiana, the proposal is being vigorously pushed on the lines of the Galliara (corridor) project of the Golden Temple. The first phase of the scheme was launched by the Punjab government under Shiromani Akali Dal (Badal) leadership and Improvement Trust, Amritsar, in 2010. In this phase, the shops on one side of the narrow passage leading to the temple were demolished and allotted an alternative place in a newly built plaza along the entrance. In the second phase, which began in 2014, an open-air theatre and multi-level parking lot were to be constructed. At the site where the amphitheatre was proposed stood Bhairon Nath temple. When I conducted a survey of this temple on 5 February 2015, its property, consisting of a residential area, concrete idols/exhibits of nine Naths, one idol of Ganga and a section that was rented out to Nalanda School, had already been demolished (Image 8.13).

Image 8.13: Demolished sections of Bhairon Nath Temple (left). Entrance of Durgiana Temple (right).

Source: Author.

The shrine complex of Bhairon Nath temple majorly consisted of 19 samadhs (linga tumuli), a gufa (underground cave for meditation) and a Gorakhtilla (referring to the famous *tilla*/

Image 8.14: Previous *gaddi-nashin* of Bhairon Nath Temple.

Source: Author.

mound near Peshawar in Pakistan; but here, Gorakhtilla refers to an exclusive *gaddi* or seat for meeting devotees) (Image 8.14). Adjacent to it is a room-cum-office. The central sacred sites consist of four old temples of which two are shivalas, a temple with *akhand jot* (eternal flame) and a Bhairon Nath temple. This place was founded by Baba Daya Nath (no date, but claimed to be around 600 years old). Jogi Shiv Nath (60 years) was the incumbent mahant of

IMAGE 8.15: Jogi Shiv Nath, who fought against the demolitions at the temple.
Source: Author.

the shrine when I visited it in 2015 (Image 8.15). Jogi Shiv Nath shared how, on his request, Yogi Adityanath (then BJP MP from Gorakhpur and the head of the Gorakhmath and later the chief minister of Uttar Pradesh since 2017) wrote a letter to Punjab's chief minister, belonging to the Akali Dal, to stop the demolitions at Bhairon Nath temple. Demolition was nevertheless carried out. The Punjab and Haryana High Court had earlier refused to grant a stay against these demolitions. The final deadline for carrying out remaining demolitions at Bhairon Nath complex, except its four old temples, samadhs and the cave, was 31 March 2015. Ninety per cent of the demolition work had already been completed by early May 2016.[19]

Not interested in the Rs 6 crore offered to him, Jogi Shiv Nath later formed a protest committee to raise his voice against demolitions and not honouring the original Durgiana Beautification Plan of 2005 under the Congress government, which apparently recognised the autonomy of the temple. The VHP leadership of Amritsar tactically denies any conflict with 'Nathji' and presents this as a conflict with the Improvement Trust.[20] A total of four members take care of Bhairon Nath temple: Shiv Nathji, Bhagat Sohan Nath, Sham (sevak) and Santosh Devi. Nathpanth has traditionally been a heterodox tradition because of its strong critique of caste and Brahmanic ritualism. The ritual practice at Bhairon Nath temple, like offering of liquor and cannabis as well as its consumption on the premises, offers an alternative to the Brahmanic religious sphere represented by the Durgiana Committee dominated by the VHP. It also offers a rare insight into the ways in which the Durgiana's periphery is being transformed and sanatan-ised. Among other temples, Shiv Ganga Temple has been transferred to the Durgiana Committee and its priest is now a salaried employee. The early links of the temple with Dasnami Sampraday have now been subsumed within the dominant sanatan sphere.

After the death of Jogi Shiv Nath on 7 December 2016, the temple came under the control of a female manager. Though still independent, it is now a minor shrine in the larger scheme of the Durgiana Tirath. The Durgiana Temple complex (Image 8.16) now consists of a redeveloped plaza complex consisting of a heritage street, an amphitheatre, fountains, open-air theatre, landscaped parks and multi-level parking lot. The foundation stone of this project was laid in August 2016 during the Akali regime. In this process, the Bhairon Nath temple has been rendered peripheral. The militant sanatan-isation of sacred spaces has been a major hallmark of post-independence India. These processes have significantly consolidated a mono-narrative of Hinduism since the formation of the VHP in 1964.[21] The Durgiana redevelopment project seeks to erase the contentious past of Amritsar with its origins in the Gurdwara Reform Movement. The successive state governments, both under the leadership of Akali Dal and the Congress, have sought to reconcile this past by assigning an important place to Durgiana and its sanatan sensibilities. This process, however, undermines the very identity of the Bhairon Nath temple.

IMAGE 8.16: Improvement Trust Amritsar's plan of the Durgiana Tirath. Bhairon Nath Temple is now a small temple close to the *darshani deori* (entrance) of the Durgiana Temple.

Source: http://www.ingeniousstudio.in/durgiana-temple.html (accessed on 21 October 2023).

GHURAM SHARIF AND GURDWARA MILAPSAR AT VILLAGE GHURAM

Ghuram Sharif celebrates a less well-known legend about Pir Bhikham Shah (d.1709), a Chishti-Sabri saint of Patiala.[22] The legend states that when the tenth Sikh Guru Gobind Singh was born in the east of India at Patna, the saint offered *sajda* (prayers) facing that direction. When questioned about this by his *murids*, he told them that he had dreamt of a new sun rising with the advent of baby (*bal*) Gobind Rai. Bhikham Shah and his disciples then travelled all the way to Patna (Bihar) for a glimpse of the infant Gobind Rai, apparently then barely three months old. Desiring to know what his attitude would be towards the two major religious traditions of India, the saint placed two small pots of sweets in front of the child, one representing Hindus and the other Muslims. As the child covered both the pots simultaneously with his tiny hands, a contented Bhikham Shah proclaimed that the new seer would treat both Hindus and Muslims alike and show equal respect to them. After meeting Bal Gobind at Patna in 1666, the Pir lamented that due to his old age he would not be in a position to travel again and wished to meet Bal Gobind at Ghuram. Later in 1702, Guru Gobind apparently visited the Pir and the place they met at is commemorated by Gurdwara Milapsar (also known as Baoli Sahib due to the location of a medieval step-well in its premises), which was 'revealed' to Sant Baba Gurbachan Singh Kambli Wale in 1965. The Gurdwara (Image 8.17) is managed by a local managing committee headed by Sant Baba Avtar Singh (*kar seva wale*). The shrine organises celebrations every new moon night (*amavas*). A huge fair (*jor mela*) is organised on the day of Baisakhi and a *nagar kirtan* (procession) from the Gurdwara visits and pays tribute at the dargah of Pir Bhikham Shah. These new shrines and rituals create an important link with the past 'through reworked myths, rituals, and histories, and re-presented and performed in ways that make sense to the leaders and followers today' (Malhotra 2017: 307).

IMAGE 8.17: Painting inside Gurdwara Milapsar commemorating Guru Gobind Singh's meeting with Bhikham Shah.

Source: Author.

The shrine of Bhikham Shah witnessed plunder and loot amidst the violence of the Partition of the province. Much is known of the alleged role of the princely state of Patiala in the ethnic cleansing of Muslims in this part of Punjab (Brass 2003; Copland 2002). It remained desolate for several years until in the 1950s Baba Mast Wareh Shah, along with Baba Mast Diwana Bulleh Shah, undertook the task of restoring it. After the demise of the former, the latter has been playing a central role in its expansion along with his wife, Bibi Mast Diwani Bholu Shah (Image 8.18). Both are the present *gaddi-nashin*s of the shrine. Baba Mast Diwana Bulleh Shah is a Kumhar (potter) by caste and was born in a nearby village, Mandheri. Under his leadership, the dargah has constructed a large *langar* hall (community kitchen) and a *serai* (inn) for pilgrims. Baba Bulleh Shah identifies his lineage with the Bhikh Chishtis, a new Chishti sub-lineage that emerged after

IMAGE 8.18: Baba Mast Diwana and Bibi Mast Diwani on either side of the flex banner commemorating the birth of Bal Gobind.

Source: Author.

Bhikham Shah. Bhikham was born in 1625 in village Siana (Pehowa) to Saiyid Yusuf, who died when the child was barely 10 years old. Bhikham Shah's mother Malka brought him to her maternal home at Sadhora (near Ambala). His maternal uncle (*mama*) Pir Fazal Shah (whose mausoleum is also located at Ghuram) sent him to Hazrat Shah Abul Maali at Ambehta (near Saharanpur) for spiritual learning. He became the foremost disciple and Khalifa of the Chishti Sabri saint and was sent to Ghuram for the propagation of the Sabri order. Bhikham Shah's blessings transformed the life of a poor Brahmin, Daula, who assumed the name Roshan Daula and rose to take charge (*wazir*) of the royal treasury under Shah Jahan. Subsequently, the emperor bestowed the land revenue of 26 villages to the shrine. A significant mausoleum was constructed over the grave of Bhikham Shah (Image 8.19a and 8.19b), and Roshan Daula was also buried in an adjacent complex.

IMAGE 8.19A: Entrance to the grave of Bhikham Shah.

IMAGE 8.19B: Mausoleum built over the grave.

Source: Author.

There is a large mound in the centre of the village. It must have been a fort of significance and is of archaeological importance.[23] Local legend relates the village to Kaushalya (mother of legendary king Rama of Ramayana) who, it was said, married Dashratha here. A temple and gurdwara (in an enclosed *baradari*) dedicated to her are located atop a mound. It was apparently built by Maharaja Karam Singh (1813–45) of the erstwhile princely state of Patiala.[24] Before the partition of the subcontinent, Ghuram was primarily a cluster of settlements dominated by prosperous Kamboh Muslims. Other Muslim communities of the village comprised Mistri, Mughals, Khojas, Lohars, Penjas, Telis and Dhobis. There were *basti*s where lower-caste non-Muslims like Kumhars, Majhabi, Chamars (now Ravidasias), Chuhras (Harijans or Balmiki) and Shorgar lived.[25] There was not even a single upper-caste Sikh household in the village. Besides Bhikham Shah's shrine, the village also had a shivala. Today, the Jat and Rajput Sikhs who migrated from Gujarat, Sialkot and Lyallpur districts of west Punjab post-Partition constitute the dominant castes in Ghuram. Niranjan Balmiki (74 years old), the prime narrator of this case study, has had a long association with the shrine from pre-Partition times. His family is native to Ghuram and lived on the outer fringe of the village.[26]

The shrine has two major entrances. A huge medieval gateway leads to the first storey of the mausoleum of Bhikham Shah (d. 1709) while the second gateway (Image 8.20) leads to the actual place of burial (see Image 8.19a). Adjacent to this shrine

Image 8.20: Ghuram Sharif's smaller entrance with religious symbols of all major religions of Punjab.

Source: Author.

is a mausoleum of Roshan Daula and probably other members of his family. Currently, langar is distributed to pilgrims from the old Langar Hall. When I visited the place in 2015, a new large hall and a serai on the first floor were being constructed adjacent to the outer wall of the shrine. The shrine has two mosques: one inside the complex, adjacent to the dargah of Bhikham Shah, and another along the major gateway of the shrine. A large hall was later added to the structure by the current gaddi-nashin. Annual celebrations during *urs* (death anniversary) go on for two weeks and include recitations of Ramayana and Guru Granth Sahib, offering *chadar* (large piece of decorated cloth offered at the graves of mystic saints) at nearby shrines, and ceremonies of *gyarvi sharif* (festival for Sheikh Abdul Qadir Jilani) and *ghusal sharif* (ceremonial washing/bathing of the tomb of Pir Bhikham Shah). Gyarvi sharif is celebrated every month on the eleventh day of the moon.

In contemporary Punjab, this shrine occupies a central place for pilgrimage and the spiritual needs of Sabri disciples who are from a wide variety of caste affiliations. Contemporary Sufi shrines and urs claiming association with this order can be found in Amritsar, Batala and Phagwara. Around 1996, a *bir* of Guru Granth Sahib was installed in one of the rooms along the enclosing hall (Image 8.21a). Granthi and his supporting 'Sikh' staff take care of the premises that have several images from Guru Gobind Singh's life. In another adjacent room, a 'Hindu' *granth* Ramayana is located, which is attended by a pujari. The room has idols of several Hindu deities. This has been a more recent addition and was in place both during my first survey in December 2010 and the second survey in January 2015 (Image 8.21b). Both these rooms are not classified by either the pilgrims or the staff as a gurdwara or a temple, but cater to the religious needs of the diverse spectrum of pilgrims who visit the shrine. The dargah management has faced objections from the SGPC over the location of the bir of Guru Granth Sahib in its premises. The criticism is being addressed by assigning a different and independent gate to the room where the Granth is located.

IMAGE 8.21A: Room where Guru Granth Sahib is kept.

IMAGE 8.21B: Room where Ramayana is kept.

Source: Author.

INTERROGATING TERRITORIALISATION

The three case studies chosen in this chapter can be situated along the peripheries of dominant debates which emerged along with sharp undercurrents territorialising religious identities in twentieth-century Punjab. Post-Partition, Baba Jalan's samadh complex was reduced to a periphery situated along a troubled Indo-Pak frontier. Durgiana Temple emerged in the background of the peripheralisation of sanatan identity since the late nineteenth century, and was also situated on the margins of the walled city of Amritsar. Its emergence can also be seen as a result of the process of sanatani 'Hindu' consolidation since the 1920s (Tuteja 2021: 29–145). In the case of Ghuram, the shrine's link with Muslim devotees and *sajjada nashins* (caretakers) was peripheralised. The study of shrines has been on the margins of the dominant historiography of post-Partition Punjab. Their experiences were intertwined with sudden changes in the network of patronage, pressures of dominant discourses, and violent events in the past and present. Some of the major events that intersect with the shrines' narratives are the Gurdwara Reform Movement of the 1920s; the partition of Punjab in 1947; violence that preceded and followed the Indo-Pak war of 1971; the rise of the Hindu right in the aftermath of the Emergency in the mid-1970s; the militancy era from the late 1970s until the early 1990s; and the period of peace that followed into the twenty-first century. However, the medieval period is also important and shapes and situates the shrines' origins in the case of Baba Jalan's samadh and Ghuram Sharif.

In all these experiences, the partition of Punjab is one important defining event which shapes state formation and the assertion of the dominant ideologies that were forged in the process. The entire Punjabi Muslim population, except in Malerkotla, either migrated to Pakistan or was killed during the Partition violence (Talbot 2008). After its reorganisation in 1966, Punjab was transformed into a Sikh-dominated province. The state was both demographically and spatially reorganised. The Radcliffe line situated Baba Jalan's shrine on the Indian side of the international border, transforming it into a frontier shrine. This spatial transformation of the shrine complex, which was otherwise situated in the middle of Lahore and Amritsar (though now on the edge of the two nation-states), makes it vulnerable to perpetual pressures of Indo-Pak tensions along the international border. Before the Indian side of the international border was fenced in the 1970s, the space at least looked porous and contiguous. Now the fence is an important feature of its existence. Both metaphorically and physically, the shrine has borne the brunt of pressures of nation-state ideologies as well as the rise of militant nationalisms from the 1970s.[27] Shrine narratives are therefore significant in our imagination of religious debates.

Shrines have complex living histories that are structured and shaped within the dominant discourse. However, these very living histories sometimes invert the dominant narratives. This vibrant dialectic within which sacred spaces are situated is embedded with possibilities of critiques, appropriation and accommodation. It is curious to notice how Baba Nirmal laments the restructuring of sacred sites associated with Baba Jalan, albeit in a reconciliatory mode by proposing a corrective to the visual imagery of Jalan. This discursive possibility of rethinking sacred spaces is ripe, particularly in popular shrines. Similarly, the altered demography of village Ghuram post-Partition opens up a possibility of situating both the Ramayana and Guru Granth Sahib in the premises of the shrine. Even though it was resisted by the SGPC, structurally inscribing an oral encounter between Bhikham Shah and Guru Gobind constitutes an important recognition of a medieval narrative. We know that contemporary Ghuram is predominantly Sikh and pilgrimage to the shrine predominantly non-Muslim. The intertwining of these realities within a given narrative of caste hierarchies can also help explain some of the post-Partition contours of shrine spaces. The *barkat* in this case flows through a Kumhar caretaker.

Popular sacred spaces do not necessarily fit into the rigid textual imagination of religious histories. As living spaces both structurally and ideologically, sacred shrines have been vibrant historical contours of the religious process.[28] Debates on the restructuring of sacred shrines remind us of Harjot Oberoi's argument on the architecture of the Sakhi Sarwar shrine at Dera Ghazi Khan. He underlines how:

> Unlike orthodox religious centres with rigidly defined principles of architecture codified by canons of great tradition, the Sarvar shrine appeared to be loosely constructed according to the devotees' conception of what constituted sacred design. Various buildings erected on the site of the shrine contributed to the shrine's religious culture. The cultural space of the shrine, its architectural fusion [and layout], and the icons it enshrined contained elements from the 'great' religious traditions of Punjab, enabling it to generate popular devotion (1994: 151).

Sakhi Sarwar's shrine therefore accommodated belief in Bhairava, Mata Masani and Guru Nanak, as also myths and legends associated with his diverse devotees like Dani Jatti, Isa Baniya and Khan Doda Pir. Modern reform movements and the discourse that these created attempted to transform sacred spaces. One notices this in the emergence of a gurdwara in the name of Baba Jalan in 1999 that radically restructures the sacred complex at Naushera Dhala, wiping out his tapasthan and peripheralising the shivala, dargah and *talab*. The samadhs of Baba Jalan, Bibi Ramki and Baba Gola, marked by votive tumuli and located inside nineteenth-century tombs, have now been enclosed into a large gurdwara-like structure. This process was followed by reimagining the visual representation of Baba Jalan. But as soon as militancy lessened in Punjab, a corrective to the pressures of the dominant discourse was initiated, which means the maintenance of the sarovar and shivala and a return to the imagery of Baba Jalan in a loincloth.

Similar processes have taken place in Durgiana temple. Though spatially similar to the Golden Temple, an aspect which cannot be altered, the sacred complex has been witness to a massive restructuring of neighbouring shrines, particularly those which do not fit into the scheme of its sanatan sensibility. It remains to be seen whether Bhairon Nath temple will be able to retain its autonomy and identity after the completion of the project.[29] The addition of a temple with the Ramayana and a room with the bir of Guru Granth Sahib at Ghuram echoes similar processes (see Images 8.21a and 8.21b), albeit with a divergent trajectory of inclusion, in the context of post-Partition realities of the region's demography. But this is not necessarily a unidirectional process. The emergence of a non-SGPC-managed Gurdwara Milapsar in 1965 attests to this vibrant process imagined within the scheme of a popular narrative around Bhikham Shah and Guru Gobind, giving it a status of a defining local narrative. But this process is not insulated from the pressures of an exclusive SGPC narrative which sees any signs of inclusion as a threat to the Sikh discourse.[30]

Shrines are therefore active spheres of debates on territoriality. The systemic takeover of the major shivalas and temples of Amritsar by the VHP is also illustrative of this process. The VHP has a dominant presence in the managing committee of Durgiana temple. Its office is situated in one of the major Shivala Bagh Bhaiyan. This has meant a growing dominance of *sanatan*ist mono-narratives in temples and the erasure of signs perceived as non-Brahmanic. It is therefore important to centre shrines in the narrative on religious reform, and not treat them as mere addenda to textual debates, pay attention to what is changing and invented, and what is being imposed by the pressures of dominant narratives. This peripheralisation of shivalas also follows from the radical Sikh taboos against the consumption of tobacco and cannabis in such temples, which were targets of Dal Khalsa militants in the early 1980s (Chawla 1982).

SITES OF ENCOUNTER

It is intriguing to note the patterns of encounters between popular sacred sites and communities, and the dominant discourses and institutions within which the three case studies can be situated. Baba Jalan was a Jat Udasi saint with an important following among Punjabi Khatris and Jats. It was a site where succession was retained in the family of Baba Jalan, barring a brief lull in the period of Sikh militancy. As compared to this scenario, the Durgiana temple management has changed hands from the Congress to the VHP in recent times. Similarly, there was a break in succession at Ghuram Sharif for at least half-a-decade post-Partition. The contemporary caretakers of each of these sites can be situated within a defined caste profile; Baba Nirmal Singh is a Jat, Durgiana committee is constituted of Hindu upper castes of Amritsar, and Ghuram Sharif is managed by caretakers who are low-caste Kumhars. Shrine narratives in the chosen case studies suggest constant negotiation with transforming spaces in given contexts. These renegotiations are possible because of a liminal narrative past. Baba Jalan's liminal identity in the present context—a Jat and Udasi—complicates the project of hegemonic appropriation of his identity in the dominant discourse of twentieth-century Punjab, where Jat has become synonymous with 'Sikh' and Udasi with 'Hindu'.

Possibilities of inversion were also present in medieval India. The encounter of Shah Jahan with Baba Jalan is one such instance. We know of Shah Jahan's patronage to miniature paintings, several of which were portraits. In one of the mid-seventeenth-century portraits, he is shown as standing on a terrestrial globe, with divine radiance depicting him as the lord of the three worlds (Ramaswamy 2007). But what we do not know is how ordinary people perceived these self-aggrandising projects of the emperor. Jalan's response to the allegation of disrespect towards Shah Jahan's portrait as envisioning 'the Ram who made him the emperor' not only helps him evade the emperor's punishment but also situates him among the mortals. This logic is similar to the Sikh narrative trope of *sacha padshah*, used to dialectically situate Sikh Gurus in relation to Mughal emperors.[31] We should also remember that Shah Jahan was wary of the growing influence of the sixth Sikh Guru Hargobind (d. 1644), which led to the Battle of Amritsar in 1628. This was a period of declining Mughal patronage to the Sikh gurus and shifting patronage to popular Sufi, Vaishnava, Nath and Udasi establishments.[32] Shrines like Ghuram Sharif and saintly figures like Baba Jalan were recipients of Mughal patronage. But this does not necessarily distance either Baba Jalan or Bhikham Shah from the Sikh Gurus. Shrine narratives, conversely, take a narrative trajectory of encounter even in times of conflict.[33]

Partition wiped out the entire population of Muslims from Ghuram.[34] Shudras (Kumhar) and Dalits ('Chuhras' and 'Chamars') are the only extant link between pre- and post-Partition Ghuram. The presence of lower castes in the managerial and spiritual contours of several Sufi shrines speaks of the legitimising process that was enabled through these abandoned spaces. This process should be situated along the historical marginality of lower castes from shrine management in Punjab. Dalits constitute more than one-third of the overall population of post-Partition Punjab (Snehi 2023: 16). Inclusive of 'Chamars' (or Ravidasias), 'Chuhras' (or Balmikis or Majhabis) and Masihs, these castes have found significant expression at the shrines of Sufi saints.[35] Desolate shrines gave these castes an opportunity to legitimise their place within the space offered by the post-Partition milieu. It is therefore important to pay attention to the process through which a Sufi shrine situated itself in a demographically transformed Ghuram—from Kamboh Muslims to Jat and Rajput Sikhs. Partition provides an intriguing insight into historical encounters of communities with new demographic realities. As stated earlier, the shrine's narrative past also provides the script on which the present encounter gets situated. Tussle with the SGPC over the Guru Granth Sahib inside Ghuram Sharif also reflects the broader pattern of social relations, albeit negotiated within the spatial lens of the village and the shrine narrative. Ghuram is a rural shrine and visited predominantly by peasants. There is a larger network of Bhikh Sabri shrines in Doaba, Majha and Malwa. Similarly, the mythic association of the archaeological mound in the village with the epic narrative of Ramayana also manifests in the temple inside Ghuram Sharif. There has, however, never been any opposition to its location in the shrine's premises.

Debates on religious reform in colonial and contemporary India have not paid attention to the ways in which shrine spaces encountered the pressures of reform. Arguments have remained confined to the ways in which major shrines, communities and religious boundaries were being formed and imagined in response to Christian missionaries and other reformist ideologies. Religious discourses were therefore reduced to the dominant frameworks of religious identities: Sikh, Muslim or Hindu. This chapter complicates religious debates by paying closer attention to the complex reception that shaped modes of religiosity in twentieth-century Punjab.[36] Textuality, in this imagination, remains one of the several components that define the territorialisation of shrines, encounter being another. Thus, in addition to the articulation of Hindu (sanatani, Arya Samaji) or Sikh (sanatani, Tat Khalsa, Kuka Namdhari) or Muslim (Anjuman, Ahmadi) sensibilities, closer attention should also be paid to intertwining with Udasi, Sufi, Nath, Jat, Kamboh, Khatri, Kumhar, Balmiki, etc., modes of social expression, which are important ingredients of any religious articulation in a given social milieu.

Marginalisation of Sufi, Nath and sanatan sensibilities was a hallmark of the critical articulation of the Tat Khalsa, Arya Samaji, Kuka or Ahmadi worldview in early twentieth-century Punjab. Anshu Malhotra has elaborated the career of an important Singh Sabhaite, Giani Ditt Singh, who dedicated popular tracts dissuading Sikhs from venerating Sufi saints, visiting Hindu temples dedicated to goddesses, and popular saint figures like Gugga and their shrines.[37] Similarly, Arya Samaj writings were inclined to critique almost every existing religious formation to propose a Shuddhi programme for a return to the Vedic religion (Jones 1989). Reformist ideas were rife in the writings of Ahmadis, Tablighi Jamaat, Anjuman, Arya Samaji, Namdhari, and Singh Sabha organisations spread across Punjab, propagating a very textual notion of piety that involved the disciplining of ordinary beliefs, affiliations and shrines. Much attention has been paid to these debates on reform, along with the works on the role of Christian missionaries. Territorialisation of shrines has been central to all these debates. This spectrum has been extended to shrines in post-Partition Punjab, ranging from militant control over the Golden Temple and leading to the bloody Operation Bluestar in 1984, to struggles over control of the Durgiana committee and peripheralisation of the Bhairon Nath temple, or violent targeting of Sufi shrines like Nigaha in Langiana or Manakpur Sharif near Kharar. Partition has been central to most of these articulations. Therefore, Vazira Fazila-Yacoobali Zamindar's argument on long partition can well be extended to the contours of shrines in post-Partition East Punjab. She argues that 'what actually happened at Partition and the ways in which Partition is rhetorically invoked and socially remembered, are tied to each other to produce what is called Partition effects' (Zamindar 2010: 238). However, closer attention should also be paid to the ways in which this terrible past is being reconciled and reimagined.

Despite post-Partition Akali rhetoric against the Rashtriya Swayamsevak Sangh (RSS) and perceived fears of Hinduisation of the Sikh tradition, a stable Akali–BJP electoral alliance shapes the contemporary narrative of shrines in Punjab. State patronage to Durgiana Tirath can be situated in this context. This trajectory also extends into other contours of the Akali–Balmiki alliance and the massive redevelopment of a Valmiki Tirath near Amritsar. This has meant a recognition of Punjab's complex sacred geography, while maintaining the dominant narrative of Khalsa by commissioning a memorial shrine for the victims of Operation Bluestar inside the Golden Temple complex in 2012.[38] This relative stability of the BJP–Akali alliance emerges from two significant moments of the anti-Emergency movement of 1975 and the condemnation of Congress's role in the 1984 Sikh pogrom. Electoral politics becomes one of the ways in which the reformist rhetoric of the early twentieth century is being reconciled, assuring a sacred geography for the sanatani Hindus of Punjab.

Acknowledgements

The author acknowledges the useful insights of Rajive McMullen and Rajnish Popi in constructing the narrative around Bhairon Nath and Durgiana Temple.

Notes

1. Mandair argues how 'terms such as "Sikh theology" have come to be regarded as native categories (in this case *gurmat*) when neither Sikh experience nor the broader Indic culture from which it is derived

can claim to possess a word for "religion" as signifying a mystical or theological core, or a unified faith community' (2005: 273).

2. I explore this notion of spiritual *wilayat* in the context of the Panj Pir shrine at Abohar and argue how textual notions of these terms do not help us to understand the emergence of memorial shrines like these whose emergence intersects with sacred geography and trade routes. Therefore, despite fundamental changes in the demographic profile of the population of this frontier town, the shrine's association with the popular origin tales and the memories of medieval encounters along the Sultanate trade route continues to have salience even today.

3. Raziuddin Aquil (2004) explores this aspect by revisiting the *malfuzat* literature of Sultanate India and reconsidering the nationalist assumption that Sufis remained aloof from political affairs of the state.

4. Refer to the work of Richard M. Eaton (2006[2003]) on the shrine of Baba Farid and the expansion of Islam in Punjab.

5. Hagiographies and writings of medieval Bhakti saints like Kabir, Namdev and Guru Nanak, and modern saints like Sai Baba are replete with references to the limits of formal religious affiliations and the dominant ritual and caste practices associated with them.

6. A recent article by Paramjit Singh Judge situates Taksals, Akharas and Nihang Deras within debates on Sikhism to suggest an in-the-making process of religious identity that is entangled with the Khalsa, Vedantic and Udasi identity, as also popular *dera* practices (Judge 2014: 372–81).

7. For an interesting discussion on Giani Ditt Singh's construction of a territorialised Sikh community, see Malhotra (2017: 201–36). Significantly, this construction was based on denouncing the *nakli* Sikh practice of venerating popular Sufi saint mystic and living gurus.

8. The plans of the Durgiana Temple Committee (dominated by the Vishwa Hindu Parishad) to expand the sacred complex of the temple at Amritsar have meant posing a challenge to *deviant* ritual practices like offering alcohol and the consumption of cannabis at Bhairon Nath Temple, though the latter is much older than Durgiana Temple.

9. Chitleen K. Sethi (2018) reports the textbook controversy in *The Print* as the 'first big test by fire' for the Amarinder Singh government.

10. On one occasion, when the author visited the Golden Temple with students from Delhi in February 2017, a young 'Sikh' devotee approached and specifically pointed at the Himachali cap covering the author's head.

The authority with which the devotee spoke about it suggested that he was a petty employee of the gurdwara. Disturbed by this incident, the author approached some old devotees performing *jal seva* at a corner of the *parikarma* to seek a resolution to this objection. They argued that the younger generation is perhaps more rigid in the interpretation of these norms, but that there was no problem in covering my head with a Himachali cap. Irrespective of the fact that the author could find a resolution to this objection, there is in general a proper code of conduct at the Golden Temple and other major religious places at Amritsar, which is mostly absent at ordinary and popular spaces of devotion.

11. This section is based on the narrative of Baba Nirmal Singh (67 years), a descendant of Bhai Gola, recorded on 4 February 2015.

12. Baba Nirmal Singh gave the author a tour of the sacred complex. He also gifted him copies of the sacred *bani* and a brief hagiography of Baba Jalan.

13. Anshu Malhotra details the semantic use of the term *samadhi* to suggest 'meditation/concentration/contemplation to a mystical experience of a trance. It also refers to immolation, especially through entombment of an ascetic, to the place where such an entombment, cremation, or a burial may have taken place, or ashes of a saintly figure may lie buried' (Malhotra 2017: 303).

14. It was under construction both at the time of my first visit in April 2013 and in February 2015.

15. Majha region has several such Persian wheels which are maintained as important symbols of material heritage at sacred spaces. One of the most significant among these is the six-wheeled Persian wheel at Chheharta near Amritsar, which commemorates Guru Arjan Dev's commissioning it for the use of the local community. These interventions played an important role in extending agriculture and shaped notions of work (*kirat*) in the popular religious discourses.

16. This section is based on the author's field visits to the shrine in 2008, 2010 and 2015.

17. Tat Khalsa discourse often classifies Udasis as Hindus. However, Udasis have had a long relationship with the Sikh tradition. Its founder Sri Chand became an ascetic but was devoted to Guru Nanak. Later Sikh Gurus recognised his spiritual lineage and the eldest son of Guru Hargobind, Baba Gurditta, succeeded Sri Chand.

18. Ranjit Singh sanctioned repairs to Ramtirath tank, giving credence to the popular legend. It is believed that Lahore was named after Luv and Kasur after Kush, the two sons of Rama. Both of these are medieval cities (Chopra 1976: 606).

19. Punjab and Haryana High Court, *Pracheen Mandir Shree Bhairav Nath Ji vs State of Punjab*, Civil Writ Petition no. 17671 of 2014 (final order dated 5 May 2016).

20. The VHP has its head office at yet another important shrine, Shivala Bagh Bhaiyan in Amritsar. I visited the VHP office and interviewed Mr Arun Khanna on 6 February 2015.

21. For a detailed reading on the rise of VHP in India, see Peter van der Veer (1994), Manjari Katju (2003) and Malavika Kasturi (2015).

22. H. A. Rose mentions this site briefly in his glossary (1919: 529–30). This discussion is based on the interviews with Sevadar Niranjan Balmiki (74 years) and Baba Bulleh Shah, the current *gaddi-nashin*, conducted on 20 January 2015. The shrine of Ghuram Sharif was first surveyed on 30 December 2010. The story of the saint is painted on the front wall, both in Hindi and Punjabi, and is also illustrated on several walls through enamel wall-paintings.

23. G. B. Sharma and Manmohan Kumar (1980) published a study based on an excavation of the site, which dates from at least first century CE.

24. *The Tribune* (28 December 2009) reported the protest of locals against the removal of the temple and gurdwara located inside the *baradari*.

25. There are several terms used to designate erstwhile untouchable communities. Majhabi is a term used to designate sweepers who gravitated towards Sikhism. 'Chamars', also known as Ravidasias, were traditionally leather-tanners and rallied as a new identity under the leadership of Mangu Ram in the early twentieth century. The term 'Chuhras' is used for sweepers who trace their origins to saint Valmiki, who composed the Ramayana. To alleviate their low-caste status, Gandhi designated them as Harijans. These communities are today known as Dalits.

26. Niranjan's father too was a devotee of the shrine. Niranjan himself has been associated with the shrine for more than four decades. He is involved as a mason for the maintenance and expansion of the dargah premises. Although not a convert to Islam, he desires to be buried after his death, a wish he has communicated to his sons.

27. It is curious to note the ways in which the iconography of Baba Jalan was transformed to erase his Udasi antecedents. Shrine management instituted a new set of dominant rituals which included the recitation of Guru Granth Sahib in the newly constructed gurdwara erected in the *tapasthan* of Baba Jalan. The transformed *samadhs* of Baba Jalan and Bibi Ramki now fit into the dominant architectural landscape. Within these transformed realities, the small shrine of the Sufi saint, the recent corrective to Baba Jalan's image and the publication of his *bani* offer a critical insight into the shrine's past.

28. While discussing the historical evolution of rituals at the Golden Temple, Navtej K. Purewal and Virinder S. Kalra underline that despite attempts towards 'disciplining the darbar', incorporation and adaptation of common idioms and practices is a dynamic process through which the SGPC re-narrativised sites into a Guru-centred history, and therefore an 'institutionalization of popular rituals'. Healing, *darshan* and *mannat* are as much a component of temples or saint shrines as they are of gurdwaras (Purewal and Kalra 2016).

29. Elsewhere in Uttar Pradesh, in Gorakhnath temple in Gorakhpur, a century-long process of sanatanisation has transformed this Nath yogi site and has instituted Brahmanic rituals in its everyday practices.

30. The SGPC has systematically taken over a large spectrum of gurdwaras which otherwise existed in the realms of popular imagination and were managed by local committees. This process is particularly marked along shared sites like Achal Sahib-Achleshwar Dham and Gurdwara Haji Ratan-Dargah Haji Ratan.

31. Pashaura Singh (2005) explores this in relation to the Mughal state in his article on the martyrdom of Guru Arjan.

32. Refer to the works of B. N. Goswamy and J. S. Grewal (1967, 1969) for an understanding of Mughal patronage at Jakhbar and Pindori.

33. This narrative is in contrast to the modern constructions of Sikh identity, particularly in the *rahit* literature, which often 'built itself against and in conflict with Islam, though there were multiple other possibilities and mitigating factors on the ground, among them demotic interaction, shared devotional traditions that venerated Sufi pirs, popular performative traditions, sects like Gulabdasis' (Malhotra 2017: 308).

34. More recently, attempts have been made to record the oral narratives of ordinary individuals in Indian and Pakistani Punjab. One such attempt is the YouTube channel, 'Sab Da Punjab'. In one such

narrative, Baba Haji Saddique tells us about the demographic profile of pre-Partition Ghuram and the circumstances which forced the Muslims from the village to migrate to Pakistan (see https://www.youtube.com/watch?v=IKHXq61q7Bk, accessed on 13 October 2023).

35. For a fascinating visual insight into the world of saint shrines, see documentary films by Ajay Bhardwaj (2005, 2012). Snehi's monograph (2019) also details several case studies of shrines in which lower castes have an active managerial involvement in the everyday functioning of the shrine.

36. While narrating the performance of Gulabdasi rituals at Rajoki, Malhotra underlines how the Sikh villagers vacated the village gurdwara temporarily for these performances at the request of Vijenderji, representing the eclectic religiosity of South Asian popular culture (Malhotra 2017: 314).

37. See Malhotra (2017: Chapter 6).

38. Radhika Chopra (2013) explores the establishment of the museum and the politics of memorialisation that it institutes.

REFERENCES

Aquil, Raziuddin. 2004. 'Scholars, Saints and Sultans: Some Aspects of Religion and Politics in the Delhi Sultanate'. *Indian Historical Review* 31 (1&2): 210–20.

Bani Bhagat Jalan Das Ji [Punjabi]. 2013[1999]. Naushera Dhala (Tarn Taran): Gurdwara Samadhan Bhagat Jalan Das Ji.

Bhardwaj, Ajay (Dir.). 2005. *Kitte Mil Ve Mahi* ('Where the Twain Shall Meet'), DVD. New Delhi: India Foundation for the Arts.

———. 2012. *Milange Babey Ratan De Mele Te* ('Let's Meet at Baba Ratan's Fair'), DVD. New Delhi: Mainstay Production.

Bigelow, Anna. 2010. *Sharing the Sacred: Practicing Pluralism in Muslim North India*. New York: Oxford University Press.

Brass, Paul R. 2003. 'The Partition of India and Retributive Genocide in the Punjab, 1946–47: Means, Methods, and Purposes'. *Journal of Genocide Research* 5 (1): 71–101.

Chawla, Prabhu. 1982. 'Miscreants Succeed in Sowing Seeds of Hatred among Hindus and Sikhs in Punjab'. *India Today*, 31 May. Available at https://www.indiatoday.in/magazine/special-report/story/19820531-miscreants-succeed-in-sowing-seeds-of-hatred-among-hindus-and-sikhs-in-punjab-771825-2013-10-12 (accessed 17 January 2024).

Chopra, Barkat Rai, ed. 1976. *Punjab District Gazetteers, Amritsar*. Chandigarh: Revenue Department.

Chopra, Radhika. 2013. 'A Museum, a Memorial, and a Martyr: Politics of Memory in the Sikh Golden Temple'. *Sikh Formations* 9 (2): 97–114.

Copland, Ian. 2002. 'The Master and the Maharajas: The Sikh Princes and the East Punjab Massacres of 1947'. *Modern Asian Studies* 36 (3): 657–704.

Eaton, Richard M. 2006[2003]. 'The Political and Religious Role of the Shrine of Baba Farid'. In *India's Islamic Tradition, 711–1750*, ed. Richard M. Eaton, 263–84. New Delhi: Oxford University Press.

Goswamy, B. N., and J. S. Grewal. 1967. *The Mughals and the Jogis of Jakhbar: Some Madad-i-ma'āsh and Other Documents*. Shimla: Indian Institute of Advanced Study.

———. 1969. *The Mughal and Sikh Rulers and the Vaishnavas of Pindori: A Historical Interpretation of 52 Persian Documents*. Shimla: Indian Institute of Advanced Study.

Haroon, Sana. 2017. 'Custodianship of Shahidganj in Colonial Lahore: Land, Land Use and the Formation of Religious Community, 1850–1936'. *Indian Economic and Social History Review* 54 (2): 183–220.

Jones, Kenneth W. 1989. *Arya Dharm: Hindu Consciousness in 19th-Century Punjab*. New Delhi: Manohar.

Judge, Paramjit Singh. 2014. 'Taksals, Akharas, and Nihang Deras'. In *The Oxford Handbook of Sikh Studies*, eds Pashaura Singh and Louis E. Fenech, 372–82. New York: Oxford University Press.

Kasturi, Malavika. 2015. *Sadhus, Sampradaya, and Hindu Nationalism: The Dasnamis and the Shri Bharat Dharma Mahamandala in the Early Twentieth Century*. Nehru Memorial Museum and Library (NMML) Occasional Paper, History and Society, New Series 79. New Delhi: Nehru Memorial Museum and Library.

Katju, Manjari. 2003. *Vishva Hindu Parishad and Indian Politics*. New Delhi: Orient BlackSwan.

Malhotra, Anshu. 2017. *Piro and the Gulabdasis: Gender, Sect, and Society in Punjab*. New Delhi: Oxford University Press.

Malhotra, Anshu, and Farina Mir. 2012. 'Punjab in History and Historiography: An Introduction'. In *Punjab Reconsidered: History, Culture, and Practice*, eds Anshu Malhotra and Farina Mir, xv–lviii. New Delhi: Oxford University Press.

Mandair, Arvind-Pal S. 2005. 'The Emergence of Modern "Sikh Theology": Reassessing the Passage of Ideas from Trumpp to Bhāī Vīr Singh'. *Bulletin of the School of Oriental and African Studies* 68 (2): 253–75.

Mir, Farina. 2006. 'Imperial Policy, Provincial Practices: Colonial Language Policy in Nineteenth-century India'. *Indian Economic and Social History Review* 43 (4): 395–427.

_____. 2010. *The Social Space of Language: Vernacular Literature in British Colonial Punjab*. Ranikhet: Permanent Black.

Murphy, Anne. 2012. *The Materiality of the Past: History and Representation in the Sikh Tradition*. New York: Oxford University Press.

Oberoi, Harjot S. 1987. 'From Punjab to "Khalistan": Territoriality and Metacommentary'. *Pacific Affairs* 60 (1): 26–41.

_____. 1994. *The Construction of Religious Boundaries: Culture, Identity, and Diversity in the Sikh Tradition*. New Delhi: Oxford University Press.

Pashaura, Singh. 2005. 'Understanding the Martyrdom of Guru Arjan'. *Journal of Punjab Studies* 12 (1): 29–62.

Purewal, Navtej K., and Virinder S. Kalra. 2016. 'Adaptation and Incorporation in Ritual Practices at the Golden Temple, Amritsar'. *Journal of Ritual Studies* 30 (1): 75–87.

Ramaswamy, Sumathi. 2007. 'Conceit of the Globe in Mughal Visual Practice'. *Comparative Studies in Society and History* 49 (4): 751–82.

Rose, H. A. 1919. *A Glossary of the Tribes & Castes of the Punjab & North-West Frontier Province*. Lahore: Superintendent, Government Printing, Punjab.

Sethi, Chitleen K. 2018. 'Amarinder Faces His First Big Test by Fire Over "Erasing" Punjab History from Textbooks'. *The Print*, 4 May. Available at https://theprint.in/india/governance/how-punjabs-history-has-been-erased-from-textbooks/55329/ (accessed 17 January 2024).

Sharma, G. B., and Manmohan Kumar. 1980. 'Excavations at Ghuram'. *Proceedings of Punjab History Conference*, 32–47. Patiala: Department of Punjab Historical Studies, Punjabi University.

Singh, Diwan, and Bikram Singh Ghuman, eds. 2012[2005]. *Bhagat Jalan Das Ji: Jeevan te Rachna*. Naushera Dhala (Tarn Taran): Baba Nirmal Singh Ji.

Singh, Mohinder. 2000. 'Akalis and the Nationalist Politics'. In *Five Punjabi Centuries: Polity, Economy, Society, and Culture, c. 1500–1990*, ed. Indu Banga, 221–42. New Delhi: Manohar.

Singh, Teja. 1922. *The Gurdwara Reform Movement and the Sikh Awakening*. Jullundur: Desh Sewak Book Agency.

Snehi, Yogesh. 2014. 'Vicissitudes of Gurdwara Politics'. *Economic & Political Weekly* 49 (34). Available at https://www.epw.in/journal/2014/34/reports-states-web-exclusives/vicissitudes-gurdwara-politics.html# (accessed on 13 October 2023).

———. 2019. *Spatializing Popular Sufi Shrines in Punjab: Dreams, Memories, Territoriality*. New Delhi: Routledge.

———. 2020. 'Border'. In *Keywords for India: A Conceptual Lexicon for the 21st Century*, eds Rukmini Bhaya Nair and Peter Ronald deSouza, 350–51. New Delhi: Bloomsbury.

———. 2023. 'From Ram Tirath to Valmiki Tirath: The Making of Valmiki Religious Identity in Amritsar'. *Nidān: International Journal for Indian Studies* 8 (1): 15–40.

Talbot, Ian. 2008. 'The 1947 Partition of India'. In *The Historiography of Genocide*, ed. Dan Stone, 420–37. New York: Palgrave Macmillan.

The Gazetteer of Amritsar District, 1892–93. 1991. Chandigarh: Government Press.

Tuteja, K. L. 2021. *Religion, Community and Nation: Hindu Consciousness and Nationalism in Colonial Punjab*. New Delhi: Primus Books.

Veer, Peter van der. 1994. *Religious Nationalism: Hindus and Muslims in India*. Berkeley: University of California Press.

Zamindar, Vazira Fazila-Yacoobali. 2010. *The Long Partition and the Making of Modern South Asia*. New York: Columbia University Press.

Nine

Commemorating Baghel Singh's 'Conquest' of Delhi

The Fateh Diwas*

Kanika Singh

On 8 and 9 March 2014, a grand event called *Fateh Diwas* (day of victory) was celebrated at the historic Red Fort in Delhi. Organised by the Delhi Sikh Gurdwara Management Committee (DSGMC), the massive public function on the lawns outside the Red Fort was held to mark the conquest of Delhi in 1783 and the unfurling of the *Nishan Sahib* (the Sikh flag) at the Red Fort by the Sikh military commander, Baghel Singh. The programme included a march through the streets of Delhi, culminating at the Red Fort. Called the *jarnaili march* or the march of the Khalsa generals, the assembly featured a large number of Sikhs on foot, vehicles, horses and elephants. Some were dressed as eighteenth-century Khalsa Sikh warriors; others performed *gatka* (martial exercises with weapons). The *Nihangs* (a lavishly armed Sikh sub-group) were the most prominent in the procession. They were armed with spears, swords and what appeared to be modern rifles. A replica of a canon was carried in procession atop a vehicle which burst out confetti (in imitation of canon fire) at regular intervals. The

*An earlier version of this chapter was published in *Studies in History* 36 (2), 2020: 280–301.

two-day celebrations included the performance of the play *Raj Karega Khalsa* ('The Khalsa Shall Rule'), *kirtan* (congregational singing) and gatka performances. *Langar* (community kitchen) was also arranged at the venue. These celebrations were repeated in the following years, becoming an annual celebration in the DSGMC calendar (Image 9.1).

IMAGE 9.1: Fateh Diwas 2016.

Source: Author.

This public celebration is significant in several ways, both for its symbolism and the historical legacy it seeks to commemorate. First, the flying of the Sikh flag over the Red Fort represents, in general terms, a clear and powerful claim to sovereignty. Second, the first-ever Fateh Diwas celebrations in 2014 followed the political victory of Shiromani Akali Dal (Badal)[1] in the DSGMC in 2013. The massive public celebration at the Red Fort and the jarnaili march re-enacting the city's conquest were entirely at the initiative of the SAD (Badal)-controlled DSGMC. The confluence of a vivid claim to sovereignty and the political will to express it suggests the need to look closely at the circumstances that allowed the emergence of this celebration, and what it might mean.

Several questions emerge from this consideration. First, how does the Fateh Diwas relate to other forms of representation of this specifically Sikh past? Second, was Baghel Singh always so remembered or is this a modern representation? Third, what is the relationship between Baghel Singh and a Sikh claim to sovereignty? Finally, how do localised political formations impinge on this representation of the past, which is then generalised beyond the local? A consideration of these questions enables us to understand the complex forces that shape this representation.

Portraying Baghel Singh

Baghel Singh (d. 1802) was the leader of the Karorsinghia *misl* (confederacy) and a prominent Sikh chief of the cis-Satluj region in the second half of the eighteenth century. He succeeded Karora Singh as the chief of the misl in 1765. He controlled portions of the Jalandhar doab and Karnal, and his headquarters were at Chhalaudi, a village in Karnal. Along with other Sikh chiefs, he frequently carried out raids in the Doab and around Delhi, which was then the Mughal capital (Gupta 1992; Seetal n.d.: 66-73). In recent popular representations of Sikh history, the most significant of these excursions was in 1783, when the Sikh armies entered the city of Delhi.[2]

The particular representation of the Sikh presence in Delhi that we see in the Fateh Diwas celebration—the conquest of the Red Fort and Baghel Singh raising the Nishan Sahib over it—does not appear there alone. It has been depicted in 'history paintings',[3] at least since the 1970s. The narrative associated with these paintings marks a departure from previous representations of Baghel Singh. It is, however, strongly aligned with the narrative associated with the Fateh Diwas. The paintings, seen together with the Fateh Diwas, emphasise Baghel Singh's unfurling of the Nishan Sahib over the Red Fort after his conquest of Delhi, representing a modern concern, which seems to appear in the popular visual sphere only in the 1970s.[4]

History paintings of Sikh subjects usually depict portraits of the Sikh Gurus, popular stories from their lives and the lives of their most dedicated followers, scenes of battle and of martyrdom. These paintings are commonly available in calendars, children's books, academic works,[5] posters, pamphlets, government advertisements,[6] animation and even sculptures.[7] One may refer to them as Sikh popular art or calendar art.[8] Significantly, these paintings also constitute the display in the museums of Sikh history. Their presence within the portals of a museum gives them great authority as providing evidence of the Sikh past. Sikh museums have been built by both the gurdwara management committees (especially, the Shiromani Gurdwara Prabhandak Committee [SGPC] and the DSGMC) and the Punjab government. These are often part of the sacred space of a gurdwara. Small gurdwaras may display paintings in a single room in the gurdwara complex and large gurdwaras may have an entire building dedicated to the museum. The paintings' existence within the sacred landscape of the gurdwara lends them additional sanctity.[9]

The imagery of the history paintings is also reproduced in performances and in non-visual modes of communicating the Sikh past, such as plays and *dhadhi* (ballad) performances. A comparison of the play *Raj Karega Khalsa*, performed at the 2014 Fateh Diwas celebrations,[10] or the jarnaili march, where the Sikhs dressed as eighteenth-century warriors, with the paintings establishes strong visual similarities between them.[11] Mughal courtiers and soldiers in the play have their turbans and beards styled to ensure their easy identification as 'Muslim'. Their beards are short, and not long-flowing like those of Sikhs; the turbans have a conical top, around which the rest of the turban cloth is wound; the Mughal soldiers are dressed in green and the conical tops of their turbans are red—a colour scheme and iconography identical to that of many history paintings.[12]

Moreover, TV programmes on the Fateh Diwas use and run the history paintings along with photographs and videos from the celebration, establishing a visual continuity between the two. For instance, the PTC news channel[13] featured the Fateh Diwas celebration of 2014[14] in their programme series '*Goonjan Sikh Virse Diyaan*' ('Echoes of Sikh Heritage'). The episode liberally used history paintings showing portraits of Baghel Singh and other misl sardars (especially Jassa Singh Ahluwalia and Jassa Singh Ramgarhia), the Khalsa army marching and in battle, and the Khalsa forces before the Red Fort, which has the Nishan Sahib on it. These visuals are interspersed and run in tandem with clips from the Fateh Diwas celebrations—of gatka performers, the jarnaili march and the congregation of Nihangs and other Sikhs dressed as warriors—before the Red Fort.[15] This juxtaposition only consolidates the striking visual similarity between the paintings and their re-enactment in the Fateh Diwas. The same episode also includes an interview of Manjit Singh GK, the president of DSGMC, where he expressed his pride and satisfaction that the present Sikh congregation at the Red Fort brought alive the glorious history of the Sikhs. He says, 'It feels as if the Khalsa has camped here, preparations are being made [for the conquest] and that we have once again conquered Delhi.'[16]

Such a convergence of visual and performative registers is by no means new. Nijhawan (2006: 153–57) notes the similarity in the depiction of martyrdom in the popular print on Bhai Mani Singh (made by Kirpal Singh)[17] and the dhadi songs. In the well-known print, Bhai Mani Singh sits on the ground facing the executioner and looks the latter in the eye, instructing him to follow the orders given to him while dismembering Bhai Mani Singh at each joint. Bhai Mani Singh presents his fingers to the executioner who holds the chopper in his hand. The same details are incorporated in the songs, which provide a blow-by-blow account, a graphic description of martyrdom, just as is depicted in Kirpal Singh's painting. Nijhawan argues that '[the image] gives concreteness and symbolic plenitude to particular historical events and experiences that mere literal representation would not achieve…symbolism in the image is multiplied by linguistic tropes and sonic images' (ibid.: 156–57). This interocularity and reproducibility make for an extremely powerful mnemonic device. Studies on South Asian visual culture recognise the 'enormous power of images to transform and mobilise self and community' (Ramaswamy 2003: xiv).[18]

Seeking to understand Baghel Singh's images, both as a mass-produced object and as evidence of Sikh history with pedagogical value, it is useful to see them in light of Chandra's work on Amar Chitra Katha (ACK), the comic books on Indian history. Chandra argues that though the ACK are books on Indian history (presented in a visual medium), they continue to engage and remain associated with the religious sphere (primarily Hindu). Here, Chandra draws upon studies of popular Hindu religious images which show that the poster or the print continues to have the aura (divine value) of the original deity. Each of the numerous mass-produced images has a strong connection with its sacred source (Chandra 2013: 7–9). While Baghel Singh is not a sacred figure in the Sikh tradition, his images also participate in the Sikh religious sphere, as has been noted earlier. Just like the 'history comics' (ACK), the history paintings and the Fateh Diwas performances are connected with the Sikh religious sphere. In addition, they have a significant commemorative value. Radhika Chopra's recent work demonstrates the relationship between Sikh popular visual culture and the community's commemorative practices in sacred spaces. Chopra studies the popular prints and souvenirs available in the bazaars around the Darbar Sahib complex and notes,

> Visual images and visually striking artefacts within and around the Darbar Sahib complex, and in the city of Amritsar, are key sites for an elaboration of visual remembrance. Both in ordinary public arenas like the bazaars around the Golden Temple complex and in set-apart spaces like the Central Sikh Museum (CSM) within the precinct of the shrines, the

visual appears as a key register of remembrance (Chopra 2018: xiv–xv).

Images 9.2 and 9.3 are examples of popular history paintings depicting Baghel Singh. Both are displayed at the Bhai Mati Das Museum at the Sis Ganj Gurdwara in Chandni Chowk, Delhi.[19] The first painting was made by Amolak Singh[20] and is undated (Image 9.2). It shows three Sikh chiefs (the one in the centre presumably being Baghel Singh) leading a victory procession. In the background is the Lahori Gate of the Red Fort with the Nishan Sahib atop. The Khalsa soldiers (dressed mostly in blue) follow the chiefs on horseback, camels and on foot. There are two men playing drums and other instruments in front of the procession. The painting shows a man wearing a white Pathani suit with a green waistcoat and a matching turban. This figure is clearly marked as Muslim, and is depicted as a willing participant in the celebratory

Image 9.2: Baghel Singh outside the Red Fort. Painting at Bhai Mati Das Museum, Delhi.

Source: Reproduced with permission from Kirpal Singh Sandhu.

procession. On the right-hand corner, a woman is shown standing with a little girl, telling her to greet the Sikh chiefs, and the girl does so with folded hands.

The second painting, by Kirpal Singh, was made in 1976 (Image 9.3). It shows five Sikh chiefs (with Baghel Singh presumably in the centre) sitting on the Mughal throne in the *Diwan-i Aam*, the hall of public audience where the Mughal emperors held court. Sikh soldiers are seated in attendance in the court. The deposed Mughal Emperor, Shah Alam (r. 1760–1806), and Begum Samru (c. 1753–1836), the ruler of the principality of Sardhana (near Meerut),[21] are shown pleading for mercy.

IMAGE 9.3: Five Sikhs chiefs in the Red Fort. Painting at Bhai Mati Das Museum, Delhi.

Source: Painting by Kirpal Singh Artist, photography by Jarnail Singh Artist. Reproduced with the permission of Jarnail Singh.

The descriptions of these paintings at the museum tell us that in 1783, Baghel Singh along with some other misl leaders conquered Delhi and the Red Fort. They raised the Nishan Sahib over the fort and led a victory procession from it to the Fatehpuri Masjid, that is, along the main street of Chandni Chowk. This procession was joined by Hindus, Muslims and Sikhs as they welcomed the Khalsa forces. The Sikhs established their domination over the city and Begum Samru had to plead with them to spare the Mughal throne. They agreed to leave the city on condition that they were allowed to construct gurdwaras in Delhi.

These paintings and similar versions (repainted by different artists) are frequently reproduced and widely circulated. For instance, *Sis Ganj*, the monthly magazine of the DSGMC, uses them to illustrate articles which describe Baghel Singh's victory over Delhi. Reproductions of these paintings were also given away as mementoes at the Fateh Diwas celebrations in 2014. There are four paintings in the Bhai Mati Das Museum illustrating this episode. Copies of the paintings are also on display in museums like the Central Sikh Museum at the Golden Temple, Amritsar, and the Baba Baghel Singh Sikh Heritage Multimedia Museum at Gurdwara Bangla Sahib in New Delhi.[22] These two depictions of Baghel Singh—one showing him conquering the Red Fort and raising the Nishan Sahib over it, and the other showing him sitting on the Mughal throne while the emperor begs for mercy—are the most common depictions of Baghel Singh in contemporary India. In these, Baghel Singh's claim to sovereignty comes across clearly: in the depiction of the Sikh flag on the Red Fort, and the seating of the Sikh sardars on the Mughals' throne.

A Prehistory of the Modern Representation of Baghel Singh: Sri Gur Panth Prakash and the Idea of Sikh Sovereignty

It is useful to compare the depiction of Sikh sovereignty in the Fateh Diwas and the history paintings with the *Sri Gur Panth Prakash*, a nineteenth-century account of Sikh history. It was written by Ratan Singh Bhangu and completed in 1841 in Amritsar.[23] There is a rationale behind the choice of this text to study differing representations of Baghel Singh: the most well-known histories of the Sikhs, such as those by J. S. Grewal and Khushwant Singh, do not mention Baghel Singh's conquest of Delhi (Grewal 1998[1990]; Singh 1999). Among the scholarly writings of those who have worked on the history of the Sikh misls, Hari Ram Gupta's book (1980) seems to be the only one which refers to the 1783 events in detail. Gupta published the *History of the Sikhs* in eight volumes, the third volume of which is titled *Sikh Domination of the Mughal Empire (1764–1803)* and describes Baghel Singh's presence in Delhi (Gupta 1980: 158–70). A summary of this event also appears in Gupta's entry on Baghel Singh in the well-known *The Encyclopaedia of Sikhism,* edited by Harbans Singh (Gupta 1992). For this particular episode of Baghel Singh's entry into Delhi and the Red Fort, Gupta's chief Gurmukhi sources are Bhangu's *Sri Gur Panth Prakash* and Giani Gian Singh's *Sri Guru Panth Prakash* written in 1880 (Giani 1970).[24] I have chosen to use only one—Bhangu's text—for the purposes of this study. All scholarship on Bhangu's text recognises its popularity as a source of Sikh history and has identified sovereignty of the Khalsa panth as the key idea in the text.[25] It therefore offers a useful comparison to the claims made at the Fateh Diwas.

As he begins the *Sri Gur Panth Prakash*, Ratan Singh Bhangu explains his project: he argues that Sikh history has been misrepresented by sources that are hostile to the community, that is, the Muslims. It is his desire therefore to present an accurate account of Sikh history. When Bhangu came to know that the British had commissioned a *maulvi* (a Muslim cleric) to write about the Sikhs, he felt duty-bound to present the correct version of Sikh history (Bhangu 2004: 6, verses 26–27, sakhi 2). Further, his account would show that the Sikhs were a sovereign people and were not subordinate feudal lords of the Mughals. Bhangu is clear that the Khalsa *Panth* (community) was made sovereign by the Guru himself and they were subjects of only the divine Gurus (ibid.: 7, verse 34, sakhi 3; 33, verse 37, sakhi 15). The Sikhs did not owe their right to rule to the Mughals. On the contrary, it was the Sikh

Gurus who had bestowed sovereignty on the Mughals. According to Bhangu, Babur, the first Mughal emperor, had approached Guru Nanak, the first Guru, with folded hands. The Guru, pleased with his humility, gave him seven handfuls of cannabis leaves, representing seven Mughal emperors, up to Aurangzeb (Bhangu 2004: 270, verses 96–98, sakhi 104). However, the Mughals turned ungrateful and began persecuting the Sikhs. That is why, explains Bhangu, Guru Gobind Singh (the tenth and the last guru), snatched away their rule and then vested the Khalsa Panth with sovereignty (ibid.: 23, verse 8, sakhi 12; 271–72, verses 108–18, sakhi 104). Bhangu places particular emphasis on the collective sovereignty of the Panth, rather than on any particular Sikh chief or follower of the Gurus (Dhavan 2009: 521-22; Hans 1975: 77–78; Murphy 2012: 123).

Scholars have explained the particular idea of Sikh sovereignty as expressed in the *Sri Gur Panth Prakash* in the context of Bhangu's own position and the times during which he was composing this history. Most scholars have located Bhangu's work in the middle of the nineteenth century after the death of Maharaja Ranjit Singh (1780–1839), which saw a weakening of the Sikh kingdom and the rise of British power in Punjab.[26] On the one hand, there was a need to convince the British that the Sikhs were a legitimate ruling power in Punjab and not feudatories of the Mughals. On the other hand, there were competing political claims amongst the Sikhs, too. In such a scenario, Bhangu's emphasis is on the sovereignty of the collective Sikh Panth, as against the claims of individual Sikh chiefs who sought to establish their dynastic rule in Punjab, with the support of the British. Dhavan (2009: 521) shows that Bhangu idealises the ways in which eighteenth-century Khalsa heroes spurned individual power for the greater good of the community. Hans (1975: 82) has suggested that Bhangu's narration of the bravery of the martyrs and triumph of the Khalsa against all odds was also to boost the morale of the Sikhs, at a time when war against the British seemed imminent. Mann differs on the context of the production of Bhangu's manuscript and its idea of Sikh sovereignty. He dates Bhangu's work between 1810 and 1813 and argues that Bhangu's idea of Sikh sovereignty anticipates the rise of Sikh power in the Punjab region, rather than being a rallying cry to mobilise demoralised Sikhs in a post-Ranjit Singh Punjab or to convince the British to leave the Sikhs alone (Mann 2016: 30). Despite these differences in dating and therefore in the context of the work, the above works agree upon the popularity and significance of the text.

That Bhangu's narrative was as much directed at his fellow Sikhs as at the British is especially noted by Dhavan (2009). The composition of the history in the style of a *sakhi* (stories from the lives of the Gurus), the use of a popular dialect of Punjabi and Braj, and frequent invocations of religious texts and oral traditions which were familiar to Sikhs—all these factors indicate that Bhangu was addressing a Sikh audience, and these factors contributed to the popularity of the stories of the *Sri Gur Panth Prakash*. While Bhangu's text was one among many being written in the nineteenth century, it has proved to be very popular, much more than any other contemporary history (ibid.: 521). His concern about how the Sikh past should be presented also finds echo in the concerns of the late nineteenth and early twentieth-century Singh Sabha reformers and the Gurdwara Reform Movement of the 1920s (ibid.: 527).

Bhangu has two episodes on Baghel Singh's presence in Delhi and his encounter with the Mughal emperor, Shah Alam (Bhangu 2004: 413–22, sakhi 157 and 158). The first describes Baghel Singh's approach towards the Mughal capital, his negotiations with Begum Samru and his efforts towards building gurdwaras in Delhi (ibid.: 416–19, verses 39–87, sakhi 157). Bhangu informs us that as the Khalsa forces marched towards Delhi, the Mughal emperor was filled with terror (ibid.: 416, verses 39–43, sakhi 157). The latter requested Begum Samru to negotiate with the Sikhs to ward off their planned attack on the capital. Begum Samru met Baghel Singh, presented him with gifts and sought the Khalsa's protection for the Mughals (Bhangu 2004: 416, verses 45–50, sakhi 157). Baghel Singh agreed to leave Delhi on the condition of payment of one-sixth of Delhi's revenue to the Khalsa forces and the right to build gurdwaras in the city (ibid.: 417, verses 51–52, sakhi 157). Bhangu goes on to describe how Baghel Singh identified sites which were associated with the Gurus and began construction of the shrines. At times, he had to demolish mosques and faced stiff opposition from the Muslims. But, by cunning and tact, he was successful in establishing seven gurdwaras in the city (ibid.: 417–19, verses 59–86, sakhi 157). Bhangu says that this was a great service to the Gurus, for which Baghel Singh will be honoured in the Guru's presence and his name will be remembered in the Panth forever:

> *Srdāra Baghela Simgha ima gaḍha mārā*
> *Rahūgu prithī usa nāma ujārā*
> *Aisī karī una gura kī kāra*
> *Pāū jagā vahi gura ke dwāra*
>
> (Sardar Baghel Singh established great landmarks
> His name shall shine till eternity
> He rendered such great service to the Guru
> That he would find a place at the Guru's gate [presence])
> (ibid.: 419, verse 87, sakhi 157)[27]

The second episode describes Baghel Singh's meeting with the Mughal emperor (ibid.: 419–22, sakhi 158). Bhangu tells us that Shah Alam was much impressed with Baghel Singh and expressed a wish to meet him (ibid.: 419–20, verses 3–4, sakhi 158). The Sikhs declared that such a meeting would be difficult as they did not bow before any Muslim and were always armed (ibid.: 420, verses 5–6, sakhi 158). The emperor agreed to meet Baghel Singh on the terms set down by the latter (ibid.: 420, verses 9–10, sakhi 158). Thus, Baghel Singh met the Mughal emperor as an equal and not a subordinate. Bhangu tells us that he arrived at the Red Fort on a decorated elephant, a flywhisk being waved around his head. The Khalsa forces marched through Delhi to reach the fort and the procession was led by minstrels who sang the glory of Sikh Gurus (ibid.: 420, verses 14–16, sakhi 158). Baghel Singh entered the Red Fort fully armed and on horseback; so confident as if he was already familiar with the layout (ibid.: 421, verses 18 and 20, sakhi 158). The emperor's court extended the Khalsa greeting of '*Gur Fateh*' (victory to the Guru) to Baghel Singh (ibid.: 421, verse 24, sakhi 158), and he reciprocated and sat on a chair across from the emperor (ibid.: 421, verse 26, sakhi 158). Many gifts were exchanged between the two (ibid.: 421, verses 29–30, sakhi 158). In Bhangu's account, this is the only instance when Baghel Singh enters the Red Fort. Towards the end of the meeting, Shah Alam expressed a desire to witness the famed plundering raids of the Khalsa, and Baghel Singh demonstrated the same in the fields opposite the Red Fort (ibid.: 421, verses 31–43, sakhi 158). Through this narration, Bhangu successfully conveys Baghel Singh's domination of Delhi and how the Mughal emperor owed his position to the former's generosity. This was in keeping with his larger objective: to demonstrate that the Khalsa is sovereign by the grace of the Gurus, and it is the Mughals who are dependent on the Khalsa for their kingship.

It should not surprise us to see such a complex relationship between Sikh and Mughal power in a text of this period. A study of the scholarship on eighteenth-century politics and conditions in Delhi tells us that the situation was indeed complex. Historians including Gupta (1980) and, most recently, Dhavan (2012) have shown how different players like the Sikhs, the Jats, the Marathas, the Rohillas and the English were active in north India, each vying for power. The Mughals had effectively lost all control over the state's income and army. This was a period of shifting loyalties and changing coalitions among the various parties involved and not motivated by religious factors alone, but also by a consideration of one's political and economic interests. This was the milieu in which Baghel Singh and other Sikhs operated—a picture which is lost in the Fateh Diwas and the history paintings.

Sikh Flag on the Red Fort

Baghel Singh's contribution to Sikh history changes dramatically in the history paintings and the Fateh Diwas. Now, the emphasis is on raising the Nishan Sahib at the Red Fort, an act attributed to Baghel Singh and the Khalsa forces after they conquered the fort. As mentioned earlier, this emphasis seems to have been in popular circulation for a few decades before being commemorated at the Fateh Diwas. Image 9.3, the painting by Kirpal Singh displayed at Bhai Mati Das Museum, was created in 1976. Image 9.2 is undated, but another painting by Amolak Singh—which shows Baghel Singh and the Khalsa forces before the Red Fort with the Nishan Sahib planted on it—is dated 1979.[28] It is likely that these were first painted as symbolic representations of Sikh (especially Akali) resistance against the Emergency and their eventual triumph against the oppressive rule(r) in Delhi. The Fateh Diwas, the grand public celebration at the Red Fort—the very site of 'conquest'—is the most spectacular manifestation of this claim. The account of raising the Nishan Sahib on the Red Fort does not exist in Bhangu's writing; neither does it exist in Gupta (1980).[29]

Bhangu *does* invoke the imagery of 'planting the Khalsa flag' in his work, except these are at the sites where gurdwaras are built, rather than at the Red Fort. Mann notes Bhangu's frequent use of the imagery of Nishan Sahib to convey Sikh sovereignty: '[it is] the excitement of its opening decades of the nineteenth century with Sikh saffron flags (*nishan/jhanda*) fluttering everywhere in the region [Punjab] that underlines the author's [Bhangu's] vision' (2016: 30). He also notes Bhangu's use of the Sikh flag for claiming Sikh sites, such as the identification and establishment of a gurdwara at Sirhind, marking the spot where the two younger sons of Guru Gobind Singh were killed (ibid.: 35).

In Delhi, too, Bhangu talks about planting the Nishan Sahib, when Baghel Singh identified the sites associated with the Gurus and established gurdwaras:

1. *Hutī sāhaba daī o sundrī māta*
Gura patanī sabha jaga bikhyāta
Srī Hari Krishana samādha āda jahīṃ
Jamnā ḍhīga gaḍḍe jhaṇḍe trai tahīṃ
(Mata Sahib and Mata Sundri were here
The world-known wives of the Guru
And, the samadhi of Sri Hari Krishan
On the banks of the Yamuna, he planted three flags)
(Bhangu 2004: 417, verse 60, sakhi 157)

2. *Pañjvōṃ jhaṇḍoṃ hari krishana jī jahīṃ bahe*
Jai Simgha pure madha bañglo jī ahe
Sugama bhānt pañja ḍehare bhae
Gaḍḍa jhaṇḍe pañja kaṛāha kara dae
(The fifth flag where Hari Krishan had been
The bunglow at Jai Singh pura
The five doorways [gurdwaras] were easily marked
Five flags were planted, and karah parshad was given)
(ibid.: 417, verse 61, sakhi 157)

3. *Srī Tegha Bahādara deha jahīṃ hutī thī dāgī ṭhaura*
ḍirho chhevoṃ tahiṃ racyo jhaṇḍo gaḍayo kara dhauṛa
(Where Sri Tegh Bahadur's body had been cremated
The sixth doorway was built and the flag planted) (ibid.: 419, verse 78, sakhi 157)

The purpose here is not to see whether the Nishans were actually hoisted or not, but to argue that this symbolic action of raising the flag differs in emphasis in Bhangu's account and in modern portrayals such as the Fateh Diwas and related painting traditions. This difference indicates a significant change in Baghel Singh's meaning and importance in Sikh history. More significantly, it indicates a change in how the Sikhs see themselves in contemporary India. For Bhangu, the site of Baghel Singh's triumph is not the Red Fort, but the gurdwaras, the establishment of which he sees as Baghel Singh's significant contribution.

For the Fateh Diwas, the achievement is firmly located at the site of the Red Fort, where the Mughals were overthrown and the Khalsa flag raised. Baghel Singh's contribution in building gurdwaras, as noted in Bhangu's account, is hardly mentioned in the Fateh Diwas celebrations. This absence is also evident in the history paintings, where Baghel Singh is always depicted as marching at or inside the Red Fort, and never as constructing gurdwaras. The descriptions of the paintings too (such as those in the Bhai Mati Das Museum at Sis Ganj gurdwara near the Red Fort, Delhi) focus on Baghel Singh's conquest of Delhi and his unfurling the flag. Both the Fateh Diwas and the paintings differ in emphasis from Murphy's suggestion that 'Baghel Singh represents today the fight for Sikh gurdwaras in the Mughal context' (Murphy 2012: 152).[30]

The Fateh Diwas is a celebration of the Sikh conquest of the Red Fort, which was the seat of the Mughal Empire and, therefore, is depicted in the celebrations as a symbol of Mughal tyranny. *Raj Karega Khalsa*, the play enacted during the 2014 celebrations, claims that the sole motivation of the Sikhs in attacking Delhi was to avenge the wrongs done to them by the Mughals, and this was ultimately achieved when Baghel Singh dethroned the Mughals and unfurled the Khalsa flag at the very site from which the Mughals had ordered the persecution of the Sikhs. In the play, Baghel Singh's character gives a speech in the Diwan-i Aam of the Red Fort:

> This is the Diwan-i Aam, where emperors like Aurangzeb and Farrukhsiyar held darbar. This is the same *takht* (throne) from which they planned the massacre of Sikhs. This is the takht from where the *farman* (summons) to kill Guru Tegh Bahadur was issued. This is the same takht from where orders to torture and kill Banda Bahadur and thousands of innocent Sikhs, was issued.... This platform should be uprooted and sent off to the Guru's darbar in Amritsar.[31]

In the play *Dilli Fateh* ('Conquest of Delhi') performed at the 2015 Fateh Diwas celebrations, the narrator declares: 'The same Delhi which used to oppress the Sikhs, now lay at their feet.'[32]

In Image 9.2, a Muslim man is markedly shown as a willing participant in the victory march. The description of this painting at the Bhai Mati Das Museum tells us, 'Hindus, Sikhs and Muslims willingly joined his [Baghel Singh's] procession from the Red Fort to Fatehpuri', implying that the Sikh forces' entry into Delhi was a welcome one as it liberated the masses from Mughal oppression. Indeed, the DSGMC press release for the Fateh Diwas celebrations in 2015 claimed that Baghel Singh's conquest 'paved the end of the mighty Mughal rule in India and beginning of war for Independence' (*The Hindu* 2015). The DSGMC therefore demanded that the Indian government announce the 'conquest of Lal Qila by the Sikh forces in 1783 as a national event celebrated annually' (ibid.). This particular demand is a claim for a place—a pride of place—in the larger narrative of Indian history. In fact, Sikh leaders frequently like to point out that the Sikhs' role in Indian history has been neglected. As the Fateh Diwas makes a claim for the Sikhs' place in Indian history, it also reinforces the broader right-wing propaganda of Mughals being considered foreigners, whose rule was characterised by the tyranny and oppression of other religious groups.

This story of Baghel Singh's conquest of the Red Fort also differs from many other popular versions of Sikh engagement with the Mughals. Often, the narrative is one of resistance, sacrifice and moral triumph; the Sikhs achieve martyrdom fighting the Mughals in defence of righteousness and faith. The history paintings and Fateh Diwas instead present actual conquest and military triumph over the Mughals. On the basis of this representation, the DSGMC can demand that this achievement of the Sikh forces be declared a national event and be made part of the sound and light show at the Red Fort (*The Hindu* 2015; *The Tribune* 2015).

Significance of the Fateh Diwas

The symbolism in commemorating Baghel Singh's victory over the Red Fort can be better understood in the context of who is organising the celebration and the timing of the event. The Red Fort, besides its association with Mughal rule, remains a deeply symbolic monument in independent India. Each year, on the occasion of the nation's Independence Day (15 August), the prime minister unfurls the Indian national flag and addresses the nation's citizens from the ramparts of the fort. The Indian flag over the Red Fort is a symbol of the Indian nation-state and its sovereignty. The Sikh flag over the Red Fort then becomes a symbol of Sikh sovereignty. The Fateh Diwas, when seen in this context, is a statement of triumph of a regional power [SAD (Badal)] over the oppressive centre at Delhi. Through their career in independent India, Akali politics and the SAD (Badal) have projected themselves as the champion of the Sikhs in Punjab. And one of the major themes around which Sikh politics is organised has been the alleged discrimination against the Sikhs by the Indian nation-state. This is especially manifest against the Indian National Congress, the political party which controlled the Central government for the longest time after India's independence.[33] The Akalis argued that the Congress-led Central governments were un-secular and discriminatory towards the Sikhs.[34] The Indian nation-state is perceived as depriving Punjab of its resources and as having caused grievous hurt to the Sikh community by invading the Golden Temple in 1984.

The long-standing rivalry between the SAD (Badal) and the Congress also explains the selective nature and timing of commemorations by the SAD (Badal)-controlled DSGMC. Soon after coming to power in the Delhi Gurdwara Committee, the SAD (Badal) declared its intention to raise a memorial for the victims of the 1984 violence against the Sikhs (*The Tribune* 2013). Predictably, this move was opposed by Paramjit Singh Sarna, the former president of DSGMC and the leader of the Congress-backed Akali Dal (Sarna),[35] which had controlled DSGMC for many years before 2013.[36] The foundation stone-laying ceremony of the 1984 memorial was organised in November 2014 at Gurdwara Rakabganj in New Delhi with the major leaders of the SAD (Badal) in attendance. Parkash Singh Badal, the Chief Minister of Punjab and SAD (Badal) leader, called the targeted violence against the Sikhs in 1984 the 'fourth holocaust'.[37]

The DSGMC has a full calendar in which they commemorate both joyous occasions and traumatic events from the community's past. Under the SAD (Badal)-led DSGMC, the frequency of these events has increased manifold and the DSGMC calendar is busier than ever. Each month, the DSGMC magazine, *Sis Ganj*, provides a listing of dates and events which are of historic significance to the Sikh community. Not only are the *gurupurab*s (birth anniversaries of the Sikh Gurus) celebrated, but there is also much emphasis on commemorating *shaheedi diwas* (anniversary of martyrdom) of various Sikh heroes, such as Banda Bahadur. These celebrations are no longer confined to the state of Punjab where the SAD (Badal)'s propensity to celebrate events from Sikh history is well-known. In addition, the scale of celebration is more spectacular than ever. For instance, the DSGMC released half-page advertisements in national dailies on 3 July 2016 which announced a *shaheedi samagam* (congregation to pay respects to martyrs) on the third centenary of the martyrdom of Banda Bahadur, 'the first sovereign Sikh ruler' (*The Sunday Tribune* 2016). The event was organised at the Indira Gandhi Indoor Stadium in New Delhi, and the invited guests included Prime Minister of India Narendra Modi and Chief Minister of Punjab Parkash Singh Badal.[38]

It is clear that the notion of Sikh sovereignty in these commemorations (especially the Fateh Diwas) is different from Bhangu's idea of Sikh sovereignty. While both invoke Baghel Singh's domination of Delhi, the symbols of sovereignty and their purposes differ, as was shown in the previous section. Just as Bhangu's idea of sovereignty was shaped by the demands of the times, Fateh Diwas's claim of sovereignty too is a product of its context. Recent scholarship on Sikh history has noted different manifestations of the idea of Sikh sovereignty. For example, Murphy discusses how Sikh sovereignty may be understood particularly through the Sikh community's relationship with sacred objects (related to the Sikh Gurus) and the gurdwaras. She argues that multiple ideas of sovereignty have been expressed over time through the community's representation of its own past and these ideas are not necessarily articulated in terms of statist aspirations (Murphy 2012: 7–18, 252–53). Dhavan's (2012) work demonstrates the multiple layers of Sikh sovereignty that existed among the misl groups in eighteenth-century Punjab, and how symbolic practices helped regulate relations among both the misl sardars on the one hand, and the Sikhs and Mughals on the other.

Further, the Fateh Diwas's claim of Sikh sovereignty is also different from that of the Khalistan movement, associated with the Sikh demand for sovereignty through the creation of a separate state. The difference lies in the fact that the movement for Khalistan demanded sovereignty in the form of an independent nation-state, a territorial entity separate from India. The Sikhs' history of persecution under the Mughals was invoked, a situation perceived as continuing under the Indian state, and the Sikhs sought liberation in the form of a separate state for themselves.[39] In contrast, the Fateh Diwas demands a kind of inclusion (through dominance) in the history of the Indian nation-state. The celebrations show the Sikh conquest over the Mughals and underline their role in liberating the entire population from the latter's oppression. The Fateh Diwas celebrations demand that all Indians remember this victory of the Sikhs. This is a greater claim upon the nation, and not a demand to secede from it. The Fateh Diwas thus becomes both a claim by the Sikhs on the nation's past and a claim by the SAD (Badal) upon the nation's political present.[40]

The Fateh Diwas becomes especially significant as it pitches the Baghel Singh story at a level where it has the potential to be accepted by a wider social community and not just the Sikhs. This can be attributed to a combination of several factors: Baghel Singh's association with the Red Fort in Delhi; his fight against Muslim oppression, which is projected as the 'first war of independence' by the Indian people; and the easy fit of this narrative with Hindu-majority nationalism, which is especially vocal now.

This process is similar to the trajectory of Prithviraj Chauhan's rise from a local clan hero to the defender of the Hindu nation, as studied by Talbot (2016). She has especially noted the importance of location (Delhi) and its association with the personality (Prithviraj) as being crucial to this process. According to Talbot, 'Prithviraj's prominence in Indian culture...derives largely from the fact that memory identified him as ruling from the most powerful political centre of North India since the early thirteenth century, Delhi' (ibid.: 104). For Baghel Singh, too, his 'conquest' of the Red Fort in Delhi (associated with sovereignty) is the reason for the DSGMC's demand that it be celebrated as a 'national event'.

Again, in the case of Prithviraj, Talbot demonstrates that the histories which were once limited to a small social group (to which Prithviraj belonged) could through retellings become relevant to a wider community (the Rajputs and the Indian nation):

> The mostly Brahmin intellectuals writing [the history of Prithviraj Chauhan] in modern Hindi gradually came to regard the *Rasō* version of the Rajput past part of a shared history that also encompassed themselves. Retellings of the Prithviraj story were now seen as relevant to a wide audience, who together constituted a collective group (2016: 258).

The modern retellings of Baghel Singh in the history paintings and the Fateh Diwas make him a hero not only for the Sikhs but also for the entire Indian nation. Politically, this can be seen in parallel with SAD (Badal)'s aspirations to be a national player and not remain a regional political party. Not only did the SAD (Badal) trump the Congress in the DSGMC elections, but it also contested the election to the Delhi legislature in 2015, and held a cabinet rank in the Central government formed by the right-wing political alliance, the National Democratic Alliance (NDA), in 2014.[41]

Invoking history to further the Sikh community's interests is not a new phenomenon, and neither is the contemporary use of history particular to the Sikh community. Many scholars have demonstrated how representations of the Sikh past must be read in their particular contexts and understood in light of the interests they further.[42] The commemoration of the Sikh past in the Fateh Diwas, and the particular representation of Baghel Singh in it, makes the event noteworthy. The unprecedented scale and location (Red Fort) of the celebration conveys a forceful message to both the Sikh community and a wider public. History paintings in museums and in popular spheres, when seen along with the dazzling celebrations at Fateh Diwas, create an extremely powerful and dominant version of the Sikh past. The visual has the agency of historical evidence and its performance in Fateh Diwas only reinforces its authority.

This chapter has examined three representations of Baghel Singh—the Fateh Diwas in 2014, the history paintings since the 1970s and the nineteenth-century text, *Sri Gur Panth Prakash*. A long-term study may reveal many more changes and continuities in how the Sikhs remember him: the trajectory of Baghel Singh's emergence as a hero; when, by whom and why he was remembered; and even contrasting accounts of him. It would be especially interesting to see whether and how Baghel Singh was invoked during the Gurdwara Reform Movement of the 1920s in Punjab—a time when Sikh history was both invoked and shaped by those reclaiming gurdwaras. An enquiry along these lines could further help us understand the Sikh community's perception of its heritage vis-à-vis the idea of India and other communities.

NOTES

1. Shiromani Akali Dal (Badal) is a political party dominant in the state of Punjab. It emerged as a political group representing the interests of the Sikh community. Its government was in power in Punjab continuously from 2007 till early 2017, with Parkash Singh Badal as the chief minister.

2. These popular representations of Baghel Singh are both visual and textual. For instance, paintings on Baghel Singh appear in the museums

at prominent gurdwaras, including the Darbar Sahib (Golden Temple), Amritsar, and the Sis Ganj gurdwara and the Bangla Sahib gurdwara in Delhi. *Sardar Baghel Singh* (n.d.) is an example of a popular tract which narrates Baghel Singh's exploits.

3. History painting refers to a genre of painting in seventeenth-century Europe which had subjects drawn from classical history and mythology. Here, I use the term to refer to modern paintings done in Western realistic style which illustrate events from Sikh history.

4. The appearance of Baghel Singh's paintings in the 1970s may be seen in the context of the political turmoil in Punjab in that decade and particularly the Emergency of 1975–77, imposed by the then Prime Minister, Indira Gandhi. Akalis, the most prominent political group representing the Sikhs, were fierce opponents of the Emergency. They launched the 'Save Democracy Morcha' and courted arrest in large numbers, some estimates putting the figure at over 40,000. See Grewal (1996: 145–46) and Narang (1983: 191–92). The paintings depicting Baghel Singh conquering Delhi can perhaps be understood as a Sikh, and particularly Akali, response to a dictatorial and oppressive ruler at the centre (Indira Gandhi).

5. An example of an academic publication using modern history paintings is Daljeet (2005).

6. For example, on 17 September 2013, the Delhi government renamed a city square after Bebe Nanaki, the sister of Guru Nanak. The state government carried a huge advertisement in the dailies, which used part of a painting by artist Bodhraj. The painting shows Bebe Nanaki, Nanak and Mardana. It was painted in 1974 and it is on display at the Bhai Mati Das Museum at Sis Ganj Gurdwara in Delhi. There are several such examples of the use of history paintings by government bodies.

7. The most notable example is the display of sculptures at Gurdwara Mehdiana Sahib, Ludhiana. The sculptures were created by artist Tara Singh of Raikot, who uses the paintings of the well-known artist Kirpal Singh as a template.

8. For more on Sikh popular art, see Kesar (2003), McLeod (1991), Uberoi (2003).

9. For more on Sikh museums, see Chopra (2010, 2013), Glover (2014), Launois (Sat Kaur) (2003), Murphy (2012), Singh (2015), Singh (2016).

10. The video of the play is available with the author.

11. The forging of a symbolic unity by bringing together events disparate in time and context has been noted by Das (1995: 121) and Chopra (2018: xv–xvi) in their study of contemporary invocations of Sikh history.

12. For a discussion on the representation of different communities (especially Muslims) in popular visual culture, see Chandra (2013: 55–65) and Sreenivas (2010).

13. Incidentally, the PTC network is owned by Sukhbir Singh Badal, the president of SAD (Badal) and the Deputy Chief Minister of Punjab from 2009 till early 2017.

14. And subsequently of the 2015 and 2016 celebrations.

15. The video of the episode is available at https://www.youtube.com/watch?v=yux0Vhdd3Fc (accessed 25 January 2024).

16. Ibid. The interview is in Punjabi. Translation by author.

17. Kirpal Singh (1923–90) was one of the most popular artists in Punjab, known for his paintings on Sikh history. He was the first artist to be employed at the Central Sikh Museum, Amritsar, and made paintings for several other museums like the Anglo-Sikh War Memorial at Ferozepur, the Baghel Singh Museum in Delhi and the Guru Tegh Bahadur Museum in Anandpur Sahib. He specialised in painting scenes of action and violence, especially battle scenes and martyrdom of the Sikhs.

18. Some other important works on visual culture in the Indian context include Jain (2007), Pinney (2004) and Saeed (2012).

19. The Bhai Mati Das Museum is maintained by the DSGMC, and it opened to the public in 2001.

20. Amolak Singh (1950–2006) was an artist employed with the SGPC at the Central Sikh Museum in the Golden Temple, Amritsar. He had worked as an artist in Bollywood in the 1970s and in close association with calendar artists like S. M. Pandit. He also trained under the well-known artist Sobha Singh. His projects included paintings on Sikh history for the Punjab and Sind Bank, PSB Finance, Bank of Punjab and museums such as the Bhai Mati Das Museum, Delhi.

21. Begum Samru is believed to have negotiated the terms of peace between the Sikh forces and the Mughal emperor during this incursion.

22. The Central Sikh Museum was established in 1958. Baba Baghel Singh Museum was established sometime in the 1970s. It was renovated as a multimedia museum and reopened to public in November 2014.

23. There is some disagreement over this date. The year 1841 is the most commonly accepted.

24. Gupta, *History of the Sikhs*, uses a range of sources to study Sikh history in the eighteenth century, including Persian, Punjabi, Marathi and English ones. My choice of a single text from his entire repertoire, while being a limited one, is explained in the main body of this chapter.

25. See Dhavan (2009), Grewal (2004), Hans (1975), Mann (2016) and Murphy (2012: Chapter 4).

26. See Dhavan (2009: 516); Hans (1975: 82); Murphy (2012: 121). Mann (2016: 28) suggests a date between 1810 and 1813.

27. All translations by the author. The diacritics follow Library of Congress recommendations for Panjabi as given at this link: https://www.loc.gov/catdir/cpso/romanization/panjabi.pdf (accessed 25 January 2024).

28. This painting is reproduced on the cover of a booklet, *Baba Baghel Singh Museum's Paintings and Their Brief History* (1998).

29. Gupta (1980: 166) does say that the Sikh chiefs entered the Diwan-i Aam of the Red Fort as the Mughals hid in the interiors of the fort. He writes that Jassa Singh Ahluwalia, one of the misl sardars, was made to sit on the Mughal throne. This was objected to by others in the raiding party and almost led to a fight among the Sikhs. Jassa Singh Ahluwalia stepped down to prevent the fight, and the Sikhs left after seizing whatever they could lay their hands on. This awkward crowning is hardly comparable to the DSGMC's claims of 'conquest' of the Red Fort.

30. According to Murphy (2012), Baghel Singh's representation at the Bhai Mati Das Museum is evidence of a modern memory of the Sikhs where Baghel Singh represents the fight for gurdwaras during the Mughal rule, and that this memory is in continuation of the Sikh community's search for gurdwaras, as seen both in Bhangu's nineteenth-century text and the modern Sikh *ardas* (daily prayer). Murphy's statement is based on a single line from the description of one of the paintings (reproduced here as Image 9.3) at the Bhai Mati Das Museum, Sis Ganj Gurdwara. However, a collective reading of the four paintings on Baghel Singh and their descriptions in the same museum indicates a modern focus on Baghel Singh's conquest of Delhi and his act of raising the Sikh flag on the Red Fort, rather than his establishment of gurdwaras. None of the paintings show Baghel Singh building gurdwaras.

31. The original dialogue is in Punjabi. The translation is by the author. Video available with the author.

32. The video is available with the author.

33. See Kumar (2004) and Narang (2014) for a study of Akali Dal's politics in Punjab.

34. According to the Akalis, this was evident in many Central government policies. For instance, the Constitution (Scheduled Castes) Order, 1950, which identified Scheduled Castes in India, did not include any Sikh castes. This was interpreted as an attempt to absorb the Sikhs into Hinduism. Further, Muslims, Christians, and Parsis in independent India were allowed their personal laws, but Sikhs were grouped under the Hindus (Narang 1983: 115–20).

35. Also referred to as SAD (Delhi).

36. The 1984 violence against the Sikhs was orchestrated allegedly by leaders of the Congress party. Admittedly, the attacks on Sikhs were to retaliate and avenge the assassination of the Congress leader and then Prime Minister of India, Indira Gandhi, by her Sikh bodyguards. While the Congress-controlled DSGMC continued to build museums and the Congress-controlled Delhi government built memorials on Sikh history (like the Guru Tegh Bahadur Memorial at the Singhu border between Delhi and Haryana, on the highway connecting Delhi to Punjab), the events of 1984 were never commemorated by them. See Chakravarti and Haksar (1987), Mitta and Phoolka (2007), and Rao et al. (1985).

37. DNA (2014). He was referring to the carnages against the Sikhs, popularly remembered in the Sikh tradition as the *chhota ghallughara* (the Lesser Holocaust, in 1746) and the *wadda ghallughara* (the Greater Holocaust, in 1762); and the attack on the Golden Temple in 1984 (Operation Bluestar) as the third holocaust. Also see Grewal (1998[1990]: 90–91).

As we note the building of a 1984 memorial in a Delhi gurdwara by the SAD (Badal)-led DSGMC, it is worthwhile to highlight here Chopra's observations on the 1984 commemorations in and around the Darbar Sahib, Amritsar, and in the diaspora. She observes that the 1984 commemorations in Amritsar are shorter in duration with fewer people participating, and argues that this may indicate a need to gradually forget the trauma. In the UK, the commemoration rituals are directed at an international audience and make claims for the inclusion of the Sikhs in these foreign lands. At each of these places—Delhi, Amritsar, London—the 1984 commemorations are performed differently and serve different purposes (Chopra 2018: xvi–xvii, xxii).

38. It is noteworthy that an event celebrating a famous Sikh martyr as the 'first sovereign Sikh ruler' was organised at a prominent venue named after Indira Gandhi. Indira Gandhi's assassination by her Sikh bodyguards is widely considered as the Sikh community's revenge for mounting the military attack on Darbar Sahib in 1984 (Operation Bluestar). While the two bodyguards (Satwant Singh and Beant Singh) were punished as assassins by the Indian state, they are often remembered as martyrs by the Sikh community. For instance, in the Central Sikh Museum at the Darbar Sahib, Amritsar, their portraits appear in a gallery dedicated to Sikh martyrs. Also see Chopra (2010) for an analysis of commemorations of the martyrs of 1984 by the Sikh community, and the official remembrance of Indira Gandhi's death.

39. See Das (1995: 118–36), Mahmood (1996).

40. It is interesting to note that the SAD (Badal) contested elections for the Delhi Legislative Assembly for the first time in 2015 on four seats—all with a majority or substantial Sikh population.

41. Harsimrat Kaur Badal, a member of Parliament from SAD (Badal), was the Union cabinet minister of food processing in the National Democratic Alliance (NDA) government during 2014–20.

42. For example, see Fenech (2000); Murphy (2012); Oberoi (1994).

References

Baba Baghel Singh Museum's Paintings and Their Brief History. 1998. New Delhi: Delhi Sikh Gurdwara Management Committee.

Bhangu, Ratan Singh. 2004. *Sri Gur Panth Prakash*, ed. Balwant Singh Dhillon. Amritsar: Singh Brothers.

Chakravarti, Uma, and Nandita Haksar. 1987. *The Delhi Riots: Three Days in the Life of a Nation*. New Delhi: Lancer International.

Chandra, Nandini. 2013. *The Classic Popular: Amar Chitra Katha 1967–2007*. New Delhi: Yoda Press.

Chopra, Radhika. 2010. 'Commemorating Hurt: Memorialising Operation Bluestar'. *Sikh Formations: Religion, Culture, Theory* 6 (2): 119–52.

_____. 2013. 'A Museum, A Memorial, A Martyr: Politics of Memory in the Sikh Golden Temple'. *Sikh Formations: Religion, Culture, Theory* 9 (2): 97–114.

Chopra, Radhika. 2018. *Amritsar 1984: A City Remembers*. London & New York: Lexington Books.

Daljeet. 2005. *The Sikh Heritage: A Search for Totality*. New Delhi: Prakash Books.

Das, Veena. 1995. *Critical Events: An Anthropological Perspective on Contemporary India*. New Delhi: Oxford University Press.

Dhavan, Purnima. 2009. 'Reading the Texture of History and Memory in Early-Nineteenth-Century Punjab'. *Comparative Studies of South Asia, Africa and the Middle East* 29 (3): 515–27.

———. 2012. *When Sparrows Became Hawks: The Making of the Sikh Warrior Tradition 1699–1799*. New York: Oxford University Press.

DNA. 2014. 'Memorial for 1984 Anti-Sikh Riot Victims to Come Up in Delhi'. 1 November. Available at http://www.dnaindia.com/india/report-memorial-for-1984-anti-sikh-riot-victims-to-come-up-in-delhi-2031339 (accessed 25 January 2024).

Fenech, Louis E. 2000. *Martyrdom in the Sikh Tradition: Playing the 'Game of Love'*. New Delhi: Oxford University Press.

Giani, Bhai Gian Singh ji. 1970. *Sri Guru Panth Prakash*. Patiala: Bhasha Vibhag.

Glover, William J. 2014. 'The Khalsa Heritage Complex'. In *The Oxford Handbook of Sikh Studies*, eds Pashaura Singh and Louis E. Fenech, 441–48. New York: Oxford University Press.

Grewal, J. S. 1996. *The Akalis: A Short History*. Chandigarh: Punjab Studies Publications.

———. 1998[1990]. *The Sikhs of the Punjab*. Cambridge: Cambridge University Press.

———. 2004. 'Valorizing the Tradition: Bhangu's Guru Panth Prakash'. In *The Khalsa: Sikh and Non-Sikh Perspectives*, ed. J. S. Grewal, 103–22. New Delhi: Manohar.

Gupta, Hari Ram. 1980. *History of the Sikhs: Sikh Domination of the Mughal Empire (1764–1803)*, Vol. 3. Delhi: Munshiram Manoharlal.

———. 1992. 'Baghel Singh'. In *The Encyclopaedia of Sikhism*, ed. Harbans Singh, 249–50. Patiala: Punjabi University.

Hans, S. S. 1975. 'Rattan Singh Bhangu's Purpose of Writing the Sri Gur Panth Prakash'. In Punjab History Conference Proceedings, 9th session, 75–82. Patiala: Punjabi University.

Jain, Kajri. 2007. *Gods in Bazaar: The Economies of Indian Calendar Art*. Durham: Duke University Press.

Kesar, Urmi. 2003. 'Twentieth Century Sikh Painting: The Presence of the Past'. In *New Insights into Sikh Art*, ed. Kavita Singh, 118–33. Mumbai: Marg.

Kumar, Ashutosh. 2004. 'Electoral Politics in Punjab: Study of Akali Dal'. *Economic & Political Weekly* 39 (14–15): 1515–20.

Launois (Sat Kaur), Anne-Colombe. 2003. 'The Khalsa Heritage Complex: A Museum for a Community?' In *New Insights into Sikh Art*, ed. Kavita Singh, 134–45. Mumbai: Marg.

Mahmood, Cynthia Keppley. 1996. *Fighting for Faith and Nation: Dialogues with Sikh Militants*. Philadelphia: University of Pennsylvania Press.

Mann, Gurinder Singh. 2016. '*Sri Gur Panth Prakash*: Its Text, Context, and Significance'. *Journal of Sikh and Punjab Studies* 23 (1 & 2): 15–56.

McLeod, W. H. 1991. *Popular Sikh Art*. New Delhi: Oxford University Press.

Mitta, Manoj, and H. S. Phoolka. 2007. *When A Tree Shook Delhi: The 1984 Carnage and its Aftermath*. New Delhi: Roli Books.

Murphy, A. 2012. *The Materiality of the Past: History and Representation in the Sikh Tradition*. New York: Oxford University Press.

———. 2015. 'Sikh Museuming'. In *Sacred Objects in Secular Spaces: Exhibiting Asian Religions in Museums*, ed. Bruce M. Sullivan, 49–64. London: Bloomsbury.

Narang, A. S. 1983. *Storm over the Sutlej: The Akali Politics*. New Delhi: Gitanjali Publishing House.

———. 2014. 'The Shiromani Akali Dal'. In *The Oxford Handbook of Sikh Studies*, eds Pashaura Singh and Louis E. Fenech, 339–49. New York: Oxford University Press.

Nijhawan, Michael. 2006. *Dhadi Darbar: Religion, Violence, and the Performance of Sikh History*. New Delhi: Oxford University Press.

Oberoi, Harjot. 1994. *The Construction of Religious Boundaries: Culture, Identity and Diversity in the Sikh Tradition*. New Delhi: Oxford University Press.

Pinney, Christopher. 2004. *Photos of Gods: The Printed Image and Political Struggle in India*. New Delhi: Oxford University Press.

Ramaswamy, Sumathi. 2003. 'Introduction'. In *Beyond Appearances? Visual Practices and Ideologies in Modern India*, ed. Sumathi Ramaswamy, xii–xxix. New Delhi: Sage Publications.

Rao, Amiya, Aurobindo Ghosh and N. D. Pancholi. 1985. *Report to the Nation: Truth About Delhi Violence*. New Delhi: Citizens For Democracy.

Saeed, Yousuf. 2012. *Muslim Devotional Art in India*. New Delhi: Routledge.

Sardar Baghel Singh: The Vanquisher of Delhi. n.d. New Delhi: Sikh Foundation.

Seetal, Sohan Singh. n.d. *The Sikh Misals and the Punjab States*. Ludhiana: Lahore Book Shop.

Singh, Kanika. 2016. 'Representation of Heritage in Museums of Sikh History: A Case Study of the Museum at Sis Ganj Gurdwara, Delhi'. PhD diss., Ambedkar University Delhi.

Singh, Kavita. 2015. 'Ghosts of Future Nations, or the Uses of the Holocaust Museum Paradigm in India'. In *The International Handbook of Museum Studies: Museum Transformations*, eds Annie E. Coombes and Ruth B. Phillips, 29–69. Chichester: Wiley-Blackwell.

Singh, Khushwant. 1999. *A History of the Sikhs*. 2 vols. New Delhi: Oxford University Press.

Sreenivas, Deepa. 2010. *Sculpting a Middle Class: History, Masculinity and the Amar Chitra Katha in India*. New Delhi: Routledge.

Talbot, Cynthia. 2016. *The Last Hindu Emperor: Prithviraj Chauhan and the Indian Past, 1200–2000*. Cambridge: Cambridge University Press.

The Hindu. 2015. 'Celebrate Conquest of Lal Qila: Sikhs'. 21 March.

The Tribune. 2013. 'Memorial to '84 Riots Victims Soon'. 3 June.

_____. 2015. 'Make Lal Qila Conquest a National Event: DSGMC'. 20 March.

The Sunday Tribune. 2016. '300th Shaheedi Samagam of Baba Banda Singh Bahadur Ji'. 3 July.

Uberoi, Patricia. 2003. 'Dilemmas of Nationhood in Indian Calendar Art'. In *Beyond Appearances? Visual Practices and Ideologies in Modern India*, ed. Sumathi Ramaswamy, 191–232. New Delhi: Sage Publications.

Ten

Caste in an Urban Business Space

A Study of the Khatri Community of Amritsar*

Gurpreet Bal

In the Hindu *varnashram* scheme, the prescribed occupation for the Vaishya varna is business and trade. The business history of India, as illustrated by Tripathi (2004), also reveals that a preponderant number of merchants and traders belonged to the Vaishya varna. Within this varna, there are a large number of castes who have been carrying on business activities for centuries, though their names vary across different regions of India. This chapter takes into cognisance the social character of Indian business by

*The preliminary findings of the study were first presented at the '12th Biennial Conference on Entrepreneurship' at the Entrepreneurship Development Institute of India, Ahmedabad, in 2017. This is a revised and modified version of the paper. Though I am highly indebted to all my respondents, I would like to especially express my gratitude to Sudarshan Kapoor, Arun Khanna, Avtar Kishan Kapoor and Kewal Kishan Kapoor for enriching my knowledge about the city and its business activities. I very affectionately acknowledge the help of Ganesh Mehra and Harpreet Singh for not only accompanying me during the collection of data, but for also making me enjoy the real delicacies of the city. It is my great pleasure to thank my husband, Professor Paramjit S. Judge, for helping me in myriad ways.

arguing that though engagement in business and trade in India has been the preoccupation of certain communities, the communities engaged in business have a specific character according to the region. These business communities are groups of castes with a common regional origin and a traditional involvement in trade. Their names typically indicate their geographical origin, such as Gujarati, Marwari, Sindhi and Punjabi. Amongst the Punjabis, the prominent castes endowed with business acumen are the Khatri, Arora, Bania and Mahajan. Taking an urban space as social and economic milieu, the argument is based on an empirical study conducted by the author in two phases (in 2017 and 2018) in the city of Amritsar in Punjab, which has a business history of more than four centuries. The business and entrepreneurial activities of some communities, castes and families in the backdrop of the evolution of the city point towards the intersection of caste, occupation and physical space.

Singh writes, 'For centuries Amritsar laid on the caravan route of traders from North-West. Every bazaar, every mohalla, every small lane and every brick laid here has some history' (1977: 105). In light of the same, this chapter has been divided into two sections. The development process of the city interwoven with the business activities of various groups of people contributing to the making of the city has been examined in the first section. The study focuses on a caste group which, in Punjab, is almost synonymous with business and trade, that is, the Khatri. It examines how Khatri as a community has evolved over time and the gradual and continuous transformation these Khatris have experienced in trade, business and manufacturing activities in the wake of technological development. How have these traditional traders, businessmen and industrialists been adapting to the changing features of the city? Further, the growth process of trans-generational family enterprises, their inter-family dependence and intra-family relationships, crucial and indispensable to running the business, have been explored in the second section.

Creating Business Space

Making of the City

Guru Ram Das, the fourth Sikh Guru, himself belonging to the Khatri caste, laid the foundation of Amritsar on 14 June 1577. Guru Ram Das had heard about the sanctity of this place and the pool. Having identified the site of the pool and the surrounding land of village Chak, the Guru decided to transform it into a city.[1] To establish the city, the land[2] was purchased by his father-in-law, the third Sikh Guru Amar Das, from the inhabitants of village Tung for a sum of 700 *Akbari tankas*. The work began with the digging of the tank, and simultaneously with its construction all care was taken to develop village Chak. In 1588, Guru Ram Das's son, the fifth Guru, laid the foundation of Harimandir in the centre of the pool. A market, *Guru Bazaar*,[3] was also established adjoining Harimandir. For the first 200 years of its history, the city was called Chak Guru or Chak Guru Ram Das or simply Ramdaspur.[4] Later, it came to be known as Amritsar after the name of the sacred tank (Amrit sarovar—pool of nectar). Fifty-two types of caste groups from Patti, Kasur and Kalanaur were called by the founder Guru to settle here to ensure a regular supply of essential commodities to the settlers. Grewal (1984) writes that there is enough evidence showing that the fourth and fifth Gurus of the Sikhs encouraged craftsmen and traders to reside in this place. A number of rich sarafs (bankers) and banjaras (traders) also settled down in the town.

On completion of the construction of the town, the Guru called the local Khatris (business community) and asked them to take charge of the holy place. However, they humbly pleaded their inability to perform religious duties and requested the Guru to engage some Brahmins and Fakirs (mendicants) for the job. Instead, the Khatris sought the blessings of the Guru for *kirt* (hard work) and *barkat* (prosperity) in their profession, which were granted (Singh 1977). Up to the eighth Sikh Guru, this place remained their abode. Thus, the city remained a sacred place for the Sikhs. Though the city, being very close to Lahore (32 miles), always remained under the threat of invasions by Mughals and Afghans, trade and business expanded gradually.

The Misls, Katras and Bazaars

The Harimandir (literally, 'God's own place') was destroyed by Afghan invaders thrice (1757, 1762, 1764) and finally built in its present form during the period of *misl*s in 1777. The town of Ramdaspur also started expanding rapidly under the misl sardars after a gap of more than a century. Datta (1967) says that Amritsar was no more than a village between the years 1767 and 1773. The sardars/chiefs of five misls[5] built bungas (rest houses) around the holy temple in order to defend it and also to provide boarding and lodging facilities for the pilgrims. Thus, the sardars gained influence over Ramdaspur and occupied areas around the temple, where they developed their quarters of influence into independent small principalities within their jurisdiction and carried on civil administration (Singh 1977). The sardars brought wealth, workmen and resources, and started building the town according to their own plans in their respective quarters. These quarters were called *katras*.[6] The entire expansion of the city took place in the form of katras. Each katra had a bazaar from where essential commodities were supplied to its residents. Many of these katras attained the status of big trading centres over time, and till date the essence of the city lies within these katras.

Expansion of a Town to a City

It was during the reign of the first Sikh ruler Maharaja Ranjit Singh that Amritsar saw its glorious time as it was consolidated and given a new shape. The city of Amritsar was taken over by Maharaja Ranjit Singh in 1805 by annexing the biggest and powerful misl, Bhangi. He made the misl sardars relinquish their control of katras and unified the town of Ramdaspur by forming a committee of responsible and prominent citizens to look after the administration. Grewal (1984) remarks that it finally became the city of Amritsar (one of the criteria prescribed by the Census of India to define a place as a city is that its population should be 1 lakh or more; a town has a population between 50,000 and 1 lakh). Amritsar being a major centre for Sikhs and their activities, besides being the location of the Harimandir, the Maharaja visited it frequently and hence built his palace (popularly known as 'summer palace', at present a protected monument) inside Rambagh garden ('on the model of Shalimar garden of Srinagar, Kashmir', as narrated by respondents of the author's study); thus Amritsar became the Maharaja's capital, and Lahore remained the main capital.

During the period of Maharaja Ranjit Singh, Harimandir was given a white marble facelift and its upper part was covered with gold sheets; from then on, it got the name Golden Temple. In the 1820s, an outer wall was constructed around the town with 12 gates, of which the Lahori gate served as the main entrance. Twenty-seven new katras were constructed with different castes and professions, each having a market centre; of these, Katra Sher Singh and Katra Mai Sewan emerged as prominent business areas. In order to develop the city as a leading trading and business centre, Maharaja Ranjit Singh invited well-known entrepreneurial communities to settle here. The prominence of Marwaris was apparent even in the early nineteenth century, and they were thus called upon to settle in the city. The Maharaja offered them shops and houses to live in. Till date, they are settled in and around Katra Ahluwalia and have remained successful businessmen in the areas of processing and trading of tea leaves, woollens shawls and blankets. Kashmir had also become a part of the Sikh kingdom in 1819 and Amritsar became a centre of the Kashmiri shawl trade by 1835. Kashmiri colonies were also established in the city. After the death of Maharaja Ranjit Singh in 1839, Punjab was annexed by the British within 10 years, in 1849. His garden palace was named as Company Bagh (garden) by the British. At this time, Amritsar was the biggest city of Punjab and continued to be so till

1881; it was later overtaken by Lahore which remained on top till 1941 and Amritsar was reduced to the third position after Delhi (Gauba 1988).

Trade to Industry

By the early nineteenth century, Amritsar had become a great centre of trade and manufacturing. There were important wholesale market centres, like Majith (name of a dye obtained from the roots of a plant) Mandi, Namak Mandi, Ghee Mandi and Kanak Mandi. The Western traveller B. C. Hugel described Amritsar in the first half of the nineteenth century thus, 'It was most bustling of all the cities of Punjab. In every street could be seen most beautiful productions of India exhibited for sale. The wealth of whole Punjab seems collected in it and great merchants have made it their abode' (1845[1970]: 393). The number of shopkeepers had grown and markets of specialised skills and crafts had developed around the Golden Temple. The most important institution to develop was its municipality in 1868 which recorded the city's population as 135,813 in that year (Grewal 1984).[7] Nearly 40 per cent of them were Muslims, of which nearly half were Kashmiris (Gauba 1988). During this time, Amritsar was a famous market for high-quality pashmina *doshalas* and *jamavar/kani* shawls which continued to dominate till the 1880s. Pasham was imported from Tibet, Bokhara, Kerman and China, and this business was mainly controlled by Kashmiri Muslims—Khojas and Sheikhs. After the 1880s, both the trade in pashmina shawl and the population of Kashmiris in the city started declining due to a number of reasons.[8] Kashmiri weavers shifted to carpet weaving, which was organised by the wealthy Hindu trading classes (Bal 2015). By 1911, Amritsar was exporting carpets worth Rs 5 lakh annually. Henceforth, carpet manufacturing remained another specialty of the city till the middle of the twentieth century, to the extent that in 1929 the Oriental Carpet Manufacturing Company (OCM) was set up. Besides these, the city also remained famous for silk cloth manufacturing. There were four prominent silk mills here.[9] By the beginning of the twentieth century, Amritsar had become the metropolis of both the silk trade and the silk industry of Punjab.

The Census Report of Punjab, 1868, states that there were 658 merchants, 2,115 bankers, 3,463 moneylenders and 12,647 shopkeepers in Amritsar (Datta 1967: 133). Therefore, flourishing economic activities attracted artisans, weavers and craftsmen to this place. The records of the municipal corporation, Amritsar, also reveal that towards the end of the nineteenth century, even a few foreigners, mainly Europeans, were living in the city for trade purposes, besides Kashmiri, Marwari, Gujarati, Jain, Bengali, Sindhi, Tibetan and Parsi traders. The city got connected by rail and road with Delhi, Lahore and Multan, thus increasing its commercial importance. Towards the end of the nineteenth century, Amritsar also had three famous colleges, separately for the three dominant religious groups—Khalsa College, Hindu College and Mohammdan Anglo Oriental (MAO) College. Amritsar always recorded a high literacy rate. In 1911, it was 12 per cent, which increased to 15 per cent in 1931 (Sangeeta 1989: 91). The Khatris, amongst the business communities, took the lead in education.

The entrepreneurial growth process of the city slowed down towards the end of the nineteenth century and remained so till the early twentieth century. But after the first two decades of the last century, after World War I, the city expanded rapidly: there were 9 factories in 1901, which increased to 37 in 1928 and 87 in 1938 (that is, before the start of World War II) (Bandhu 1989). The Census of India, 1931, depicts the natural growth of the city as well as the migration of industrial workers to the city when the population increased by 65.30 per cent, making it 2,64,840 (Gauba 1984). It may be argued that the world wars provided ample opportunities to the local businessmen and that was the time when there was a sharp rise in industrial development in the city. The business of raw hides and leather goods manufacturing also started. A Government of India harness and saddlery factory was established in 1912. The local business communities, mainly the enterprising and affluent Khatris, took the lead to venture into new spheres of economic activity, particularly the industry. Some of them imported Japanese machinery and Japanese rayon yarn; later, a powerloom for manufacturing rayon was set up in 1933. The India Woollen Mill was the first to instal a powerloom (Sangeeta 1989: 110). A few fine fabrics like crepe and shantoon began to be manufactured by local weavers through the putting-out system, wherein capital was provided by some Khatri families who purchased raw silk and gave it to weavers through the agents. Weavers were paid wages while the profits were earned by the Khatri capitalists. Sugar and flour[10] mills came up in the 1930s, besides the brass and copper industry. A Marwari started Partap Steel Rolling Mills in 1935 (ibid.: 97). Artisans were engaged in wood works, metal works, ivory carving, marble cutting, jewellery making, gold and silver leafing, perfumery, utensils, and the art of dyeing and hand (gold/salma) embroidery. Gauba (1980) argues that while in the nineteenth century mostly luxury items such as pashmina and silk products were manufactured, in the twentieth century, popular consumption goods like ruffle shawl, rayon silk, soap and glass, alongside electrical and engineering goods, were manufactured. Essma Woollen Mills and Hansa (Swadeshi) Woollen Mills were started by the local Khatris in 1971 and 1975, respectively.

The policies of the British government also remained favourable towards the industrialists. The Chheharta[11] area of Amritsar was developed for this purpose; they gave incentives and issued a notice that no octroi or property taxes would be charged from the factories established in the area. It remained an important industrial centre until many industrialists were forced to migrate to other places, first due to Partition and later owing to the two wars between India and Pakistan in 1965 and 1971.

The modern banking system emerged between 1930 and 1940 in Amritsar. Three foreign exchange banks—the Chartered Bank, the Lloyds and Grindlays Bank—were established to facilitate business activities in the city. A new shopping centre, Hall Bazaar, was named after Charles Hall, then deputy commissioner of Amritsar. Trade and manufacturing continued to flourish in this industrial city, with an investment of Rs 18 lakh in big industries (Bandhu 1989), and with a population of nearly 4 lakh on the eve of Independence when the country was partitioned (Census of India 1941). Amritsar bore the major brunt of violence and displacement. Muslims left the city for Pakistan, and Hindus and Sikhs from West Punjab came to settle here, resulting in the transformation of the socio-economic life of the city. The vacuum created by the departure of Muslims was filled by the local affluent Khatri businessmen, who controlled most of the trade of Punjab and Afghanistan. Uma Shankar, a Khatri, had a direct link with England and till the 1930s he continued to import artificial silk from Japan. Kedar Nath Kapoor and Inderpal Khanna had also been prominent traders of silk in the 1930s (Sangeeta 1989). Significantly, they were also educated; some of them even held foreign degrees. They were scholars, lawyers, doctors and engineers, and much of the social change could be credited to their efforts. They, at this time, bought land and engaged in cultivation and grew fruits. New buildings were constructed. In the words of Gauba,

> The revenue records show that the land around Amritsar, which once belonged to the Sikh nobility, passed into the hands of the bourgeoisies, notably the Khatris. In 1935 most of the orchards and market gardens around the city were owned by them. Most of the industry was in the hands of the Khatris, especially those of Khannas, Kapoors and Mehras (1988: 266).

They demonstrated an enterprising attitude towards the adoption of modern techniques and machines in their work and soon started controlling the trade and manufacture of woollens and cotton textiles, which they continue to do even now. It is significant to note their personal traits, such as their ability to adapt to situations, ingenuity and innovative skills. The more important question is: How could this community keep the trade and industry going? The answer can be sought in the social and cultural capital (Bourdieu

2011) they accumulated, and this is the subject of discussion in the following section.

Khatris: The Empirical Context

This section takes cognisance of empirical explorations into the social basis of economic activities of the city. It focuses on a community comprising the Charzati, that is, Kapoor, Khanna, Mehra and Seth sub-castes, popularly known as *chaar rattan* (four gems) of the Khatri caste. Most of them have come from Lahore and are therefore popularly known as *Lahorie*. The Census of 1881 reveals the number of principal Khatri sections in Amritsar district as: Bunjai—12,097; Sarin—10,516; Charzati—3,859; Jauson—1,279; Jammun—1,279; Khanne—1,725; Kapur—1,615; and Malhotra—1,171 (Gazetteer, Amritsar District 1884). As per the Census Report 1891, in Amritsar city, there were 151,737 Hindus, 110,347 Sikhs and 199,083 Muslims, besides Jains, Christians, Parsis and others (Gazetteer, Amritsar District 1893). Based on the 1891 census, Bingley (1893[1985]: 48–50) has mentioned the Khatri population as 447,000, of which 52,000 were Sikhs, and found more in Ludhiana, Hoshiarpur, Amritsar, Lahore, Gujranwala, Rawalpindi and Jhelum districts.

Presently, Amritsar city has 49.36 per cent Hindus while Sikhs constitute 48 per cent of the total population (Census of India 2011). Both these religious groups have Khatris. Though Khatris are mostly Hindus, they are also found prominently among the Sikhs (Malhotra 2002). For the purpose of this study, only Hindu Khatris have been examined. This chapter is based on the data collected for a larger project on business communities of Amritsar. Data have been collected through both quantitative and qualitative techniques. In the absence of any recorded information on the number of Khatris, respondents were selected randomly and contacted through the snowball technique. In all, 94 Charzati Khatris (27 Khanna, 26 Kapoor, 21 Mehra and 20 Seth) were interviewed with the help of an interview schedule containing mainly open-ended questions arranged in a non-hierarchical manner. The businessmen were anxious to participate in the research. In addition, it was decided to prepare detailed cases of some prominently successful businessmen who had been running businesses for the last four to five generations. One of the main points of interest was to know how they look back at the city: how they perceive the business culture that was prevalent earlier in the city, the type of transformation they have experienced over time and the factors that have kept business activities alive in the city despite some major policy shifts. Thus, eight in-depth case studies were prepared by using an interview guide. These include: Khanna (2, including Arun Khanna, formerly president of Khatri Sabha), Kapoor (4, including prominent personalities like Sudarshan Kapoor and Kewal Kishan Kapoor), Mehra (1, owner of the famous Essma woollen mills) and Seth (1, an industrialist). All of them were between the ages of 75 and 91 years, and at the time of the study, besides their business activities, they were engaged in a number of social welfare and philanthropic activities. Once the appointments were fixed, they all were very forthcoming with information. I have primarily interpreted the case studies in this chapter, in addition to providing a few inputs on the basis of observations and interviews. On the basis of narratives of the cases, it may be discerned that certain behavioural and social practices, work ethics, risk taking, business acumen, besides the quality of water and pilgrims to the Golden Temple, have remained the accelerating factors for their success.

Tracing the Descent

Ibbetson (1916[1974]: 247) writes that the Khatris claim to be the direct representatives of Kshatriyas, as given by Manu (of *Manusmriti*). Bingley (1893[1985]), too, in his book *The Sikhs*, writes that the Khatris claim a Rajput or Kshatriya descent. 'Even though following vaishya pursuits, Khatris claimed Kshatriya descent for themselves, a claim that was by and large accepted by British ethnographers' (Malhotra 2002: 32). Jones mentions, 'The Khatris claimed, with some justice and increasing insistence, the status of Rajputs, of Kashatriyas, a claim not granted by those above but illustrative of their ambiguous position on the great varna scale of class divisions and their importance within Hindu community' (1976: 5). As there is a close association between caste and occupation in India, there are numerous instances (Patidars of Gujarat, Thathiars of Punjab) of those who claimed to belong to a higher caste/varna in the hierarchy on the basis of success in a particular occupation (Bal 2006; Kaur 2017). Ibbetson elaborates that

> There are three different kinds of divisions of Khatri caste. First division is that there are four real tribal sections, then the four most important of the artificial divisions alluded to above, and finally six of the most important clans. The origin of the division into four sections called Bunjahi, Sarin, Bahri and Khokhran is said to be that Ala-ul-din Khilji attempted to impose widow-marriage upon the Khatris. The Western Khatris resolved to resist the innovation, and sent a deputation of 52 (bawan) of their members to represent their case at court. Thus they were called Bawanjai …hence Bunjahi, but the Eastern Khatris were afraid to sign the memorial. They were therefore called followers of Mahomedan customs—hence—Sarin. The Khokhran section is said to consist of the descendants of certain Khatris who joined the Khokhars in rebellion (who rejected the idea of widow remarriage) and with whom the other Khatri families were afraid to intermarry; and lastly, the Bahri section (1916[1974]: 248).

The present study focuses on the Bahri section of the lineage. Ibbetson informs

> of Mehr Chand, Khan Chand and Kapur Chand, three Khatris who went to Delhi in attendance upon one of Akbar's Rajput wives, and who, thus separated from the rest of the caste, married only within each other's families. …The most

> important in order of social rank are the Mehrotra or Mehra, Khanna, Kapur named after these three men, while Seth is a term used for any rich banker. They constitute the Dhaighar (who marries in two and half houses because a grouping of three is considered unlucky), Charzati (later they included Seth in the grouping who now marries into four sub-castes), Chhezati (he who marries into six tribes), and Barazati (marries in twelve gotras) divisions and so on. Dhaighar and Charzati divisions stand the highest of all in the social ranking. The origin of the term Dhaighar lies in the fact that the families of that division exclude not only the fathers' clan, but also such families of the mothers' clan as are closely connected with her and thus reduce the clans available for intermarriage to two and half. Each division will take wives from one below it though it will not give its daughters to it in the marriage (ibid.: 248–50).

'These again are split up into various families and septs' (a term given by Rivers [1996], which means clans—those who are related through common descent) (Bingley 1893[1985]: 49). It was also to protect the lineage that the Dhaigarh Khatris did not marry their daughters out of Dhaigarh, while they took daughters-in-law from other Khatris. The Bunjahi Khatris owe their influence and importance to the fact that they include the Bedi and Sodhi clans, to which belonged the founders of the Sikh faith. Guru Nanak was a Bedi, whereas all the Gurus from Guru Ram Das (fourth Guru) onwards to Guru Gobind Singh (tenth Guru) were Sodhis (McLeod 1975). They have a high social position by caste.

Tripathi (2004: 195) writes, 'Though claiming descent from ancient Kshatriyas in the Hindu caste hierarchy, most Punjabi Khatris had taken to trading by the beginning of the middle of the 19th century. Commerce and trade is their main occupation, however many of them hold land, cultivate, take service, and follow various avocations.' Bingley quotes what Sir George Campbell wrote in *The Ethnology of India*, 'Besides monopolizing the trade of the Punjab and Afghanistan and doing a good deal beyond those limits, they are, in the Punjab, the chief Civil Administrators, and clerical work is almost in their hands' (1893[1985]: 48). Civil service was another attractive occupational choice for them. Oldenburg (2002: 75), while mentioning her Punjabi Khatri informants, writes that they are educated, wealthy and had traditionally served the government and army as officers, and were also commonly involved in farming, trade, shopkeeping and moneylending. The Khatris acted as 'traditional innovators' and leaders into new worlds (Jones 1976: 5). According to Levi (2015), it was due to their ingenuity and the spirit of enterprise that Punjabi Khatri merchants travelled across Afghanistan, Central Asia, Iran and Russia during the sixteenth through the nineteenth centuries in caravans to sell their produce. In the Punjab, no village can get on without its Khatri who keeps the accounts, does the banking business, and buys and sells the grain. The Khatris are a very fine, fair and handsome race, and are generally very well-educated. The Khatri Sikhs nearly always prefer services in the cavalry, where their individual smartness and intelligence give them a great advantage (Bingley 1893[1985]: 48–49).

Amritsar could emerge as a multifaceted society which fascinated people from far and wide, who saw the city as a hub of trading activities for centuries. Among its inhabitants are people of all the major religions, castes and communities. The respondents represent all four gotras of the Khatri caste. With the blessings of the fourth Guru, the Khatris successfully carried on trading activities in all phases of the development of the city. Looking for business opportunities in the city, Khatris have migrated to Amritsar from Lahore, Multan, Peshawar and Karachi, mainly in the nineteenth century.

Two respondents (about 75 years old) shifted here from Lahore. These two brothers' great-grandfather belonged to Phagwara and went to Banaras (Varanasi) in the middle of the nineteenth century where, in 1863, he started the business of selling shawls procured from Kashmir. From there, around 1900, their grandfather shifted to Amritsar as it was emerging as a textile hub. The respondents were born and brought up in Amritsar, though their forefathers had taken different routes to reach this centre of trade. All the other respondents were settled in *Tiwaria di gali* (*kuchha Tiwaria*, located inside *Lohgarh* gate) in the walled city. Later on, as the families grew bigger and affluent, they moved to big houses on the outskirts of the city—civil lines area—in the early twentieth century. Khatris, being an endogamous group, have married mainly within the Charzati inside the city. However, they avoided marrying within their own gotra; marriages took place across gotras. Matchmaking is done through the kinship network.[12] When asked to list the four gotras in order of their ranks, the respondents were unable to do so. All of them invariably informed that there was no hierarchy among the four of them. They form a community and each member is concerned with the growth and uplift of the community. However, one of the respondents remarked, '*Iss sheher vich Kapoor ziadha dimagi han te parhe-lekhe aa*' ('Kapoors are brainy as they are more educated and are found in greater numbers in the city'); however, Mehras and Khannas are now more in Mumbai than in Amritsar. He probably meant that in Amritsar, Kapoors may be considered to be at the top in the intra-caste hierarchy.

Another respondent claimed that Khatris trace their descent from Sher Shah Suri and a large number of them shifted to Amritsar before Maharaja Ranjit Singh's rule. In 1902, they formed a Khatri Sabha in Amritsar and in 1984 they organised the All India Khatri Sammelan in which Khatris from all over India participated. The Khatri respondents even claimed that Amritsar is the headquarters of Khatris and it is from here that they have moved on to all other parts of India.

Khatri Entrepreneurship: Narrative Analysis

Damodaran (2008) demarcates three paths to successful entrepreneurship in India. The first is from markets for traditional traders; the second from the office for traditional service classes; and third, from the fields for traditional farming communities. But he concedes that in north India and for north Indian groups, it was the first path—from markets to modern entrepreneurship—that was predominant. Ray (1994) also, in his account of entrepreneurship from 1800 to 1947, argues that entrepreneurship and industry in India have emerged out of the bazaar economy. People operating in the bazaar earned money which they could later invest in industries. Khatris represent a class of businessmen from the market; their enterprising and flexible nature and ability to create trust made them successful, thereby also accelerating the growth of the city. There is a common saying in the community, '*Kisi bhi khatri ko teen kapron me duniya me kahhi bhi chhor do, aek saal ke bad uske pass sub kuchh hoga*' ('You just leave a Khatri anywhere on the planet with three pieces of cloth, and when you meet him after a year, he would have all the fortunes'). This means that a Khatri is determined, hard-working and courageous in facing and overcoming any adversity.

They took to the textile business, and they have been running the same business for the last four to five generations. But they have experienced a lot of transformation in the industry as well. Textiles include three basic yarns—wool, silk and cotton. They were found to be engaged in all. But business in pure silk has long been lost to art silk and Japanese silk. Earlier, woollen cloth of good quality was being imported from England. In the mid-1930s, around World War II, the Khatris shifted from trading to manufacturing wool. To begin with, yarn was imported from Japan and Australia, but later they realised that it would be better if they produced the yarn themselves; they thus thought of installing ginning and spinning mills. And then, ginning, spinning, weaving and finishing were all done at Amritsar. There was a huge handloom textile industry which around 1942–43 transformed into a powerloom industry. Between 1945 and 1950, two spinning mills, including the famous Dyalbagh Spinning Mill (which was started by a Khatri in Putligarh but has now closed down) were established. The respondents informed that there were only a few spinning mills left in the city. Now, many Khatris have popularised the Sulzer powerlooms which, though expensive, are the latest and more efficient. As stated by one of the respondents, 'The techniques of work have changed. Now pen drives can be used in these machines. The designers just send the design in a pen drive which is assigned a number. They can at any time place the order to manufacture a shawl or ladies suit by referring to that number.' According to him, at the time of the study, only four Khatri families were running top businesses in woollen items like shawls, blankets and dress material.

Finishing a cloth requires a lot of water; the respondents were of the view that Amritsar's *aabo hawa pani* (soil, air and water) play a significant role in determining the quality of the finished material. That is why the industry flourished in Amritsar. It was learnt during the course of the study that mink blankets, woollen cloth, and heavy cloth like spun and brasso are still the famous products of Amritsar. But all respondents lamented that Bhilwara, Ahmedabad, Surat, Panipat and Ambala had progressed much faster and taken over most of their business. Manufacturing of textile is mainly done in Bhilwara and Surat and it then comes to Amritsar for printing, finishing and embroidery; from here, it is sent as far as Bhutan, Sikkim and other parts of India. It is relevant to mention that this community continuously created new combinations of raw material, kinds of cloth and weaving styles. For the last few years, embroidery on dress material was in fashion; thus, they bought embroidery machines to produce goods in bulk. As embroidery on other household items was also popular, most of them installed big embroidery machines, popularly known as *Sifali* machines, for embroidering curtain cloth, bedcovers, sofa cover cloth, etc. The characteristic feature of the Sifali embroidery machine is its length, which is up to 70 feet, and imported mainly from Switzerland and other European countries. One of the respondents' families has five such machines; others even have six or more. For this type of embroidery, they purchase cloth imported by big companies in Delhi.

It is significant to find that they kept changing the nature and quality of products and techniques of work with the changing trends and demand. As the demand for embroidery started declining, many of them shifted to different kinds of printing techniques. It was noteworthy that all those amongst them who had shifted from trading to industry at the right time and continued to innovate managed to survive the challenges of the time. But all those who remained focused on trading only—wholesale or retail—were reduced to running businesses of odd types. Almost 90 per cent of the business now involves textiles. As of June 2018, Amritsar had nearly 15 processing units which produced approximately 1 lakh metre cloth in one month.

Considering the geographical location of the city—it is located near the international border with Pakistan—respondents were asked about the challenges they had faced over time. It was learnt that though Partition struck a big blow to the businesses of Amritsar, these people were able to surge back in the 1950s and 1960s. As a border city, Amritsar has always remained under the threat of war between India and Pakistan. It witnessed two wars in 1965 and 1971, which caused a serious setback to the industry. Many families, as a survival strategy, have sent at least one of the family members to safer places like Mumbai, Surat, Ahmedabad and Dehradun. In the 1980s and the first half of the 1990s, Amritsar was a centre of terrorism, which also dealt a serious blow to its business and industry. Many Khatris—besides Mahajan and Bania businessmen—shifted their machines to Panipat. The textile industry declined tremendously while Panipat flourished and Ludhiana emerged as an alternative. The respondents narrated that their customers were frightened to travel to Amritsar for business as Panipat and Ludhiana traders, to safeguard their own interests, impressed upon them the dangers of that city.

One of the major blows to traditional business around the Golden Temple came during the period of militancy in Punjab (1979–93). To protect the sanctity and beauty of the Golden Temple, the Government of India launched a Galliara scheme in 1988, the objective of which was to remove all the habitations and markets up to 30 metres (later extended to 300 metres) in the vicinity of the temple. The project was carried out in five phases and the first three were completed by 1996 (Kalia 2010). As a result, a large number of businesses were displaced and relocated to different parts of the city. Kalia (ibid.) informs that rehabilitated respondents (75 per cent) were either Khatris or Aroras. New markets emerged at isolated places in the civil lines area.

With liberalisation and globalisation, products from China started pouring into the market. The small traders started importing mink blankets which threatened the local manufacturing of blankets. Among textiles, the woollen garments industry also started declining. A number of respondents narrated that there used to be 110 textile processing and finishing units in Amritsar. One of them, a Khanna, stated, 'My plant used to be the best in north India. I had to shift to embroidery and for the purpose imported one machine from Japan for 70 lakh in the late 1990s. Later, the same machine was imported for Rs 10 lakh from China by many community members.'

A new government policy in 1995–96 further discouraged the business community. All the respondents mentioned that the Punjab government has never given any incentive for the industry to flourish in the city. It has imposed excise duty, which is not levied in the neighbouring state of Haryana. Rather, all the recent development has taken place to develop the city as a pilgrimage centre due to the Golden Temple. Lakhs of tourists from all over India throng the city every day. Beyond doubt, tourists would give a boost to the retail trade. However, big business and industry will suffer further. It will be relevant to see how they encounter the changes in the structure of the city.

The ongoing problem of terrorism in Jammu and Kashmir has also affected the business of the city. Amritsar has a direct trade with Kashmir. The famous jamavar/*kanni* shawls and ladies' woollen suits and dress materials manufactured in Amritsar are sold in Kashmir. The demand for these has declined considerably. The respondents also said that there has been a change in the intensity and duration of winter (due to climate change) in the north, thus reducing the demand for woollen clothes.

All the respondents categorically mentioned that labour unionisation has led to great loss to the industry. At that time, Chheharta, on the outskirts of the city, had a concentration of industry, mainly textiles and related items like bukram, lace-making and embroidery factories. There must have been some exploitation of workers, but their politicisation led many of the industrialists to either shift to other locations within the city or move to other cities. At the time of the study, there was only one big factory functional in this area; it too had changed many hands over time and was virtually on the brink of closure, largely due to the lack of an entrepreneurial ecosystem.

Many of the markets situated in the katras too were facing setbacks due to the serious problem of parking. Customers hesitate to go to traditional shops and prefer malls or the civil lines area. Labourers are not interested in factory work; they prefer odd jobs in the malls where they get better wages and a far better work environment. The respondents who have been successful businessmen lamented that the younger generation does not want to do business. They are moving to Mumbai or other metropolitan cities, where they already have many relatives, for higher studies to become professionals.

Social and Cultural Capital

Despite the many challenges being encountered, these Khatri sub-castes may be credited for having kept the business activities going on in the city. This may be analysed in the context of their social and cultural capital (Bourdieu 2011). The cultural capital is their acquisition of knowledge and skills in business and trade activities. Their business acumen points towards it. It is significant to find that all the respondents are educated; two of them even earned a specialisation in textile processing and finishing from England. Their fathers and grandfathers were also educated and successfully ran the businesses as well. Datta (1967) writes that a prominent businessman had realised the utility of having someone who knew English to interact with government officials. So he planned to give his sons an English-type of education which, for him, was a process by which wealth could be accumulated; he believed that success was another name for influence, prestige and power. Among the 67 assistant surgeons employed by the British in Punjab, 52 were Hindus, out of which 20 were Khatris (Census of India 1892; Gazetteer, Amritsar District 1893). Though they are predominantly businessmen, it was informed that many elite Khatris in the city entered the civil services and the legal and medical professions, both often counterpoised on each other. One of the respondents' great-grandfather was a lawyer; his grandfather, Rai Bahadur Dr Guranditta Kapur, was a doctor with the Punjab Civil Medical Services (PCMS); and his father was also a lawyer. Even though they were professionals and were in jobs, they were still engaged in their family occupations, that is, wholesale and retail trade, manufacturing, and sometimes even moneylending. Over generations, they learnt to take risks, manage the finance and ways to operate in the market. They maintained joint families and their businesses were owned and managed by the family members. Besides business, some also owned land, used mainly to grow orchards. It is relevant to mention that the city had a very well-developed inlaid system of water supply. Canals were passing through the city from the Rambagh garden up to the Golden Temple.

Amritsar, since its inception, has remained under the constant threat of invasions. As already pointed out, to counter the uncertainty faced by businesses in the city, Khatris established parallel community businesses in other cities like Mumbai, Surat, Faridabad, Gurgaon and Panipat. How do they maintain their linkages with migrant families and kin in socio-economic terms? They do so through their social capital, in terms of interrelationships, trust in family members and associations like the Khatri Sabha. Their kinship network expanded to other bigger cities of the country. The respondents pointed to the landmark bungalows in the city, whose residents had shifted to Mumbai, as it was almost a practice amongst the prosperous Khatris to have one of their sons establish a business in another big city. Many of the Khannas and Mehras migrated to Mumbai for business. Initially, they remained traders, but soon established their factories. One of the respondents narrated, 'If you count, you will find the majority of textile millers in Mumbai had moved from Amritsar at some point in time.' They narrated that film star Rajesh Khanna's family also lived in the vicinity of *Galli Tiwaria*, but his parents migrated to Mumbai to look for greener pastures. There are innumerable such instances of Khatri families migrating to big cities that offered opportunities in the textile business. Their kinship networks remain very helpful, especially in marketing; a respondent's daughter-in-law was from Kashmir, and he stated that manufacturing of woollen garments was done here and the sale carried out by his relatives in Kashmir.

These four sub-caste groups—Khanna, Mehra, Kapoor and Seth—combine to form an endogamous group. They marry amongst themselves, mainly within the city itself. Being an endogamous group, most of the Khatris of the city and Khatris settled in other business centres are related, either through marriage or lineage. They have frequent interaction with kinsmen in other bigger cities, and hence they come to know the trends, fashion and modifications in the type of the textiles. All the respondents mentioned that the inter- and intra-family relations based on trust have helped in carrying on the business; interestingly, none of them interpreted this kinship network in terms of competition amongst them. They help each other by providing finance, market inputs and technology transfer. One of the respondents mentioned that if one of them bought a machine, many others would also soon buy that particular machine. Therefore, their social capital in the form of family ties and kinship networks has remained a resource.

Further, on probing their domination in the market, most of them emphasised their style of functioning. One, they continue to have a strong tradition of credit. They know that cash transactions are now predominant, but their style of communication has worked to their benefit, even though they sometimes face problems.

'A Khatri businessman is usually very articulate, shows humility and is courteous, yet very shrewd in business dealings,' one of the respondents commented. Their main competitors in the textile business are Ludhiana, Panipat and Delhi, and they all ask for cash payment prior to the delivery of goods. But in Amritsar, the businessmen usually accept credit terms. '*Aap lae jao, paise appe aa jaange*' ('Take the commodity now and give the money later on') is a commonly spoken statement. In order to sell the product, they would not ask for money but would convincingly tell customers to take the goods and pay later. Though such a relationship benefitted them by establishing their control over the market, they invariably failed to get the payments on time. Therefore, it often adversely affected the practice of investing profits back into the business, which further hampered production due to the lack of timely availability of resources.

Another reason for their success in business is that they strongly follow business ethics and practices—trust has a central place in one's business life. One of the respondents narrated, 'My father was a wholesaler who would import cotton and woollen cloth from Manchester, England, and would sell in the city and would travel to Peshawar, Karachi and Kashmir. There was honesty in business. Moneylending was based on trust and hence carried out by word of mouth. Human values were paramount.' Another respondent claimed, 'At one point in time there was no factory in Amritsar which did not borrow money from our family, but it was all done on trust.' Timberg (2014: xxii) chooses to use the word *sakh* for trust in the context of Marwaris. Sakh is at the heart of creditworthiness and business integrity, and means much more than wealth and financial strength. The system was well-established with the help of mediators. While describing G. D. Birla's life as a jute trader, Kudaisya (2006) also highlights that most of the buying and selling in the bazaar was based on traders' words. The Khatri business community helped each other to expand the business or to start a new business. There is an automatic transference of business activities from father to son. As one of the respondents said, 'Knowing that now the son is grown up and needs to marry, the usual practice has been to instal 3 to 4 powerlooms for him and he is settled and ready to be married.' It was so easy and taken for granted that the son would take up the family business for which he possessed the innate skills.

The earlier (SAD–BJP) government (2007–17) launched various schemes and plans to make the city a tourist attraction. Most of the respondents felt that the industry and wholesalers would face setbacks, but retailers may have a flourishing business through catering to the needs of the tourists. But Amritsar, having had a long history of business mainly due to the social and cultural capital of its enterprising communities, may survive yet another setback. The major difference they find in the way of doing business is that earlier customers used to go to them, but now they go to take orders from all over India and then supply goods. Now, it is again a trading city; manufacturing is limited and large industry has almost disappeared.

To conclude the discussion, we may say that Khatris have followed adaptation as well as transformation in the business. Continuing with the old practices but also introducing changes in business have helped them survive the challenge of globalisation. The respondents mentioned the setbacks to their business, but they also mentioned the continuous innovations and expansions. They never remained with only one business, but whenever chance permitted, they shifted to a new one. Schumpeter (2000) argues that an entrepreneur is one who continuously innovates; the moment he stops innovating, he ceases to be an entrepreneur. Entrepreneurship thus cannot be a profession or cannot be inherited. It is the Khatri community, including the four sub-groups, that has managed to retain the essence of business, lifestyle, food and integrity in the city. The factors responsible for their survival are linked with their ability to adapt and to use social capital through the expanded kinship network. If we map the social space of their social capital, we find that particular traditional family linkages have become functional in the running of universal business enterprises. The example of the Khatri community, which is far less prominent than Gujaratis, Marwaris, Parsis and Sindhis, helps us to argue that the understanding of modern Indian business systems cannot be isolated from the traditional moorings of the communities. Therefore, the idea that rationality is a binary opposite of tradition is an ideal construction which has never been followed anywhere in India.

The case of the urban social space and its connection with communities in India is an important aspect of understanding how Indian society has evolved, changed and continued over a period of time. Despite the colonial intervention with capitalist moorings, the Indian social and economic overlapping sustained due to the cultural capital in the form of skills and knowledge. The communities which overcame their socio-economic solitude by adapting to new circumstances have succeeded. The Khatris of Amritsar is one such community.

NOTES

1. Fauja Singh (1977) has mentioned that the Guru selected this place for two reasons. One, it is an old *tirath* (sacred place). This place was sanctified by the visits of great saints and sagas. Thirteen kilometres away is Ram Tirath, the abode of Maharishi Balmik. It is said that it was in Balmik's hut that Sita spent her exile and that her sons Luve and Kush were born here whom Balmik trained in the art of warfare. The forces of Ram were also challenged here by Luve and Kush and were defeated in battle. The first Sikh Guru, Nanak Dev, also visited this place during his *udasis* and even Buddha around 2,500 years prior had visited this place. It is also associated with the legend of Rajni, daughter of a Kardar (tax collector) of town Patti, who was married to a leper. She accepted her lot and served her husband. One day, they happened to pass through the spot. When she went to beg for food, her husband saw two crows fighting over a piece of bread, which then fell into the pool. Both birds swooped down upon it. On emerging from the water, they were transformed into white swans. On seeing this, the husband crawled out of his basket and into the water. His leprosy was cured instantly. When Rajni returned, she

saw him and refused to believe that he was her husband. Then Guru Ram Das convinced her that her husband had been cured of his disease by the miraculous water of the pool.

2. One of the plausible explanations for acquiring land is that the land bought by the Guru was rendered revenue-free by the orders of Mughal Emperor Akbar. Grewal (1984) writes that there is a great probability that Akbar gave the land to Guru Amar Das. It is also very likely that revenue-free land was given contiguously with the piece of land which had already been purchased by Guru Amar Das. As per the Imperial Gazetteer of India, quoted by Kahan Singh Nabha (1999: 76), 'Guru Ram Das first settled near the tank about 1574 and obtained a grant of the site with 500 *bigha*s of land from Akbar in 1577.' According to Fauja Singh (1977), it goes like this. Akbar used to pay occasional visits to Lahore. During one of his visits, he met the third Guru on the way at Goindwal (60 kilometres from Amritsar). Akbar was highly impressed by the Guru's piety and devotion. He also took his food from the *langar*. He was greatly impressed by the teachings of the Guru and his humanitarian approach to social problems and religion. Akbar offered a *jagir* for the maintenance of the Guru's kitchen. The offer was politely declined by the Guru. Then, it is said that the emperor made the offer to the Guru's daughter Bibi Bhani, which she accepted. Therefore, there is every possibility that Akbar did play a significant role, either to procure the land or he might have extended the land already in possession. Mulk Raj Anand, in his seventh novel *The Big Heart* (1945[1980]), writes that Akbar donated the money for the construction of the Harimandir.

3. Guru Bazaar remained the hub of business activities till the Galliara scheme around the Golden Temple replaced it. People coming from far and wide to pay obeisance make it a point to visit it to purchase general merchant goods.

4. The town hall building, which housed the office of the municipal corporation (now comprising the partition museum), has '*Ramdaspura*' inscribed on its main gate.

5. The five misls are Kanhaiya, Bhangi, Ahluwalia, Ramgarhia and Faizullapuria.

6. The Kanhaiya misl had three famous katras—Jai Singh, Jaimal Singh and Bhggian. The Bhangi misl had four katras—Hari Singh, Bhag Singh, Dulo and Desa Singh. The Ahluwalia, Ramgarhia and Faizullapuria misls too had their own katras.

7. Data collected from the office of the municipal corporation and Census of India show that the population of Amritsar after 1911 increased continuously except for 1951 due to the displacement of people owing to the partition of the country. The population from 1921 to 1941 increased at a fast rate. Industrial development and trading activities led to the growth of the city and increase in urbanisation. The 1981 and 2001 censuses, respectively, reveal 35 per cent and 42 per cent growth of the city, which was much higher than in the immediate years after Independence. As per the Census of India 2011, Amritsar city has a population of 1,132,761 with a growth rate of 15.5 per cent, and is thus already a metropolitan city (Gazetteer, Amritsar District 1884, 1893, 1915, 1934, 1947; Census of India 1911; District Census Handbook 1982, 2007, 2014).

8. Bal (2015) points out the reasons for this as follows: there was a shortage of pasham, on the one hand, and entry of mixed wool in the market on the other hand; wearing of shawls went out of fashion in Europe and thus the orders for weaving of shawls declined from abroad after the 1880s; the number of Kashmiris in Amritsar also decreased due to poverty, malnutrition and deaths. The most famous of all Kashmiris of Amritsar was Dr Saifuddin Kitchloo, who belonged to a wealthy family dealing in pashmina shawls and saffron.

9. Mehra Silk Mill (1931–32), Amritsar Rayon Silk Mill (1932), Kailash Textile Mill (1941), Khanna Silk Mill (1941–42) and Chuni Muni Silk Mill (1942–45) developed during the last decade of British rule.

10. The famous Maqbool Road was named after Sheikh Mir Maqbool Ahmed, who owned a flour mill (Gauba 1988: 269).

11. Chheharta, which at that time was located on the outskirts of the Civil Lines area, remained a hub of industrial activity. But due to the two Indo-Pak wars in 1965 and 1971 (especially when a Pakistani bomb fell on this place during the 1965 war), many industrialists preferred to relocate to safer places like Panipat, Faridabad and Mumbai.

12. Sixty-nine per cent of the total respondents were married within Amritsar city and nearly half of them were married within the Charzati. Sixty per cent of them mentioned that about 10 to 20 relatives from their in-laws' side resided in the city. There is every possibility that the food delicacies and eateries for which the city is known are also due to the patronage of the affluent Khatris. The traditional communities of the city have their rituals and customs, particularly with regard to the women of the house, to be carried out throughout the year. Each occasion is

connected with some special food (usually sweets), which is prepared by the specialists (*karigars*) for a few days for the community and then prepared and sold to other customers almost the whole year.

References

Anand, Mulk Raj. 1945[1980]. *The Big Heart*. New Delhi: Arnold-Heinemann.

Bal, Amandeep. 2015. *A Nationalist Muslim in Colonial Punjab: Life and Times of Dr. Saifuddin Kitchlew*. Chandigarh: Unistar.

Bal, Gurpreet. 2006. 'Entrepreneurship among Diasporic Communities: A Comparative Examination of Patidars of Gujarat and Jats of Punjab'. *The Journal of Entrepreneurship* 15 (2): 181–203.

Bandhu, Vishav. 1989. 'Industrial Development in the Punjab: A Case Study of Amritsar (1849–1947)'. M.Phil. diss., Guru Nanak Dev University, Amritsar.

Bingley, A. H. 1893[1985]. *The Sikhs*. Delhi: National Book Depot.

Bourdieu, Pierre. 2011. 'The Forms of Capital'. In *Cultural Theory: An Anthology*, eds Imre Szeman and Timothy Kaposy, 81–93. New Jersey: Wiley-Blackwell.

Census of India. 1892. Vols XIX–XXX (E. D. Maclagan), 1891. Calcutta: Government Printing.

———. 1912. Vol. XIV, Punjab Part-1 (Pandit Hari Krishan Kaul), 1911. Lahore: Civil and Military Gazette Press.

———. 1941. Punjab, Vol. 6 (Fazl I. Ilahi). Director of Census Operations, Punjab. Available at https://censusindia.gov.in/nada/index.php/catalog/31663 (accessed on 26 September 2023).

———. 2011. National Population Register and Socio Economic and Caste Census. New Delhi: Office of the Registrar General and Census Commissioner India. Available at https://censusindia.gov.in/nada/index.php/catalog/42619#metadata-description (accessed on 28 September 2023).

Damodaran, Harish. 2008. *India's New Capitalists: Caste, Business and Industry in a Modern Nation*. Ranikhet: Permanent Black.

Datta, V. N. 1967. *Amritsar: Past and Present*. Amritsar: Municipal Committee.

District Census Handbook. 1982. Amritsar, Part XIII, A and B, Series 17, Punjab, Census of India 1981. Director of Census Operations, Punjab, Chandigarh. Available at https://censusindia.gov.in/nada/index.php/catalog/28546 (accessed on 10 March 2023).

____. 2007. Amritsar, Part A and B, Series 4, Punjab, Census of India 2001. Director of Census Operations, Punjab, Chandigarh. Available at https://censusindia.gov.in/nada/index.php/catalog/44001 (accessed on 27 February 2023).

____. 2014. Amritsar, Part XIIA, Series 04, Punjab, Census of India 2011. Directorate of Census Operations, Punjab, Chandigarh. Available at https://censusindia.gov.in/nada/index.php/catalog/982 (accessed on 22 October 2023).

Gauba, Anand. 1980. 'Amritsar (1849–1947): A Study in Urban History'. PhD. diss., Guru Nanak Dev University, Amritsar.

____. 1984. 'Demographic Study of a British Indian City: Amritsar (1849–1947)'. In *Studies in Urban History*, eds J. S. Grewal and Indu Banga, 135–49. Amritsar: Guru Nanak Dev University.

____. 1988. *Amritsar: A Study in Urban History (1840–1947)*. Jalandhar: ABS Publications.

Gazetteer. 1884. Amritsar District, 1883–84. Compiled and published under the authority of the Punjab Government, Calcutta.

____. 1893. Amritsar District, 1892. Compiled and published under the authority of the Punjab Government, Calcutta.

____. 1915. Amritsar District, 1914, Part A. Compiled and published under the authority of the Punjab Government, Lahore.

____. 1934. Amritsar District, Statistical tables, 1933. Compiled and published under the authority of the Punjab Government, Lahore.

____. 1947. Amritsar District, Punjab, Chandigarh (A. Macfarquhar). Jullundur: Qaumi Press. Available at https://www.abebooks.com/first-edition/Punjab-District-Gazetteers-Amritsar-Macfarquhar-A/19288390099/bd (accessed on 21 October 2023).

Grewal, J. S. 1984. 'Ramdaspur to Amritsar: From a Town to a City'. In *Studies in Urban History*, eds J. S. Grewal and Indu Banga, 115–22. Amritsar: Guru Nanak Dev University.

Hugel, B. C. 1845[1970]. *Travels in Kashmir and Punjab*. Patiala: Punjab Language Department.

Ibbetson, D. 1916[1974]. *Panjab Castes*. Delhi: B. R. Publishing Corporation.

Jones, K. W. 1976. *Arya Dharm: Hindu Consciousness in 19th Century Punjab*. Berkeley: University of California.

Kalia, Rajesh. 2010. 'Displacement and Rehabilitation: A Sociological Study of Galliara Scheme in Amritsar'. PhD. diss., Guru Nanak Dev University, Amritsar.

Kaur, Manjot. 2017. *Caste Occupation and Social Transformation: A Study of Artisans of Punjab*. New Delhi: Kalpaz Publications.

Kudaisya, Medha M. 2006. *The Life and Times of G.D. Birla*. New Delhi: Oxford University Press.

Levi, Scott C. 2015. *Caravans: Punjabi Khatri Merchants on the Silk Road*. New Delhi: Penguin.

Malhotra, Anshu. 2002. *Gender, Caste and Religious Identities: Restructuring Class in Colonial Punjab*. New Delhi: Oxford University Press.

McLeod, W. H. 1975. *The Evolution of the Sikh Community: Five Essays*. Delhi: Oxford University Press.

Nabha, Kahan Singh. 1999. *Mahan Kosh*, sixth edn. Punjab: Bhasha Vibhag.

Oldenburg, Veena Talwar. 2002. *Dowry Murder: Imperial Origins of a Cultural Crime*. New York: Oxford University Press.

Ray, Rajat K. 1994. 'Introduction'. In *Entrepreneurship and Industry in India 1800–1947*, ed. Rajat K. Ray, 1–69. New Delhi: Oxford University Press.

Rivers, W. H. R. 1996. *Social Organization: The History of Civilization*. Reprint. New York: Routledge.

Sangeeta. 1989.'Business Communities in the City of Amritsar: Late19th–Early 20th Century'. M.Phil. diss., Guru Nanak Dev University, Amritsar.

Schumpeter, J. A. 2000. 'Entrepreneurship as Innovation'. In *Entrepreneurship: The Social Science View*, ed. Richard Swedberg, 51–75. New Delhi: Oxford University Press.

Singh, Fauja, ed. 1977. *The City of Amritsar: An Introduction*. Patiala: Department of Punjab Historical Studies, Punjabi University.

Timberg, T. A. 2014. *The Marwaris: From Jagat Seth to the Birlas*. Gurgaon: Penguin Books, India.

Tripathi, Dwijendra. 2004. *The Oxford History of Indian Business*. New Delhi: Oxford University Press.

Contributors

Gurpreet Bal was formerly Professor of Sociology, Guru Nanak Dev University, Amritsar, Punjab.

Purnima Dhavan is Giovanni and Ann Costigan Endowed Professor in History and Associate Professor, Department of History, University of Washington, Seattle.

Inderpal Grewal is Professor Emeritus of Women's, Gender and Sexuality Studies, Yale University.

Radha Kapuria is Assistant Professor, South Asian History, Durham University, UK.

Anshu Malhotra is Professor and Chair, Department of Global Studies, and Kundan Kaur Kapany Chair of Sikh and Punjab Studies, University of California, Santa Barbara.

Arti Minocha is Associate Professor, Department of English, Lady Shri Ram College, Delhi University.

Anne Murphy is Associate Professor, Department of History, University of British Columbia, and Chair of Punjabi Language, Literature and Sikh Studies.

Nicole Ranganath is Assistant Professor, Middle East/South Asia Studies, University of California, Davis.

Kanika Singh is Director, Centre for Writing and Communication, Ashoka University, India.

Yogesh Snehi is Assistant Professor, School of Liberal Studies, Dr B.R. Ambedkar University, Delhi.

Index